FAMILY VIOLENCE IN A CULTURAL PERSPECTIVE

FAMILY VIOLENCE IN A CULTURAL PERSPECTIVE

DEFINING, UNDERSTANDING, AND COMBATING ABUSE

KATHLEEN MALLEY-MORRISON
Boston University

DENISE A. HINES
University of New Hampshire

SAGE Publications
International Educational and Professional Publisher
Thousand Oaks ■ London ■ New Delhi

For information:

 Sage Publications, Inc.
2455 Teller Road
Thousand Oaks, California 91320
E-mail: order@sagepub.com

Sage Publications Ltd.
6 Bonhill Street
London EC2A 4PU
United Kingdom

Sage Publications India Pvt. Ltd.
B-42, Panchsheel Enclave
Post Box 4109
New Delhi 110 017 India

Printed in the United States of America

Library of Congress Cataloging-in-Publication Data

Malley-Morrison, Kathleen.
Family violence in a cultural perspective : defining, understanding, and combating abuse /
by Kathleen Malley-Morrison, Denise A. Hines.
    p. cm.
Includes bibliographical references and index.
ISBN 0-7619-2596-1 (pbk.)
  1. Family violence—United States. 2. Minorities—United States—Family relationships.
3. Interpersonal relations and culture—United States. 4. Social work with minorities—United
States. I. Hines, Denise A. II. Title.
HV6626.2.M35 2004
362.82′92′0973—dc211
                    2003013376

06 10 9 8 7 6 5 4 3 2

Acquisitions Editor:	Jim Brace-Thompson
Editorial Assistant:	Karen Ehrmann
Production Editor:	Sanford Robinson
Typesetter:	C&M Digitals (P) Ltd.
Proofreader:	Scott Oney
Indexer:	Molly Hall
Cover Designer:	Edgar Abarca

CONTENTS

PREFACE

There is enormous concern in the United States today concerning family violence. Making decisions affecting the lives of family members at risk of maltreatment is an enormous responsibility. A willingness to scrutinize one's own assumptions is essential in the process, especially when making judgments about families differing from one's own on dimensions such as poverty and ethnicity. In this book, we contribute to the burgeoning literature on violence in ethnic minority communities within the United States by taking an ecological approach to its incidence, correlates, and consequences. This means we consider factors operating at the level of the macrosystem (e.g., racism and poverty), the exosystem (e.g., neighborhoods, social service agencies), the microsystem (e.g., the family), and the individual (e.g., tolerance for aggression, substance abuse). We also provide numerous cases of family violence from the four major types of ethnic communities we consider (Native American Indian, African American/Black, Hispanic/Latino, and Asian American) and ask you to make judgments concerning the cases. We hope that as you consider each case, as well as the available research, you will ask yourself how your own experiences, and your own assumptions and values, affect your judgments.

The information and cases presented in this book are organized within a cognitive-affective-ecological conceptual framework. We believe that violence within the nuclear family, the extended family, and the global human family has many causes, but an approach considering cognitive as well as emotional/motivational factors within an ecological framework is particularly useful. To understand family violence, we need to consider not just environmental stresses but also personal, familial, and cultural values legitimizing aggression as a response. Although emotions such as rage have a strong biological component, they are also intimately tied to cognitions about the circumstances producing them. Individuals typically become enraged by a child talking back, a wife talking to another man, or an elderly parent becoming less independent only when these behaviors are viewed as attacks on oneself or one's values and deserving of punishment.

Thus, our focus is not just on the prevalence of various forms of abusive behavior in families within the United States as a whole and several ethnic minority communities, but also on the perceptions of violence and definitions of abuse and maltreatment that appear to underlie tolerance for aggression. We also consider varying conceptions of the roles of men, women, children, and the elderly that either contribute to or serve as protective factors against interpersonal aggression. Finally, we address the broader historical and environmental forces contributing to the potential for frustration, rage, scapegoating, and displaced aggression within different communities.

Our thanks go to the many people who were supportive and helpful as we developed this book. These include the staff at Sage, including Jim Brace-Thompson and Karen Ehrmann, Joseph Trimble for his feedback on the Native American Indian chapters, our anonymous reviewers, the authors of our four Personal Reflections boxes (Drs. Doe West, Vostina DeNovo, Soledad Vera, and Anita Raj), and our many helpful research assistants (Martha Stevens, Victor Hsuing, Olivia Tun, Robyn Bercovici, Liana Shelby, DaShanne Stokes, Melissa Hagan, Ellyn Turer, Natalia Duke, Autumn Sierra, and Kristin Burke). Kathie also wants to thank her mother, who helps endlessly in more ways than can be described, her brother Tim, who kept the computer going, her husband, Frank, who kept her going, and Dr. Eli Newberger, who provided the endlessly valuable experience of a postdoctoral fellowship in family violence at Children's Hospital in Boston. Denise would like to especially thank her parents, and her other family members and close friends, who have been a constant source of support throughout this process.

PART I

FAMILY VIOLENCE IN CULTURAL
CONTEXT: BACKGROUND ISSUES

1

ISSUES AND DEFINITIONS

Every day in the United States, judgments are made about interactions taking place within families. These judgments can lead to the removal of a child or an elderly parent from a family home, to a restraining order barring a spouse from his or her home, to an arrest, to a conviction for criminal behavior—or to services for particular family members. Sometimes these judgments contribute to the survival of a family member who is in danger, and sometimes they lead to further pain and danger for the individuals they are intended to help. The judgments that people make about interactions in families—for example, whether they are normal, acceptable, and justifiable, or violent, abusive, and intolerable—are influenced by many factors, including personal experience, religious values, personal and community biases, education, and professional training. When experts from different professions decide whether a family member is being maltreated, and whether there is a need for intervention, these professionals often disagree among themselves. Consider the case in Box 1.1 and the questions posed in the box.

Box 1.1   "Child Abuse" Scenario

A social work agency receives an anonymous call on May 28th from a caller who states that he is aware of a case of child neglect and abuse. The caller gives the name of the family and the address. Chris, a social worker with many years experience, responds to the call. The address that was given is located in a very poor area of the city that is predominantly populated by Blacks. At 4:15 p.m., the social worker knocks on the door. It is answered by a young child approximately 8 or 9 years old. At first glance, Chris sees that the child is dirty. There are bruises on both the child's knees and there is a scrape on the child's right elbow. Looking past the child, Chris views the residence. It seems quite messy. Upon closer inspection, Chris finds that there is little food in the refrigerator. Chris questions the child on the whereabouts of the parents, and the child's response is "I don't know." Chris also asks how long the child has been alone. The child responds, "All day." After considering the situation, Chris decides to take the child into care.

Indicate on a scale from 1 (strongly disagree) to 7 (strongly agree) the extent to which you agree with the statement that this child has experienced some maltreatment. Then indicate on a scale from 1 (strongly disagree) to 7 (strongly agree) the extent to which you agree with Chris's decision to remove the child from the home and take the case to court. Explain the reasons underlying your level of agreement.

SOURCE: Mandel, Lehman, and Yuille (1994).

After you have made a judgment concerning this case, and before proceeding beyond this section, please answer these questions: What were the assumptions and values that led to your judgments about whether the child had been abused? If you really were to make a decision about this case, is there any additional information you would want?

The scenario presented in Box 1.1 was developed by Mandel, Lehman, and Yuille (1994), who suggested that unwarranted assumptions about the nature of child maltreatment cases could sometimes interfere with appropriate decision making. They presented the scenario to undergraduate college students as well as to professionals from the United States and Canada enrolled in workshops focusing on child maltreatment. Of particular interest were the participants' qualitative responses—that is, requests for more information, assumptions (e.g., "The social worker was biased against Blacks" [p. 1056]), and hypotheses about the case ("the social worker may be jumping to conclusions" [p. 1056]). Although the researchers provided insufficient evidence of maltreatment to justify removing the child, almost 40% of the professionals agreed with the social worker's action—and there were no significant differences in judgments between those "experts" and the untrained college students! In a later study, social workers, compared with police officers, agreed significantly less with removing the child and provided significantly fewer reasons supporting removal (Mandel, Lehman, & Yuille, 1995). What aspects of their background or training might account for these differences?

ISSUES OF DEFINITION

The difficulties involved in defining words such as "abuse," "neglect," and "maltreatment" have long been a major challenge to workers in the family violence field. In the United States, labels such as "battering" go in and out of popularity, as much for political as for other reasons. Moreover, although phrases such as "family violence," "wife abuse," "child abuse," and "elder abuse," are becoming parts of the general lexicon, there are enormous discrepancies among professionals and members of the lay public in how those terms should be defined. Social scientists, human service workers, and medical and religious personnel constantly debate whether spanking is abusive and even whether wives who do not fulfill their "duties" to husband and home deserve to be "punished."

The issue of definitions is extremely important. The decision to label a particular behavior as abuse, maltreatment, or violence affects such matters as people's willingness to disclose a problem, professionals' sense of obligation to report incidents, the likelihood of families receiving help, and involvement of the social service or criminal justice system. Among the major controversies is the extent to which broad or narrow definitions of maltreatment should be used. Should we define abuse of a spouse, a child, or an elderly parent only in terms of physical injury, or include verbal aggression, neglect, and financial exploitation? Should any behavior, or lack of behavior, that appears to interfere with the well-being of a family member be considered a form of maltreatment? The broader the definition, the greater the number of cases that will be labeled abuse, and the greater the number of lives, for better or worse, in which intervention may be seen as necessary. Broad definitions can increase the number of spouses, children, and elderly who receive services, but they may also contribute to the backlog of cases overwhelming social service agencies, and actually harm family members. Thus, confronting definitional issues is essential to adequate intervention and prevention.

In this book, our use of the three terms "abuse," "violence," and "maltreatment" generally reflects the choices of the researchers, practitioners, and theorists whom we discuss. Our own preference, however, is for the term "maltreatment," which we define as behavior likely to have "mal" (bad) consequences for the family member experiencing it—or at least unlikely to have positive effects. The term "abuse" is so emotionally loaded in its negative connotations that for many, it calls up images of the most extreme forms of violence. Consequently, even when serious harm may be occurring in the context of physical, verbal, psychological, and sexual aggression, people may be reluctant to use the term, especially in relation to their own family members. Similarly, although the term "violence" tends to imply extreme physical aggression, psychological aggression can also have extremely harmful consequences. Our reasoning to use the term "maltreatment" is similar to that of Emery and Laumann-Billings (1998), who distinguish between two levels of *abuse*— "maltreatment" (i.e., minimal or moderate forms of abuse, such as hitting, pushing, and name-calling) and "violence" (i.e., more violent abuse involving serious endangerment, physical injury, and sexual violation), but we suggest using maltreatment as the more inclusive term.

Some of the complexities involved in defining maltreatment and abuse can be seen in the following actual family case study (with nonessential details changed to protect the privacy of the family):

Robert, Anne, and Jenny Kenmore grew up in an affluent suburban community with their father, Mark, manager of a major bank, and his wife Tricia, a successful artist. Mark was active in his church, and well-respected in his community. He was also an extremely strict disciplinarian. When Robert, between the ages of 4 and 11, wet his bed, which he did frequently, Mark made him stand by the front door for hours with his wet sheets draped over his head, an unavoidable sight for anyone entering and leaving the house. When Robert was guilty of other infractions, such as losing his homework or tearing his clothes, Mark made him go out into the yard and find a switch for a "good beating." If Robert did not bring back a big enough switch for the gravity of the offense, Mark sent him back for another. Whatever the offense, Robert received a vigorous beating that left him howling. Tricia occasionally begged her husband not to be so hard on their son, but Mark's response was one of coldness and rejection, wherein he accused her of stupidity and weakness and insisted that the boy obviously needed discipline.

Mark rarely beat his daughters, although both he and his wife occasionally spanked them when they "deserved it." Each girl had her mouth washed out with soap once for using bad language. The girls, however, had other problems with their father. Anne recalls that as early as she can remember, her father would come into her room at night, often with his penis hanging out of his pajamas, lie down next to her, and fondle her. Even in front of his wife, Mark would pull Anne onto his lap and rub himself against her. When Anne complained to her mother, Tricia said not to be silly—her daddy was just being affectionate. After going to overnight camp when she was 12, Anne learned that her father's behavior was not common. On her return home, she started locking her bedroom door at night, and his visits stopped. Only years later did she find out that her father then took up his activities with her younger sister.

The family in which Robert, Anne, and Jenny grew up looked ideal from the outside, but was a source of torment from the inside. The children did not become sources of support or comradeship to each other; rather, they were full of rivalries and hostilities and frequently fought, mostly with psychological weapons— snipping at each other, tattling on each other, lying about each other, snooping into each other's things.

How would you characterize the behaviors of each of the individuals in this family? Do you consider the father abusive when he exposes himself to his daughters and rubs up against them? How about when he forces his son to stand in the hall for hours with a urine-soaked sheet over his head? Is it pretty easy to judge those situations as forms of maltreatment? As abusive? How about when he whips his son with a switch for losing his homework? Or when he and his wife wash the girls' mouths out with soap for saying a bad word? How about spanking them? Would you consider all those behaviors to be forms of maltreatment? Many professionals would use the terms abuse or maltreatment here, but these judgments are more controversial. Many Americans believe washing a child's mouth out with soap for using a bad word or spanking—and sometimes even whipping—a disobedient child are not only acceptable and nonabusive, but necessary to raising "good" children. Finally, how about Mark's calling his wife "stupid" and "weak"? Is that abusive?

Next, consider the mother's behaviors. What are your views of the mother's failure to protect her children from their father? Was that a form of maltreatment? Because of evidence that observing family violence can be very damaging to children, there have been recent cases in which children were taken from their mother and put in foster care because their mother did not remove them from a home in which their father constantly abused *her*. Should Tricia have taken Robert, Anne, and Jenny away from their abusive father? Because she did not do so, should she have lost custody of her children? Finally, what about the children? Were they guilty of "sibling abuse" because they snooped into each other's things, tattled on each other, tried to get each other in trouble—or was that just "normal" sibling behavior?

Clearly, the definitional issues are complicated and subject to disagreement. Among the issues debated are whether the criteria for maltreatment or abuse should include

- Chronicity—If someone slaps his or her spouse across the face *once*, is that abusive?
- Motivation—If a parent spanks a child to keep the child from doing something dangerous, is that abusive?
- Injury—If an adult shakes an elderly parent but no apparent injury results, is that abusive?
- Perspectives of the "victim"—If a wife thinks she "deserved" to be beaten because she showed disrespect to her husband, is the beating not abusive?

Along with several professionals in the field (e.g., Straus, 1990), we believe that many physical acts, such as hitting (except when that is the only possible way to defend oneself from attack) and psychological acts, such as humiliation and neglect, are *inherently* forms of maltreatment, regardless of chronicity, motivation, *apparent* injury, and perspectives of the victim. However, what makes the acts inherently abusive is the potential costs—for the recipient, the perpetrator, and society—of using such behaviors. Demonstrating these costs is an ongoing task for social scientists.

Judgments about maltreatment in families and appropriate responses to behaviors judged to be abusive are influenced not just by definitions of abuse but also by the context in which they occur. The Kenmores are a White, upper-middle-class family. Neighbors may have had some inkling of the harsh discipline towards Robert, but did not interfere. If it is your view that some of Mark's behaviors were abusive, what do you think should have been done? Should he have been arrested, had a trial, and been sent to jail? Forced to have mandatory counseling? What if he had been poor and from a minority culture? Would your recommendations be the same? What if he had done everything described in the scenario except the sexual behaviors? Would you still recommend some kind of intervention into the family? Of what sort?

How do people develop their ideas as to what behaviors in a family relationship are abusive? Clearly, their own experiences—such as the deeds and words of the adults who reared them—are important, and clearly, practices and values are rooted in particular cultural contexts. We suggest that individual cognitions concerning the acceptability or abusiveness of particular behaviors are among the *proximal* (immediate) causes of those behaviors. The values of the cultures in which the individuals operate are among the important *distal* causes of the behaviors. Thus, attention to culture is essential to understanding the extent to which various practices used with children and other family members are considered to be abusive or not. Similar to Smith and Bond (1994), we view culture as a relatively organized system of *shared meanings*. Within any ethnically and religiously diverse country, there can be numerous subcultures; to understand family practices, it is important to examine patterns of behavior and values in both the subculture and the larger culture in which the subculture is embedded.

Although individual cognitions are significant, proximal, causal factors in the decision to use or not use aggressive behaviors to achieve goals, it is important to recognize that intense emotional and motivational forces are also proximal contributors to violence. In fact, batterers often refer to their emotions when providing reasons for their violence—for example, "I couldn't stand her nagging anymore" or "His constant infidelity finally drove me up the wall and I lost it." However, as in the case of cognitions, it is clear that not all negative emotions lead to aggression. Indeed, a negative emotional response to particular circumstances, and the intensity of that emotional response, are both closely interrelated with cognitive appraisals of the circumstances; moreover, the appraisals and the emotional responses are embedded in a cultural context in which particular circumstances are identified as warranting or not warranting feelings such as rage or empathy. In some cultures, disobedience by a child or infidelity by a husband are seen as justifiable reasons for anger; in other cultures, with different values, very different emotions may be associated with those behaviors.

The cognitions of most relevance to understanding family violence can be considered "implicit theories" of family roles, family relationships, and appropriate forms of interpersonal behavior within families. *Implicit theories* are laypeople's conceptions of particular psychological constructs, such as intelligence, love, and success. By contrast, *explicit theories* are "constructions of psychologists or other scientists that are based on or at least tested on data collected from people performing tasks presumed to measure psychological functioning" (Sternberg, 1985, p. 607). Thus, assumptions and values influencing judgments concerning cases of potential abuse are components of implicit theories. In this book, we give considerable attention to the implicit theories of family members' acceptable and abusive ways of interacting with each other—both as these theories are found in laypeople's definitions and examples of abuse, and as reflected in the principles of both governmental and nongovernmental agencies.

Probably the *explicit theory* that has received the most attention in studies on the development of interpersonal aggression is social learning theory, which states that people learn interpersonal aggression through observing aggressive models and being the recipient of aggression (Hotaling & Sugarman, 1986; MacEwen, 1994). However, the theoretical framework underlying the current book has a broader focus, which extends to genetically influenced traits and cognitive, emotional, and motivational processes influenced by social learning, but operating at a more proximal level in producing interpersonal aggression. Specifically, based on experiences within their social environment, individuals may come to formulate implicit theories that "to

spare the rod is to spoil the child," or that the greatest insult a husband can direct at a wife or a wife at a husband is an act of infidelity. Because of what is probably an innate human tendency valuing psychological consistency, acts that violate implicit theories concerning roles and norms in particular cultures can lead to strong emotional reactions in members of those cultures. Thus, implicit theories concerning the behaviors of others within the family, emotional reactions related to cognitions influenced by those implicit theories, and personal motivations in regard to close relationships all contribute to the relative likelihood that aggression against family members will be used and considered as appropriate and nonabusive.

Although implicit theories are fairly available to consciousness, they are influenced by unconscious processes such as denial—the psychological mechanism by which we unconsciously avoid thinking about painful realities. Making judgments about the threatening and immoral attributes of individuals, groups, and countries that differ from us in ethnicity, religion, or nationality is a relatively easy and conscious process. Recognizing our own failings, selfish motivations, hurtful intentions, and immoral behaviors is much more difficult psychologically. Consider the following statement:

> If we deny reality, if we don't feel the pain of what is happening in Bosnia or the house next door, we don't act, even in the small ways available to us, to change those realities. . . . As children, we learn in our families to deny reality, to repress feelings, and to construct imaginary worlds. As adults, we deny aspects of contemporary reality that remind us of the emotional pain we suffered in childhood: the rage, the helplessness, and the sadness. (Milburn & Conrad, 1996, p. 3)

Denial allows Americans to avoid dealing with the unpleasant realities associated with (a) a history of slavery, racism, and prejudice; (b) reliance on extreme punitiveness to deal with those whose behavior we judge negatively; and (c) family violence in our own and/or neighbors' homes, where some family members may be beating, burning, strangling, stabbing, and in other ways torturing other family members. Denial makes it easy to judge the reprehensibility of man's inhumanity to man as long as the inhumanity is not be committed by ourselves in our own homes or by others like us in our own backyards (Milburn & Conrad, 1996). Denial probably also contributes to implicit theories of maltreatment—whatever causes maltreatment, it is not something that has happened to us, and whatever forms maltreatment takes, it is not something we do.

IMPLICIT THEORIES: INTERNATIONAL LEVEL

Implicit theories are reflected not only in the views of individuals but also in a variety of documents that represent perspectives on human beings and their relationships—for example, child-rearing manuals, laws, religious writings, and human rights conventions. These representations of culture are not static; indeed, historically, implicit theories concerning men, women, children, and the elderly have undergone considerable change both within the United States and internationally. Currently, implicit theories as to appropriate child-rearing methods, relationships between spouses, and roles of the elderly vary enormously cross-culturally within the United States, and implicit theories as to what is appropriate behavior in one culture may clash with implicit theories as to what is abusive in another culture. Such clashes reflect an enormous dilemma: How do we decide when a particular subculture is continuing long-standing practices that may once have had adaptive value for the community (or at least for the people in power in the community) but are now widely recognized as harmful to the recipients of those practices? Conversely, how do we decide when the majority culture is failing to understand the adaptive usefulness of practices that have very different implications and consequences in one cultural setting than in another? Can international human rights documents provide standards that may be helpful to the definitional and decisional processes within the United States?

In many cultures for much of human history, women and children were considered the "possessions" of men, and there was little interference in men's treatment (and maltreatment) of the "dependents" in their families. Now, within the international community, the human rights movement has been increasingly concerned with protection of vulnerable individuals from misuse of power and authority within their own families. For example, the United Nations Convention on the Rights of the Child specifies

> the right of the child to freedom from all forms of physical or mental violence, injury or abuse, neglect or negligent treatment, maltreatment or exploitation, including sexual abuse, while in the care of parent(s), legal guardian(s) or any other person who has the care of the child. (Article 19, Statement 1)

Although this right may seem incontrovertible, nowhere does the Convention define the major terms—that is, mental violence, abuse, maltreatment, and exploitation. As of the writing of this book, the United States was one of two member nations of the United Nations that had *not* ratified this document—the other being Somalia, which has had no centralized government since the passing of the Convention. One of the principal objections on the part of the United States is that the Convention prohibits treating children below the age of 18 as adults and thereby forbids subjecting them to the death penalty for capital crimes. In your view, is this a good reason for the United States not to adopt the Convention? (For a fuller discussion of this issue, see Levesque, 2001.)

Another international human rights controversy concerns the issue of corporal punishment of children in the school, juvenile justice system, and home. The European Network of Ombudsmen for Children (2002) has argued that *no* level of corporal punishment is compatible with the U.N. Convention on the Rights of the Child and that corporal punishment should be eliminated in the home and other institutions. They comment,

> As spokespeople for the children of Europe, we believe that eliminating violent and humiliating forms of discipline is a vital strategy for improving children's status as people, and reducing child abuse and all other forms of violence in European societies. . . .
>
> Hitting children is disrespectful and dangerous. Children deserve at least the same protection

from violence that we as adults take for granted for ourselves. (¶ 2-3)

This implicit theory of children's rights is quite different from the prevailing view in the United States today. What do you think of it?

The United Nations has also promulgated the "Declaration on the Right of Women to Freedom From Violence." Within the international human rights community, there is considerable impetus for considering that the provisions of the "Declarations on the Right of Women to Freedom From Violence" apply to the home. In March of 2001, Amnesty International (AI) declared that wife abuse is a form of torture and a violation of international law. Noting that "women's greatest risk of violence comes from men they know, often male family members or husbands" (as cited in Family Violence Prevention Fund Newsflash, 2001, ¶ 7), AI concluded that governments should be held accountable for violence against women, regardless of where it occurs. Would wife abuse within American communities lessen if more Americans adopted this point of view?

IMPLICIT THEORIES: NATIONAL LEVEL

Maltreatment of Children

Implicit theories concerning family violence and maltreatment have undergone considerable evolution in the United States, although there continues to be enormous debate over the issue of corporal punishment in schools and the home. The first legislative definitions of child abuse (from the late 19th century) focused on three types of parental failure: endangering the morals of the child, exhibiting morally reprehensible behavior, and endangering the life and health of the child. Given that much of Western Europe and the United States were under the sway of cultural values dubbed "Victorianism" and a rather conservative Protestantism, it is not surprising that the implicit theory of abuse underlying early laws centered on morality. With the increasing involvement of social service, medical, and legal communities in cases of child maltreatment, the definition of

abuse in various statutes broadened to include notions of neglect and suffering. In the United States today, there is a bewildering array of child abuse statutes focusing on such problems as "an unfit place by reason of neglect, cruelty, depravity, or physical abuse," "mental suffering," and "endangering health." Although these contemporary implicit theories of child abuse place much less stress on moral corruption, one could argue that there continues to be an implicit concern with moral behavior underlying all efforts to define abuse (Giovannoni, 1989).

Consider the case presented in Box 1.2. What would you do if a neighbor of Mary Ellen's told you about this case? Perhaps you would want to report it to an appropriate authority. Back in the time of this case (1871), there was no "appropriate authority." When the cruelty of Mary Ellen's life became known to a humanitarian, Mrs. Etta Angell Wheeler, Mrs. Wheeler appealed to the Society for the Prevention of Cruelty to Animals, which presented the case to the New York Supreme Court. When she appeared before the court, Mary Ellen was bruised, her face was disfigured, and she had a gruesome gash on her face from being struck by scissors. The abuser was sentenced to a year in prison; Mary Ellen developed into a healthy, well-functioning adult as part of Mrs. Wheeler's family, and within a few years, the protective service movement in the United States was under way.

Currently, child abuse reporting laws at both the national and state level are a source of legal definitions of child maltreatment. According to federal law (What Is Child Maltreatment, 2002),

> Child abuse and neglect is, at a minimum, any recent act or failure to act on the part of a parent or caretaker which results in death, serious physical or emotional harm, sexual abuse or exploitation of a child or an act or failure to act which presents an imminent risk of serious harm.

Each state has its own particular subsidiary laws and regulations. Physicians, social workers, teachers, and other professionals are "mandated" by law to report situations in which they suspect child abuse. Phone numbers of child

---

Box 1.2   The Story of Mary Ellen

Mary Ellen is a 9-year-old girl—so small that she looks more like 5—who lives with her two unrelated adults, European immigrants, in a tenement in New York. She is rarely seen by other tenants, but glimpses of her reveal that she is pale and thin, generally barefoot even in winter, wearing little but rags. Sounds coming through the thin walls of the apartment indicate that she is frequently beaten despite pleas for mercy. She is often left alone in the apartment all day, locked in a back room, with the windows darkened. Despite her small size, she is responsible for many household tasks, including washing the dishes, pots, and pans, and putting them all away. Her arms and legs show the signs of her beatings. Her face is the face of a child who is never shown love or affection.

SOURCE: American Humane Association, 2002.

---

abuse hotlines are on billboards and TV channels and thousands of cases of child abuse are reported and investigated every year—although a substantial portion of such cases are "unsubstantiated." Still, a number of questions must be asked: How much maltreatment is taking place that is not labeled as abuse? In how many of the unsubstantiated cases was actual abuse taking place?

The legal definitions, like the federal statute provided above, typically define child abuse in terms of harm or potential harm to children. Unfortunately, although there is considerable agreement that it is abusive to harm children physically or emotionally, there is considerably less agreement on the specific behaviors that lead to physical, and especially to emotional, harm. Indeed, across the United States, people appear to subscribe to the belief that whatever pain or fear may have been inflicted on them during childhood, they "turned out all right," so the behaviors producing the pain and fear could not have been abusive. This implicit notion as to the inconsequential nature of corporal punishment is one of the "myths" that many professionals in the field aim to refute (e.g., Straus, 2000).

Clearly, the behavioral, social science, and clinical communities should play a role in providing answers to some of the questions raised by the legal statutes. Many researchers in the family violence field have devoted considerable attention to the problem of documenting the types of harm that can come from experiences of physical and psychological aggression, inside the family and in the larger community. The National Clearinghouse on Child Abuse and Neglect, whose goal is to acquire and disseminate information about child maltreatment, has provided guidelines for defining child maltreatment to the legal and judicial communities. According to these guidelines, "physical abuse" is characterized by physical *injury* through such behaviors as punching, beating, kicking, biting, burning, or shaking a child, whether the parent intended such injury or not. Such an injury may have resulted from "over-discipline or physical punishment." Spanking or slaps that do not cause broken skin, bruises, or other signs of physical injury, do not fit within this rather narrow definition, although many workers within the field of family violence and child abuse (e.g., Straus, 1996, 2000) have argued that whether it is labeled abuse or not, spanking is at the root of all violence in the family and society.

Despite ongoing acceptance of corporal punishment in the United States, the American Academy of Pediatrics and the American Psychological Association, among other professional organizations, have taken a stance against spanking as a form of discipline. One sign of a possible modification in values is the banning of corporal punishment in the schools in many states. However, in areas of the country where strong conservative Protestant values predominate, there is enormous resistance to ending corporal punishment in schools or homes.

Maltreatment of Spouses

Implicit theories concerning the right of women to be free of wife abuse are also evolving, as evidenced by changing laws and judicial decisions throughout U.S. history. From the sixteenth century through most of the nineteenth century, American laws, based on English common law, permitted men to beat their wives to correct misbehavior—a legal stance that did not change much until 1871, when both Alabama and Massachusetts rescinded this right of husbands. The twentieth century witnessed a growing concern with violence against women and children, and in 1967, the state of Maine opened one of the first shelters in the United States. In 1976, a Domestic Violence Act was passed that allowed temporary exclusion of a violent partner from the home. Although Nebraska made marital rape a crime in the same year, by 1996 there were still only 11 states that had completely repudiated marital rape (Stevenson & Love, 1999).

The most dramatic evidence that implicit theories concerning the roles and rights of women were evolving came in 1994, when Congress passed the Violence Against Women Act (VAWA). VAWA funded services for rape and wife abuse, and allowed women to seek civil rights solutions for gender-based crimes. It also provided protections for women whose partners took them across state lines before abusing them. Modifications of the original VAWA were enacted in October, 2000, to establish new programs, strengthen federal laws, and better address problems in the areas of wife physical abuse, sexual assault, and stalking. Currently, there continues to be some variation in laws across states, but most states define abuse as actual physical abuse, an attempt to harm another, placing another in fear of serious physical harm, or causing another to engage in sexual relations by force, threat of force, or duress.

Although spousal maltreatment laws emerged primarily to protect women, the language of the laws at both the federal and state levels is gender neutral. Despite this gender neutrality in the laws, the implicit theories of most people in the United States and elsewhere assume that perpetrators of spousal maltreatment are generally male and victims are generally female. This assumption has itself been increasingly a source of controversy, as a number of researchers have found that women, like men, are capable of considerable violence against their partners, and the violence is not always done in self-defense (see Hines & Malley-Morrison, 2001; see also chapter 3 of this book).

Maltreatment of Older Individuals

At the national level, implicit theories of family violence excluded considerations of elder abuse until very recently (late 20th century). According to the American Bar Association Commission on Legal Problems of the Elderly, there are no federal laws funding services and shelters for victims of elder abuse. Although the federal Older Americans Act includes definitions of elder abuse and authorizes the use of federal funds for a National Center on Elder Abuse and specified elder abuse activities in states and local communities, it does not fund adult protective services (APS) or shelters for abused older persons. However, according to the report, all fifty states and the District of Columbia have enacted legislation authorizing the provision of APS in cases of elder abuse, systems for the reporting and investigation of elder abuse, and mechanisms for the provision of social services to help victims. Similar to child abuse reporting laws, the elder abuse statutes vary widely in their definition of abuse, the types of maltreatment covered, and the age at or circumstances under which a victim is eligible to receive protective services.

IMPLICIT THEORIES OF PROFESSIONAL AGENCIES

Implicit theories of family violence and abuse also operate at the level of agencies and professionals whose responsibility it is to identify and assist victims of abuse. It is with these agencies and professionals that families and individuals interact directly, and the beliefs and practices of these agencies have major implications for the treatment and prevention of violence in families. Difficulties in defining abuse and lack of consensus about "harm" are among the dilemmas facing human service workers and medical and legal authorities whose responsibilities include providing services to, and protecting the rights of, needy individuals and families.

Symptoms of family crisis and childhood injury have become "medicalized" (i.e., conceptualized as a medical problem needing to be treated by the medical profession), "legalized" (i.e., identified as a violation to be reported by mandated professionals), and called "child abuse" because of major conflicts between the medical and legal perspectives on child abuse regarding (a) judgments of the seriousness of the risk to children of particular parental behaviors, (b) evidence concerning the mental state of the abuser, (c) the tendency to see the abusers themselves as victims of some sort, and (d) the role of law in helping children and families. Furthermore, the debate over children's rights is charged by two fundamental dilemmas:

1. Family autonomy versus coercive intervention—Do parents have the right to rear children however they want with no intervention from professionals or "authorities"?

2. Compassion versus control—Do abusive parents need sympathy and social services or are court action and criminal prosecution more appropriate responses? (Newberger & Bourne, 1978)

These dilemmas are equally relevant to other forms of family aggression.

Society's response to evidence of harm to children is more likely to be coercive and controlling if the families are poor and socially marginalized. Moreover, those poor and marginalized families are more likely to be labeled as abusive and neglectful in the public health settings they must use. By contrast, injuries to children from affluent families are more likely to be labeled as "accidents" by the private pediatricians whose assistance those families seek (Newberger & Bourne, 1978). It is likely that this bias transfers to other forms of family violence, as well. This perspective on identifying and responding to abuse is important because some of the minority communities discussed in this book tend to

have greater problems of poverty and social marginalization than others, and biases within the professional and community services may operate such that the label of "abuse" is more often applied to them than to families from more socioeconomically advantaged communities.

FAMILY VIOLENCE AND ABUSE IN A MULTICULTURAL SOCIETY

In a country as culturally diverse as the United States, how can one best approach an analysis of the varieties and conceptions of abuse in families across different subjective cultures? With some reservations, we decided to organize this book around the major ethnic classifications of minority communities most commonly found in the literature on families and family violence—that is, Native American Indian, African American, Latino or Hispanic, and Asian American. However, each of these labels represents a type of "ethnic lumping"—that is, each classification is itself an umbrella encompassing related but not identical cultural groups, with their own particular heritages. Consequently, within each chapter we provide any pertinent available information that is available on the subgroups—for example, African Americans versus Caribbean Americans, Korean Americans versus Japanese Americans. Moreover, we consider the forces that brought members of each group to this continent. Undoubtedly, their current value systems have been influenced not just by the cultural heritages of their families in their countries of origin but also by historical facts— did they or their ancestors come to this country to escape religious or ethnic persecution, in chains as slaves, or to seek economic opportunity? What are their lives like now: full of opportunity, stress, discrimination, or success? We also give consideration to the fact that problems related to the confounding of ethnicity with social class contribute to the difficulties of analyzing the prevalence, causes, and consequences of family violence.

This organizational system shares some commonalities with the current U.S. Census Bureau system of classification for "race." From 1977 to 2000, "Race and Ethnic Standards for Federal Statistics and Administrative Reporting," established by the federal Office of Management and Budget (OMB), designated four "racial" categories (American Indian or Alaskan Native, Asian or Pacific Islander, Black, and White) and two "ethnicity" categories (Hispanic origin and Not of Hispanic origin). In 1997, recognizing the increasing diversity of the U.S. population, the OMB announced revised standards for federal data on race and ethnicity. The categories for race are now American Indian/Alaska Native; Asian; Black/African American; Native Hawaiian/Other Pacific Islander; White; and "Some Other Race," and the two "ethnicity" categories are Hispanic or Latino and Not Hispanic or Latino (Yax, 2000).

For the 2000 census, the Census Bureau also added an item for racial self-identification. Responses to the self-identification item are categorized as follows: (a) "White," which includes all those who indicated their race as "White" or used labels such as Canadian, French, Irish, Greek, Lebanese, Near Easterner, Arab, or Polish; (b) "Black," which includes those labeling themselves as "Black or Negro" or as African American, Afro-American, Black Puerto Rican, Jamaican, Nigerian, West Indian, or Haitian; (c) "American Indian, Eskimo, or Aleut," which includes individuals who indicated their race as "American Indian," "Eskimo," or "Aleut," entered the name of a particular tribe, or used labels such as Canadian Indian, French-American Indian, or Spanish-American Indian; (d) "Asian or Pacific Islander," which includes individuals who reported in one of the Asian or Pacific Islander groups listed on the questionnaire (Chinese, Filipino, Japanese, Asian, Indian, Korean, Vietnamese, Cambodian, Hmong, Laotian, Thai, Other Asian); and (e) "Other Race," which includes individuals with a Hispanic/Latino origin (such as Mexican, Cuban, or Puerto Rican) or entries such as multiracial, multiethnic, or interracial (Yax, 2000).

The Census Bureau noted that it does not use the term "race" to denote any clear-cut scientific definition of biological stock and recognizes that the categories of the race item encompass racial and national origin as well as sociocultural groups (Gibson & Lennon, 1999). Consistent with much of the current social science literature, we prefer the term "ethnic" to "racial," partly because of the lingering view that "races" are biologically or genetically determined groupings. Furthermore, many workers within the social science community have argued that the label "race" should be abandoned altogether (e.g., Dole, 1995; Phinney, 1996) or that the term "ethnicity" should be used instead when investigators are focusing on cultural characteristics (Helms & Talleyrand, 1997). Because our emphasis is on culture, we use the term "ethnicity," without presuming that the conceptual debates over the terms "race" and "ethnicity" have been resolved.

PLAN OF THIS BOOK

In chapter 2, we introduce major theories concerning the causes of various forms of family violence. We introduce these theories within the context of an integrative conceptual framework, based on an ecological theory. We also review the major empirical approaches to family violence, and discuss the advantages and disadvantages of different methodological approaches. Chapter 3 presents the major findings concerning family violence in the country as a whole and problems inherent in arriving at exact rates of family violence.

In Parts II through V, we focus on the four major ethnic minority communities in this country—Native American Indian, African American/Black, Hispanic/Latino, and Asian American. The first chapter in each section considers the historical/cultural contexts for family interactions, the views on abuse held by members of those communities, and identified risk and protective factors. It also includes a "Personal Reflections" box from a member of that community experienced in issues of family violence. The subsequent chapter or chapters in each section focus on incidence, predictors, correlates, and consequences of family violence within that community from an ecological perspective. We present the chapters on ethnic minority communities in the order in which they faced domination by the White, majority community—that is, the Native Americans whose land the Europeans came to settle in the 1500s and 1600s; the Africans who were brought here in chains to serve the European community; the Hispanics, both indigenous and descendants of Spanish invaders, into whose territories the expanding young nation advanced in the 1900s; and the Asians who came first primarily to help build the railroads in the mid- to late 19th century, and then in a larger wave in the 20th century. In the final section of the book, we consider approaches to intervention and prevention within and across groups, including programs to combat poverty and discrimination.

To supplement the available scholarly literature, throughout this book we provide examples of implicit theories of abuse obtained through responses to an open-ended survey on cross-cultural definitions of abuse. In this survey, we asked respondents from a wide variety of backgrounds to answer, in their own words, the following questions:

1. What is your definition of "abuse" in the context of family relationships? Please give an example.

2. In your view, what makes a behavior "extremely abusive"? Please give an example.

3. In your view, what makes a behavior "moderately abusive"? Please give an example.

4. In your view, what makes a behavior "mildly abusive"? Please give an example.

We also invited these respondents to share any experiences of abuse that they or someone they knew had experienced. Additionally, in a second section of the survey, we requested examples of parent-child, husband-wife, wife-husband, adult-elderly, and other types of interpersonal abuse. We provide sample responses not as scientific evidence that a particular community has a particular implicit theory of intrafamilial abuse, but simply to illustrate perspectives found within that community. Most chapters begin with a sampling of responses from participants whose implicit theories are representative of the voices of members of those communities and illustrate the research findings discussed in the chapter.

2

THEORIES AND METHODS

- *"Psychiatric problems. Self-centeredness, e.g., when a spouse demands to exert control over the other spouse (or friend or relative) by words and actions—constantly."* (68-year-old Irish-American Catholic Caucasian male)
- *"Any member hitting another one out of anger."* (17-year-old Catholic Caucasian male)
- *"A husband not letting [his wife] leave the house because he is jealous or doesn't trust her."* (33-year-old Jewish Caucasian female)
- *"Made to feel inferior at all times, not allowed to make any decisions, must be totally dependent on the dominant person."* (66-year-old Baptist Caucasian male)
- *"Repetitive harmful (physical/emotional) behavior, e.g., someone who continually takes their frustrations out on his/her family."* (25-year-old Caucasian Catholic female)
- *"[Mild abuse is] when the person was raised with extreme criticism and grow up to think it is their job to express unfavorable judgment."* (50-year-old Christian Caucasian female)

WHAT IS ABUSE?

In answering the question "What is your definition of 'abuse' in families?" these respondents to our survey provided evidence of the kinds of implicit theories they have concerning the causes of abuse within families. Review their responses again, and identify the implicit assumptions concerning the factors that produce abuse in family relationships. Consider also your own implicit theories concerning the causes of family violence.

Although theoretical formulations abound, no single factor has been identified that can account for all the different kinds of family violence and abuse. Indeed, no single theoretical explanation seems adequate to the task of explaining all cases of even a single type of abuse (such as physical, psychological, or sexual). Similarly, there is as yet no fully adequate explanation of the cognitive judgments people

make concerning the acceptability of violence as a means of dealing with frustration and other negative feelings and evaluations related to the behavior of others. What is needed is an integrative theory of family violence that addresses the relevant behavioral, affective, and cognitive factors within a multilevel ecological model incorporating both distal factors and proximal processes leading to maltreatment. In this chapter, we build on relevant work to construct such a model, incorporating several useful illustrative theories, but by no means all of them. This model is consistent with cumulative risk models developed to explain both psychopathology and violence as outcomes of an accumulation of risk factors within individual lives (Goebert et al., 2000; Verlinden, Hersen, & Thomas, 2002).

The theories to be incorporated into such an integrative model can be distinguished on the extent to which they focus on *factors* rather than on *mechanisms* or *processes*; this distinction has implications for the nature of the integrative model. *Factor theories*, typically associated with sociology and social psychology, often focus on *characteristics* of contexts or individuals within contexts that may lead to, or be associated with, acts of family aggression but are not the direct and immediate causes of those acts. Most commonly, what are considered in these theories are risk factors. *Process theories*, typically associated with behavioral or developmental psychology, often focus on the *dynamics* or *mechanisms*—for example, cognitions and emotions—that operate within an immediate interactional context and directly produce aggression. Like factors, such mechanisms can be conceived of as operating at more distal levels (e.g., social learning of aggressive tactics in childhood) or more proximal levels (e.g., judgments that one has just been shown disrespect). Neither type of theory is complete. Moreover, none of the factors or processes identified in available theories can be considered to be necessary and sufficient as explanations of family violence.

AN ECOLOGICAL APPROACH

Currently, the most useful conceptual models in the field of family violence and abuse are ecological models incorporating both distal and proximal causes (Garbarino, 1987; Heise, 1998; Newberger & Newberger, 1981; Schiamberg & Gans, 2000). At the heart of contemporary ecological theorizing is the view that human development and behavior should be analyzed within a nested set of environmental contexts, labeled the microsystem, mesosystem, exosystem, and macrosystem. The *microsystem* consists of the relations between the developing individual and the immediate settings (e.g., home, school) in which that individual interacts with others in particular roles (e.g., son, daughter, parent). The *mesosystem* consists of relations among the settings in which the developing person is involved at any particular life stage (e.g., between home and school). The *exosystem,* an extension of the mesosystem, includes the larger neighborhood, the mass media, state agencies, and transportation facilities. Finally, the *macrosystem* in which

these other systems are embedded consists of broad cultural factors, including views about the role of children and their caretakers in society. Boundaries across contexts are fluid, such that events, systems, and relationships at each level can affect events, systems, and relationships at the other levels (Bronfenbrenner, 1979). For example, when a society is involved in a war, interactions among family members may become more conflictual.

Building on this model, Belsky (1993) identified three contexts in which etiological bases of child maltreatment have been found:

1. The developmental context, which refers to characteristics of both the parent (e.g., personal experience of violence, insecure attachment style) and the child (e.g., age, health, disruptive behavior) that can increase the likelihood of child maltreatment

2. The immediate interactional context of maltreatment, which focuses on the parenting and parent-child interactional processes associated with abuse and neglect (e.g., punitive and coercive parenting behaviors)

3. The broader context, which embraces the community, cultural, and evolutionary contexts of child maltreatment

At the community level, there is evidence linking social isolation and lack of social support to child maltreatment. At the sociocultural level, many aspects of American society historically and currently have generated a cultural context supportive of child maltreatment, including an enormous tolerance for violence, acceptance of corporal punishment, a view of children as unentitled to separate rights of their own, and the heritage of slavery. Within this framework, there is strong support for the view that child abuse and neglect are influenced by factors operating at multiple levels of analysis—that is, individual/developmental, immediate/situational, demographic, and cultural/ historical.

Our own model in this book is a synthesis and adaptation of Bronfenbrenner's (1979) and Belsky's (1993) frameworks. We use the terms "individual" or "individual/developmental" to refer to aggression-relevant individual

Box 2.1   The Evan Ramsey School Shooting Case

On February 18, 1997, Evan Ramsey, a 16-year-old high school student from Bethel, Alaska, walked into his school before classes started, shot and killed the principal and a student, and wounded two others. Evan was described by his teachers and peers as having problems with uncontrolled rage, which was reflected in acts like throwing trashcans, pushing adults, and punching a hole in the wall at his foster home. He was a marijuana user, had tried to commit suicide at the age of 10, had been diagnosed as depressed, but had never received mental health services.

Evan had lived with his mother and father and two brothers till the age of 7, when his father was sent to prison on a conviction for violent assault and his mother became a severe abuser of alcohol and entered into relationships with several violent domestic partners. After Evan and his brothers ran away from home to escape violence, and were found sleeping on the street by a local official, they were separated and placed into foster homes. Between that time and adolescence, Evan moved from foster home to foster home, and in at least one of those placements experienced abuse, humiliation, and neglect.

SOURCE: Verlinden, Hersen, and Thomas, 2000.

characteristics of aggressors within families. These characteristics include conceptions of abuse, alcohol dependency, and personal experience with family violence. Bronfenbrenner's "microsystem," which corresponds to Belsky's "immediate interactional context," encompasses interactions among family members and characteristics of victims of aggression that have been identified as risk factors for abuse (e.g., dependency). "Exosystem" (which includes the mesosystem) is the social/political/religious/geographical/economic community in which families function. Finally, "macrosystem" refers to the broader set of cultural values and structures, and their historical underpinnings, which influence the more proximal values and behaviors of families in the United States. Given the generally unfair allocation of wealth and resources in the United States and given its history of racism and discrimination, we believe that factors such as poverty, socioeconomic class, and level of education serve as proxy variables representing macrosystem level forces.

OVERVIEW OF ILLUSTRATIVE PREVAILING THEORIES

In this section, we present a brief overview of a sample of the representative anthropological,

sociological, and psychological theories that center on constructs at each of the ecological levels. This overview is by no means totally inclusive; our emphasis is on theories that focus on major risk factors identified in the relevant research. Specific findings concerning the role of the factors in family violence within the ethnic minority communities are provided in later chapters. Before beginning this discussion, read the case in Box 2.1. Based on your own implicit theories of violence, what do you think are the causes of Evan's violence? Can you identify causal factors at more than one level of the ecological framework?

Macrosystem Factor Theories

Fundamental to any macrosystem theory of family violence is the basic assumption that although family violence may be widespread, it is *not* inherent in all human societies—which indeed appears to be correct. A study of archival anthropological data from 90 different societies around the globe showed that although family violence is a pervasive phenomenon (e.g., wife beating was found in 84% of the societies studied, and physical punishment of children was found in 74%), it is not an inevitable result of family life: In 16 of the societies studied, family violence was largely nonexistent (Levinson, 1989).

Patriarchy Theories

Patriarchal theorists (typically feminists) describe a patriarchal social structure as a system of social organization with a predominant ideology justifying and maintaining male authority in all institutions, including the family, and condoning violence as a means of maintaining that authority and resolving conflicts. Recently, in a meta-analysis of studies addressing the link between wife assault and maintenance of a patriarchal ideology, the only component of patriarchal ideology that consistently predicted wife assault was the perpetrator's attitude toward violence (Sugarman & Frankel, 1996). Nevertheless, a patriarchal system is often viewed as a major contributor to the victimization of women (Yllo & Straus, 1990).

Exosystem Factor Theories

Environmental Stressors

Predominant among exosystem perspectives are theories focusing on stressors as predictors of family violence. Life stressors have been defined as relatively discrete life events or experiences perceived as exceeding the individual's resources and as a negative threat or harm. Included within this definition are life events at many levels of the ecological framework—for example, in the context of work (job demotion, loss of pay) and family (separation, extramarital affair), as well as in relation to other events, such as moving to a new residence, experiencing an arrest in the family, daily hassles (e.g., waiting in lines, paying bills), and chronic stressors (e.g., racism; Cano & Vivian, 2001). A review of research on life stressors and wife abuse showed that (a) the majority of studies conducted with batterers indicated a direct relationship between frequency and perceptions of stressors and husband-to-wife violence, and (b) the majority of studies conducted with "nonviolent men" (i.e., men who use violence against their wives but are not in treatment for this problem) indicated that life stressors (either frequency or impact) are positively related to husband-to-wife violence (Cano & Vivian). Which life stressors are likely to be exacerbated

in communities of color in the United States? In what way?

However, some argue that stress results in violence against family members *only* when certain other factors are present because violence is only one of many possible responses to stress. Although there is evidence of a positive association between number of stressors (e.g., troubles with an employer, death of someone close, large increase in hours worked) experienced in a year and rate of child abuse (e.g., kicking, biting, punching, and/or beating a child), especially by husbands, a number of intervening variables play a role in this relationship—specifically, growing up in a violent family, low marital satisfaction, and social isolation (Straus, 1980a). For example, among people who had learned to use violence during childhood and who believed that hitting other family members was justified, stress was related to child abuse. However, when those conditions were absent, the relationship between stress and child abuse was minimal or even absent. Thus, stress is an important, but not necessary, cause of family violence. Because we know that not all families of color in the United States are characterized by family violence, even when subject to extreme stresses related to poverty and discrimination, this emphasis on the importance of beliefs (implicit theories) is a vital reminder of intervening factors in the ecological model that can counteract risk factors.

Social Isolation

Some researchers have argued that child abuse and neglect are both associated with isolation of the parent-child relationship from "potent, prosocial support systems" that can provide nurturance and feedback (e.g., Garbarino, 1977). Therefore, to understand child maltreatment, we must study not just high-risk families, but also high-risk neighborhoods (i.e., neighborhoods with higher rates of child maltreatment). A study of communities matched on SES and race, but differing in reported rates of child maltreatment, indicated that in high-risk neighborhoods, family problems seemed to be exacerbated by their contexts—by neighborhoods where isolated families competed for scarce resources rather than assisted each other (Garbarino & Sherman, 1980). In a study of communities within the Chicago metropolitan area, the areas at high risk for child maltreatment were characterized by social disorganization (e.g., criminal activity) and lack of social coherence (e.g., lack of availability and knowledge of social services and support networks; Garbarino & Kostelny, 1992). Although a more recent study with a nationally representative sample found no support for the hypothesis that social isolation is a predictor of parental abuse-proneness (Jackson et al., 1999), much of the research on ethnic minority communities implicates social isolation as a risk factor.

Microsystem Factor Theories

Intrafamilial Stress

As previously mentioned, different stress theories focus on different levels of the ecological network. Whereas exosystem stress theories focus on contextual factors that are *external* to the individual and the family (e.g., poverty, unemployment), microsystem level stress theories place greater emphasis on stresses that are *inherent* in the family as a social structure. Microsystem stress factors can include overcrowding, too many children, and children with disabilities. The assumption is that parents who become overwhelmed by immediate stressors and abuse their children would not necessarily abuse their children under less stressful circumstances. The ecological perspective suggests that stress and parenting beliefs may interact in such a way that the association between parental stress and risk for physical child abuse varies depending on the parent's belief in the value of corporal punishment (Crouch & Behl, 2001).

Dependency Relations

A focus on the role of dependency in family violence can be found particularly in theories of child abuse and elder abuse, but also to some extent in theories of wife abuse. For example, one reason why the victimization of children is so common may be because of their dependency status; they are typically weaker and smaller than adults and have relatively little ability to escape from an abusive family or violent neighborhood (Finkelhor & Dziuba-Leatherman, 1994). Moreover, the "traditional" view on elder abuse can be summed up in the following way: "Elderly people . . . become sick, frail, dependent, and difficult to care for. They then cause stress for their caregivers; as a result of this stress, these otherwise responsible and well-meaning relatives lose control and become abusive toward the elders" (Pillemer, 1993, p. 239). There is evidence that older people, like children, can become dependent on family members for help with eating, dressing, bathing, and transportation; this dependency, in turn, can operate as a risk factor for abuse (Steinmetz, 1993). However, even though many elderly become dependent on relatives for some degree of care, only a very small percentage of the elderly are abused, and some researchers have found no support for the notion that elder abuse results from the dependency of the elderly victim on the perpetrator (Pillemer, 1993). This research indicates that abusers, who "tend to suffer from a variety of mental health, substance abuse, and stress-related problems" (p. 245), are likely to be dependent—particularly financially—on their elderly victims rather than the other way around.

With regard to wife abuse, the most common view is that wives' dependency, particularly their economic dependency, is what keeps many women in abusive marriages. Maltreated wives may have little or no income of their own, be unable to support themselves, or be able to support themselves but not their children. Moreover, they may have internalized society's message that a woman is not complete without a husband and children, and consequently find it emotionally difficult to leave (Wallace, 2002). These sources of dependence may be exacerbated in immigrant women, who may be fearful of being on their own in a country where they are not fluent in the language, feel compelled to send money back home to relatives, and be fearful of bringing shame on their families by divorcing their abusers (Dasgupta, 1998).

As shown with regard to elder abuse, attention to dependency as a factor in family violence has long focused on the dependency of the victim. Here again, however, we find evidence that dependency in the abuser may be the more important risk factor. Perhaps the most dramatic examples of violence sparked by the dependency needs of the perpetrator can be found in what has been described as reactive spousal homicides resulting from a perception that a spouse is either leaving or has left (Dutton, 2002). In a study of such cases, most of the men had personality disorders and nonaggressive criminal histories; when faced with the possibility of being abandoned by their spouses, their dependency needs exploded into uncontrollable rage and led them to murder their wives rather than be left alone without them (Dutton & Kerry, 1999).

Individual/Developmental Context Theories

Behavioral Genetics

Family violence researchers working within a behavioral genetics conceptual framework (Hines & Saudino, 2002) have pointed out that genetic factors, as well as social learning, may account for similarities among family members in the use of violence. In a recent review of literature, Hines and Saudino noted that "behavioral genetic studies on antisocial behavior and aggression support the notion that individual differences in these characteristics are genetically influenced" (p. 220). Moreover, they noted important similarities between aggression in intimate relationships and aggression in the community in their predictors (e.g., alcohol abuse) and their outcomes (e.g., mental health disorders, such as anxiety and depression).

Drug and/or Alcohol Abuse

"Demon rum" and illicit drug explanations for family violence and abuse have a long history of acceptance in both the popular and professional literature and were in part responsible for the prohibition movement in the United States in the 1920s (Gelles, 1993). However, support for this association is mixed. Several clinical studies support the following roles of alcohol as an intervening *causal* variable in

family violence: (a) alcohol is an *instigator* of violence; (b) alcohol is a *disinhibitor* of social control; (c) alcohol is a *destroyer* of the normal growth and development of the individual and the family system, establishing a milieu that tolerates violence; (d) alcohol provides a *rationalization* for violence, allowing the individual to avoid taking responsibility for his/her aggression; and (e) alcohol *influences brain functioning*, operating to increase irritability and anger (Flanzer, 1993). However, other researchers (e.g., Gelles) argue that with the exception of amphetamines, there is little evidence that alcohol and drugs play a disinhibitory role that makes them prime causes of family violence. Furthermore, the best evidence against the disinhibitor theory of alcohol comes from cross-cultural and experimental studies indicating that the effects of drinking on behavior vary widely, and evidence that even men who have been drinking before assaulting their wives are typically not legally intoxicated at the time of the wife beating. Therefore, although alcohol use may be associated with family violence, it may not be either a necessary or a sufficient cause.

Process Theories of Learning: Social Learning Theory

Social learning theory is one of the most popular theories for explaining the process by which individuals come to behave aggressively against family members and others. According to this theory, aggressive behaviors are learned both through operant conditioning (i.e., the strengthening of some behaviors through positive and negative reinforcement, and the suppression of other behaviors through punishment) and through modeling observed behaviors in important role models. Studies addressing this theory of the intergenerational transmission of violence have found at least partial support for hypotheses that individuals abused in childhood will be at risk for later abuse of their own children (Gershoff, 2002; Jackson et al., 1999; Kaufman & Zigler, 1987; Straus & Smith, 1990a), that men who observed their fathers abusing their mothers will be at increased risk for abusing their own wives (Corvo & Carpenter, 2000; Dutton, 1995), and that young adults who observed and experienced aggression in childhood will be more likely to be in abusive relationships with their partners (Cappell & Heiner, 1990; Kalmuss, 1984; Marshall & Rose, 1990; Straus & Smith, 1990a; Widom, 1989).

Process Theories of Cognition: Social Exchange/Control

According to social exchange/control theory (Gelles, 1983, 1987; Goode, 1971), human social behavior is motivated by a "minimax strategy"—that is, it operates to minimize costs and maximize benefits. In an early application of exchange theory to family violence, Goode noted that force, the threat of force, violence, and the threat of violence are commonly used by the more powerful members in families (e.g., fathers, parents) to gain compliance from less powerful members (e.g., children, wives)—to keep them from behaving in ways considered undesirable and to get them to behave in ways considered desirable. Among the lessons children may learn is that force is a very effective tool for controlling others, that some situations call for violence (e.g., when there is a threat to one's honor), and that there are circumstances in which others will justify the use of violence. When family members believe their needs are being met because of the love, loyalty, and respect they gain from each other, they may refrain from using violence. However, family relations often turn sour, divergent values may emerge, what each is willing to do for the others may diminish, one or more family members may feel intensifying anger and frustration at the failure of the others to give as much as they seem to get, and violence may erupt (Goode). How might some of these dynamics operate in communities of color, especially in newly arrived immigrant families?

Process Theories of Emotion: Emotional Reactivity

According to Berkowitz's (1983) theory of reactive aggression, the following sequence of events occurs when an individual faces an unpleasant situation: (a) an aversive stimulus leads to a negative emotional response; (b) the negative emotional response leads to an urge to

hurt, and to associated cognitions, which may further stimulate the urge to hurt; and (c) unless there are inhibiting events, the urge to hurt leads to aggressive behavior. Workers in the field of family violence have found evidence that anger, emotional reactivity, and impulsivity are associated with violence, including family violence. For example, there is a positive correlation between parental self-reports of anger and the use of physical discipline, harsh discipline, and risk for child abuse (Kolko, 1996; Whiteman, Fanshel, & Grundy, 1987), even after controlling for parental stress (Rodriguez & Green, 1997). Furthermore, domestic stalkers and a group of wife-batterers labeled "borderline/cyclical batterers" have been observed to react with rage to perceived or actual rejection or abandonment (Douglas & Dutton, 2001).

Process Theories of Motivation: The Punishment Motive

Many family violence researchers have focused on the desire to punish, without, to our knowledge, formalizing their views into an explicit theory of a punishment motive. However, several major workers in the field have at least an implicit theory concerning the role of a "punishment motive" in interpersonal violence. Consider this argument:

> Everyone understands that corporal punishment is carried out to correct or control misbehavior. What is not understood is that almost all assaults by adults and about two thirds of homicides are also carried out to correct what the offender perceives as misbehavior. (Straus, 1996, p. 837)

In addition, "Corporal punishment provides a model for what to do when someone misbehaves. . . . Unfortunately, sooner or later, almost all spouses misbehave, at least as their partner sees it" (Straus, 1996, p. 839). The development of a motive to punish may be fueled by the suppressed anger that can accompany frequent corporal punishment. Messages that the punishment is deserved may reinforce the related motivation to see that others get their "just deserts."

Box 2.2   The Case of Mrs. Jones

Mrs. Jones grew up in a very wealthy Long Island family. She had very little contact with her cold, rejecting parents, who never wanted a child, and was raised mostly by a nanny who was an extremely strict disciplinarian. She was spanked hard and often early in childhood for making any sort of noise or "disrupting" the household. She married young to get away from home, and immediately became pregnant. She had a difficult pregnancy and was convinced that the child developing within her was "out to get her." From the time Adam was born, she was constantly angry at him, finding him "nothing but trouble." Her husband was away a good deal of the time, but when he was home, he tried to make up for her hostility to the child by giving him lots of attention—which further fueled Mrs. Jones' anger and jealousy, and contributed to increasingly abusive behavior when Mr. Jones was away. By the time Adam was 6, he was engaging in a good deal of delinquent behavior, including the constant pulling of fire alarms, which brought him to the attention of authorities.

SOURCE: Based on a case from Malley-Morrison's files.

Applications of Theories

Review the implicit theories in the responses presented in the opening of this chapter. Which of the formal theories seem to be reflected in those responses? Also, maltreatment is generally considered to involve acts of omission (e.g., neglect), as well as acts of commission (e.g., name-calling, hitting). Which, if any, of the theoretical frameworks presented above seem to have relevance for explaining neglect? Consider now the case study in Box 2.2. Analyze this case in light of the theories that have been introduced in this chapter. Which theories seem to apply best to the case? Which do not apply?

RESEARCH APPROACHES TO FAMILY VIOLENCE

Several major research approaches have been used to study the frequency, predictors, correlates, and outcomes of maltreatment in families. The major approaches are (a) behavioral self-report surveys from national and local community samples as well as more selected samples (e.g., college students, convicted felons) concerning the extent to which they have used particular aggressive behaviors (e.g., hitting, beating) in specified family relationships within a specified time limit; (b) reports from statewide or local professionals or agencies on identified or "caught" cases; (c) attitudinal and experiential self-report questionnaires, often designed to assess potential for abuse at the individual/developmental level; (d) vignette procedures; and (e) observational methods designed to assess intrafamilial dynamics (e.g., at the microsystem level). The behavioral self-report and identified case methods are the most common approaches to the direct assessment of family violence and have provided most of the data on the frequency of family violence and its predictors and outcomes. Attitudinal/experiential surveys have been useful in prospective and other studies designed to identify factors that can help stop abuse before it takes place. Vignette studies have contributed important information on the social-cognitive (i.e., implicit theory) processes that help predict family violence. Finally, observational studies provide a direct snapshot of interpersonal dynamics in abusive couple or parent-child relationships.

Each of these approaches has advantages and disadvantages. A major advantage of the self-report surveys lies in the fact that many incidents of family violence are never reported to authorities, and we would learn nothing about these cases if we relied solely on reports of "caught" cases. The most widely used self-report measures are Straus's original *Conflict Tactics Scales* (*CTS*; Straus, 1979), the *Parent-Child Conflict Tactics Scales* (*CTS-PC*; Straus, Hamby, Finkelhor, Moore, & Runyan, 1998), and the *Revised Conflict Tactic Scales* (*CTS2*; Straus, Hamby, Boney-McCoy, & Sugarman, 1996). Various versions of the *CTS* seek information from respondents about how often they have used or observed such behaviors as swearing, hitting, and pushing, in the context of particular family relationships (e.g., parent-child, husband-wife) and how often these behaviors have been used on them. The *CTS* have been administered in national and regional studies and to specific groups, such as college or high school students, social service and medical personnel, and child and spousal abusers. One disadvantage of these surveys is that many people who are abusive do not admit to it, even on an anonymous survey. However, these self-report surveys consistently provide higher estimates of family violence than studies of caught cases. Therefore, even though studies using the *CTS* may still underestimate rates of family violence, they are probably the best estimates we have.

Data from mandated reporters and social service agencies have the advantage of providing information about cases of family violence that are noteworthy or extreme enough to have come to the attention of authorities. Among the most well-known reports on identified cases of family violence are (a) the National Incidence Studies of Child Abuse and Neglect, (b) the National Child Abuse and Neglect Data System, which receives annual reports from every state on child maltreatment cases reported to protective service agencies, (c) the Department of Justice Reports on Intimate Partner Violence, using estimates from the National Crime Victimization Survey, and (d) the National Elder Abuse Incidence Study. Information from these surveys is probably essential to the goal of eliminating family violence, but the data are subject to biases, such as the underreporting of cases from the more advantaged levels of society and the overreporting of cases from impoverished and minority communities.

In addition to behavioral self-report measures, other self-report questionnaires assess a wide range of personal attitudes, cognitions, judgments, feelings, and other attributes and experiences that may be predictive of or associated with the use of aggression in relationships. Some of the measures in this category are essentially implicit theory measures, providing information on respondents' implicit theories of appropriate forms of discipline (Ashton, 2001; Daro & Gelles, 1992), definitions of maltreatment (Portwood, 1998), attitudes toward wife abuse (Falchikov, 1996), and judgments concerning elder abuse (Moon & Williams, 1993). A limitation to all forms of self-report is people's willingness to answer them honestly.

Another type of self-report measure provides an even more indirect approach to risk for maltreatment. For example, Milner's *Child Abuse Potential* (*CAP*) inventory, developed to distinguish between physically abusive and nonabusive parents in clinical and child protection settings, does not ask direct questions about maltreatment. A recent version of *CAP* (Milner, 1994) includes a 77-item physical child abuse potential scale, which includes subscales for distress, rigidity, unhappiness, problems with child and self, problems with family, and problems from others—all factors that are considered to be predictive of child abuse. Although there is considerable evidence that the *CAP* distinguishes between parents who have been identified as abusive and parents who have not, some researchers (Melton & Limber, 1989; Milner, Gold, Ayoub, & Jacewitz, 1984) have argued that it is risky to use the *CAP* in legal and protective service proceedings to help determine whether a child has been abused. This risk stems from a high rate of "false positives"—that is, the identification of parents at high risk for abuse even though they are not abusive. What level of the ecological model does "potential for child abuse" reflect? What about "distress, rigidity, and unhappiness"? "Problems with family"? "Problems from others"? What does Milner's approach tell you about his implicit theory of child abuse?

Vignette studies provide an indirect approach to individuals' judgments concerning such issues as the appropriateness, acceptability, justifiability, and/or abusiveness of certain behaviors (e.g., slapping a child for telling a lie). Some vignette studies have also asked respondents to indicate whether the behaviors described are serious enough to warrant reporting them to authorities (Crenshaw, Crenshaw, & Lichtenberg, 1995; Kalichman, Craig, & Follingstad, 1989). Vignettes may be less subject to bias than surveys asking people to report on their own aggressive behaviors. Moreover, a major advantage is that different details in the vignette can be manipulated to determine whether characteristics such as race affect judgments of maltreatment. Consider the findings of a study in which participants judged one of two nearly identical versions of a vignette about a child being hurt, with the *only* difference between the vignettes being the race of the family. The participants who judged the version in which the family was Black were significantly more likely to judge the act as abuse than the participants who judged the version in which the family was White (Nalepka, O'Toole, & Turbett, 1981). What does that suggest about implicit theories concerning the nature or causes of child abuse? If we asked professionals directly whether they would report a particular child injury case if the family was Black, but not if it was White, would we get the same evidence of likely bias that came from the vignette study? The disadvantage of vignette studies is that they do not provide evidence about what people actually do, only about what they think and what they indicate they might do.

Observational research methods have been used to study interactions between parents and abused children and between husbands and wives in conflictual marriages. Most typically, these observational methods have been used in case-comparison studies, where the interactions in families identified as abusive are compared with interactions in nonabusive families. What level of the ecological system is being targeted in these studies? Observational studies have the major advantage of giving researchers direct access to interactions that may themselves be abusive or may lead to abuse, but the ethical issues of conducting such research are weighty. Moreover, perhaps because observational studies are very costly, we found few examples of observational studies of family violence within ethnic minority samples.

Major Measures of the Frequency of Family Violence

There are many difficulties in determining *incidence rates* (i.e., the frequency with which acts occur within a specific population during a specified time period) and *prevalence rates* (i.e., the percentage of the population experiencing those acts within a particular time period) for the various forms of family violence in different ethnic communities. Among the problems are sampling and methodological differences across surveys, differences in operational definitions of violence and abuse, differing criteria for ethnic categorization, and reporting biases. The measures that have been used most commonly to determine rates of family violence in different ethnic communities, and to compare rates across communities, are described briefly in the following sections. Findings based on these surveys are discussed in subsequent chapters.

Child Abuse Surveys

National incidence surveys of child maltreatment include the National Family Violence Surveys (NFVS), the National Studies of the Incidence of Child Abuse and Neglect (NIS), and the annual surveys of the National Committee on Abuse and Neglect Data System (NCANDS). Important features of each of these surveys are described briefly here, with an emphasis on the differences among surveys that can lead to discrepancies in estimates of the frequency of child maltreatment.

Both the original 1975 National Family Violence Survey (NFVS; Straus, Gelles, & Steinmetz, 1980) and the 1985 National Family Violence Resurvey (Straus & Gelles, 1986) were administered by Harris pollsters to nationally representative samples of American families. There were 2,143 respondents in the first, face-to-face interview study, and 6,002 respondents in the second, telephone interview study. In each case, half of the respondents were wives or female partners, and the other half were husbands or male partners. In addition to a national probability sample of 4,032 households, the second study oversampled Black and Hispanic households to allow ethnic group analyses. Moreover, unlike the 1975 study, the

1985 study included separated or divorced individuals and single parents. In both studies, the measure used to obtain self-reports concerning parental use of corporal punishment (e.g., grabbing, shoving, hitting, spanking the child) or more extreme violence (e.g., kicking, biting, beating up, burning the child) was the *CTS* (Straus, 1979, 1990). In each study, parents were asked how many times they used each behavior with a target child in the year before the interview. If a parent did not report using a behavior in the previous year, the interviewer asked if the parent had *ever* used the tactic. Typically, investigators using the responses to the NFVS have summed the frequency responses to form corporal punishment and severe violence or abuse scales.

Other major surveys providing incidence rates by ethnicity typically focus on identified cases of child abuse rather than on representative community samples. The three National Studies on the Incidence of Child Abuse and Neglect (NIS, 1980, 1988, 1993) solicited information from community professionals mandated to report child abuse cases, specifically, professionals from schools, hospitals, law enforcement agencies, and welfare offices. These mandated professionals were asked to report all cases of child maltreatment with which they had come in contact and to indicate which ones they had reported to child protective services (CPS). The NIS investigators also solicited reports from CPS agencies, so that they could compare the cases reported by the professionals with the reports received by CPS from either professionals or nonprofessionals, such as neighbors, family members, and friends.

In identifying maltreatment cases as physical, sexual, and emotional abuse, and physical, emotional, and educational neglect, the NIS respondents were instructed to use a definition of maltreatment emphasizing deliberate acts or marked inattention to the child's basic needs that could result in foreseeable and avoidable injury or impairment to a child, or worsen an existing condition. The findings of the most recent NIS survey are based on a nationally representative sample of over 5,600 professionals in 842 agencies serving 42 counties. This study and the NIS-2 used two sets of standardized definitions of abuse and neglect.

Under the "Harm Standard," the only standard used in NIS-1, children were identified as maltreated only if they had already experienced harm from abuse or neglect. Under the "Endangerment Standard," added to NIS-2 and NIS-3, children were included in the maltreatment group if they had experienced abuse or neglect that put them at risk of harm (Sedlak & Broadhurst, 1996).

Another source of data on the incidence of child maltreatment in different ethnic groups in the United States can be found in annual reports from state CPS agencies to the National Child Abuse and Neglect Data System (NCANDS) and reported by the U.S. Department of Health and Human Services (DHHS). Data submitted to the NCANDS are of two types: the Summary Data Component (SDC) and the Detailed Case Data Component (DCDC), which collect state child abuse and neglect data at different levels of detail. The SDC collects aggregate data through annual surveys in which states report the number of children and families receiving preventive services, the number of reports and investigations of child abuse and neglect, the number of children who were subjects of reports of abuse or neglect, the number of child victims of maltreatment, the number of child fatalities, and other statistics. For the 1999 calendar year, all states submitted a report, but varied in the extent to which they responded to items required by the 1996 amendments to the child abuse reporting law. For example, although 49 of the 51 states provided information on the number of children reported as victims of abuse and neglect, only six states reported data on the average number of out-of-court contacts between court-appointed representatives and child victims. The second NCANDS component, the DCDC, collects case-level data on the children identified in reports alleging maltreatment. These data include the age, race, and sex of the children, types of maltreatment, apparent risk factors, services provided, and characteristics of children and perpetrators. For 1999, 23 States submitted DCDC data that passed the rigorous validation process within the NCANDS.

The annual reports based on the NCANDS data provide several types of summary information of the "dispositions" that follow the investigation of a child maltreatment report:

Box 2.3   Baby X—Another Failure of the System?

Child X was only 7 weeks old when seen by a doctor for a fractured leg. She was placed in foster care following the physician's report that the fracture could not have been accidental and a CPS assessment of the family as at high overall risk for maltreatment. Both parents denied causing the injury, though the father admitted that the injury had happened while the child was living in his home and probably in his physical care. Psychological evaluations indicated that the mother was somewhat more pathological than the father, who was described as having a strong religious orientation, as being troubled by difficulties acculturating to life in the United States, and as being guarded and defensive on the tests. Both parents were referred to both individual and couples therapy and cooperated reasonably well.

Child X's case was reviewed about 11 months after the initial injury. The father's therapist strongly recommended that the child be returned home that day, and the family's social worker changed her original negative recommendation to the court to match the therapist's recommendation. The attorneys for mother, father, and child all agreed with the recommendation that the child be returned home. The court ordered that the child continue to be formally in foster placement status, but be returned to her parents' home. Therapy continued; meanwhile, a second child, Child Y, was born to the family. About 5 months after Child X was returned to the home, she was taken to an emergency room with a subdural hematoma. It was later discovered that she also had a blunt injury skull fracture. Both children were removed from parental custody, and Child X was still on life support at the time of follow-up. The father left the country and supervised visitation was ordered for the mother.

SOURCE: Miller, Fox, and Garcia-Beckwith, 1999.

(a) "substantiated" investigations, where the allegation of maltreatment or risk of maltreatment was supported or founded on the basis of law or policy in that state; (b) "indicated" or "reason to suspect" dispositions, where the allegation could not be substantiated under state law or policy, but there was reason to believe that the child may have been maltreated or at risk of maltreatment; and (c) "not substantiated" dispositions, where there was insufficient evidence under state law or policy to conclude that the child had been or might be mistreated. Data from the NCANDS provide the lowest estimates of the frequency of child abuse in the United States.

There are a number of reasons why cases reported to state CPS agencies may not be substantiated. For example, there may be no maltreatment occurring in the family, or the maltreatment may be taking place without sufficient evidence to prove it. Consider the case in Box 2.3. How could a case go so wrong? Who is responsible for what happened to Baby X? At

how many levels of the ecological system did things go wrong?

Summary of Differences. In trying to provide an adequate estimate of the pervasiveness of child abuse, different investigators refer to the findings of different surveys and, therefore, provide different estimates. The estimates for child physical maltreatment are highest when data from the NFVS are analyzed, because many respondents admit to behaviors, such as beating their children, that are never reported to any child protection agency. The next highest estimates come from the NIS surveys, which gather data on the cases that mandated reporters have identified as abusive, but have not necessarily reported. Somewhat lower rates come from the DHHS reports on NCANDS, which provide data on number of child maltreatment reports, because the actual number of substantiated cases is even lower and clearly an underestimate of the actual number of child maltreatment cases. In later chapters, we provide more specifics as to the estimated frequencies of the various forms of abuse within different ethnic communities.

Race Classifications in the Different Surveys. Although several investigators have provided estimates of the incidence of child maltreatment in different ethnic groups, based on each of the surveys already described (NFVS, NIS, and NCANDS), obtaining accurate estimates is complicated further by the fact that different investigators have grouped respondents differently in the process of identifying "ethnic" groups. For example, in some of the NFVS analyses for corporal punishment and physical abuse (e.g., Straus & Donnelly, 2001), participants' race was coded as either White or "minority" (i.e., all minority group members combined); clearly, this strategy can mask many potential differences among ethnic groups. Several other studies (e.g., Wolfner & Gelles, 1993), using NFVS data, have separated ethnic groups (i.e., Hispanics, Blacks, and Native Americans) to allow greater specificity in comparisons. In contrast to the analyses of NFVS data in which Hispanics were included in the "minority" sample, the original analyses of NIS-3 data combined Whites with Hispanic Whites and compared them to Nonwhites, thus also making comparisons difficult (Sedlak & Broadhurst, 1996). As is discussed in Chapter 7, NFVS data indicate ethnic differences in parental levels of physical discipline (Straus & Stewart, 1999), whereas NIS-3 data show no racial differences in child maltreatment (Sedlak & Broadhurst). Other investigators (e.g., Hampton, 1987) doing secondary analyses of NIS data and analyzing the data separately for Whites, Blacks, and Hispanics have found ethnic group differences. Finally, DHHS reports of NCANDS data, which provide frequencies of child maltreatment separately for Whites, Blacks, Hispanics, American Indians, and Asians, also indicate ethnic group differences.

Estimates of the Incidence of Adult Maltreatment

The NFVS also included the *CTS* for husband-to-wife violence and wife-to-husband violence. Again, participants were asked to indicate the number of times during the previous year that they had perpetrated or received specific behaviors, such as swearing, hitting, threatening with a knife or gun, and using a knife or gun. If they had not used any of these behaviors that year, they were asked if they had *ever* used them. Items from the NFVS have also been included in a number of federally sponsored national surveys, including the 1995–96 National Violence Against Women Survey (described later in this section), the 1992 National Alcohol and Family Violence Survey, and the 1995 National Alcohol Survey.

Although different versions of the *CTS* have been used to study family violence in hundreds of studies in the United States and abroad, the scales are not without their criticisms. A particular point of contention is that several studies using the *CTS* (e.g., Straus & Gelles, 1986) have found that rates of violence against partners are as high for women as for men (for reviews of these issues, see Hines & Malley-Morrison, 2001; Sugarman & Hotaling, 1989). Straus (1990) has frequently addressed the criticisms of the *CTS*, has provided extensive reliability and validity data in support of the scales, and in our view has well established their usefulness. He and his colleagues (Straus et al., 1998) have also revised the scales to address many criticisms; to our knowledge, the *Revised Conflict Tactics Scales* (*CTS2*) have not yet been administered to a nationally representative sample.

The National Violence Against Women (NVAW) Survey, a national telephone survey jointly sponsored by the National Institute of Justice (NIJ) and the Centers for Disease Control and Prevention (CDC), was administered between November 1995 and May 1996 to a representative sample of 8,000 U.S. women and 8,000 U.S. men. To measure physical abuse, this survey incorporated items from the original *CTS* concerning whether any other adult had slapped or hit them, kicked or bit them, choked them, hit them with an object, beaten them up, threatened them with a weapon, or used a gun, knife, or other weapon on them. The survey provided information about men's maltreatment of women, women's maltreatment of men, and maltreatment in same-sex relationships. It also included questions on sexual abuse and stalking (Tjaden & Thoennes, 2000).

Annual rates of physical assault generated from the NVAW Survey are substantially lower than those generated by the NFVS, partly for methodological reasons. In the NFVS, participants were told they were answering questions about their spousal relationships, were assured that conflicts between spouses are a normal aspect of any marriage, were told that different couples utilize different methods of resolving conflicts, and were asked about both their own and their partners' behaviors. In the NVAW, participants were told that they were participating in a study on personal safety, and were asked to indicate whether the specified behaviors had been perpetrated on them in the previous year. If they indicated that an aggressive behavior had been perpetrated against them, they were asked about their relationship with the perpetrator. The NFVS may elicit higher frequencies of spousal abuse because spouse's aggressive acts may not come to mind when one thinks about threats to personal safety, but be more readily available when one thinks about conflicts within that particular relationship.

Somewhat different questions and procedures have been used in the National Crime Victimization Surveys (NCVS) of the U.S. Department of Justice (DOJ). Through a standard interview, the NCVS collects victimization data from a sample of approximately 100,000 individuals living in approximately 50,000 households, whether or not those crimes were reported to law enforcement. Among the questions asked are: "Has anyone attacked or threatened you in any of these ways: a) with any weapon, for instance, a gun or knife; b) with anything like a baseball bat, frying pan, scissors, or stick; c) by something thrown, such as a rock or bottle?" Respondents are also asked if they have been grabbed, punched, choked, or threatened, and whether anyone has raped or attempted to rape them or committed any other form of sexual attack or unwanted sexual act against them. If they report any of these incidents, they then identify their relationship with the perpetrator. These data, in contrast to the NFVS data, show substantially higher levels of violence by men against women than by women against men. They also report substantially lower violence rates overall for *both* men and women.

The National Elder Abuse Incidence Study (NEAIS) of 1996 was prepared by the National Center on Elder Abuse for the Administration for Children and Families and the Administration on Aging and made available in September of 1998. Similar to NIS, the design for NEAIS employed a stratified multistage sample of 20 nationally representative counties. Moreover, the data for this study included information from two types of sources: (a) reports of domestic elder abuse to protective service agencies, in this case, to Adult Protective Services Agencies (APS), and (b) "sentinel agencies," including financial institutions, law enforcement agencies, hospitals, and elder care providers. Thus, data from the NEAIS, similar to data on other forms of family violence from mandated reporters, are likely to significantly underestimate the actual incidence of elder abuse in the United States. Analyses of the data include separate analyses by five major ethnic groups: White, Black, Hispanic, Asian, and American Indian.

Differences in the nature of samples and methodologies constrain more than just estimates of the incidence or prevalence of various forms of family violence. Researchers in the field desire to identify the predictors, correlates, and outcomes of family violence. When researchers take advantage of protective service records to identify characteristics of perpetrators, how far can they generalize their findings? If physical and mental frailty of the elderly person is a predictor of substantiated cases of elder mistreatment, does that mean physical and mental frailty are good predictors of the types of elder abuse that never get reported?

Another problem facing researchers who are interested in the predictors, correlates, and outcomes of family violence, especially the extent to which these variables may vary by ethnicity, is the confounding of social class and ethnicity. As shown in subsequent chapters, minority group members typically differ from majority group members not just in ethnicity, but also in social class. Because social class is very often a statistical predictor of family violence, disentangling the effects of social class from those of ethnicity is an extremely important yet difficult task. Finally, with very few exceptions, the studies of family violence in ethnic minority communities are characterized by "ethnic lumping"—the assumption that all Native Americans, African Americans, Latino Americans, and Asian Americans are alike. We discuss this problem more extensively in subsequent chapters, and report every study known to us that attended to differences within the broader classifications.

Summary

Many theories of family violence have been advanced, and these can be categorized as to whether they address its causes at the macrosystem, exosystem, microsystem, or individual level of the ecological model. Moreover, these theories differ among themselves in the extent to which they focus on risk factors or processes. The primary research methods that have been employed to gain information about different forms of maltreatment in families include national and local self-report surveys focusing on abusive acts, information on identified cases by mandated reporters, attitudinal surveys, vignette studies, and observational studies. Different approaches provide different estimates of the incidence/prevalence of family violence in ethnic minority communities, and a major limitation of most of the relevant studies is ethnic lumping. As you read the rest of this book, consider the extent to which particular research findings seem consistent with one theoretical framework rather than another, the usefulness of considering the findings from an ecological perspective, and the ways the findings were likely to have been influenced by the particular research methods used. Ask yourself which findings seem most valid, and why, and what further research you think is necessary if we are to do a more effective job of combating family violence in all ethnic communities (including White).

3

Types and Extent of Maltreatment in the United States

Families within the United States, including minority families, are imbedded in a macroculture in which violence is a pervasive and acceptable means of behavior. Every institution within this country is affected in some way by, or in some way perpetuates, violence. For instance, cultural attitudes about violence can affect laws at the federal and state levels enacted to either protect people from violence or maintain it. These attitudes are in many ways either mirrored or affected by the media. This chapter is an overview of the many types of violence occurring in families in this country. We discuss the difficulties in deciding on an exact definition of each type of violence and statistics on each type. First, we briefly discuss the broader context in which these families operate—that is, macrosystem influences, such as American cultural beliefs and laws, coupled with exosystem influences, such as state laws and the media.

On a macrosystem level, broad cultural beliefs have contributed to our inability to eliminate or even ameliorate the problem of family violence. Foremost among these beliefs is the sanctity of family privacy. Family life in general, and parenting in particular, has traditionally been viewed as a private matter in this country, and the government has been reluctant to interfere in parents' rights to raise their

children as they see fit (Harrington & Dubowitz, 1999). Cultural norms also allow parents to use violence against children, and most parents view physical punishment as an acceptable and even desirable method of child rearing (Harrington & Dubowitz; Straus & Stewart, 1999). Furthermore, many people do not believe that, for instance, a wife can be raped or a husband can be abused (Russell, 1990; Walker, 1999) and, therefore, these forms of family violence may not even be recognized when they occur. Finally, studies show that many Americans believe it is sometimes acceptable for people to hit their intimate partners (Mills & Malley-Morrison, 1998) and financially exploit their elderly parents (Mills, Vermette, & Malley-Morrison, 1998).

Because there is a considerable tolerance for family violence in general, it is not surprising that family violence is a problem in the United States and is supported in many cases by legislation consistent with cultural beliefs. For instance, although physical abuse of children is illegal in all 50 states, all states allow parents to physically discipline their children (Davidson, 1997). Moreover, the revisions of the child welfare act passed in 1996 weaken the definition of child maltreatment and may exclude many less severe cases; in addition, the act indicates that parents are not required to get necessary medical care for their children if doing so interferes with their religious beliefs (Harrington & Dubowitz, 1999). Legislation to end wife abuse has been less problematic in that it is always illegal to assault one's wife. However, legislation to prohibit sexual abuse of wives makes it legal in some states for husbands to rape wives under certain circumstances. Moreover, there are no specific laws to fight the maltreatment of husbands, and because of broad cultural beliefs that husbands cannot be abused, many abused men face an uphill battle when trying to convince the system that their wives are violent.

It is also no surprise that laws against family violence are problematic when we consider the broader culture of violence within the United States. For instance, the death penalty, which is still a legal means of punishment in several states, has never been empirically validated as an effective means of deterring crime. In fact, studies show it has absolutely no effect on level of crime: States with a death penalty do not have lower homicide rates than states without one; when states drop the death penalty, crime rates do not increase, and when states institute it, crime rates do not decrease (Costanzo, 1997; Haney & Logan, 1994). Furthermore, as of 2001, teachers in 23 states are allowed to use corporal punishment on students (National Coalition to Abolish Corporal Punishment in the Schools, 2001)—a right upheld by the Supreme Court even on children with disabilities (*Ingraham v. Wright,* 1977; Lohrmann-O'Rourke & Zirkel, 1998).

This implicit acceptance of violence is also inherent in our media, which expose family members to an inordinate amount of violence every day. Widespread viewing of violence on television, in movies, and in video games is evidence of this country's acceptance of violence (Harrington & Dubowitz, 1999) and can lead to more violence—in general, and in the family. Indeed, people who watch violent TV programs do imitate the aggressive models: The more violent programs children watch, the more aggressive their behavior toward their peers (Eron, 1987)—an association that holds even when controlling for many possible confounding variables (Eron & Huesmann, 1980, 1985). Furthermore, children exposed to violent TV programs behave more aggressively following the

programs than children exposed to nonviolent programs (Boyatzis, Matillo, & Nesbitt, 1995). In addition, a comprehensive review of media violence and children's behavior showed that viewing violent media *causes* children to behave aggressively (Wood, Wong, & Chachere, 1991). If children learn that using violence is acceptable, how are they going to behave when they become parents, and their children, spouses, or elder parents upset or frustrate them? Furthermore, the sexualization of children in the media and elsewhere has been implicated as culturally sanctioning child sexual abuse (Goldsen, 1978); the availability of child pornography may also lead to adult sexual interest in children (Baker, 1978); and the availability of adult pornography, both violent and nonviolent, has been implicated as a contributor to violence against women (Baron & Straus, 1984). Although an empirical link has yet to be established, the proliferation of child and violent adult pornography on the Internet certainly cannot be helping to end the sexual abuse of children and wives in this country.

Although minority families in the United States may not subscribe to the same views as the majority culture and legislators in this country, they are imbedded in a culture in which violence is pervasive. Moreover, many minorities, particularly African Americans and Native American Indians, have been the direct victims of violence by the majority culture, through such institutions as slavery and manifest destiny. This exposure to, and victimization by, violence cannot in any way lead to a reduction in the amount of violence within ethnic minority families—in fact, it can only serve to make it worse.

CHILD MALTREATMENT

Table 3.1 contains major studies of child maltreatment that are repeatedly mentioned throughout this book. This table, and all other family violence incidence tables in this book, are separated first by National versus Regional studies, and then again by Reported versus Self-Report studies. Table 3.1 summarizes the results of studies that are both large-scale and contain results for at least three ethnic groups in the United States.

(Text continues on page 36)

Table 3.1 Major Studies of Child Maltreatment

Study	Sample Description	Definition/Measure of Abuse	Findings
National Studies—Reported Cases			
Preliminary Report on Child Maltreatment, 2000 (U.S. Department of Health and Human Services, 2000)	Reported cases of child abuse (3 million reports concerning approximately 5 million children)	Substantiated cases (879,000 children) of one or more of the following: physical abuse, neglect, medical neglect, sexual abuse, psychological maltreatment, and/ or other abuse	• Whites accounted for 50.6% of victims and 79% of U.S. population. • Blacks accounted for 24.7% of victims and 15% of U.S. population. • Hispanics accounted for 14.2% of victims and 12.5% of U.S. population. • American Indian/Alaska Natives accounted for 1.6% of victims and 0.9% of U.S. population. • Asian-Pacific Islanders accounted for 1.4% of victims and 4.5% of U.S. population.
Report on Child Maltreatment, 1999 (U.S. Department of Health and Human Services, 1999)	826,000 cases of child maltreatment substantiated by state child protective service agencies	Same as above	• Overall, 11.8 children per 1,000 were victims of child maltreatment. • 58.4% of cases suffered neglect, 21.3% suffered physical abuse, and 11.3% suffered sexual abuse. Victimization rates by race and ethnicity: • 10.6 White child victims per 1,000 children. • 20.1 American Indian child victims per 1,000 children—substantially higher than national average. • 25.2 African American child victims per 1,000 children—highest among all groups. • 12.6 Hispanic child victims per 1,000 children. • 4.4 Asian American child victims per 1,000 children—lowest among all groups. Of the 773,786 cases in which race was reported: • 419,858 cases were White, or 54% of victims; proportion of Whites in U.S. population is 72%. • 13,588 cases were American Indian, or 1.8% of victims; proportion of American Indians in U.S. population is 0.9%. • 204,193 cases were Black, or 26% of victims; proportion of Blacks in U.S. population is 13%. • 10,722 were Asian American, or 1.5% of victims; proportion of Asians in U.S. population is 4.5%.

Study	Sample Description	Definition/Measure of Abuse	Findings
			Of the 768,980 cases in which Hispanic ethnicity was reported: • 108,105 cases were Hispanic, or 14% of victims; proportion of Hispanics in U.S. population is 12.5%. • 583,397 cases were non-Hispanic, or 76% of victims.
Third National Incidence Study (Sedlak & Broadhurst, 1996)	Nationally representative sample of over 5,600 professionals in 842 agencies serving 42 counties; nationwide reports to child protective services plus sentinel reports	• *Harm Standard:* experienced harm from abuse or neglect • *Endangerment Standard:* at risk of harm from abuse or neglect	According to the Harm Standard: • 1,553,800 children in United States maltreated. • 217,700 children in United States sexually abused. • 338,900 children in United States physically neglected. • 212,800 children in United States emotionally neglected. • 381,700 children in United States physically abused. According to the Endangerment Standard: • 2,815,600 children in United States maltreated. • 300,200 children in United States sexually abused. • 1,335,100 children in United States physically neglected. • 532,200 children in United States emotionally neglected. • 614,100 children in United States physically abused. • As was true for the NIS 1 and NIS 2, no race differences in maltreatment incidence were found.
National Studies—Self-Report			
1990 National Longitudinal Survey of Youth (Giles-Sims, Straus, & Sugarman, 1995)	7,725 women and their 8,513 children	Mother's answer to following: "Sometimes kids mind pretty well and sometimes they don't. About how many times, if any, have you had to spank your child in the past week?"	• 60.7% of mothers of 3- to 5-year-olds spanked them in previous week; 36.5% of mothers of 6- to 9-year-olds spanked; 16% of mothers of children over 10 spanked. • Chronicity of being spanked >1 time per week decreases after preschool; chronicity does not decrease after this period though. • Spanking decreases as SES and maternal age increase. • 69.4% of Blacks spanked; 59.5% of Whites spanked; 61.8% of Hispanics spanked; 68.7% of American Indians spanked. • A significantly higher percentage of Black mothers spank their children than do mothers of other ethnic groups.

(Continued)

Table 3.1 Continued

Study	Sample Description	Definition/Measure of Abuse	Findings
National Family Violence Surveys of 1975 and 1985 (Cazenave & Straus, 1979; Connelly & Straus, 1992; Straus & Gelles, 1990a; Straus & Smith, 1990a, 1990b; Wolfner & Gelles, 1993)	Nationally representative surveys of U.S. families 1975 survey: 2,143 families; 75 Black families 1985 survey: 6,002 families; 4,052 White families; oversample of 580 Black and 721 Hispanic households	• *Child Abuse I*: any act of severe violence as measured by the Conflict Tactics Scales, except hitting with a stick/belt, and so on • *Child Abuse II*: any act of severe violence as measured by the Conflict Tactics Scales	1975 Rates Overall: • Child Abuse I: 36 per 1,000 child victims in previous year. • Child Abuse II: 140 per 1,000 child victims in previous year. 1985 Rates Overall: • Child Abuse I: 19 per 1,000 child victims in previous year. • Child Abuse II: 107 per 1,000 child victims in previous year. • 1985 rates represent a significant decline from the 1975 rates. • In 1985, greater child abuse rates associated with minority status (African American and Hispanic). Black vs. White comparisons: • In 1975, 51% of Blacks and 59% of Whites reported slapping a child in previous year. • In 1975, Child Abuse I rate was 15.7 per 100 for Blacks and 14.1 per 100 for Whites (difference not significant). • In 1985, Black rate remained stable, but White rate had declined to 10.3 per 100 (significant difference). • In 1985 survey, Black respondents did not differ from White respondents in level of Child Abuse II but did report higher frequencies of Child Abuse II. Hispanic vs. White comparisons (from 1985 survey only): • Hispanic children were significantly more likely than Whites to be abused in 1985, as measured by Child Abuse I (4.8% vs. 1.8%) and Child Abuse II (13.4% vs. 9.8%). • Approximately 288,000 Hispanic children nationwide were victims of Child Abuse I and 804,000 were victims of Child Abuse II. • When other significant predictors of child abuse were held constant, Hispanic children were still significantly more likely to be abused.
Regional Studies—Reported Cases			
California Children's Services Archive (2002)	115,158 (21%) substantiated cases out of 548,821 alleged cases of child maltreatment	Case records from California Children's Services Archive	Substantiated abuse allegations: • Hispanic: 44% of substantiated cases. • White: 34% of substantiated cases. • Black: 16% of substantiated cases. • Asian: 4% of substantiated cases. • Native American Indian: 1% of substantiated cases. • Representation of each group in the population as a whole not provided.

Study	Sample Description	Definition/Measure of Abuse	Findings
Rao, DiClemente, & Ponton (1992)	2,007 cases of sexual abuse victims at the Child and Adolescent Sexual Abuse Resource Center at San Francisco's General Hospital, 1986–1988; the 69 Asian charts and 80 charts each of Black, Hispanic, and White children were chosen at random for analysis	Substantiated cases	• Of the 2,007 cases, 37.6% were Black, 25.9% were White, 21.9% were Hispanic, 6.6% were Asian, 6.7% were racially mixed, and 0.5% were Other. Of the 309 randomly chosen subjects: • Hispanics: more likely than Whites, but less likely than Asians, to be abused by a male relative. • Hispanics and Blacks: more likely than Whites or Asians to experience vaginal or anal intercourse. • Hispanics and Asians: more likely to be living in the same home as the assailant. • Hispanics and Asians: older at time of first assault. • Hispanics and Asians: higher percentage of primary caretakers refused to believe that the child had been sexually abused (11.3% of Hispanics).
Regional Studies—Self-Report			
Roosa, Reinholtz, & Angelini (1999)	2,003 Arizona women ages 18–22 years (14.2% Black, 27.5% Mexican American, 16% Native American, 39.3% White)	Prior to age 18, child sexual abuse (CSA) defined as: 0 = *none* 1 = *contact molestation* 2 = *coercion* 3 = *attempted rape* 4 = *rape*	• ~ One third of each ethnic group reported CSA. • ~ One fifth of each ethnic group reported rape.
Urquiza & Goodlin-Jones (1994)	243 community college females in California: 56.4% White, 11.9% Black, 15.6% Asian, and 16% Latina (69.2% Mexican American, 7.7% South American, 23.1% unspecified) randomly selected	• Wyatt Sexual History Questionnaire; Sexual Experience Questionnaire • Child sexual abuse, either: (a) physical contact of a sexual nature when under 12 years old and perpetrator at least 5 years older, or (b) sexual contact between ages 13 and 17 if perpetrator a relative	• 25.6% of Hispanics reported CSA. • 38% of Whites reported CSA. • 44.8% of Blacks reported CSA. • 21.1% of Asians reported CSA. • Rates highest for Blacks and Whites, and lowest for Asians and Latinas.

Physical Abuse

Exact rates of physical abuse of children are hard to obtain for several reasons. As discussed in chapter 2, different studies have different definitions of physical abuse; even within the same study, data may be reported from several sources differing in their definitions of physical abuse. While CPS workers vary in biases and interpretations of the cases they investigate, each CPS agency and each state provide data to the government for physical abuse rates, data that are used by both the U.S. Department of Health and Human Services (DHHS) and the National Incidence Studies (NIS). One aspect of the definitional problem is that the lines between physically abusive versus subabusive versus nonabusive acts are blurred, and there is no consensus on the exact severity, frequency, or duration of physical aggression necessary for a behavior to be deemed abusive. Is injury a necessary criterion? Is risk of injury enough? What if no physical injury occurs, but the child is slapped on a daily basis for no apparent reason? What if the child was punched "only" once with no lasting injury? Do you think an agreement on an exact definition of physical abuse is even possible?

According to DHHS (1999), rates of substantiated physical abuse from CPS agencies reveal that physical abuse is the second most prevalent form of child abuse, second only to neglect and comprising 21.3% of all abuse cases. This DHHS report also indicated that in 1999, approximately 176,000 children were physically abused by their parents, following a steady decline since 1993 in numbers of reported cases. Furthermore, physical abuse was the least recurring type of abuse, probably because its indications are the most concrete. According to the Third National Incidence Study of Child Abuse and Neglect (NIS-3; Sedlak & Broadhurst, 1996), the actual rates of physical abuse are higher than the DHHS rates indicate, probably because the investigators had access to more sources of data than just CPS agencies (see chapter 2 in this book). According to the Harm Standard, 381,700 children were physically abused in 1993, a 42% increase from the previous survey in 1986. According to the Endangerment Standard, 614,000 children were physically abused, a 97% increase.

One other source of data, although older than the NCANDS and the NIS-3, suggests that actual rates of physical child abuse are even higher than indicated in the reports on identified cases. In the 1985 National Family Violence Resurvey, approximately 100% of parents hit their children at least once in the previous year. According to Child Abuse I, 23/1,000 children were victimized by their parents in 1985, a rate which translates to 1,500,000 children nationwide. According to Child Abuse II, which is considered to be the best indicator of physical abuse, 110/1,000 children (that is, 6,900,000 children) were victimized by their parents in 1985 alone. Moreover, even these large numbers are likely to be underestimates, as many parents may be unwilling to disclose the number of times they beat up, choked, kicked, or punched their children (Straus & Gelles, 1990a). In addition, although the rates were highest for the youngest children and steadily declined as the children got older (Wauchope & Straus, 1990), teenagers were not immune from physical aggression: 3,800,000 (340/1,000) teenagers experienced some form of aggression from their parents; 800,000 teens (70/1,000) experienced Child Abuse II, and 235,000 (21/1,000) experienced Child Abuse I in 1985 (Straus & Gelles).

Sexual Abuse

Defining sexual abuse is also not an easy task. Most studies have, as one criterion for judging sexual acts as abusive, an arbitrary age difference of at least 5 years between the victim and perpetrator (e.g., Finkelhor, 1979). However, this criterion does not take into consideration that siblings with less of an age discrepancy can perpetrate sexual abuse. Furthermore, there is no consensus on what acts constitute abuse. Sometimes noncontact acts, such as voyeurism, exhibitionism, and exposure to pornography, are included in definitions of sexual abuse, which leads to very high incidence rates. If only contact sexual abuse is included (e.g., fondling; oral, anal, vaginal intercourse), then rates are lower. Most studies do not specify the frequency or duration of sexual contact necessary for an act to be considered abusive, although many workers in the field hold that just one instance of sexual contact is enough. However, when we consider the consequences of sexual abuse, a child who was intentionally exposed once to pornography is going to differ dramatically from children who experienced repeated vaginal penetration.

All states have laws prohibiting sexual maltreatment of children (Myers, 1998), but each state has its own definition of sexual abuse and, therefore, of what is prohibited; thus, official statistics need to be interpreted with caution. Generally, adult sexual contact with a child under the age of 14 is illegal, as is any kind of incest. According to the DHHS, in 1999, 11.3% of all substantiated maltreatment cases were sexual abuse cases, and parents were the perpetrators in half of these cases. Nationwide, for every 1,000 females, 1.6 were sexually abused, and for every 1,000 males, 0.4 were sexually abused. Although these rates of substantiated cases are high, they reflect a decrease from 1995, when the sexual abuse rate was 1.3 for every 1,000 children.

NIS-3 (Sedlak & Broadhurst, 1996) shows a similar picture. According to the Harm Standard, the number of sexual abuse cases rose from 119,200 in 1986 to 217,700 in 1993, an increase of 83%. Similarly, according to the Endangerment Standard, the number of cases rose from 133,600 to 300,200, an increase of 125%. Overall, the data indicate that sexual abuse reports rose during the late 1980s and then declined in the mid- to late 1990s. As with the DHHS reports, reported victims of sexual abuse were three times more likely to be girls than boys, but in contrast to reports of DHHS, only one fourth of children were abused by their birth parents.

Although these official statistics are very informative, most sexual abuse is not reported at the time it occurs; indeed, often it is never reported (Finkelhor, Hotaling, Lewis, & Smith, 1990). In addition, there is reason to believe that sexual abuse perpetrated by a family member is even less likely to be reported to officials than extrafamilial sexual abuse. Consequently, better sources for an estimate of the prevalence of sexual abuse rates may be retrospective reports of sexual abuse in nonclinical populations (Berliner & Elliott, 2002). A review of these studies (Finkelhor, 1994) revealed a sexual abuse rate of 20–25% for women and 5–15%

for men, a rate that included both intra- and extrafamilial abuse and contact sexual abuse only. The mean age of victimization was 9 years; the peak age range was 7 to 13 years. In the general population, parents were the perpetrators in 6–16% of the cases; any relative was the perpetrator in one third of the cases, and overall, 85–95% of the perpetrators are known to the child victim (Finkelhor).

In nonclinical samples, half of the sexual abuse victims reported multiple episodes of abuse, and 25% of the victims reported completed or attempted oral, anal, and/or vaginal intercourse (Saunders, Kilpatrick, Hanson, Resnick, & Walker, 1999). These self-reported rates of sexual abuse in nonclinical samples are dramatically lower than rates found in clinical samples. People who seek mental health help because of childhood sexual abuse probably have had more severe abuse experiences, and the data confirm that supposition. For example, participants in clinical samples have identified 25–33% of sexual abuse perpetrators as parents, and any relative as the perpetrator in half the cases. Three fourths of the clinical victims experienced multiple episodes of abuse, and in most cases, the multiple episodes consisted of completed or attempted oral, anal, and/or vaginal intercourse (Elliott & Briere, 1994; Ruggiero, McLeer, & Dixon, 2000).

Neglect

Only in recent decades have the profound negative consequences of neglect led to its public recognition as a severe form of child maltreatment. But what exactly is neglect? Do we need to see immediate psychological damage to children in order for parents' behaviors to be considered neglectful? Should intentions be taken into account? Does it matter whether stressors in the parents' lives limit their caretaking abilities, or should omission of adequate care be considered neglectful only if parents deliberately ignore the needs of their child?

Neglect is commonly viewed as a failure to meet minimal community standards of care. Unlike physical and sexual abuse, neglect refers to acts of omission rather than of commission. Several different forms have been identified (Erickson & Egeland, 2002). *Physical neglect* is when parents fail to provide for a child's basic physical needs, such as food, bathing, and shelter, or when they fail to protect the child from harm and danger. *Emotional neglect*, which usually leaves no physical evidence, is when parents fail to attend to a child's basic emotional needs (e.g., they may not comfort their children when they are hurt, or may routinely ignore a child), but there is considerable controversy over exactly what a child's basic emotional needs are. *Medical neglect*, which has generated considerable controversy in regard to several religious sects in this country, is the failure to provide for the basic medical needs of the child, such as routine checkups, immunizations, and prescribed medicine. Finally, *educational neglect* is when parents do not comply with state ordinances for their child's attendance in school or fail to cooperate or become involved in the child's education (Erickson & Egeland).

Overall, at the core of conceptions of neglect is the assumption that parents are responsible for protecting their children from known hazards. As more hazards become known, the definition of neglect and its different forms will continue to evolve (Garbarino & Collins, 1999). One of the basic problems facing scholars concerned with neglect is that it is frequently not investigated or analyzed independently of physical abuse—probably because, legally, both are forms of maltreatment (Erickson & Egeland, 2002). Consequently, problems that may be due specifically to neglect often are ignored, perhaps because our culture is more obsessed with violence and acts of commission than it is with acts of omission. Severely beaten children attract more attention because the scars are evident, but the emotional scars from which neglected children suffer may be more insidious and traumatic (Garbarino & Collins).

It is ironic that physical abuse garners so much attention, because, according to DHHS, neglect is by far the most common type of child maltreatment—58.4% of all maltreatment cases substantiated by CPS in 1999 were cases of neglect, and 6.5 children per 1,000 in the United States were the victims of neglect. Although the CPS data indicate that reported cases of neglect have been steadily declining since 1995, it still exceeds other forms of maltreatment. Moreover, neglected children are 44% more likely than

physically abused children to experience a recurrence of maltreatment.

Data from NIS-3 (Sedlak & Broadhurst, 1996) reinforce DHHS findings on the relative prevalence of neglect, and show a significant increase in its incidence between 1986 and 1993. Perhaps this increase was due to the fact that neglect finally gained notice in the late 1980s and professionals became able to recognize it better. Whatever the cause, under the Harm Standard, the number of neglected children rose between 1986 and 1993 from 474,800 to 879,000; under the Endangerment Standard, the numbers rose from 917,200 to 1,961,300, an increase of 114%. Physical neglect was the most often reported type of neglect (338,900 under the Harm Standard; 1,335,100 under the Endangerment Standard), but emotional neglect was also a significant problem (212,800 under the Harm Standard; 585,100 under the Endangerment Standard).

Despite the great wealth and resources of the United States, neglect is a grave problem for children in this country. Even though it is commonly thought that maltreated children are most likely to die from fatal physical abuse, neglect accounts for more child fatalities than any other form of maltreatment (DHHS, 1999). In 1999, 38.2% of maltreatment deaths were due to neglect, and when neglect was combined with physical abuse, it accounted for an additional 22.7% of fatalities. Moreover, the rates of fatalities due to neglect may be even higher than these statistics show because identifying neglect as a cause of fatalities is more difficult than identifying physical abuse as a cause of death. There is also considerable controversy over how to define and assess fatalities due to neglect (Bonner, Crow, & Logue, 1999; Lung & Daro, 1996). Take the examples in Box 3.1. Which of the fatalities would you attribute to neglect?

As these examples indicate, the determination of "fatality by neglect" may be in the eye of the beholder. Most cases of this sort may not be determined to be neglect-related, and even if neglect is seen as the cause, the determination would not necessarily be noted on the death certificate. Therefore, neglect fatality rates should be assumed to be much higher than the reported figures indicate (McClain, Sacks, Froehlke, & Ewigman, 1993). Furthermore,

Box 3.1   Possible Cases of Fatal Child Neglect

1. "A 4-month old infant died from massive trauma after being ejected from the front seat of a car in a traffic collision. The child was not secured in an infant car seat" (p. 156).

2. "An 18-month old toddler fell from a second-story window and suffered fatal head injuries. The window had no window guards, and the child had climbed onto the windowsill when his mother thought he was asleep in the room" (p. 156).

3. "An 8-year-old boy drowned in a neighbor's covered above-ground pool after he became trapped under the cover to retrieve a toy he dropped in the pool. There was no fence around the pool" (p. 156).

4. "A 6-year-old boy fatally shot his 4-year-old brother with a handgun he found in the pocket of a coat hanging in the closet. The parents were in the next room watching television" (p. 156).

5. One night, a mother was giving her 2-year-old son, Bob, a bath. She then left him in the tub and went to take care of something in the kitchen for about 10 minutes. She then sent her 8-year-old in to check on Bob, who was lying face-down in the tub. Bob was taken to the hospital, where he was unresponsive with a temperature of 90°F. After some treatment, Bob began breathing again, and he was transported for inpatient care. After 9 days in the pediatric intensive care unit, Bob still had minimal brain functioning and was unresponsive to any stimuli. He died two days later. On the death certificate, which the attending physician signed, the cause of death was deemed to be pneumonia with anoxic brain injury after a near-drowning. The CPS worker told the mother that 10 minutes was too long to leave a 2-year-old unattended in a tub, and the mother replied that she did it all the time with no problems.

SOURCE: Bonner, Crow, and Logue, 1999.

although fatalities can result from a failure to provide supervision, protection, medical care, or nutrition (Bonner et al., 1999), where exactly do we draw the line between a momentary lapse in supervision and chronic neglect? Does this distinction necessarily make a difference when determining whether neglect was involved in a child fatality? Consider again the cases in Box 3.1. Are any of these neglectful acts more egregious than the others? Can any be associated with merely a lapse in supervision, or do they all appear to reflect chronic neglect?

Psychological Maltreatment

Historically, the concept of psychological maltreatment suffers from the greatest number of definitional and conceptual problems of all the maltreatment types. Therefore, it has been very difficult for legal and medical services to provide accurate estimates or services for families suffering from this problem. To give an example, imagine what would happen if a child called the police because his parents called him a dirty name. Has he been psychologically maltreated? What is the likely legal response?

Society has traditionally subscribed to the implicit theory that physical and sexual abuse are more harmful than psychological maltreatment (Kashani & Allan, 1998). It is possible that society could not be more wrong. Studies have shown that people who experienced both physical and emotional abuse at the hands of their caregivers consistently say they were bothered more by the emotional trauma than the physical trauma (e.g., Jurich, 1990). According to DHHS (1999), the rate of psychological maltreatment is low—only 0.9/1,000 children were victimized by it in 1999; the only form of maltreatment reported less frequently was medical neglect. NIS-3 (Sedlak & Broadhurst, 1996) indicated that psychological maltreatment is the third most prevalent form of maltreatment (behind neglect and physical abuse), with

532,200 children victimized by it in 1993. By contrast, several researchers (e.g., Binggeli, Hart, & Brassard, 2001; Garbarino, Guttman, & Seeley, 1986) have argued that psychological maltreatment (a) is at the core of *all* other forms of child maltreatment, including physical and sexual abuse and neglect; (b) may be the strongest predictor of negative psychological outcomes; and (c) may have the longest-lasting and strongest negative effects. Furthermore, psychological maltreatment can occur on its own. Therefore, as opposed to being one of the *least* prevalent forms of child maltreatment, it is more likely the *most* prevalent.

In 1995, the American Professional Society on the Abuse of Children (APSAC) attempted to resolve some of the definitional issues by offering a basic definition and conceptualization of psychological maltreatment. In their view,

1. "Psychological maltreatment means a repeated pattern of caregiver behavior or extreme incident(s) that convey to children that they are worthless, flawed, unloved, unwanted, endangered, or only of value in meeting another's needs" (p. 2) and

2. "Psychological maltreatment includes (a) spurning, (b) terrorizing, (c) isolating, (d) exploiting/corrupting, (e) denying emotional responsiveness, and (e) mental health, medical, and educational neglect" (p. 4).

Based upon the APSAC conceptualization, a better estimate of the incidence of psychological maltreatment may be gained by looking at studies that include measures for the factors in Statement #2. Based on adults' retrospective reports of their own psychological maltreatment, somewhere between 25% and 37% of people experienced it in childhood (Gross & Keller, 1992; Moeller, Bachman, & Moeller, 1993). These percentages are likely to be an underestimate because the participants in these studies were mostly middle to upper-middle class, White, relatively well-educated people. In addition, adults may not accurately recall the psychological maltreatment episodes of their childhood. According to a nationally representative survey (Vissing, Straus, Gelles, & Harrop, 1991) of parent reports of verbal aggression

(e.g., name-calling, swearing at, or insulting their children), 63% of parents had used at least one type of verbal aggression on their children the previous year, and the average number of verbally aggressive acts was 12.6 acts. If 10 acts per year is used as a cutoff for psychological maltreatment, then 26.7% of the children were victims of that form of maltreatment that year. This study is also likely to have underestimated the incidence of psychological maltreatment, because parents are likely to underreport their own use of verbal aggression, and only a limited number of verbally aggressive behaviors were assessed.

ADULT MALTREATMENT

Table 3.2 contains the major studies of adult maltreatment to which we refer throughout this book. Like Table 3.1, it summarizes large-scale studies with results for at least three of the ethnic groups in the United States.

Spousal Maltreatment

Wife Physical Abuse

The physical abuse of wives has been the most extensively studied form of adult maltreatment. Perhaps because of widespread attention to the problem in both the scientific community and the popular media, the major prevalence studies have shown steady declines in physical wife abuse since the 1970s, even though different methods of assessing it sometimes lead to vastly different estimates (see chapter 2). For example, according to the Department of Justice (DOJ), in 1998, there were 876,340 reported cases of female victims of assault by an intimate partner, which was a decline from the 1993 rate of 1.1 million (Rennison & Welchans, 2000). Reported cases of lethal violence against women by an intimate have also declined in recent years. Between 1976 and 1998, women killed by an intimate partner declined an average of 1% per year to approximately 1,500 women in 1998. The National Family Violence Surveys (NFVS) also show declines in rates of wife beating. Specifically, between 1975 and 1985, there was a 27% decrease in the

(Text continues on page 48)

Table 3.2 Major Studies of Adult Maltreatment

Study	Sample Description	Definition/Measure of Abuse	Findings
National Studies—Reported Cases			
U.S. Department of Justice Report on *Intimate Partner Violence and Age of Victim, 1993-99* (Rennison, 2001a)	National Crime Victimization Survey of nationally representative households in United States; between 1993 and 1999, 651,750 individuals interviewed about experiences with crime	Murder, rape, sexual assault, aggravated assault, and/or simple assault committed by a current or former spouse, boyfriend, or girlfriend	Wife Abuse: • In 1999, 671,110 females victimized by intimate partner, or 5.8 victimizations per 1,000 females; females age 16–24 had highest rates of intimate partner violence: 15–16 per 1,000. • 74% of persons murdered by an intimate partner were female, or 1,218 females; females in 35–49 age group had highest rates of being murdered. • For Black and White females, the rates of intimate partner violence peaked at age 20–24 and then steadily declined. • Black and White females experienced similar rates of intimate partner violence in all age groups, except age 20–24 (Black females experienced a rate of 29 per 1,000 and Whites experienced a rate of 20 per 1,000). • All other races (e.g., Asians and American Indians) and Hispanics experienced similar victimization patterns as Whites and Blacks, but rates for "Other" and Hispanics were consistently lower. • Hispanic females ages 16–34 were significantly less likely than non-Hispanics of same age to report intimate partner violence. Husband Abuse: • In 1999, 120,100 males were victimized by an intimate partner. • Males age 20–49 had the highest rates of being murdered. • No other comparisons were done with males.
U.S. Department of Justice Report on *Violent Victimization and Race, 1993-98* (Rennison, 2001b)	National Crime Victimization Survey of nationally representative households in United States; between 1993 and 1998, 574,000 individuals interviewed	Murder, rape, sexual assault, aggravated assault, and/or simple assault committed by a current or former spouse, boyfriend, or girlfriend	Wife Abuse: • Between 1993 and 1998, American Indian females experienced more intimate partner violence than any other ethnic group. • Rate for American Indians: 23 per 1,000; for Blacks: 11 per 1,000; for Whites: 8 per 1,000; for Asians: 2 per 1,000. • Rate of intimate partner violence against White females declined steadily from 1993 to 1998; rate did not decline for Black females.

(Continued)

41

Table 3.2 Continued

Study	Sample Description	Definition/Measure of Abuse	Findings
			Husband Abuse:
			• In 1998, 1.6 per 1,000 White males were victimized by an intimate partner; no discernible trend was found in violence between 1993 and 1998.
			• Analyses on ethnic differences were not conducted (too few cases).
U.S. Department of Justice Report on *Intimate Partner Violence* (Rennison & Welchans, 2000)	National Crime Victimization Survey of nationally representative households in United States; between 1993 and 1998, 574,000 individuals interviewed	Murder, rape, sexual assault, aggravated assault, and/or simple assault committed by a current or former spouse, boyfriend, or girlfriend	**Wife Abuse:**
			• In 1998, overall 876,340 (7.5/1,000) females were victimized by an intimate partner, a decline from the 1993 rate (9.8/1,000).
			• White victims of intimate partner violence: 8.2 per 1,000.
			• Black victims: 11.1 per 1,000; Other race victims: 4.1 per 1,000.
			• Black females experienced violence at a rate 35% higher than White victims and 2 times the rate of other races.
			• No significant differences for Hispanic ethnicity in reported rates of intimate violence: 8/1,000 Hispanic females vs. 8.5/1,000 non-Hispanics.
			• Between 1993 and 1998, White female victims of intimate partner homicide remained steady.
			• Homicide rate of Black female victims decreased by 45%.
			• Homicide statistics were not performed on any other race/ethnicity.
			Husband Abuse:
			• Between 1993 and 1998, White male victims of intimate partner violence: 1.3 per 1,000; Black victims: 2.1 per 1,000; Hispanic victims: 1.5 per 1,000; Other race victims: not reported.
			• Black males experienced violence at a rate 62% higher than White males and 2 times the rate of other races.
			• No significant differences in husband abuse rates by Hispanic ethnicity.
			• Between 1993 and 1998, White male victims of intimate homicide decreased by 44%; homicide rate of Black males decreased by 74%.

Study	Sample Description	Definition/Measure of Abuse	Findings
National Elder Abuse Incidence Study of 1996 (National Center on Elder Abuse, 1998)	Reported cases of elder abuse to APS or by sentinels in 1996 from a nationally representative sample of 20 counties in 15 states	Reported cases of physical abuse, sexual abuse, emotional abuse, financial exploitation, abandonment, neglect, and self-neglect	• 449,924 elderly were abused and/or neglected in 1996. • With self-abuse added, 551,011 were abused. • 402,287 were abused; 182,368 neglected, 138,980 self-neglected. • Whites: 84% of cases; overrepresented overall and for all types of elder abuse, except abandonment. • Native American Indians: 0.4% of cases; underrepresented for all types of elder abuse. • Blacks: 8.3% of cases; overrepresented for neglect, emotional abuse, financial exploitation, and abandonment. • Hispanics: 5.1% of cases; equals their representation in the population. • Asians: 2.1% of cases; underrepresented for all types of elder abuse.

National Studies—Self-Report

Study	Sample Description	Definition/Measure of Abuse	Findings
National Comorbidity Survey (Kessler, Molnar, Feurer, & Appelbaum, 2001)	Nationally representative sample of 8,098 people aged 15 to 54, 1990–1992: no ethnic breakdown of sample provided; analyses done on married/cohabiting men and women	Conflict Tactics Scales	Wife Abuse: • 17.4% of women reported experiencing minor physical violence. • 6.5% of women reported experiencing severe physical violence. Husband Abuse: • 18.4% of men reported being victimized by minor physical violence. • 5.5% of men reported being victimized by severe physical violence. • Severe violence was significantly higher for Blacks and Hispanics than for Whites for both genders, even after controlling for SES.
1995 National Study of Couples (Caetano, Cunradi, Schafer, & Clark, 2000)	1,635 couples: 555 White, 358 Black, 527 Hispanic; nationally representative of 48 contiguous states; oversampling of Blacks and Hispanics	Conflict Tactics Scales	• 11.5% of White, 23% of Black, and 17% of Hispanic couples reported wife abuse. • 15% of White, 30% of Black, and 21% of Hispanic couples reported husband abuse. • Rates for Blacks were significantly higher than rates for Hispanics and Whites.
National Violence Against Women Survey (Coker et al.,	Nationally representative survey of 8,000 men and 8,000 women overall:	• *Rape:* "an event that occurs without the victim's consent and involves the use of	Wife Abuse: • 25.5% of females were the victims of physical assaults by an intimate partner over the course of their lifetimes.

(Continued)

Table 3.2 Continued

Study	Sample Description	Definition/Measure of Abuse	Findings
2002; Tjaden & Thoennes, 2000)	6,452 female and 6,424 male Whites; 105 female and 88 male American Indian/Alaska Natives; 780 female and 659 male African Americans; 133 female and 165 male Asians/Pacific Islanders; Hispanic ethnicity: 628 female and 581 male Hispanics; 7,317 female and 7,335 male non-Hispanics	• threat or force to penetrate the victim's vagina or anus by penis, tongue, fingers, or object or the victim's mouth by penis"; includes both attempted and completed rape • *Physical assault:* "behaviors that threaten, attempt, or actually inflict physical harm. . . ; includes a wide range of behaviors from slapping, pushing, and shoving to using a gun" (Tjaden & Thoennes, 2000, p. 5)	• 1.8% of females reported victimization within the prior 12 months. • Whites: 24.8% victimized over lifetime; American Indians: 37.5%; African Americans: 29.1%; Asians: 15%; Hispanics: 23.4%. • American Indian/Alaska Native women reported significantly higher rates of both rape and physical assault than all other racial groups. • 15.9% of American Indian women reported rape; 30.7% reported physical assault. • 7.7% of White women reported rape; 21.3% reported physical assault. • 7.4% of Black women reported rape; 26.3% reported physical assault; rates higher than Asian American women, lower than American Indian/Alaska Native, and similar to White. • 3.8% of Asian women reported rape; 12.8% reported physical assault. • Rates for Asian American women significantly lower than for African American, American Indian, and mixed race. • 7.9% of Hispanics reported rape; significantly greater than the 5.7% of non-Hispanics who reported rape. • 21.2% of Hispanics reported physical assault (vs. 22.1% of non-Hispanics, difference not significant). • Differences in rates of physical assault among minority groups diminished when controlling for other sociodemographic and relationship variables. Husband Abuse: • 7.9% of males were victimized by an intimate partner over the course of their lifetimes; 1.1% were victimized in the previous year. • Whites: 7.2% physically assaulted over lifetime; American Indians: 11.4%; African Americans: 10.8%; Asians: 3%; Hispanics: 6.5%. • No ethnic differences in rates of physical assaults.

Study	Sample Description	Definition/Measure of Abuse	Findings
National Family Violence Surveys of 1975 and 1985 (Bachman, 1992; Cazenave & Straus, 1979; Hampton & Gelles, 1994; Straus & Gelles, 1986, 1990a; Straus, Gelles, & Steinmetz, 1980; Straus & Smith, 1990b; Straus & Sweet, 1992)	Nationally representative surveys of U.S. families 1975 survey: 2,143 families; 75 Black families 1985 survey: 6,002 families; 4,052 White families; oversample of 580 Black and 721 Hispanic households; 204 Native American Indian households	Conflict Tactics Scales	Wife Abuse: • In 1975, 121 per 1,000 wives were victimized by any violence in the previous year; 38 per 1,000 reported severe violence. • In 1985, 113 per 1,000 wives were victimized by any violence in the previous year; 30 per 1,000 reported severe violence; a decline from 1975 rate. White vs. Native American Indian Comparisons (1985 Survey): • 12.2% of wives experienced spousal assault in the previous year, or 29,000 Native American Indian women. • 3.2% experienced severe violence in the previous year, or 6,000 Native American women. • No differences were found in violence rates between Native Americans and Whites. White vs. Black Comparisons: • In 1975, severe violence against wives: 11.3% of Blacks, 3% of Whites. No tests of statistical significance reported. • In 1985, any husband to wife violence: 17.4% of Blacks, 11.2% of Whites; minor violence: 10.3% of Blacks, 8.2% of Whites; severe violence: 7.1% of Blacks, 3.0% of Whites. Rates of wife abuse significantly higher for Blacks than for Whites. • In 1985, when controlling for income, Black rates significantly higher than White rates except at the poverty level ($6,000–$11,999), where Black rates are marginally ($p = .055$) higher. White vs. Hispanic Comparisons (1985 Survey): • 10.8% of Whites vs. 17.3% of Hispanics physically abused wives (519,000 Hispanic wives nationwide). • 3% of Whites vs. 7.3% of Hispanics severely abused wives (219,000 Hispanic wives nationwide). • Differences held across income, occupation, and employment statuses.

(Continued)

Table 3.2 Continued

Study	Sample Description	Definition/Measure of Abuse	Findings
			Husband Abuse:
			• In 1975, 116 per 1,000 husbands were victimized by any violence in the previous year; 46 per 1,000 reported severe violence.
			• In 1985, 121 per 1,000 husbands were victimized by any violence in the previous year; 44 per 1,000 reported severe violence; no apparent trend from 1975 to 1985.
			White vs. Black Comparisons:
			• In 1975, severe violence against husbands: 7.6% of Blacks, 7.6% of Whites. No tests of statistical significance reported.
			White vs. Hispanic Comparisons (1985 Survey):
			• 16.8% of Latinas abused their husbands (504,000 nationwide), compared to 11.5% of White women; difference is significant.
			• 7.8% of Latinas severely abused their husbands (234,000 nationwide), compared to 4% of White women; difference is significant.
			Emotional Abuse:
			• In 1985, 74% of men and 75% of women reported engaging in one or more acts of verbal/symbolic aggression in the previous year.
			• Race and SES were not related to verbal/symbolic aggression.
Regional Studies—Self-Report			
1998 California Women's Health Survey (Lund, 2002; Weinbaum et al., 2001)	4,006 women: 196 African American, 222 Asian/other, 965 Latina, and 2,025 White over 18 years of age from California; random computer-assisted telephone interview	Conflict Tactics Scales in either English or Spanish	• Black and Latino women had significantly higher prevalence rates of domestic violence (11.4% and 9.4%) than White and Asian women (4.5% and 4.4%)
			• Age at entry into the United States was significantly negatively associated with wife abuse rates (Asians and Hispanics combined in this analysis).
			• Black women had the highest rates of serious physical violence (5.5%), followed by Hispanics (3.6%), Asians (2.6%), and Whites (1.5%).
			• Black women also had the highest rates of minor physical violence (10.2%), followed by Hispanics (7.9%), Asians (4.5%), and Whites (4%).

Study	Sample Description	Definition/Measure of Abuse	Findings
Neff, Holamon, & Schluter (1995)	1,374 married, divorced, or separated San Antonio residents: multistage probability sample; 1,286 drinkers and 498 nondrinkers aged 20–60; 451 Whites, 252 Blacks, 671 Mexican Americans	Answered yes to following: "Have you ever been slapped, hit, kicked, or pushed by husband/wife/partner?" (pp. 5-6)	White vs. Black Comparisons: • 61% of Black females reported experiencing physical aggression. • 57% of Black females reported perpetrating physical aggression. • Black females were significantly more likely than Whites to report beating and having been beaten. • Difference not accounted for by stress or SES. White vs. Mexican American Comparisons: • 26% of White females vs. 30% of Mexican American females reported physical abuse victimization. • 14.6% of White males vs. 25.6% of Mexican American males reported perpetrating wife abuse; difference is significant. • 19% of White vs. 20.4% of Mexican American males physically abused; 26.3% of White vs. 26.5% of Mexican American females reported physically abusing their husbands. • No ethnic differences in husband abuse rates.

self-reported rate of severe violence by husbands, which translated into 432,000 fewer cases of severe violence against wives, and a projected national incidence of 1.6 million wives. The apparent decline may be due to increased attention to wife-beating and consequences instituted for men who assault their intimate partners (Straus & Gelles, 1986).

Although it does not provide data across time on the incidence of wife abuse, the National Violence Against Women Survey (NVAW) is another important source of information. According to NVAW, 25.5% of women were the victims of physical assaults from a current or former intimate partner over the course of their lifetimes, and 1.8% reported victimization within the prior 12 months. The average frequency of attacks was 7.1 incidents, and the abuse tended to last an average 3.8 years (Tjaden & Thoennes, 2000). The prevalence rates reported in all of these national studies show that despite the apparent decline in rates of physical wife abuse and lethal violence, it continues to be a major social problem in the United States.

There appear to be two main nonoverlapping types of violence against women: (a) aggression within the context of *common couple violence*, which is typically reported in studies of the general population and is marked by more or less "minor" reciprocal violence; and (b) more extreme *terroristic violence*, which is mostly found in shelter populations of battered women and criminal justice surveys (Johnson, 1995). Women experiencing terroristic violence are usually subject to systematic, serious, and frequent beatings, and are usually only violent themselves in self-defense. Although this second type of violence, in comparison to common couple violence, is quite rare, it has fascinated both the public and the scientific community, and several researchers have tried to describe its dynamics. For instance, one well-known theory, the "cycle of violence" theory, states that interactions between the batterer and his wife start with a period of tension-building, followed by a battering incident, then the batterer's expression of remorse, and then a period of calm. When tensions resume, probably because of some stressor, the cycle begins again; this time the violence is more severe. Over time, the cycle

escalates, and violence becomes more frequent (Walker, 1979).

Although this cycle may characterize some terroristic abusive relationships, it is not typical of common couple violence, nor does it necessarily apply to all terroristic abusive relationships. For instance, some researchers (e.g., Douglas, 1991) have observed that in early stages of abusive relationships, there seem to be many good times and exchanges of loving feelings. However, over time, a pattern of conflict emerges, with old issues going unresolved and frequently argued over. Soon, conflicts become more intense and more frequent, and positive aspects of the relationship seem to disappear. At this point, any violence that was previously enacted in arguments becomes deliberate, dangerous, and premeditated, and there is no relief from the violence: The abusive husband will endlessly dominate, punish, and criticize his wife.

Wife Emotional Abuse

In comparison to physical abuse, there is a dearth of research on the emotional abuse of wives by their husbands. This fact is surprising, given the following:

1. Emotional abuse predicts the occurrence of physical abuse in relationships (Murphy & O'Leary, 1989).

2. Emotional abuse tends to co-occur with physical abuse (Stets, 1990).

3. Emotional abuse also occurs in the absence of physical abuse (Stets, 1990).

4. Most battered women, when interviewed about their emotional abuse, state that the emotional abuse was much worse than the physical abuse they received (Follingstad, Rutledge, Hause, & Polek, 1990).

There seem to be three reasons for the lack of research on emotional abuse, mirroring the reasons for minimal research on the psychological maltreatment of children: (a) physical abuse and its consequences are much more apparent than emotional abuse and its consequences; (b) there is an implicit assumption that the consequences of physical abuse are more severe than those of emotional abuse (a bias that is probably erroneous); and (c) it has been even harder for investigators of emotional abuse to come to a consensus on its definition than it has been for investigators of physical abuse (Arias, 1999).

The original *Conflict Tactics Scales* (*CTS*) administered in the NFVS of 1975 operationally defined emotional abuse with six acts that either verbally (e.g., insulted or swore at other person) or symbolically (e.g., threw, smashed, hit, or kicked something) hurt the other person (Murphy & Cascardi, 1999). However, several researchers argue that the *CTS* definition of emotional abuse is too narrow. Research on emotional abuse in battered women has had several additional possibilities for defining the construct:

1. In addition to the subtypes assessed by the *CTS*, psychological humiliation and verbal harassment may also be components of emotional abuse (Walker, 1979).

2. There may be six distinct types of emotional abuse: verbal attacks; isolation; jealousy and possessiveness; verbal threats of harm, abuse, and/or torture; threats to divorce, abandon, and/or have an affair; and damage and/or destruction of personal property (Follingstad et al., 1990).

3. There may be five subcategories of emotional abuse: isolating and restricting the partner's activities and social contacts; attacking the partner's self-esteem through humiliating and degrading comments; withdrawing in hostile ways; destroying property; and threatening harm or violence (Murphy & Cascardi, 1999).

Furthermore, attempts to operationalize the posited subtypes of emotional abuse have not been fully successful. Even the most widely used scale, Tolman's (1989) Psychological Maltreatment of Women Inventory (PMWI), which was designed to measure six conceptually distinct components of emotional abuse, revealed only two components: Dominance/Isolation and Emotional/Verbal abuse (Murphy & Hoover, 2001).

The rates of emotional abuse of women appear to be quite high. The 1985 NFVS showed only 25% of the couples reported no emotionally abusive acts in the previous year (Stets, 1990). Even higher rates of husband-to-wife emotional abuse were found among couples attending a marital therapy clinic: 94% of the men insulted or swore at their wives, 94% did or said something to spite their wives, 90% stomped out of the room, house, or yard, and 97% sulked or refused to talk about an issue (Barling, O'Leary, Jouriles, Vivian, & MacEwen, 1987).

To measure emotional abuse, these studies used the *CTS*, which, as stated previously, are considered to have the narrowest definition of emotional abuse. The few studies that have used the most comprehensive assessment tool for assessing emotional abuse, Tolman's (1989) *PMWI*, suffer from a different problem: They tend to have samples restricted to battered women. Among battered women in a shelter, over 75% reported experiencing the vast majority of the 58 behaviors on the *PMWI* within the past 6 months. Over 90% reported that their husbands swore at them and tried to blame them for their violence; over 80% said their husbands ordered them around, called them names, insulted them in front of others, and monitored their time; and more than half the sample said their husbands did not allow them to socialize with friends, did not allow them to see their families, restricted their use of the telephone, tried to convince them they were crazy, and restricted their use of the car (Tolman, 1989). Obviously, emotional abuse is a problem for both battered and nonbattered women. Battered women will most likely experience it in combination with the physical abuse, but many women who are not physically battered will be emotionally abused.

Wife Sexual Abuse

Sexual abuse of wives has been the least studied type of wife abuse—perhaps because until recently, most people assumed it was impossible, by definition, for a husband to sexually assault his wife. Another reason for lack of attention to wife sexual abuse is problems in defining it. Consider the cases presented in Box 3.2. Which of these would you consider "sexual abuse"? Why? Are there any cases that you do not consider to be sexual abuse?

Box 3.2   Possible Cases of Sexual Aggression Against a Wife

"It happens very often. If I refuse he will go to other women. Then it would be my fault and a sin. Whether I like it or not I have to give in" (Mrs. Fisher, p. 83).

"Sometimes when I didn't want to have intercourse and he did, he pushed it. He used verbal tactics. He laid guilt trips on me. Like when we would go for a long time without any sex he would demand it, and I would feel like I had to have sex though I didn't want it. I'd just be passive and let him have his way. I felt I had no way out" (Mrs. Carter, p. 77).

"He wanted me to have sex with him when I didn't want to. I had no desire. I didn't want him to touch me, so he forced me. He said I was his wife and I had to do it. I wanted to sleep on the couch but he forced me. . . . He said he was going to beat me. He called me names. He said I was his wife and he had a right to sleep with me when he wanted to" (Mrs. Morgan, p. 44).

"We had come back from a party and he had drunk too much. He became obnoxious when drunk. At six feet four inches and two hundred pounds he was quite powerful. . . . When we got home I went to bed immediately. He came in, got in bed, and wanted to make love. I wasn't in any mood to do that. He forced himself, by using his strength to pin my arms down. He started kissing me, touching me, aggressively grabbing me, all the time holding my arms down. I would turn my head away and he would turn my head around to kiss me. I fought him for a long time. I tried to free my arms, but I couldn't. I yelled abuse at him, told him to leave me alone and to stop it. Finally, because it was obvious I wasn't going to get my way, I ended up just lying there" (Mrs. Atkins, p. 165).

SOURCE: Russell (1990).

Consider also that most researchers who study the sexual abuse of wives focus on "wife rape." Which cases in Box 3.2 should be considered "wife rape"? Why?

Wife rape is now illegal in all 50 states. Therefore the DOJ collects data on raped women's relationship to their assailants. In 1998, 63,490 women were raped or sexually assaulted by an intimate partner, a number that projects to 55.6 per 100,000 women (Rennison, 2002). However, several caveats must be made about these numbers. First, the "intimate partners" were husbands, boyfriends, dates, or ex-husbands—not just spouses. In addition, rather than being clearly defined, "rape" and "sexual assault" were left to the interpretation of the respondent, which is a problem because many women are reluctant to label sexual aggression by an intimate as "rape." Consider the woman whose husband demanded sex three times a day, physically abused her if she did not comply, forced her to have sex in front of their child four times, and threatened to rip out her vagina with pliers. When asked if she had ever been raped,

this woman said no (Finkelhor & Yllo, 1985). Furthermore, women are less likely to talk about intimate partner rape than stranger rape to friends, relatives, and professionals (Ullman & Siegel, 1993).

Our best estimates of the extent of wife rape come from two large representative surveys of women from San Francisco (Russell, 1990) and Boston (Finkelhor & Yllo, 1985). The researchers in these studies did not ask the women directly if they had ever been raped by their husbands. Rather, they asked if the women had ever experienced "unwanted sex" from their husbands, and if so, how was the husband able to get them to have sex. Women who were forced in some way (or even just threatened with force), or unable to consent (e.g., were drugged or asleep at the time), were considered raped. More than 25% of the San Francisco women reported unwanted sex with their husbands, and 14% reported that their husbands had forced them (Russell). In Boston, 10% of married women had been forced to have sex with their husbands (Finkelhor & Yllo). Generalizing from these two representative surveys, 1 out of every 7 to 10 women are raped by their husbands.

Moreover, these figures may underestimate the actual rate (Russell, 1990). The researchers did not ask about forced oral or anal sex. Although some of the participants spontaneously volunteered that information, many probably did not. This omission is important, because victims of marital rape are more likely than victims of acquaintance rape to have experienced forced oral or anal intercourse (Peacock, 1995). In addition, several respondents refused to disclose any incidents. Finally, some women assumed it was their wifely duty to submit to sex; because they did not feel they could say no, they were in a sense "unrapeable." A better way of estimating the prevalence of marital rape may therefore be to calculate the percentage of women who were forced into sex but also felt that they had the right to refuse (Russell).

There appear to be four types of coercion that can be used during marital rape: (a) social coercion, in which the wife feels it is her duty to submit; (b) interpersonal coercion, in which the husband uses threats to leave, cheat, or humiliate his wife to get her to submit; (c) threats of physical force; and (d) actual physical force (Finkelhor & Yllo, 1983). Which cases in Box 3.2 show which type of coercion? Does it matter which type of coercion a husband uses to get his wife to have sex with him? Is Mrs. Fisher "unrapeable" just because she accepts societal mores obligating wives to have sex with their husbands on demand as part of the marriage vows? What happens if a woman does not physically resist her husband because she knows she will lose the battle or be hurt worse if she resists, as in the case with Mrs. Morgan? Does lack of resistance mean the act is not "rape"? Consider Mrs. Atkins. If she passively gives in to her husband's demands in the future because of her experience, can these future cases be considered "rape"?

Even if the prevalence rates of wife rape extrapolated from these studies are an underestimate, they demonstrate that wife rape is almost three times as likely as stranger rape (Finkelhor & Yllo, 1985). Furthermore, the more intimate the relationship between perpetrator and victim, the more likely the rape is to succeed and the

more frequently the victim is raped (Russell, 1990). Indeed, 33% to 50% of raped wives are raped more than 20 times during their marriages (Finkelhor & Yllo, 1985; Russell). In the majority of cases (58%), the husband uses only the minimal force necessary to carry out the rape, and sometimes rapes without battering—about 14% of wife rape incidents in the San Francisco study were perpetrated by husbands who did not batter their wives (Russell). In that study, wife abuse was classified into three types: wife rape only or primarily wife rape (23%); wife rape and battering as equal problems (22%); and battering as the primary problem or only form of abuse (54%). Other studies have indicated that 33 % to 59% of battered women are also raped by their husbands (Campbell & Alford, 1989).

Husband Abuse

Although incidence reports of women abusing their husbands have appeared since the study of spousal maltreatment began in the early to mid-1970s (e.g., Gelles, 1974), the literature on husband abuse has not expanded much beyond the point of trying to establish whether or not it actually exists. Many researchers in the field of family violence are concerned that if husband abuse is deemed a significant problem, attention and resources will be diverted away from abused wives, who are the real victims of spousal maltreatment (Mignon, 1998). Consider the cases presented in Box 3.3. Do you consider either or both of these cases abusive? Why or why not? Are the circumstances and dynamics similar in any way to the ones experienced by abused women? Do these recipients of aggression present a simple reversal of the roles played in your picture of the "typical case of spousal maltreatment"? Are there ways in which these cases seem different from those of abused wives? Are there problems that appear to be unique to husbands? Conversely, are there problems that abused husbands may never experience but abused wives would? Finally, consider these cases again, but reverse the roles of the abuser and victim. Do you now view the cases as more, less, or equally abusive? Why?

Rates of violence by wives have come from many of the sources from which we obtain rates of violence by husbands. Crime statistics from

---

Box 3.3   Can Husbands Be Physically Abused?

Richard C, an upper-income man working in financial services, says he was attacked 50–60 times in their 14 years together, most of the time while she was drinking: "A lot of times, I would be working on some papers and there would be a coffee cup there, and she would intentionally spill the coffee; she went from that to throwing the coffee, and then throwing the cup and the coffee. She would throw hot scalding coffee in my face. It was a gradual thing that built over a three-year period, until it got to the point where she would physically strike me. . . . She would physically attack me, tear the glasses off, kick me in the testicles five, six, seven times. . . . You couldn't control her. A couple of times, I would wrestle her to the ground, pin her arms around her, and wrap my legs around her, and tell her to calm down, calm down. She'd say, 'O.K. I'm calm now, I'm under control now.' And you let her go, and she'd be right back at you, doing it again" (pp. 39-41).

Jake T., a 6-foot-tall construction worker, married 3 years to a woman who was 5 feet 3 inches: "I think a lot of her problems had to do with the drug use. I mean, I could never tell when she might come unglued. It would happen all of a sudden, usually in the bedroom. For example, one night I was sitting on the side of the bed, taking off my shoes, and she just came at me, kicking and swinging, no warning, nothin'. Just bang, she starts in. That's the way it was with her. She would never say why. One time, she did throw a knife at me; it missed. But most of the time, she would hit with her fists and kick. I'd just either hold her arms, or put up my arms, and then leave, till she had a chance to settle down" (p. 49).

SOURCE: Cook (1997).

---

the DOJ show that in 1998, 160,000 males were the victims of assault by an intimate partner (Rennison & Welchans, 2000). In addition, although rates of reported partner violence against females declined between 1993 and 1998, the rates for males did not. As mentioned in chapter 2, crime surveys are likely to provide an underestimate of intimate violence victimization because many people are unwilling to label the physical violence they receive at the hands of an intimate partner a "crime." This reluctance may be even more pronounced in men because men are supposed to be the physically dominant and aggressive partner; consequently, admitting to being victimized by a woman and labeling it a "crime" may be viewed as emasculating (Steinmetz, 1977).

A second source of data on violence by wives has come from the NVAW survey: 7% of the men reported being physically assaulted by a current or former wife or cohabiting partner over the course of their lifetimes, and 0.8% of the men reported being physically assaulted in the previous year (Tjaden & Thoennes, 2000).

These figures may also be an underestimate of the amount of violence against men because the respondents were told that they were being interviewed about "personal safety" issues; many men may not view the violence they receive at the hands of their wives or girlfriends as a threat to personal safety.

A final source of data on violence against men comes from studies using the *CTS*. The NFVS of 1975 showed that 11.6% of husbands reported having experienced some sort of violence from their wives within the previous year. Moreover, 4.6% reported having been the victims of severe violence by their wives, which translated into 2.6 million husbands nationwide (Straus, 1980b). The 1985 NFVS showed that 12.4% of husbands reported some level of physical assault by their wives in the previous year, and 4.8% reported being the victims of severe violence (again 2.6 million male victims nationwide)—a marked contrast to the apparent declines in the rates of wife abuse indicated in these surveys (Straus & Gelles, 1988).

These apparently equal, and sometimes higher, rates of male and female violence in intimate relationships as shown in the NFVS and other studies (e.g., Morse, 1995; O'Leary et al., 1989) using the *CTS* have been the subject of much debate. One major criticism is that the *CTS* do not measure motives, and most of these women, if not all, may be acting out of self-defense (Pleck, Pleck, Grossman, & Bart, 1977-1978). Data from several studies on violence by *battered* women support this proposition (e.g., Saunders, 1986; Walker, 2000), but self-defense is not the primary motive for violence by women in the bulk of the studies on motivations for common couple violence in intimate relationships (Hines & Malley-Morrison, 2001). Primary motives for violence by women include expressing jealousy or confusion, showing anger, retaliating for emotional hurt, expressing feelings that they had difficulty communicating verbally, and gaining control over the other person (Cate, Henton, Koval, Christopher, & Lloyd, 1982; Follingstad, Wright, Lloyd, & Sebastian, 1991; Henton, Cate, Koval, Lloyd, & Christopher, 1983; Makepeace, 1981). Although women cited self-defense as a motivation significantly more often than men did, it was never the most cited motivation for violence. In addition, two studies (Morse; O'Leary et al.) show that in 16% to 38% of violent couples, the violence is committed only by the females—in these relationships, the violence is obviously not a matter of hitting out of self-defense.

Emotional abuse of husbands has received even less attention. The little research done tends to be with community convenience samples (e.g., college men in dating relationships), not battered men. As is true in regard to women, there is as yet no consensus as to what constitutes emotional abuse of men, although research on dating relationships supports the view that men can be emotionally abused, sometimes even more so than women (Hines & Saudino, 2003; Simonelli & Ingram, 1998). However, some researchers (e.g., Walker, 1999) have argued that women cannot abuse men, even emotionally. What do you think? Is there any need for a consensus about the meaning of emotional abuse of husbands? Do you think the identified forms of emotional abuse of women also apply to men?

Elder Maltreatment

Research on domestic elder maltreatment has also been beset with definitional problems—particularly in regard to the constructs of neglect and financial exploitation. For instance, although neglect is considered a common form of child maltreatment, is it possible to maltreat adults by neglecting them? Adults are usually self-sufficient and self-determining, unless they are in some way impaired. Therefore, how can they be neglected? How impaired must they be in order for us to apply the label "neglect" meaningfully? What about the label "self-neglect," which can be found in many studies on elder maltreatment and refers to cases where older people neglect to eat properly or show good hygiene? If an older person neglects his or her own well-being, should we say that person is being maltreated? Or should we reserve such labels for acts committed (or omitted) by someone other than the individuals themselves? Finally, many researchers argue as to whether or not financial exploitation (e.g., when family members use the elderly person's income for their own benefit) should be considered abusive. The controversy surrounding this type of maltreatment concerns cultural differences in the perceptions of family obligations. Many cultures would not consider behaviors such as taking an elderly person's money to be abusive (or even exploitive) because of the implicit theory that family members have an obligation to share resources with one another.

For the purposes of this chapter, we discuss the various types of maltreatment identified by the National Center on Elder Abuse (1998), which conducted the first National Elder Abuse Incidence Study (NEAIS) for the year 1996 (see chapter 2). To arrive at the various subtypes of elder abuse, the investigators analyzed state definitions of elder abuse, convened roundtables of professionals dealing with elder abuse, reviewed definitions offered by elder abuse experts, and pilot tested their definitions with the Adult Protective Services agencies (APS) and sentinels that would be part of the study. According to the NEAIS, elder abuse perpetrated by family members can be of the following types:

1. Physical abuse, "the use of physical force that may result in bodily injury, physical pain, or impairment," including the unwarranted administration of drugs and physical restraints, force-feeding, and physical punishment of any kind.

2. Sexual abuse, "nonconsensual sexual contact of any kind."

3. Emotional abuse, "the infliction of anguish, emotional pain, or distress".

4. Neglect, "the refusal or failure to provide an elderly person with such life necessities as food, water, clothing, shelter, personal hygiene, medicine, comfort, personal safety, and other essentials included as a responsibility or agreement."

5. Abandonment, " the desertion of an elderly person by an individual who has assumed responsibility for providing care or by a person with physical custody of an elder."

6. Financial or material exploitation, "the illegal or improper use of an elder's funds, property, or assets."

7. Self-neglect, "behaviors of an elderly person that threaten his/her own health or safety" (National Center on Elder Abuse, 1998, Section 3.1, ¶ 7-13).

Table 3.2 presents some of the major findings from the NEAIS. In 1996, the data show that 449,924 elders were abused and/or neglected (excluding self-neglect) in domestic settings. Of these incidents; 16% were reported to APS for investigation, thus five times more abusive incidents were unreported than were reported. When self-neglect is added to the definition, 551,011 elders were maltreated in 1996, 21% were reported to APS agencies for investigation, and four times as many cases went unreported as were reported. Of the types of elder abuse that were reported and substantiated by APS agencies, the largest percentage were for neglect (48.7%), followed by emotional abuse (35.4%), financial exploitation (30.2%), physical abuse (25.6%), abandonment (3.6%), sexual abuse (0.3%), and other types (1.4%). Physical abuse was the most likely to be substantiated (61.9% of cases), followed by

abandonment (56%), emotional abuse (54.1%), financial exploitation (44.5%), neglect (41%), and sexual abuse (7.4%).

The NEAIS is probably the most comprehensive study of elder maltreatment to date. However, it does suffer from methodological problems (see chapter 2), and its results should be interpreted with caution. Other studies of representative samples of elders have also established preliminary rates of elder maltreatment. For instance, in the Boston metropolitan area, 32 of every 1,000 elders were the recipients of maltreatment (physical, emotional, and/or neglect). If these results could be generalized nationwide, between 701,000 and 1,093,560 elders would have been abused that year (Pillemer & Finkelhor, 1988).

The dynamics of elder maltreatment appear to be complex. In child maltreatment, a dependent child is maltreated by a parent, and in spousal maltreatment, spouses either maltreat each other or one spouse is the primary victim. In the case of elder maltreatment, there is a wider range of possibilities for elder-caretaker relationships. For instance, long-standing spousal maltreatment situations could continue into old age; a family member who is caring for an impaired elder can become frustrated at the elder and become abusive, or a well-functioning elder can be taken advantage of by a family member who is dependent upon him or her.

Spousal Elder Maltreatment

According to the NEAIS data, only 19% of cases reported to APS, compared to 30.3% of unreported cases, are committed by spouses. In the Boston study, nearly three fifths of the perpetrators were spouses (Pillemer & Finkelhor, 1988). Yet even though a substantial percentage of elder abusers are spouses, this type of maltreatment has been the least researched, perhaps because the image of elderly spouses hitting each other is not as abhorrent as the idea of a stronger, healthier, middle-aged adult hitting an elder. Although many people may assume that the consequences of spousal elder maltreatment are not as severe as other forms of elder maltreatment, there seem to be no differences in level of violence, number of injuries sustained, nor degree of upset engendered in the victim when the abuser is a spouse than when the abuser is an adult child. Therefore, spousal elder maltreatment needs more attention, because the elderly are much more likely to live with their spouses only than with their adult children only, and because the rate of maltreatment by elderly spouses may be 41 per 1,000 elders (Pillemer & Finkelhor).

Elder Maltreatment by Caregiving Relatives

In contrast to spousal elder maltreatment, the maltreatment of elders by adult relatives entrusted with their care is the most researched and most widely recognized type of elder maltreatment. Statistics from the NEAIS indicate that frail, confused, elderly women over the age of 80 are the most likely group to be identified by mandated reporters for elder maltreatment, primarily at the hands of family members with whom they reside. The more stressful adult children perceive caregiving for elderly parents to be, the more likely they are to resort to using abusive behaviors on the elder (Steinmetz, 1988). On the basis of her research, Steinmetz (1993) concluded that "the stress, frustration, and feelings of burden experienced by caregivers who are caring for dependent elders can result in abusive and neglectful treatment" (p. 223).

Maltreatment by Adult Dependent Children

Proponents of the view that elder maltreatment is primarily committed by adult dependent children rather than by adult caregivers (e.g., Pillemer, 1993) argue that (a) the majority of case control studies on this issue (e.g., Pillemer, 1986; Pillemer & Finkelhor, 1989) have found that victims of elder maltreatment do *not* differ from nonvictims on their health status and level of dependency; (b) the popular assumption that elders are maltreated by their middle-aged, stronger caregivers stems from media attention and the attention of public officials; and (c) more rigorous studies of elder maltreatment show that we need to look at the characteristics of the abuser, not the characteristics of the victim, if we are to clearly understand elder

maltreatment (Pillemer, 1993). Research on characteristics of the abusers does seem to show that they are the ones who are dependent. For example, two thirds of the elder maltreatment cases in Massachusetts were characterized by the adult child's financial dependence on the abuser (Wolf, Strugnell, & Godkin, 1982). Of reported cases in Wisconsin, 75% of the abusers were living in the elder's home, and 25% were financially dependent upon the elder (Greenberg, McKibben, & Raymond, 1990). Furthermore, in comparison to nonvictimized elders, those elders who were maltreated were more likely to have their adult children dependent upon them in several areas, including housing, household repair, financial assistance, transportation, and cooking and cleaning (Pillemer, 1986; Pillemer & Finkelhor). The abusers may have been subject to maltreatment themselves when they were children, often by the elderly parent they are now maltreating (Steinmetz, 1978), and abusers are likely to have problems with drugs and alcohol and chronic psychological problems (Greenberg et al.). Finally, abusers are likely to have mental and emotional problems, be hospitalized for those problems, and be violent and arrested in other situations (Pillemer & Finkelhor; Pillemer & Wolf, 1986).

SUMMARY

Families in the United States, including minority families, are imbedded in a culture that legitimizes and perpetuates violence as a means of behaving. Through cultural beliefs, laws, media influences, and governmental practices, this "culture of violence" has contributed to the perpetuation of all forms of family violence, both child and adult maltreatment. Although exact rates of child maltreatment are difficult to pinpoint, mostly because of difficulties in operationalization, it has been shown that it can exist in several forms, including physical and sexual abuse, neglect, and psychological maltreatment. Although some types of child maltreatment are more troubled by conceptual issues than others, researchers have not been able to come to a consensus on definitions of any of these types. The same problem arises when researchers have studied adult maltreatment. Wife physical, sexual, and emotional maltreatment have all been the subject of much debate: How hard and how often must a husband hit his wife for it to be physical abuse; can a husband sexually abuse his wife; and what exactly are the behaviors that constitute emotional abuse? The definition of husband abuse, sometimes the most hotly debated type of family violence, may face even more definitional problems, in part because many researchers do not even believe that husbands can be abused by their wives. Finally, elder maltreatment, the newest family violence type to be researched, is not without its definitional problems: Should self-neglect be considered a form of maltreatment; in what relationship is elder maltreatment most prevalent; is it meaningful to talk about neglecting an adult? Even though researchers cannot agree on the precise definitions of these types of family violence, they have been studied within the major minority groups in this country. When reading about the forms of family violence in minority communities, keep these definitional issues in mind. Also keep in mind the broader cultural context in which these minority families operate: the culture of violence in the United States. Then, combine what you learned in this chapter with what you learn about the cultural context of each minority community. How do these forces in combination contribute to family violence? We hope that through reading this book, you will gain a better idea of how family violence is instigated and perpetuated, and how we can work to eliminate family violence in the United States.

PART II

Native American Indian Cultures

4

NATIVE AMERICAN INDIAN CULTURAL CONTEXTS

Many of today's Native American parents have parents or grandparents who were "snatched" from the reservation and placed in foster care or sent off to boarding school. Consequently, there exists a genuine and deep-seated fear of government agencies that have the power to place children. . . . Today's Native American parents and grandparents have grown up with the reality-based belief that once a child goes into foster care, he or she never returns home. In other words, in their experience and from what they were told by their parents and grandparents, foster care is always permanent. This belief increases the parent's fear of [Child Protective Services] and accounts for the frequent observation that once a child is placed, parents seem to "give up" and "walk away." Unfortunately, this reaction is sometimes misinterpreted as a lack of motivation or a lack of concern for the child. A more accurate interpretation is to view the parents as making an effort to get on with their life after the "death" of a loved one.

—(Horejsi, Craig, & Pablo, 1992, pp. 335–336)

This quotation provides a dramatic description of the cultural/historical macrosystem in which contemporary judgments about abuse in Native American Indian communities must take place. It illustrates succinctly the historical maltreatment of members of Native communities by members of the White majority power establishment, and possible misinterpretations that can be made by members of a majority culture in judging behaviors in a minority culture.

For a long time, acknowledging that family violence existed in Native cultures was essentially viewed as criticizing the culture itself (Carson, 1995; Piasecki et al., 1989). Furthermore, many tribal members feared research into family violence because information about the extent and nature of family violence in Native communities could potentially be misused to reinforce and perpetuate negative stereotypes of Native American Indians (Hamby, 2000; Wolk, 1982). More recently, family violence has been acknowledged as a problem within many Native communities. To understand these problems adequately, it is essential to understand both the systemic abuse to which Native families have been subjected by the majority culture, and Native Americans' own conceptions of what behaviors constitute abuse.

In this chapter, we first consider two definitional issues central to the study of family violence in these communities: How do Native American Indians define different types of family violence and who exactly are Native Americans? We then address strengths of the Native culture that serve as protective factors against family violence. Finally, we review the historical relationship between Native American Indians and the majority culture and the role of oppressive practices of the U.S. government in the rise of family violence in these communities.

What Is Abuse?

Because it has been a closet subject, there have been few studies addressing Native American Indian views of abuse in families. There is some anecdotal information showing that the Native American and majority communities have some discrepancies in their views of abusive behavior. The opening paragraph of this chapter is an example of these differences: It is not unusual for child welfare agencies to view Native parents as neglectful because once the children are placed in foster care, the parents tend to react with passivity and avoidance—they leave their home area, avoid further contact with the agency, and seemingly abandon their children. However, Native Americans have a long history of losing their children to the White culture. Their children have been forcibly and permanently removed from their homes for generations in attempts to assimilate them into the majority culture; thus, parents feel that once the child is taken away, there is no hope for return (Horejsi et al., 1992).

Moreover, often the majority culture perceives Native parents as emotionally neglecting their children because of cultural differences in parenting practices. Within the Native American Indian microsystems, parents tend to be more silent, noninterfering, and permissive in their child-rearing practices, and they are often more than willing to let their children live with an extended family member if the child wishes (Ishisaka, 1978). The majority culture may see these acts as neglectful or abandonment, but the Native culture views the practice as appropriate parenting; moreover, their reliance on their extended family members for support in

parenting is viewed as a cultural barrier against child abuse (Cross, Earle, & Simmons, 2000; Ishisaka).

Our own data on definitions of child abuse from Native American Indians give examples of very strict criteria for judging the abusiveness of child-rearing behaviors. Two Natives, from two different tribes, gave examples of specific types of family violence, and provided two different examples of extreme child abuse. The example given by one respondent was "not feeding a child for not doing well in school," indicating that he considered intentional neglect of a child's basic needs to be extremely abusive, even when intended to teach the child an important lesson. The second respondent stated that "alcoholic parents continually beating their children because of their drunken stupor" is extremely abusive, which conjures up images of a widespread problem among many Native tribes, that of alcoholism.

There is less research on views of spousal abuse in Native communities, although there is evidence that at least some view aggression against a spouse not as a gender issue, but as a human or family issue. This view probably stems from the tradition of relative equality and complementarity existing between men and women in many of these communities prior to European contact. Currently, many Native Americans acknowledge that not only do men use violence against their wives, but women use violence against their husbands. In their view, in order for family violence (or violence in general) to be eliminated from their communities, both types of violence must be acknowledged and dealt with. Natives who have this view feel alienated by domestic violence shelters espousing a feminist perspective (Brave Heart-Jordan & DeBruyn, 1995), and dismayed at the tendency of the majority judicial system to blame the male for conflicts while seeming to ignore the woman's actions or behaviors (Durst, 1991).

In our study of the definitions of wife and husband abuse, the two Native American Indian respondents acknowledged that both wives and husbands can be the perpetrators of abuse. However, they had stricter criteria for wife abuse than for husband abuse. Both respondents mentioned that "beating," especially "repeatedly," is extremely abusive when either the wife or the husband is the perpetrator. For mildly abusive behaviors, both respondents mentioned some type of verbal abuse for both husbands and wives as perpetrators. But for moderately abusive behaviors, a different picture emerges. When a husband either "slapped his wife once" or "verbally and emotionally abused her," the husband was being moderately abusive. These responses stand in stark contrast to the "moderately" abusive behaviors that wives perpetrate: "throwing hot water at her husband" and "throwing dishes at her husband." It is interesting that these "moderately" abusive behaviors performed by the wife have a much greater likelihood of causing injury that the "moderately" abusive behaviors performed by the husband.

Although elder abuse is the least researched and least acknowledged area of family violence among Native American Indians, there is, ironically, research on Native views on elder abuse. This research (e.g., Brown, 1989, 1998) indicates that one of the greatest discrepancies between majority and Native cultures concerns the concept of financial exploitation. Many elderly Native Americans admit that they share or give their money to other family members who may need financial help, which majority culture researchers label financial exploitation and hence elder abuse (see chapter 3 in this book). However, Native elderly say they are not exploited; they voluntarily give money to family members because they are living up to an important communal cultural value.

There has also been research on differences in definitions of elder abuse between Native American Indians and the majority culture and between two different Native tribes. Hudson and Carlson (1999) presented various hypothetical examples of elder abuse to Native Americans and White adults and asked (a) whether each example was abusive and (b) how abusive it was. Native Americans gave higher ratings of severity of the abuse than did Whites. Furthermore, Native Americans were more likely than Whites to strongly agree that physically or verbally forcing elders to do something they did not want to do was elder abuse. Although White respondents indicated that yelling and swearing at an elder needs to occur more than once to be considered abuse, Native American respondents believed even one

occurrence of yelling was abusive. They were also more likely to view verbal force (swearing, yelling, belittling) as a form of elder abuse.

When comparisons were made between two different Native tribes, one of which was more culturally and geographically isolated than the other, the two groups largely agreed on the situations they considered abusive, with the exception of only four items. A larger percentage of the more acculturated tribe agreed that elders who are seen as physically weaker now than when they were younger were more at risk for abuse. In addition, a greater percentage of the more isolated tribe disagreed with the following statements: Elder abuse does not decrease the elder's quality of life; the use of verbal force is not a form of elder abuse; and in order for an act to be abuse, the elder has to be dependent on the person who does the abuse (Hudson, Armachain, Beasley, & Carlson, 1998).

Respondents in the Hudson et al. (1998) study also provided valuable qualitative data in their answers to an open-ended question on what elder abuse meant to them. The following statements were the most widely mentioned: hurting or harming an elder or causing them pain or suffering; treating an elder wrong, unkindly, unfairly, or in an unjust manner; being mean or cruel to an elder; and being disrespectful to or not honoring an elder. Respondents said that elder abuse could be demonstrated in physical, psychological, social, or financial ways, and could have a negative effect on elders in any or all of those ways. Moreover, some respondents stated that elder abuse is "being disrespectful of or not honoring the elderly and their place in history," "to treat an elder as less than human," and "injuries to an elder's body, heart, mind, or spirit" (Hudson et al., p. 544).

Our own qualitative data on Native definitions of elder abuse in some ways mirror the results from the two Hudson studies. One respondent mentioned that in addition to physically abusive behaviors, "leaving an elderly person, who cannot move, home without food" and "extreme neglect" are extremely abusive behaviors. Moderately abusive behaviors included "refusing the elderly adult medicine" and "insults; punches that don't cause permanent damage." Finally, mildly abusive behaviors included "purposely disturbing the elderly person" and "deliberately not visiting if the elderly person is lonely." As can be seen, the majority of these responses show that neglecting or disrespecting the elderly in any way is considered abusive.

Overall, although there may be some overlap between the majority culture's and Natives' conceptions of abuse, there are also important differences. These differences need to be considered as we discuss the incidence, predictors, and consequences of the various forms of family violence in these communities. Consider this Aboriginal (Canada's Natives) definition of family violence:

> A consequence to colonization, forced assimilation, and cultural genocide; the learned negative, cumulative, multi-generational actions, values, beliefs, attitudes, and behavioural patterns practiced by one or more people that weaken or destroy the harmony and well-being of an Aboriginal individual, family, extended family, community or nationhood. (Marackle, 1993, as cited in National Clearinghouse on Family Violence, 1996, pp. 1-2)

The definition also included *spiritual abuse*, defined as "the erosion or breaking down of one's cultural or religious belief system," as a type of family violence, and note that the majority of studies addressing family violence in Native communities have been done by non-Native researchers. Do you think that the definitions that these studies used conformed to the above-mentioned Aboriginal definitions? Do you think non-Native researchers would ever study spiritual abuse as a form of family violence? What type of study could be done to ensure that Native voices and definitions of abuse are heard?

WHO ARE NATIVE AMERICAN INDIANS?

To address the problem of family violence in Native communities, it is important to determine who should be labeled as a Native American Indian. Approximately 70 distinct definitions of Native American Indian have been identified (U.S. Department of Education, 1982). For example, the U.S. Census Bureau, from which we obtain population estimates, now allows people to self-report their ethnic background. A problem with this means of defining Native Americans emerges when the value of being Native American increases. In recent decades, Native cultures have been romanticized, such that people with very little Native American blood are defining themselves as Native American Indian (Clifton, 1989). Native American Indian can also be defined by tribal enrollment. However, terms and conditions vary by tribe, such that some tribes require at least half-blood quantum to be eligible (e.g., Northern Arapahoe and Hopi), whereas others merely require members to trace back their roots to original signatories (e.g., Cherokee Nation of Oklahoma). Furthermore, the Bureau of Indian Affairs (BIA) issues Certificates of Degree of Indian Blood to determine who can be considered Native American Indian (U.S. Office of Technology Assessment, 1986). These complexities in defining who is Native should be kept in mind when evaluating studies of family violence in these communities (see also Trimble & Thurman, 2002).

According to Census 2000, there currently are approximately 2.5 million American Indians and Alaska Natives in the United States. If we include people who consider themselves at least part American Indian, there are approximately 4.1 million, which is 1.5% of the U.S. population and an increase of 110% from the 1990 Census (U.S. Bureau of the Census, 2001a). American Indians and Alaska Natives belong to culturally heterogeneous and geographically dispersed communities that maintain their own language, family structure, social and religious functions, and health practices (Norton & Manson, 1996). Currently, there are 651 federally recognized American Indian and Alaska Native tribes.[1] The largest tribes include the Cherokee, Navajo, Latin American Indian, Chippewa, and Sioux tribes, which account for approximately 40% of the nation's Native population. The majority of tribes have fewer than 1,000 members, and many tribes have no formal recognition in the U.S. government (U.S. Bureau of the Census). The states with the most American Indians are California, Oklahoma, Arizona, Texas, New Mexico, New York, Washington, North Carolina, Michigan, and Alaska, in that order; these states contain approximately 62% of the nation's Native population, but only 44% of the total population. The majority are in the West and South, but the largest number of urban American Indians can be found in New York City, and only eight other cities have Native populations over 10,000.

In 1995, there existed approximately 209 Native languages, which is about half the number spoken 500 years ago. Many of these languages face extinction, as only the elderly members of the community speak them fluently (Goddard, 1996). Slightly less than 50% of Native Americans have become urbanized, mostly in order to find gainful employment. The rest live in rural villages, small rural communities, and on reservations (Trimble & Thurman, 2002). Indeed, 42% of Native Americans reside in rural areas, compared to 23% of Whites (Rural Policy Research Institute, 1999), and one in five Natives reside on reservations or trust lands (U.S. Department of Health and Human Services [DHHS], 2001).

Gainful employment is especially important to Native American Indians, who tend to be so poor that they are largely unaffected by macrosystem economic cycles. They are twice as likely as Whites to be unemployed (Population Reference Bureau, 2000). Between 1997 and 1999, approximately 26% of Native Americans, in comparison to 13% of the population as a whole and 8% of Whites, lived below the poverty line (U.S. Bureau of the Census, 1999). One researcher who visited a Navajo reservation said her first impression was that she had entered a Third World country. Only 20.9% of the homes had telephones and only 44.7% had complete plumbing. Not all Navajo view themselves as living in abject poverty because they value nonmaterialism, but many younger Navajo perceive and are distressed by their relative lack of material goods in comparison to the majority culture (Dawson, 1994; Navajo Nation, 1988). Although Native communities are culturally heterogeneous, they tend to share this extreme poverty and its antecedents and consequences. However, even level of poverty varies across tribes depending on the location of reservations. For example, the Gila Reservation near Phoenix is located near a modern urban center, and therefore, has better access to jobs and casino revenue than do more

geographically isolated tribes, which suffer more abject poverty (Hamby, 2000).

The antecedents to poverty flow from the oppression of Native American Indians at the hands of western Europeans when they settled America. These settlers forced Natives off their ancestral lands; restricted their means of obtaining food, shelter, and clothing; imposed their own forms of government on the Native Americans; mandated the education of Native children in White schools; and consequently, destroyed the Native language and religion (Norton & Manson, 1996)—practices that continue to have repercussions today and are essential components of the macrosystem in which Native communities are embedded. Substandard housing, poverty, and unemployment have contributed to malnutrition, inadequate health care, and shortened life expectancy. Indeed, they have the second highest infant mortality rate in the nation (National Center for Health Statistics, 2000), one third of Native American Indians do not have access to a source of health care, such as a doctor or clinic (Brown, Ojeda, Wyn, & Levan, 2000), and the life expectancy for Native American Indians is nine years shorter than for the population as a whole (DHHS, 2001; Indian Health Service, 1997).

Moreover, Native American Indian educational attainment is relatively low; in 1990, only two thirds of Native American Indians graduated high school, compared to 75% of the population as a whole (DHHS, 2001; U.S. Bureau of the Census, 1993). Native children seem to perform equally to the population as a whole until somewhere between 4th and 7th grades, when their academic performance declines and their entry into mental health treatment increases (Barlow & Walkup, 1998; Beiser & Attneave, 1982; DHHS). An inability to escape abject poverty has led to very high rates of mental disorders among Native Americans, who experience greater psychological distress than the population as a whole (Centers for Disease Control and Prevention, 1998; DHHS). Alcoholism is a long-standing problem, and although rates of alcoholism vary from tribe to tribe, they are typically very high. In one Southwestern tribe, over 70% of the participants in one large study qualified for a lifetime diagnosis of alcoholism (Robin, Chester, Rasmussen, Jaranson, & Goldman, 1997). Native

Americans also have the highest rates of infants born with fetal alcohol syndrome in this country: 2.97 for every 1,000 births, in comparison to 0.6 per 1,000 births for African Americans, the next highest rate (Chavez, Cordero, & Becerra, 1988; DHHS).

Alcoholism and substance abuse disorders are also a significant problem for Native children and adolescents. Higher rates have been found among Native children than among Whites in Appalachia (Costello, Farmer, Angold, Burns, & Erkanli, 1997), and Northern Plains Native adolescents, whose rate of substance abuse disorders was 18%, were more likely to be diagnosed with substance abuse or substance dependence disorders than the population as a whole (Beals et al., 1997). In addition, Native adolescents tend to drink more heavily than other ethnic groups, and tend to suffer more negative social consequences (DHHS, 2001; Mitchell et al., 1995; Oetting, Swaim, Edwards, & Beauvais, 1989; Plunkett & Mitchell, 2000). Rates of delinquency and crime committed under the influence of drugs and alcohol for Native Americans are the highest of any ethnic group in the United States (Greenfeld & Smith, 1999), and Native Americans are five times more likely to die from an alcohol-related cause than are Whites (DHHS; Indian Health Service, 1997).

Most of the discussion thus far pertains primarily to Native American Indians in the 48 contiguous states. Alaska Natives, although very similar to Native Americans, experience important differences that may put them at particular risk for family violence. First, isolation is particularly problematic for Alaska Native tribes. For example, 217 of the 322 Alaska Native communities are not on a road system and are accessible only by plane, boat, snow machine, or dog sled. Because these villages are so isolated, law enforcement is a problem—at times, it can take hours, or even days, for police to arrive to help someone in need, and it can cost over $500 to charter a flight to an urban center to escape abuse, assuming the individual is willing to leave the only community he or she has ever known. Second, the relative isolation of these communities leads many tribal members to rely on hunting and fishing for sustenance; therefore, the presence of weapons is ubiquitous and can make a

violent family situation even more dangerous. Finally, the severe weather and entire days of darkness during the Alaskan winters lead to further problems for families experiencing violence (Shepherd, 2001). As one abused Alaska Native woman stated, "When it's 40 below 0 and dark and you have several kids, what are you going to do? Where are you going to go?" (p. 496).

These conditions in Alaska have led to an alarming rate of violent crime, and Native women are at particular risk. Alaska Native women are killed at 4.5 times the rate of the women in the nation as a whole, and in three rural villages, they were 4 to 10 times more likely to be severely injured or die from wife abuse than were women in the general population. People in small Alaskan communities see 6 times more violent deaths than people in the nation as a whole. In 1995, 80% of the homicides in Alaska were related to family violence, and in 1996, 4 of 16 family violence deaths in Alaska were children (Council on Domestic Violence and Sexual Assault, 1997; Shepherd, 2001; Shinkwin, 1983). Although the overwhelming majority of studies done on family violence in Native communities do not consider the experience of Alaska Natives, the conditions of many of their communities may make the problem of family violence even more severe than in Native American communities.

Clearly, Native American Indian communities are extremely heterogeneous. Prior to European contact, most communities had little or no contact with each other (Hamby, 2000). Even today, there is diversity in the social conditions of the hundreds of tribes, as some are more isolated and more poverty-stricken than others (Hamby). However, some generalizations can be made because all Natives experienced European domination—for example, their social conditions today are primarily a result of the elimination and assimilation techniques Europeans used to solve the "problem" of the Native Americans.

PROTECTIVE FACTORS: STRENGTHS OF NATIVE FAMILIES AND CULTURAL VALUES

Native communities have various familial, cultural, and tribal strengths that have allowed them to survive centuries of European domination in North America. The extent to which these strengths are still ingrained and maintained in these communities varies from tribe to tribe (Carson & Hand, 1999), and depends on such factors as the tribe's degree of poverty, stress associated with acculturation, and poor health (Hudson et al., 1998). Traditional strengths, when they have survived, have served to protect Native Americans from family violence.

Native communities are known especially for their emphasis on the familial and tribal community as sources of support. They value acts such as sharing, humility, and not hurting others, and they emphasize the success of the community, not the success of the individual. This emphasis is evident in their valuing of cooperation and noncompetition, and in a community conscience and sense of responsibility for the survival of the tribe (Carson, 1995). Prior to European domination and to varying extents today, all members of Native communities fulfilled their role as part of the community with strict adherence to a social order devised and controlled by the community. If tribal practices were violated, it was understood that transgressions would be dealt with harshly (BigFoot, 2000). Other strengths of Native communities relate to their history of deep spirituality, strict religious practices, and rituals. They believe in living in harmony with all of creation, and have a cosmic identity leading to optimism and contentment with life (Carson). These beliefs have helped Native communities survive for centuries, and values specific to children, women, and the elderly have served to protect these members from abuse.

Views on Children

Children hold a special place in Native communities. They are considered sacred gifts from the Creator, innately endowed with wisdom, and their opinion is valued (Cross, 1986; Cross et al., 2000). Child care is a highly esteemed responsibility (Brave Heart-Jordan & DeBruyn, 1995) and is shared by several people in the child's family and community. This sharing of child-rearing responsibilities leads to a natural safeguard for children, whose parents are being watched by aunts, uncles, grandparents, and tribal elders. Prior to European domination, this system ensured that no one felt overburdened by child care (Cross).

According to tradition, prior to European domination, Native parents were extraordinarily patient and tolerant in their child-rearing practices. Physical punishment and restraint were typically not used. Instead, children were instilled with the traditional beliefs of their culture—for example, that supernatural beings kept strict watch over children and punished them for wrongdoing (Cross et al., 2000). In some tribes, children learned through the myths that certain behaviors were expected and that if they did not obey, a supernatural being would come and discipline them for their misdeeds (Cross, 1986; Cross et al.). Alternatively, the role of disciplinarian was sometimes placed in the hands of a specific tribal member, as in the case of the Warm Springs tribe in Oregon (Cross). This tribe had a "whipperman," a designated member of the tribe, who would come and visit a family and punish the children for their wrongdoings. He would also spend much time telling stories and legends to teach the children the value of behaving properly. Although parents were not entirely relieved of responsibility in disciplining their own children, they were held to community standards, and transgressions from these standards could lead to chastisement and ridicule (Cross). For these reasons and because it was believed that the mistreatment of children would result in the child's spirit returning to its Creator (Cross), many scholars believe that child maltreatment was seldom a problem in tribal communities prior to European domination (Cross et al.).

Views on Women

Because of the historical tribal emphasis on community and sharing, interdependence of the sexes was traditionally considered necessary for survival of the tribe. Prior to European domination, women and men shared many activities, and women sometimes assumed a stereotypically male role. For instance, in the Lakota tribe, both genders could initiate a divorce, and because women owned the tipi and its contents, a man could keep only his clothes, hunting equipment, and sacred objects if a divorce occurred (Powers, 1986). Also, when men were not out hunting, they would stay home and assist the women with child care and meal preparation.

Prior to European domination, many Native communities were matrilineal (bloodlines were determined by the women; e.g., Iroquois, Hopi, and Zuni), matrilocal (place of residence after marriage was determined by the women; e.g., Hopi and Zuni), or matriarchal (family decisions were made by the women; e.g., Iroquois and Apache). Furthermore, some nations were governed by women, and women held positions as healers and spiritual leaders. If they did not hold a position of authority in the tribe, women often had a say in tribal decision making. Moreover, in contrast to the creation story of the Christian culture, Native communities often told creation stories in which both sexes were created simultaneously by a gender-neutral or female god (Buffalohead, 1985; Chester, Robin, Koss, Lopez, & Goldman, 1994; Columbus, Day-Garcia, Wallace, & Walt, 1980; Gridley, 1974).

According to the Sacred Shawl Women's Society (2002) on the Pine Ridge reservation, the abuse of women rarely occurred in this Native community prior to European domination, probably because of the high value placed on women and their contributions to the tribe. As one Winnebago man stated, "Our grandmother, the earth, is a woman, and in mistreating your wife, you will be mistreating her. Most assuredly you will be abusing our grandmother if you act thus" (Chester et al., 1994, p. 249). If wife abuse did occur, it was dealt with harshly. A wife batterer was considered irrational, and his wife had the option of exiling him from her family. In addition, the wife's brothers were obligated to retaliate in some way against the batterer and his family. On the community level, the batterer, because of his irrationality, was not allowed to own a pipe, hunt, or lead a war party (Sacred Shawl Women's Society). This method of dealing with wife abuse is a prime example of the harsh punishment that tribal members would receive if they were to transgress against one of the community's social norms.

Views on the Elderly

Native American Indians have a long-standing tradition of respect for the elderly (Carson, 1995). The Ojibwa Tribal Code, for example, has the following as one of its tenets: "Honor the aged: In honoring them you honor life and wisdom" (Carson & Hand, 1999, p. 167). There is evidence (Burgess, 1980; John, 1988) that prior to European domination, the elderly were typically not neglected, deserted, or isolated from the tribe; to this day, they often hold esteemed positions in tribes and perform many political, social, and religious duties. They are the keepers of the traditions, language, rituals, and legends of the tribe, and they pass on this knowledge to the younger generations (Edwards, 1983; Schweitzer, 1983). They tell traditional stories, and assist in the care and upbringing of children (Benokraitis, 1996; Staples & Mirande, 1980; Yates, 1987). Among the Navajo, reciprocal caregiving among three generations has been observed. Grandmothers assist their daughters in caring for their children and the grandmothers expect to be the recipients of care when they need it (Shomaker, 1990; Weibel-Orlando, 1990).

Elders also hold esteemed positions in tribal political and religious life. For instance, among the Arapaho in Wyoming, elders control religious rituals and functions (Fowler, 1990). Elderly Navajo women are essential elements in kin relationships and tribal dealings and help maintain reciprocity between the family and tribe. In recent decades, with the new emphasis on preserving tribal culture, language, and history, elders have experienced renewed importance in the community, as they are the only ones left with knowledge of the culture and language (Curley, 1987).

Links Between Beliefs and Behavior

Although Native communities have strong beliefs in community and nonaggression, there is evidence that some forms of what can be considered family violence occurred prior to European domination. Many of the assertions made about the absence of family violence during this time period are based on an analysis of relatively nonviolent tribes. However, as stressed previously, there were hundreds of tribes with different languages, cultures, and beliefs, and therefore, blanket generalizations about the nonexistence of family violence based upon the analysis of only a few tribes should be critically evaluated. Furthermore, given various ecological conditions, there was not necessarily a perfect correlation between the beliefs and values of the Native cultures and their behaviors toward each other.

For example, although children were deemed as sacred gifts in many tribes, tribes were known to kill a twin or starve a physically deformed child. Moreover, in some tribes, if a child disrespected fire, that child would be allowed to test the flame and possibly even be burned in the process to teach respect for fire (BigFoot, 2000). In some tribes, a man could cut off his wife's nose if she committed adultery (Mayhall, 2001), or he could have other members of the tribe rape her if she insulted him in their marriage (BigFoot). An Inuit man could reprimand his wife if her housework was not acceptable to him, and could arrange sexual exchanges with other men without his wife's consent (Guemple, 1995; Hamby, 2000). Among the Apache, a man had to severely reprimand his wife if she was adulterous by either beating or disfiguring her; otherwise, he was considered unmanly (Hamby; Opler, 1996). Furthermore, in some tribes, a woman could destroy her husband's hunting and fishing tools if he did not provide sufficiently for the family. A husband could be ostracized from the community and left without shelter or family if he violated a sacred rule, and a wife could be ostracized if she violated teachings regarding her social interactions with men other than her husband (BigFoot). According to your own implicit theories of abuse, which would you consider to be abusive? To what extent do you think those behaviors were abusive even if they conformed to cultural practices?

These examples and the fact that there were prescribed ways of dealing with wife batterers show that aggressive behaviors among spouses occurred prior to European domination. Moreover, in a study that assessed wife abuse both prior to and after industrialization in two Arctic communities, wife abuse was a problem prior to industrialization, but was kept private because people were not as willing to confront and acknowledge the issue before industrialization as they were afterwards (Durst, 1991). Furthermore, even though many researchers cite the matrilineal, matrilocal, and matriarchal organization of many tribes as evidence that Native American males and females were deemed equal prior to European domination, two caveats must be made: (a) The social organization of tribes varied, and many were patrilineal, patrilocal, and patriarchal. In addition, most patrilineal tribes were also patriarchal, but most matrilineal tribes were not matriarchal. (b) Furthermore, even if a tribe was matrilineal, matrilocal, or matriarchal, there were variations in the social conditions of the women. For example, even if bloodlines were matrilineal, women may not have been allowed to participate in political life or religious ceremonies. Thus, it is faulty to assume that because many tribes were matrilineal, matrilocal, or matriarchal, family violence did not exist in all Native communities prior to European domination, and it is also faulty to assume that because a tribe had that kind of social organization that women were not subject to violence. The lineage of the bloodlines may have little to do with dominance within a spousal relationship (Hamby, 2000).

There is also evidence that prior to European domination, elderly Native Americans were treated in ways that would be considered by contemporary American social service definitions to be abusive. For example, tribes were known to abandon the elderly (BigFoot, 2000). In addition, Native American Indians viewed elders as falling into two categories: "intact" and "decrepit," and there were three means of dealing with the elderly: supportive, nonsupportive death hastening, and death hastening (Glascock, 1990). The death hastening and nonsupportive means were usually directed at those elderly who went from being productive members of the community to being inactive and nonproductive, and usually occurred in societies located in harsh environments, such as deserts, where it was difficult to support nonproductive and dependent members. The Ojibwa practiced the death hastening method with their elderly. A decision was usually made jointly by the elder and his or her family to kill the elder if that person was becoming a burden on the family. These death hastening and nonsupportive means of dealing with nonproductive elderly served to protect and maximize the chances of survival of a tribe facing overwhelmingly difficult living conditions (Glascock). Given these conditions, should death hastening and nonsupportive practices be considered forms of maltreatment? Should we say that the behaviors were forms of maltreatment but unavoidable because of ecological conditions, or should we say that because of the ecological conditions, the behaviors should not be considered forms of maltreatment?

In sum, although Native communities have a long-standing tradition of revering children, women, and the elderly, there is evidence that many family members were subjected to harsh practices, sometimes with and sometimes without community support. There is also evidence of considerable variation in the extent and nature of family violence from tribe to tribe. For example, the frequency of family violence is historically low among the Fox, but higher for the Apache, for whom spousal abuse was sometimes an acceptable punishment (Hamby, 2000). In addition, family violence was often associated with geography. Tribes experiencing harsh environmental conditions were more likely than other tribes to abandon or kill nonproductive members of the community. Perhaps the variations in forms of aggression and neglect depended upon the environmental conditions the communities were forced to deal with, and perhaps the variations depended upon how violent and warlike the community's relationships with other communities were. We have no definitive answers to these questions, primarily because there is no written or visual history of Native communities prior to European domination. What we do know, however, is that regardless of the level of family violence in individual tribes in the earlier period, rates of family violence in their communities have risen dramatically in the last 150 years (Hamby). These increased rates are probably due to the oppression, racism, and profound losses Native American Indians have experienced, as discussed in the next section.

ROLE OF OPPRESSION AND RACISM IN NATIVE AMERICAN INDIAN FAMILY VIOLENCE

Unlike other minorities in this country, Native American Indians were not brought to this country, nor did they arrive after the establishment of the United States as a nation. They occupied the land of North America long before the first European settlers arrived, and have been all but wiped out since that time. When the European settlers first discovered that others were occupying the land, they deemed the occupants to be uncivilized, barbaric savages, who were intellectually, culturally, and religiously inferior to Whites. In the early days, the general policy of destroying the Natives was accomplished through the introduction of foreign disease on reservations (sometimes intentionally by trading smallpox-infested blankets to tribes), mass killings, and enslavement. Alcohol was used purposely to intoxicate tribal leaders and coerce them into signing treaties to benefit the United States. A further tactic used to decimate the Native population was the displacement of Eastern Native tribes to areas west of the Mississippi; wars broke out between the displaced nations and the tribes who had already occupied the land for many centuries. Later, when the U.S. officials displaced tribes to reservations, they purposely put rival tribes on the same reservations. Furthermore, historical, cultural, and family differences among the tribes made it difficult for them to unite to address common problems (Bohn, 1993; Brave Heart-Jordan & DeBruyn, 1995).

Table 4.1 presents a brief history of oppressive practices of the U.S. government toward the Native American Indians. As can be seen, the U.S. government used boarding schools, treaties, and removals to undermine the structure and integrity of the tribes. The effects of these practices have been devastating to Native Americans. Moreover, Native people were taught not to resist U.S. demands, because every time they did, something—ranging from land, to food, to shelter, to homes, and to children—was taken away (BigFoot, 2000). As can also be seen from Table 4.1, the practice of destroying

Table 4.1   History of U.S. Government Oppression of Native American Indians

1620—Pilgrims landed on Plymouth Rock and followed what they saw as their "Manifest Destiny"—their right, responsibility, and privilege as law-abiding citizens to take this new land as their own gain. The inhabitants were deemed *savages*, and religious arguments were used to justify their unfair treatment.

1684–1880—Invasion (Indian) Wars occurred between the United States and the Indians; especially fierce out west, as the United States continued to expand into the frontier lands; priority was removal of the Indians.

1824—Creation of the Bureau of Indian Affairs in the U.S. War Department; oversaw U.S. relations with Indian tribes.

1830—Indian Removal Act forced Eastern Indian tribes to relocate cross-country to areas west of the Mississippi River. The U.S. government then guaranteed them these lands forever.

1850-1890—Reservation Treaties violated the Indian Removal Act; the United States paid little cash and promised services to the Indians in exchange for more land cessions; Indians gave more land to the United States and were relocated to reservations owned by individual tribes.

1855—Court of Claims was established so that private parties could sue the United States for violation of contracts; tribes tried to sue the United States for taking more land from them; Congress then prohibited claims to be made from violations of treaties.

1867—Purchase of Alaska from the Russians; Alaska Natives were not forced to move to reservations until 1891, when only a few were established for a small number of tribes.

1879—Carlisle Indian School was established with the goal of complete assimilation or annihilation of Indian children. Indian children were taught reading, writing, math, home economics, and manual trades; marked the beginning of the *boarding school movement*, in which Indian children were taken from their families to "civilize" them and make them lose their Indian ways.

1887—General Allotment Act (Dawes Act) terminated communal ownership of reservation lands and awarded individual Indians taxable tracts of land to further civilize the Indians by converting them to an individual system of land ownership; leftover lands were open for White settlement; many Indians were cheated out of ownership.

Early 1900s—Population of Native American Indians: 5% of original population.

1924—Indian Citizenship Act granted Indians U.S. citizenship.

1928—Merriam Report to Congress documented harsh treatment of Indian children in boarding schools; abuse typically went unreported in schools and the offending official was not held responsible for acts; became part of the *1930 Congressional Hearings on the Status of American Indians*.

1934—Indian Reorganization Act allowed Indians to organize their own government with limited jurisdiction; designed to help tribes recover sufficient power to represent their interests in political and economic arenas; traditional forms of tribal government discouraged.

1950–1968—Urban Relocation Program began relocating reservation Indians into the industrial or commercial areas in major cities in order to assimilate Indians into the mainstream economy and improve their financial situations; Indians could not compete with the working poor in these cities because they did not have marketable skills.

1953—Resolution 108 led to the disbanding of more than 200 tribes and their governments; those benefits that were still offered to other Indians were no longer offered to these disbanded tribes; *Public Law 280* gave some states civil and criminal jurisdiction over the tribes that were not disbanded.

1968—Indian Civil Rights Act prohibited states from assuming jurisdiction over reservations without tribal consent; reestablished tribal control of health, education, and social services.

1971—Alaska Native Claims Settlement Act passed after the discovery of huge oil deposits on Alaska's North Slope to organize Alaska Native tribes into regional corporations with control of over 44 million acres of land; Alaska Natives waived their rights to their original lands.

(Continued)

Table 4.1 Continued

1975—Indian Self-Determination and Education Assistance Act allowed the federal government to establish grants and make contracts with tribal governments for federal services; tribal governments could control housing, education, law enforcement, social services, health programs, and community development programs on their lands.

1978—Indian Child Welfare Act was enacted to reduce the number of Indian children who were taken from their families and placed in non-Indian foster care or adoptive homes as a result of abuse or neglect; provided minimal federal guidelines for removal of Indian children and allowed tribal governments to place Indian children in Indian homes in order to preserve their culture.

1978—Indian Religious Freedom Act finally validated the Native American church as a true religious structure with all the rights and protections of other religious structures.

1990—Indian Child Protection and Family Violence Protection Act mandated that reports of child abuse or neglect on Indian lands be made to the appropriate authorities; called for the establishment of treatment programs for victims of child sexual abuse, the training of people to investigate and treat cases of child maltreatment, the establishment of programs to reduce the incidence of family violence on reservations, and the authorization of other programs necessary to protect children; no funds were appropriated for this act.

1994—Federal Crime Control Bill was devised to allow for greater police presence on reservations, the expansion of efforts to improve relations between the police and community members, and the enhancement of public safety because crimes were growing on tribal lands and there were insufficient resources to deal with this problem; allowed for more federal support to prosecute and reduce crimes against women and children and to strengthen victim services.

SOURCES: BigFoot, 2000; DHHS, 2001; Duran, Duran, Brave Heart, and Yellow Horse-Davis, 1998; Henson, 2002; O'Brien, 1989.

Native Americans eventually turned into attempts to "civilize" and "assimilate" them. Although no empirical examination has ever been conducted on the influence of European domination on the current conditions of Native American Indians, it is generally accepted that the many social and economic problems they face are a result of this systematic oppression (Hamby, 2000). Perhaps the single most devastating means of "civilizing" Native Americans was the establishment of boarding schools for Native children. These schools are arguably the most important contributor to the widespread problems that face Native American Indians today—problems such as suicide, homicide, alcoholism, and family violence.

Boarding Schools

The height of the use of boarding schools to "civilize" Native American Indians occurred between 1880 and 1960. However, the earliest boarding school opened in the 1700s. The schools started in the East, but as tribes were forced west, boarding schools were also relocated to remote areas. By 1887, there were more than 200 boarding schools with a total of over 14,000 Native children as students (BigFoot, 2000). During the 1930s and 1940s, approximately one half of all educated Native Americans received their education in these schools (DHHS, 2001), which were operated by both the federal government and established religious orders (Carson & Hand, 1999). The official intention was to assimilate the Native children to the dominant White culture. Why were only children chosen to be converted to the mainstream way of life? Perhaps the answer can best be summed up by the 1886 Commissioner of Indian Affairs:

It is admitted by most people that the adult savage is not susceptible to the influence of civilization, and we must therefore turn to his children, that they might be taught to abandon the pathway of barbarism and walk with a sure step along the pleasant highway of Christian civilization. . . . They must be withdrawn, in tender years, entirely from the camp and taught to eat, to sleep, to dress, to play, to work, to think after the manner of the white man. (Price, 1973, as cited in George, 1997, p. 166)

To accomplish the conversion to White ways, Native children were forbidden to speak their tribal language, practice their own religion, wear their traditional clothes or hairstyles, participate in their cultural events, or spend time with their families (Carson & Hand, 1999). Instead, they were to speak only English, move in regimental lines, wear uniforms, never question authority, maintain silence, and work. Violation of any rule led to severe punishment, the most common punishments being grade failure, commitment to reformatory schools, excommunication from the church, being forced to stand still at their bedside for hours, physical assaults with such things as rulers, and thrashings with a strap (George, 1997). Other punishments included denial of medical care; limitations on food, clothing, and shelter; and being used as indentured servants. At the extreme level, boarding school officials beat and whipped children to death to serve as examples to the other children of what would happen if they violated the strict rules (BigFoot, 2000). Is there any reason to suspect that such practices would not have devastating effects on the Native children subjected to them? What might these effects be? Are there any such practices that would not be considered abusive today?

The boarding school movement reached deeply into Native communities. Often, children as young as three years of age were forced to attend. Sometimes, this force consisted of threatening to cut off food and supply rations to Native families if they did not comply with federal authorities (Bohn, 1993; Cross et al., 2000). The children were sent away for at least nine months at a time, and often for many years (Bohn). Many times, the removal would be extended beyond the academic year by placing the children with White families for the summer (George, 1997). Because the boarding schools valued military discipline and complete regimentation (Bohn), they attracted a certain

type of personnel, few of whom possessed an understanding of Native cultures. Often, the staff included ex-military personnel who had engaged in destroying Native Americans prior to the assimilation era (BigFoot, 2000). The personnel were encouraged to use strict discipline with the children and often were not held accountable for any severe injuries or deaths that occurred. They were held accountable only if they failed to convert the children from their "savage" ways (BigFoot).

In addition to the deplorable conditions these children suffered, many times they were never able to return to their families simply because their parents could not find them. When the children were taken from their families at an early age, their families knew only their Native name. However, to encourage assimilation, the children were immediately given Christian names. If children were transferred to another school or died, families had no way of finding out because they did not know the children's Christian names and schools did not record their Native names. Furthermore, the schools were not responsible for informing the parents of transfers or deaths, and authorities were not held accountable for any missing children (BigFoot, 2000).

When children did return home to the reservations, they were often confronted with a difficult situation. Having felt like strangers in the dominant culture, they now felt like strangers in their families (George, 1997). Sent away for years at a time, they could not learn their traditional culture, did not have role models for learning to function within a tribal unit, and were never allowed to develop nurturing relationships in their families (BigFoot, 2000). Instead, in the boarding schools, they were exposed to harsh physical discipline, which they probably would not have experienced in an intact Native tribe. Is it any surprise that many of these children, so severely maltreated by the system officially intended to rescue them, turned into abusive and neglectful parents, whose children were taken away and placed into adoptive homes by the BIA (George)? Many generations of Native children experienced the harsh discipline of the boarding schools, and consequently, many generations of children grew up to be abusive and neglectful parents who never had the opportunity to learn proper child-rearing skills from their own parents (BigFoot). Recall from chapter 2 that one of the strongest predictors for the perpetration of child abuse is abuse in one's family of origin. Although boarding school children did not grow up in their own families, can we say they were subject to the "intergenerational transmission" of child abuse? In what ways?

In addition to harsh physical discipline of the children in boarding schools, there is also a legacy of sexual abuse by personnel in these schools (BigFoot, 2000; Schafer & McIllwaine, 1992). Historically, Native tribes have a strong taboo against incest, such that violators were subjected to banishment, death, and loss of all rights and honor (BigFoot). However, there is evidence that in the recent past, some Native American Indians were and are pedophiles. How is this possible when there is such a strong cultural taboo against incest? According to research in the majority culture, many child sexual abusers report a history of sexual abuse during their own childhoods (e.g., Watkins & Bentovim, 1992). Therefore, the existence of child sexual abuse in Native communities today can be traced back to the sexual abuse that many Native Americans experienced in these boarding schools (Schafer & McIllwaine).

In the mid-1930s, the boarding schools began closing in response to the Indian Reorganization Act, which gave tribes control over their reservations (George, 1997). The damage, however, was done. Many generations of Native children grew up in extremely abusive environments with no parental or tribal nurturing and guidance. Moreover, even when the legacy of boarding schools was coming to a close, a new era—the Adoption Era—was beginning. This new era further decimated the culture and identity of Native tribes and continued the generational cycle of abuse.

Indian Adoption Project

With the closing of the boarding schools, the government was faced with the problem of many Native children returning home to the reservation, where poverty was rampant. Poverty, according to the government, was a breeding ground for neglect, and, therefore, the children must be removed. Placement with extended family was not considered to be a solution, as they also existed in poverty. Therefore, the BIA began hiring social workers to place Native children in non-Native homes for long-term care (BigFoot, 2000; George, 1997). The policy of the Indian Adoption Project was to take Native children out of their homes and place them far away, culturally and geographically, from the reservation, a practice that continued until 1978, when the Indian Child Welfare Act was passed. This act gave tribal authorities, not federal or state authorities, the power to decide whether placement of children was needed, and if so, where they would go. After the Indian Child Welfare Act was passed, children in need of placement were usually placed either in the homes of extended family members (as is tribal custom) or in other Native foster homes. Prior to 1978, as many as 25% to 35% of all Native children had been separated from their families and placed in non-Native homes (BigFoot; George).

Other Issues in Oppression

European domination also served to undermine the respectful and equal relationships that Native men and women had in many tribes. For example, when U.S. federal authorities negotiated treaties with Native American Indians, they would do so only with the men. As discussed previously, in many tribes, women were leaders or at least had a say in decisions made by the tribes. Therefore, this practice of the U.S. government undermined the status of Native women within their tribes (Brave Heart-Jordan & DeBruyn, 1995). What are likely outcomes of such undermining of women's status?

The transplantation of Eastern tribes west of the Mississippi and the removal of all tribes to reservations also undermined the traditional role of some Native men as hunters, protectors, and providers. Continual shifts in power due to problems in the reservation economy led to Native women becoming more employable than Native men. Native women secured employment off the reservation as clerical and domestic workers, which were more permanent sources of income than were available to Native men, who tended to be restricted to temporary manual labor positions. Thus, Native men lost positions of status and honor within their tribes (Brave Heart-Jordan & DeBruyn, 1995). Indeed, it appears that the roles of Native men have eroded more than women's, and that this loss has led to a decreased self-esteem and increased violence among men (Duran, Duran, Woodis, & Woodis, 1998; Hamby, 2000; Wolk, 1982). What are likely implications of such changes for family relationships?

The lessening status of both Native women and men, and especially of the relative status of Native women to men, are among the likely causes of the many social ills seen in Native communities today, including family violence. Men may still revere women when they speak of them. However, their actions frequently contradict their words (Brave Heart-Jordan & DeBruyn, 1995). Furthermore,

> once complementary relationships are now fraught with tension and ambivalence. Gender roles are no longer enacted in ways that help people feel powerful and honored. . . . Male-dominated and female-subservient social systems have infiltrated and become a part of reservation communities as individuals are forced to adopt an alien model of government. (Brave Heart-Jordan & DeBruyn, 1995, p. 353)

Historical Trauma and Unresolved Grief

The longstanding history of European domination, genocide, cultural genocide, and involuntary assimilation of the Native Americans can be viewed as having two enduring psychological consequences: (a) *unresolved* or *disenfranchised grief*, the grief experienced when one cannot publicly mourn, openly acknowledge, or receive social support for one's loss, either because the perpetrators will not allow it or because one trauma is immediately followed by another, and (b) *historical trauma* or *soul wound*, the social transmission of one generation's trauma to subsequent generations (DeBruyn, Chino, Serna, & Fullerton-Gleason, 2001; Duran, Duran, Brave Heart, & Yellow Horse-Davis, 1998; Trimble & Thurman, 2002).

According to one major perspective, this historical trauma, described as a "wound to the

soul of Native American people that is felt in agonizing proportions to this day" (Duran & Duran, 1995, p. 27), is multigenerational and cumulative, such that each subsequent generation suffers more than the previous one. The centuries of incurable diseases, massacres, forced relocation, poverty, broken treaties, abuse, and loss that have been experienced by the Native Americans at the hands of the European settlers have led to a compounding of health problems in these communities (Duran, Duran, Brave Heart, et al., 1998; Trimble & Thurman, 2002). Furthermore, the unresolved grief of one generation's traumas leads to depression, which is then absorbed by the children of the next generation, and the cycle continues (Duran, Duran, Brave Heart, et al.).

Although not studied empirically as predictors of psychological distress among Native Americans, historical trauma and unresolved grief have been shown to exist among an analogous group—children of German Holocaust survivors (Kestenberg, 1990). The symptoms of historical trauma these people display

> include depression, suicidal ideation and behavior, guilt and concern about betraying the ancestors for being excluded from the suffering, as well as obligation to share in the ancestral pain, a sense of being obliged to take care of and being responsible for survivor parents, identification with parental suffering and a compulsion to compensate for the genocidal legacy, persecutory and intrusive Holocaust as well as grandiose fantasies, dreams, images, and a perception of the world as dangerous. (Duran, Duran, Brave Heart, et al., 1998, p. 342)

Compounding the problem of historical trauma in children of Holocaust survivors is unresolved grief, for it is difficult to mourn at a mass grave and to live amongst the people who perpetrated these atrocities and murdered millions of other Jewish people. Consequently, many Jews, especially in Europe, have had a hard time coping with the reality of the Holocaust. Many feel an uncontrollable rage against the perpetrators, but fear to acknowledge these feelings, for to do so may lead to an overwhelming desire to avenge the deaths of their loved ones (Brave Heart-Jordan &

Box 4.1   My Family, My Responsibility, by Doe West, Ph.D.

When I was 8, my grandmother told me I had a calling as a healer. "I am of The People," she began. "I am an Indian. You are of The People. You are an Indian." I had not known this.

Born in 1893, my grandmother lost both parents before she was 8. The "church people" placed her and her sister with a White family. "I was called 'the help,' but I knew I was a 'slave.'" When she matured, a young White man fell in love with her. He warned his family that if he could not bring her home as his wife, he would leave with her. She learned to pass within the community, for she was light-skinned, and brought my mother up thinking of herself as White.

My mother had another issue that set her apart. She was mentally ill. My grandmother's way was to take care of her and teach me to do so, too. I learned to cope with trauma in my family by stoicism and silence. When both my sisters became involved in violent relationships, I often got into confrontations with the men. Gra would draw me aside and shush me. When I suggested calling the police or getting them into therapy, she explained this was "a family problem." I understood that for her keeping the family together was a price worth paying. As I have worked as a social scientist, I have come to understand that my grandmother's cultural background was the foundation of both of our lives. Especially important was spirituality, a connectivity of all Creation and a responsibility to life, but to my grandmother, this responsibility was expressed primarily in silence and stoicism, bending to violence to protect the family structure. I came to understand that my grandmother's way was not unique to her, and to wonder if her silence and stoicism fed into the ways we, as Native Americans, are killing ourselves even today. In my middle age, I still live a life of great transition due to past and present family caretaking issues. It is a price I am willing to pay. For I am of The People and this is my family, my responsibility. But not in silence, not about violence, any longer.

DeBruyn, 1995; Duran, Duran, Brave Heart, et al., 1998; Fogelman, 1988, 1991).

Consider the similarities between the German Holocaust of the Jews and the American genocidal practices against the Native Americans. For instance, both the Jews and the Native American Indians experienced attempts at genocide, and both the Germans and the Americans, through decades of denial and repression, have flourished as countries and as people, with no more psychological distress among their people than any other countries (Lebert & Lebert, 2000). Also, consider this overwhelming difference: Whereas Jews oppressed in Europe before, during, and after the Holocaust were able to emigrate to the United States and other countries to escape further persecution and genocide, Native American Indians have had no place to escape to. No other country offered asylum to these victims of persecution, and the very country that welcomes refugees was the one that committed the persecution and genocide (Brave Heart-Jordan & DeBruyn, 1995; Duran, Duran, Brave Heart, et al., 1998; Kehoe, 1989).

Historical trauma and unresolved grief resulting from European domination have been clinically linked with all types of family violence in Native communities (DeBruyn et al., 2001). Psychologically, the link makes sense. When Native Americans repress the rage they feel toward perpetrators of the many atrocities committed against their people, the anger can become manifested in other ways, such as alcohol abuse or family violence. Family violence also makes sense when one considers the multigenerational lesson that Natives have been taught: that they are unworthy of life or love (Duran, Duran, Brave Heart, et al., 1998).

SUMMARY

As this chapter shows, although Native American Indians are a culturally heterogeneous community, they have some similarities in their cultural values and their history of oppression by Whites. Consider again the opening paragraph of this chapter. Now that you have read about who the Native American Indians are, what their cultural values are, and what types of abuse they have experienced in this country, think about the likely response to the boarding school movement from the Native Americans' point of view. What cultural ideals would prompt them to be stoic in this situation? What experiences would lead them to distrust White social workers and White institutions?

In comparison to the sections on African and Latino Americans, the family violence research on Native American Indians fits into only one chapter in this book. Considering that Native Americans have been on this continent much longer than either African or Latino Americans, why do you think the research on Native Americans is so much more limited than the research on these other ethnic groups? Based on their history with White people in this country, do you think that the Native American Indians would allow themselves to be the subjects of research on this topic? Furthermore, would they invite the intrusion into their family lives? Why or why not? What cultural values and historical experiences are relevant? As you read the next chapter, keep these cultural values and historical experiences in mind. Based on the history of this community, what do you anticipate in terms of levels of family violence? Why?

NOTE

1. In these chapters, we use the names of tribes that most Americans are familiar with. However, many Native tribes are again going by their original names. For a listing of these names, please see the following Web site run by Phil Konstantin: http://www.snowwowl.com/altnames.html.

5

NATIVE AMERICAN INDIAN FAMILY VIOLENCE

....

Definition of "abuse" in the context of family relationships:

- *Extreme discipline and/or actions with the intent or result of physical, mental, or emotional harm or pain. A parent beating their child with a bat.* (21-year-old male, half Native American Indian, half African American)
- *Emotional and/or physical intimidation; anything of an abusive sexual nature.* (51-year-old female, half Native American Indian, half White)
- *Verbal, physical, sexual. Verbal, saying things that would be intended to degrade. Physical, hitting, other contact (also alluded to contact for intimidation) that hurts a person physically or emotionally. Sexual, forcing sexual relations (oral, vaginal, anal, masturbatory) on another individual.* (22-year-old male, half Native American Lakota Indian, half White)
- *Abuse is any behavior, verbal or physical, which repeatedly causes suffering—be it emotional, physical, or spiritual. Insults and violence would fall into this category.* (24-year-old male, half Native American Indian from South Dakota tribe, half White)

Consider these answers by Native American Indians to the question, "What is your definition of abuse in the context of family relationships?" What themes seem to run through these quotes? Are there any differences between what these respondents state versus what you would answer? All of the respondents mention various types of abuse, including physical, emotional, sexual, and even spiritual. Now consider these quotes from other Native respondents to the same survey: "A person is able to hit someone, but that does not give them a right to do so. Relating this as a value implies that one person has domination over the other," and "I don't believe that violence

teaches love. . . . Love really should be what guides us in our hearts. . . . It is in my belief structure that victims do not exist, that we all, deeply, choose ALL events that occur to us . . . that they help us to define ourselves." Think about these responses with respect to the material on the Native cultural context. How might their historical experiences and their religious beliefs influence their conceptions of abuse, violence, and victimization?

Although conceptions of abuse may vary across ethnic communities, sources of information on family violence in Native communities tend to use the majority culture definition. One useful source of information on family violence comes from the U.S. Department of Justice (DOJ), which provides rates of criminal victimization from family members (caught cases). According to the DOJ (Greenfeld & Smith, 1999), approximately 1 in 6 of the violent victimizations occurring among American Indians between 1992 and 1996 involved an offender who was an intimate or family member of the victim—which is about the same rate for victims of all races. This degree of comparability is quite dramatic, given that overall, Native Americans are at much higher risk for most forms of violent victimization than Americans from other ethnic groups.

Scope of the Problem

Child Maltreatment

Table 5.1 presents studies on child maltreatment that either focus specifically on Native communities or at least have a sizeable subsample of Native American Indians. In the only national studies of reported child maltreatment cases in Native communities, reports from the U.S. Department of Health and Human Services (DHHS) for the year 1999 and from the DOJ (Greenfeld & Smith, 1999) for the years 1992–1995 reveal that American Indian/Alaska Native children appear to be overrepresented as victims of child maltreatment. In 1999, DHHS found that the nearly 13,600 American Indian/Alaska Native cases of child maltreatment reported to CPS accounted for 1.8% of the country's victims, but American Indian/Alaska Natives accounted for approximately 0.9% of the population as a whole. Overall, the victimization rate for American Indians was high: 20.1 victims per 1,000 Native children in 1999, compared to 11.8/1,000 children in the overall population.

Between 1992 and 1995, a similar picture emerged. For the population as a whole, the number of reported cases of child maltreatment declined by 8%. However, for American Indians/Alaska Natives, the number of reported cases increased by 18%. Moreover, for the overall population, 1 of every 58 children was a victim of maltreatment, but for Native American Indians, this ratio was higher: 1 of every 30 children was a victim of maltreatment

(Greenfeld & Smith, 1999). Because these national studies consider only reported cases of child maltreatment (see chapter 2 of this book), they may not indicate the true incidence of child maltreatment in Native communities, where many cases of maltreatment are likely to go unreported, as in the U.S. population as a whole. Moreover, the tendency not to report child maltreatment to authorities may be exacerbated in Native communities because tribes have sovereignty and are, therefore, not required to report cases to any U.S. national registry. One study of this issue showed that, at best, 61% of the Native American child maltreatment cases get reported to any U.S. state or federal agency (Earle, 2000).

In contrast to research on other ethnic groups in this country, there has been no population-based study, such as the National Family Violence Surveys, that has estimated the incidence of child maltreatment in Native communities. Thus, we do not know how much maltreatment is occurring in the Native populations as a whole—we know only about the reported cases. Moreover, even studies of reported or self-reported cases of child maltreatment in Native communities are relatively rare and involve only a small segment and a small sampling of tribes. To further hinder our knowledge, these rare studies have been scattered over the past 30 years, and it is difficult to ascertain whether differences in rates of maltreatment are due to true differences between tribes or to changes over time or in reporting tendencies. Therefore, incidence rates gleaned from these studies are tentative at best. In the following discussion on the incidence of the different types of child maltreatment in Native communities, we mention, when the information is available, the specific tribe studied. However, until recently, many tribes agreed to let researchers study them only if their tribe name was not mentioned in reports. We provide any information available, even if it is just the region in which the tribe is located.

Physical Abuse and Neglect

Most research on child physical abuse and neglect has been done with the Navajo tribe

(Text continues on page 82)

Table 5.1 Child Maltreatment in Native American Indian Communities

Study	Sample Description	Definition/Measure of Abuse	Findings
National Studies—Reported Cases			
U.S. Department of Justice Report on American Indians and Crime, 1992–1996 (Greenfeld & Smith, 1999)	Data from the National Child Abuse and Neglect Data System (NCANDS)	Substantiated cases by CPS and sentinel reports of child abuse	• In 1992, 2,830/100,000 American Indian children were victims of child abuse. • In 1995, 3,343/100,000 American Indian children were victims of child abuse. • Between 1992 and 1995, there was an 18% increase in American Indian child victims of abuse; for the population as a whole, there was an 8% decline in child abuse cases. • In 1995, approximately 1 out of every 30 American Indian children were victims of abuse, in comparison to 1 out of every 58 children overall.
Regional Studies—Reported Cases			
Vernon & Bubar (2001)	Clientele at Alaska Cares Children's Advocacy Center in Anchorage	Substantiated cases	• Alaska Natives represent 17% of state's population, but 45% of the sexual abuse cases at the center.
Nelson, Cross, Landsman, & Tyler (1996)	77 families with a history of neglect and low income: families were primarily from the Mesquakie tribe in Iowa, the Siletz tribe in Oregon, and urban Native Americans from Portland, Oregon	Substantiated cases	• Neglect was more common than physical abuse in both tribes. • Neglect was less prevalent among the Mesquakie (45%) than among the Siletz (82%). • Sexual abuse was more prevalent among the Siletz tribe (75% of cases) than among the Mesquakie tribe (4% of cases).
Northern Navajo Medical Center (1996)	Cases of abuse and neglect in the Northern Navajo Medical Center between 1992 and 1995	Substantiated cases	• 3.3–4.3/1,000 children were physically abused or neglected.
DeBruyn, Lujan, & May (1992)	117 target children, plus siblings, parents, and grandparents, identified to a southwestern	Substantiated cases	91.7% of target children were physically abused and/or neglected. • 22.4% neglected only • 3.7% abused only • 64.5% both abused and neglected

Study	Sample Description	Definition/Measure of Abuse	Findings
	Indian Health Service hospital as abused and 137 matched controls, plus siblings and caretakers: families represented 11 Pueblo and 1 Apache tribe on reservations; nonreservation Native American Indians were from a wide variety of tribes		42.6% of control children were physically abused and/or neglected. • 28.7% neglected only • 9.3% abused only • 4.7% both abused and neglected • Relative rates of reported physical abuse to neglect: 46.6% to 87.9% among target children. • 32.9% of target sample were emotionally abused. • 50% of control sample were emotionally abused.
Piasecki et al. (1989)	1,155 American Indian children from Arizona and New Mexico who were (a) currently in mental health treatment, (b) in need of mental health treatment, or (c) were known to have been abused or neglected	Substantiated cases	67% of sample were abused and/or neglected. • 20.7% neglected only • 9.9% abused only • 37.2% both abused and neglected Types of abuse for females: • 32.5% emotionally abused • 18.3% physically abused • 12.3% sexually abused Types of abuse for males: • 27.6% emotionally abused • 14.5% physically abused • 2.0% sexually abused
Hauswald (1987)	Reported cases to the Navajo Tribe Division of Social Welfare in 1985	Substantiated cases	• 600–900 physically abused and/or neglected children per year in the Navajo tribe. • 13.5/1,000 Navajo children were physically abused or neglected.
Fischler (1985)	Cases of child abuse and neglect recorded by the American Humane Association in 1976: off-reservation Native American Indian children, approximately one half of the Native American Indian population at that time	Substantiated cases	• 5.7 substantiated cases of child abuse and neglect per 1,000 Native American Indian children. • Ratio of child neglect cases to abuse cases was 2.5:1.

(Continued)

Table 5.1 Continued

Study	Sample Description	Definition/Measure of Abuse	Findings
White & Cornely (1981)	Reported cases to the Bureau of Indian Affairs, state social services, and ambulatory pediatric cases in the Navajo tribe in 1975	Substantiated cases	• 10.34 children per 1,000 were abused or neglected in the Navajo tribe in 1975. • Ratio of child neglect cases to abuse cases was 6.1:1.
Wichlacz, Lane, & Kempe (1978)	Reported cases in the Cheyenne River Sioux Reservation in South Dakota between September 1974 and December 1975	Substantiated cases	• 65 reported cases of child abuse and neglect. • Average age: 4.5 years. • Equal distribution of boys and girls. • 1 out of 3 cases involved physical abuse. • 11.07 per 1,000 children reported for child abuse or neglect.
Regional Studies—Self-Report			
Hobfoll et al. (2002)	160 Native American women between ages 16 and 29 years from community centers that foster social and educational activities at the Little Big Horn, Dull Knife, Blackfoot, and Fort Bellnap reservations in Montana; part of a larger study on health promotion	Childhood Trauma Questionnaire	• 42% reported child sexual abuse; 25% reported multiple kinds and times of sexual abuse. • 56% reported physical/emotional abuse during childhood.
Kunitz, Levy, McCloskey, & Gabriel (1998)	352 adult male and female alcoholics in alcohol treatment, plus 434 alcohol dependent and 300 nonalcohol dependent matched controls: all from Navajo tribe	Answered yes to the following: "Had you ever been abused physically as a child? If yes, describe incident."	• 12.7% reported retrospective child physical abuse.
Pharris, Resnick, & Blum (1997)	13,923 American Indian/Alaska Native 7th–12th graders who resided close to or on Indian reservations	Answered yes to the following: "Have you ever been sexually abused?" which was defined as "when someone in your family or someone else touches you in a place you did not want to be touched or does something sexually which they shouldn't have done."	• 14% of females and 2.4% of males reported sexual abuse (both intra- and extrafamilial combined). • Rates for females steadily increased with age. • Rates for males remained the same across ages.

Study	Sample Description	Definition/Measure of Abuse	Findings
Robin, Chester, Rasmussen, Jaranson, & Goldman (1997)	375 adults (217 females and 158 males) from a southwestern Indian tribe; representative sample; retrospective reports	Direct physical sexual contact with a victim prior to age 16 by a perpetrator at least 5 years older than the victim	• 49% of females and 14% of males reported childhood sexual abuse. • Females were more likely than males to have been abused. • 78% of perpetrators were immediate, step, or extended family members. • 2% of perpetrators were strangers. • 49% of victims reported at least two perpetrators. • 78% of cases were male-on-female abuse cases. • 11% of cases were male-on-male abuse cases. • 8% of cases were female-on-male abuse cases. • 4% of cases were female-on-female abuse cases. • More than one half of cases occurred prior to age 10. • One sixth of cases occurred prior to age 6. • 55% of cases involved penetration—the most frequent type of abuse for both males and females. • The second most frequent type of abuse was touching sex organs with hand.
Lodico, Gruber, & DiClemente (1996)	5,290 White, 440 African American, and 494 Native American Indian 9th–12th graders in a midwestern state	Answered yes to whether any "adult or older person outside the family ever touched you sexually against your wishes or forced you to touch them sexually," or to whether "any older or stronger member of your family every touched you sexually or had you touch them sexually."	• 10.1% of adolescents reported sexual abuse. • 17.2% of Native American Indians reported history of sexual abuse (both intra- and extrafamilial). • Native American Indian rate was 2 times the rate for White adolescents, but was no different than for African American adolescents. • Native American females reported 3.3 times the rate of sexual abuse that Native American males reported. • Minority males reported 2.9 times the rate of White males. • 2% of Native American Indians reported intrafamilial sexual abuse: 2.8% for females, 1.6% for males. • No ethnic differences in intrafamilial sexual abuse rates.

NOTE: For information on Native American child maltreatment according to the U.S. Department of Health and Human Services (1999, 2000), the Third National Incidence Study (Sedlak & Broadhurst, 1996), the 1990 National Longitudinal Survey of Youth (Giles-Sims et al., 1995), California Children's Services Archive (2002), and Roosa, Reinholtz, and Angelini (1999), please see Table 3.1.

(northwestern New Mexico and northern Arizona), and in most studies, the researchers do not report rates separately by maltreatment type. In the 1970s and 1980s, the reported rate of physical abuse and/or neglect among the Navajo was between 10.34 and 13.5 per 1,000 children (Hauswald, 1987; White & Cornely, 1981). Between 1992 and 1995, the rate was between 3.3 and 4.3 per 1,000 children (Northern Navajo Medical Center, 1996). However, in a sample of Navajo obtained through inpatient and outpatient visits at the Indian Health Service catchment areas, the rate of childhood physical abuse only (not neglect), as retrospectively reported by adult patients, was 12.7% (Kunitz, Levy, McCloskey, & Gabriel, 1998)—much higher than the physical abuse, in combination with neglect, reported to authorities.

Physical abuse and/or neglect rates have also been reported for off-reservation Native American Indians and for the Pueblo and Apache (New Mexico) and Cheyenne River Sioux (South Dakota) tribes. Based on cases of physical abuse and neglect recorded by the American Humane Association in 1976, the rate of child physical abuse and/or neglect was 5.7 per 1,000 children in off-reservation Native Americans, who accounted for approximately one half of the Native population at that time (Fischler, 1985). A higher rate of physical abuse was found in a sample of Apache and Pueblo Indians (DeBruyn, Lujan, & May, 1992). In this study, the researchers matched known abuse cases with controls, and found that, even in their control group, approximately 14% were reported for physical abuse. Finally, among the Cheyenne River Sioux, the reported rate of physical abuse and/or neglect in the mid-1970s, derived from a register of suspected cases, was 11.07 per 1,000 children (Wichlacz, Lane, & Kempe, 1978).

Although there is not enough evidence to make any definitive conclusions, these studies show that the rates of physical abuse and/or neglect may vary from tribe to tribe and within the tribes themselves. However, the data are from only a small sampling of tribes, most of which are in the Southwest. Therefore, it is difficult to know the rate of physical abuse and neglect in other tribes or even within the tribes

in which there have been physical abuse/neglect reports. What is known is that the reported cases of physical abuse seem to be lower than the reported cases of child neglect (DeBruyn et al., 1992; Lujan, DeBruyn, May, & Bird, 1989). Statistics from the 1970s show that 2 of every 3 child maltreatment cases reported to authorities among the Cheyenne River Sioux involved neglect (Wichlacz et al., 1978). Statistics from the 1980s show that among off-reservation Native Americans, the ratio of neglect to physical abuse was 2.5:1 (Fischler, 1985), and among the Navajo, the ratio was 6.1:1 (White & Cornely, 1981). These rates are striking when compared to the proportion of neglect to physical abuse cases in the United States as a whole around that time: 1.5:1 (Scheper-Hughes, 1987). In the 1990s among Pueblo and Apache children, the relative rates of reported physical abuse to child neglect were 46.6% to 87.9% among children who were targeted for a history of child maltreatment (DeBruyn et al.). Finally, in a recent sample that was specifically selected for neglect cases and/or low-income, neglect was more common than physical abuse among the Mesquakie tribe (Iowa) and in the Siletz tribe (Oregon; Nelson, Cross, Landsman, & Tyler, 1996).

Perhaps our best estimates of child physical abuse come from retrospective self-report studies. Although two studies give estimates of physical abuse, these two studies report very disparate estimates. Among adults recruited for a study on alcohol abuse among the Navajo, 12.7% reported that they had been physically abused as children (Kunitz et al., 1998). However, the measure of childhood physical abuse was flawed—not only was it retrospective, but the definition of physical abuse was subject to the participants' interpretations. Among adult Native women recruited for a study on health promotion on reservations in Montana, 56% reported physical and emotional abuse during childhood (Hobfoll et al., 2002). Although the measure used in this population was more comprehensive than the one used with the Navajos, the researchers combined the scales of physical and emotional abuse, making it impossible to extract estimates of physical and emotional abuse independent of each other.

Overall, the following conclusions about child physical abuse and neglect can be made: (a) Neglect is more common than physical abuse; (b) the respective rates of each may vary depending upon the tribe studied; and (c) there is preliminary evidence that the rates of physical abuse and neglect among Native American Indians may be higher than those of the population as a whole, but the evidence is not conclusive. Consider what you learned about the cultural context of Native American Indians in the previous chapter. What are possible reasons why the rates of child maltreatment may be higher among Native American Indians?

Sexual Abuse

Preliminary data show that sexual abuse occurs less often than physical abuse and neglect, but again, exact estimates are difficult to establish. To our knowledge, five self-report studies and two studies of reported cases have been conducted since 1990 on the sexual abuse of Native American Indian children. Among studies of substantiated cases of sexual abuse, the statistics show that (a) sexual abuse may be more prevalent among Alaska Natives than among non-Natives living in Alaska, (b) sexual abuse rates may vary by tribe, and (c) sexual abuse rates of Native Americans as a whole may reflect those of the population as a whole.

First, even though Alaska Natives represent only 17% of that state's population, 45% of the sexual abuse cases seen at the Alaska Cares Advocacy Center in Anchorage are from Alaska Native families (Vernon & Bubar, 2001). Although conclusions cannot be made on this one report of a small center in Alaska, it suggests that Native children may be at a higher risk for sexual abuse than non-Native children. In contrast, in a study of unidentified southwestern Indian children with histories of suspected maltreatment, the rate of sexual abuse was 12.3% for females and 2% for males (Piasecki et al., 1989). Again, although conclusions cannot be made based upon this one study, these statistics suggest that the rate of sexual abuse cases among Native Americans reflect those of the population as a whole. Finally, in a study of families that either had a history of child neglect or who had low income, the Mesquakie tribe (Iowa) had

significantly lower rates of childhood sexual abuse (4% of cases) than the Siletz tribe (Oregon, 75% of cases; Nelson et al., 1996)—confirming again that abuse statistics may vary considerably across tribes.

Two recent studies of adolescents may provide better estimates of sexual abuse among Native children. Among White, African American, and Native adolescents in a midwestern state, approximately 17.2% of Native Americans reported a history of sexual abuse, which was almost twice that of the Whites, but no different than the African Americans. These numbers, however, reflect both extra- and intrafamilial sexual abuse. Only 2% of Native Americans (2.8% for females; 1.6% for males) reported intrafamilial sexual abuse, and there were no ethnic differences in intrafamilial sexual abuse; therefore, the ethnic differences that were observed were accounted for solely by extrafamilial sexual abuse (Lodico, Gruber, & DiClemente, 1996). Among Native adolescents nationwide, 14% of females and 2.4% of males reported a history of sexual abuse (Pharris, Resnick, & Blum, 1997). In this study, intrafamilial and extrafamilial sexual abuse were also combined, but the perpetrator of the abuse was not reported. Consequently, the differential rates of these two types of sexual abuse cannot be disentangled.

Overall, according to adolescents' reports, rates of sexual abuse among Native American Indians seem to reflect those of the population as a whole: Between 14% and 18% of females and between 2% and 3% of males report sexual abuse. A different picture emerges from adult Native Americans providing retrospective data: A higher percentage report sexual abuse experiences. Among women from reservations in Montana, a full 56% reported experiences of child sexual abuse (Hobfoll et al., 2002), and among adults from a southwestern tribe, 49% of females and 14% of males reported it (Robin et al., 1997). Compare these rates with those from adolescent reports. What may account for the higher percentages of adults reporting childhood sexual abuse?

This last study of a southwestern tribe also provides a unique insight into the dynamics of sexual abuse among Native Americans. The majority of cases for males and females involved penetration, and the overwhelming majority of perpetrators were family members or people known to the victim. Furthermore, more than half of the cases involved children under the age of 10 (Robin et al., 1997). Compare these findings with those presented in chapter 3 from the population as a whole. Are there similarities in the age, severity, or relationship to the perpetrator? Differences? What possible cultural or other differences discussed in chapter 4 may account for any differences? How may such differences lead to different consequences?

Psychological Maltreatment

Perhaps the least researched child maltreatment problem in Native communities is psychological maltreatment. To our knowledge, only two studies have reported rates of this form of maltreatment. In a sample of maltreated southwestern Indian children, 32.5% of females and 27.6% of males were labeled emotionally abused. Emotional abuse was less common than neglect but more common than physical and sexual abuse (Piasecki et al., 1989). Among a sample of children targeted for maltreatment, 32.9% were considered emotionally abused, as were, more strikingly, 50% of the control group (DeBruyn et al., 1992).

Spousal Maltreatment

Spousal maltreatment, especially the maltreatment of wives, has been deemed a widespread social problem in Native communities, but has received little attention in the literature (Bohn, 1993). Although there is less research on spousal maltreatment than on child maltreatment, the literature on spousal maltreatment in the Native communities offers one advantage over the child maltreatment literature: All but one of the studies were published after 1990. Therefore, because all of the studies are from the same time period, we can perhaps reach more definitive conclusions as to the rate of wife abuse than we can for child maltreatment. Table 5.2 lists the studies on spousal maltreatment in Native communities.

Wife Abuse

The only national studies of reported cases of spousal maltreatment come from the DOJ. Based on reported cases of all types of violent crimes between the years 1992 and 1996, the DOJ (Greenfeld & Smith, 1999) found no difference between American Indians and the population as a whole in the percentage of violent crimes committed against intimates (~ 9%). Moreover, there were no differences between American Indians and the population as a whole in the percentage of intimate violence cases involving alcohol (~ 55%). However, there were ethnic group differences in two important areas. First, American Indians were significantly more likely to be injured in an incident of spousal abuse, and second, the majority of American Indian victims of intimate violence (75%) were victimized by someone other than an American Indian. This figure stands in stark contrast to the 11% of the overall population of spousal abuse victims victimized by someone of another race. What might the implications of this repeated victimization by members of other groups mean to the overall mental health of Native Americans?

A second DOJ (Rennison, 2001b) report indicates that American Indian females were victimized by an intimate at rates that were much greater than other ethnic groups. Their rate of 23 victims per 1,000 females was more than twice that of the next highest group; specifically, Blacks had a rate of 11 victims per 1,000 females (see Table 3.2). In addition, as mentioned in the previous section, much maltreatment is likely to go unreported—a problem that may be exacerbated among Native Americans because of tribal sovereignty.

Data from the 1985 National Family Violence Resurvey (NFVR) do not support the conclusions from the DOJ reports that there are differences in wife abuse between Native Americans and other cultures. In a study focusing specifically on the Native Americans in the NFVR (Bachman, 1992), 12.2% of Native couples (and a projected national estimate of 29,000) reported violence against the wife in the previous year, which was not much different than the rate found for the White population (11%). Similarly, in comparison to 3% of the

Table 5.2 Spousal Maltreatment in Native American Indian Communities

Study	Sample Description	Definition/Measure of Abuse	Findings
National Studies—Reported Cases			
U.S. Department of Justice Report on American Indians and Crime, 1992–1996 (Greenfeld & Smith, 1999)	Reported cases of spousal abuse	Reported cases	• 9% of violent crimes committed by American Indians were against intimates; no difference from the overall population. • 75% of intimate victimizations among American Indians involved an offender of a different race (11% for the overall population involved offender from a different race). • Alcohol involved in ~55% of intimate victimizations for American Indians (no difference from overall population). • American Indian victims of intimate violence injured in ~50% of the cases; significantly more likely than overall population.
Regional Studies—Reported Cases			
Kuklinski & Buchanan (1997)	Residents of the Hualapai Indian Reservation in Arizona receiving medical attention for an assault injury between 1992 and 1994	Reported cases	• 35.9% of all assault cases were cases of family violence. • 56% of all female assault victims receiving medical attention were victims of wife abuse. • 11% of all male assault victims were victims of husband abuse.
McIntire (1988)	Minnesota women	Utilization of battered women's shelters in Minnesota	• Native American Indian women utilized battered women's shelters at 14 times the proportion of their state representation.
Regional Studies—Self-Report			
Bohn (1993, 2002)	30 pregnant Native American Indian women from an urban community in Minnesota	Index of Spouse Abuse	• 90% experienced some type of abuse in their lifetime. • 60% were currently involved in a physically abusive relationship. • 33% were physically abused while pregnant. • 67% reported 2 or more physically abusive adult relationships. • 17% reported adult sexual abuse.
Bohn (1998)	230 pregnant women at a certified nurse-midwife in an urban area in the Midwest: 43 Native American Indian women	Unidentified	• 56% of non-Native women reported physical and/or sexual abuse. • 77% of Native women reported physical and/or sexual abuse.

(Continued)

85

Table 5.2 Continued

Study	Sample Description	Definition/Measure of Abuse	Findings
Fairchild, Fairchild, & Stoner (1998)	341 Native American Indian women presenting at an Indian Health Service comprehensive health care facility on the Navajo reservation	Unidentified "domestic violence screening instrument"	Lifetime rates: • 52.5% reported at least 1 episode of spousal abuse; 40.5% reported verbal abuse; 41.9% reported physical abuse; 31.7% reported severe physical abuse; 12.1% reported sexual abuse. 1-year prevalence: • 16.4% reported at least 1 episode; 14.4% reported verbal abuse; 13.5% reported physical abuse; 11.1% reported severe physical abuse; 3.8% reported sexual abuse.
Hamby & Skupien (1998)	169 Apache women and 65 Apache men; recruited through ads on local cable television, local newspaper, and public flyers and signs	Conflict Tactics Scales	Females: • 48% experienced wife abuse within the previous year; 75% experienced wife abuse at some point in their current relationship. Males: • 50% experienced husband abuse in the previous year; 57.5% experienced husband abuse at some point in their current relationship.
Robin, Chester, & Rasmussen (1998)	48 Native American Indian men and 56 Native American Indian women recruited by local members of a southwestern tribe	Conflict Tactics Scales	Females: • 91% reported any incident of spousal abuse victimization. • 75% reported verbal and physical violence victimization. • 36% reported children involved in spousal abuse incident. • 28.6% reported forced sex by partner. • 33% reported involvement in an abusive incident within the previous year. Males: • 91% reported any incident of spousal abuse victimization. • 75% reported verbal and physical violence victimization. • 33% reported involvement in an abusive incident within the previous year.
Norton & Manson (1995)	198 Native American Indian women presenting at an urban Indian health care center in the Rocky Mountains	Conflict Tactics Scales	• 46% reported a history of spousal physical abuse victimization.

NOTE: For information on Native American Indian spousal abuse according to the U.S. Department of Justice (Rennison, 2001a, 2001b; Rennison & Welchans, 2000), the National Violence Against Women Survey (Coker et al., 2002; Tjaden & Thoennes, 2000), the National Family Violence Surveys of 1975 and 1985 (Bachman, 1992; Cazenave & Straus, 1979; Hampton, & Gelles, 1994; Straus & Gelles, 1986, 1990a; Straus, Gelles, & Steinmetz, 1980; Straus & Smith, 1990b; Straus & Sweet, 1992), please see Table 3.2.

Box 5.1   The Story of a Native American Battered Woman

Debbie entered a shelter for battered women in the Spring of 1987 after the following incident with her husband. He was out drinking with his friends one Saturday night, and Debbie, who was eight months pregnant, stayed home with their son. Her husband came home drunk and shouting; he accused her of having an affair and shouted that the child she was carrying was probably not his. Subsequently, he padlocked the front door so that Debbie couldn't escape, and he locked their son in a closet so that he could not run for help.

While continuing to drink, Debbie's husband poured cleaning fluids, ketchup, syrup, and other substances on her head. He then ordered her to clean up, and after she did, he would do it again. This pattern continued all night. In the morning, after locking Debbie in the bedroom, the husband let their son out of the closet so that he could go to school. After the son left, the physical abuse began. He repeatedly hit Debbie with both a curling iron and a curtain rod, and he kicked her all over. Several hours passed when a friend finally knocked on the front door. When her husband went to answer the door, Debbie snuck out a window. She was taken by neighbors to a hospital, where several injuries were observed, including large bruises and welts on her back, cigarette burns on her foot, a black eye, and missing hair. She needed seven stitches on her head, and she also started having contractions, which subsided after a while.

Debbie took out a restraining order on her husband, who was arrested by tribal police. However, he was released within 24 hours. When Debbie went to her home with a police escort to collect her possessions, she found her and her son's burnt clothes scattered over the front lawn.

SOURCE: Bachman, 1992

White population, 3.2% of Native husbands (or 6,000) used severe violence against their wives. Now consider one of the qualitative accounts of Native battered women from this study in Box 5.1. Does this account seem to differ substantially from those of the majority culture?

In contrast to the findings from the NFVR, but in support of the DOJ reports, data from the only other national study of spousal maltreatment in Native communities, the National Violence Against Women Survey (NVAW), show that Native Indian women report significantly higher rates of physical spousal abuse than any other ethnic group. Over 30% of Native women reported physical assaults from their husbands, compared to 22.1% of women overall (Tjaden & Thoennes, 2000). Differences in the relative rates of spousal abuse from the DOJ, NFVR, and the NVAW probably depend on their differing methodology (see chapter 2 in this book). Therefore, it is difficult to ascertain whether Native women are at a greater risk for spousal maltreatment than women in the

population as a whole. Based upon these studies, it is probably safe to conclude that Native women are maltreated at a rate that is at least equal to, if not higher than, the rate for the population of women in the United States as a whole.

The NFVR and the NVAW samples, although representative of the U.S. population, have limitations as sources of data on Native communities. First, they were telephone surveys, and because the poorest of the Native Americans may not have access to a telephone, these people could not be included in the survey. It is these uninterviewed people who could also be the ones with the highest rates of violence in their intimate relationships because they tend to live in remote, isolated, poverty-stricken areas. Second, the surveys were given only to English or, in the case of the NVAW, Spanish speakers, and there are still a number of Native Americans who speak only their tribal language. Finally, researchers did not collect data on tribal affiliation or residence, and there could be significant variations in violence among tribes and between urban, reservation, and rural areas.

Results from more localized studies of wife abuse in Native communities suggest a more serious problem than the figures from the DOJ, NFVR, and even the NVAW, indicate. For example, in a series of studies of pregnant women (Bohn, 1993, 2002), 90% of pregnant Native women experienced some type of abuse in their lifetimes, and 60% were currently involved in a physically abusive relationship with their partners. Moreover, 33% reported physical abuse while they were pregnant, and the majority of the women (67%) reported that they had had two or more physically abusive partners as adults. In another study of pregnant women (Bohn, 1998), 77% of the Native women reported experiencing physical and/or sexual abuse in their lifetimes, in comparison to 56% of the non-Native women. Although the prevalence of physical abuse in these studies is dramatic, the samples were small, tribal affiliations were not given, and these women were not from a reservation; therefore, generalizability is very limited.

One dramatic statistic from the Minnesota Department of Corrections is that Native women seek help at battered women's shelters at a rate 14 times their proportion in the state population (McIntire, 1988). Although this figure may indicate that Native women are subjected to more battering, it is also possible that because Native women are among the poorest of the poor, they are more likely to utilize shelters than women who are not quite as destitute. Lower rates of wife abuse were found among urban women from an Indian health center: Approximately 46% of women reported a history of wife abuse (Norton & Manson, 1995). This study also has limits to generalizability because the sample was urban. Because of their isolation, rural women may actually have a higher rate of wife abuse.

As with studies on child maltreatment, the majority of studies of wife abuse in Native Americans have been done on tribes in the Southwest. Similar to the findings already mentioned, researchers have found high rates of wife abuse in this part of the United States among many different groups. For example,

91% of women from an unidentified southwestern tribe reported being the victims of any intimate violence, 75% reported verbal and physical violence, and one third had been involved in at least one abusive incident within the previous 12 months (Robin, Chester, & Goldman, 1998). Among Navajo women presenting at an Indian Health Care facility, 52.5% reported at least one episode of domestic violence by a male partner. The most frequent types of violence were verbal (40.5%) and physical (41.9%), and 31.7% experienced severe physical violence (Fairchild, Fairchild, & Stoner, 1998). Finally, in the only community-based study of wife abuse in Native communities, similarly high rates of wife abuse were found among the Apache: 48% of women had experienced wife abuse within the previous year, and 75% had experienced it sometime during the course of their current relationship (Hamby & Skupien, 1998).

An even less researched area is sexual abuse by an intimate partner. The studies that do report these rates indicate that between 12.2% (Navajos; Fairchild et al., 1998) and 28.6% (southwestern tribe; Robin et al., 1998) of Native women are sexually victimized by an intimate partner. Moreover, nationally, the rate of Native women sexually victimized by an intimate partner was significantly higher than for women of other races (Tjaden & Thoennes, 2000).

Although the exact rate of wife abuse is difficult to ascertain from these studies, it can be concluded that wife abuse is a significant problem affecting at least a substantial minority, if not the majority, of Native American Indians—probably more than the national incidence studies show. Moreover, there are important variations in the extent of wife abuse across tribes. Among 17 Native communities within the United States, 3 communities, the Iroquois, Fox, and Papago, had no or minimal levels of wife abuse, but the others, such as the Arapaho, had evidence of the occurrence of wife abuse at least as far back as the 19th century (Levinson, 1989).

Husband Abuse

The other form of spousal maltreatment, husband abuse, has been even less researched.

Six of the previously cited studies make reference to violence against husbands, and show that those rates are also quite high (see Table 5.2). What characteristics of contemporary Native community life might account for these high rates? The DOJ statistics discussed previously indicate that the majority of the reported perpetrators of husband abuse against Native husbands are from other ethnic groups, and the majority of reported husband abuse cases involve alcohol and injury (Greenfeld & Smith, 1999). The rate of couple violence from the 1985 NFVR reveal that 15.5% of Native couples (or 37,000 overall), in comparison to 14.8% of White couples, experienced violence in the previous year, and 7.2% of Native couples (18,000), in comparison to 5.3% of White couples, experienced severe violence (Bachman, 1992). The rates for husband abuse were approximately equal to the rates of wife abuse in the NFVR sample as a whole (Straus & Gelles, 1990a). The NVAW showed that 11.4% of Native husbands were the victims of husband abuse, a rate that was not significantly different from other ethnic groups (Tjaden & Thoennes, 2000).

The localized studies that included statistics on husband abuse show that, similar to the majority culture, Native males are more likely to be assaulted by an acquaintance who is a male, rather than by an intimate female partner (Kuklinski, 1997). However, the majority of men are the recipients of violence from their intimate partners. For example, among Apaches, 50% of men reported a physical assault from their wives in the previous year, and 57.5% reported a physical assault at some point in their current relationships (Hamby & Skupien, 1998). Among southwestern Native Americans, approximately 91% of men reported being the victims of intimate violence over the course of their lifetimes, and 75% reported verbal and physical violence. However, a higher percentage of women than men reported being the victims of every form of physical violence listed except being hit with an object. Moreover, a higher percentage of men than women reported that their partner used a weapon in self-defense. Women were significantly more likely than men to be injured and seek medical attention, and significantly fewer men reported that the children were involved in the violence. One man, as compared to 16 women, reported forced sex by a partner, but nearly one third of both men and women reported an incident of physical violence in their relationships within the previous 12 months (Robin et al., 1998). How do such patterns compare with what you have learned about the majority culture?

The above studies, although certainly not representative of all Native men, tribes, and areas, show that men are also the victims of violence in these communities. The problem is probably more significant for women than men (Hamby & Skupien, 1998; Robin et al., 1998), but men are also victimized. The studies did not show that all incidents in which women used violence were in self-defense. Therefore, Native men are victimized, too, and more research in this area is sorely needed.

Elder Maltreatment

Even less researched than the incidence of child or spousal maltreatment is the incidence of elder maltreatment in Native communities. However, like spousal maltreatment, all but one of the incidence studies were conducted in the 1990s; because all of the studies are from the same recent time period, it may be easier to draw some conclusions about incidence. As mentioned in Table 3.2, the National Elder Abuse Incidence Study (NEAIS) revealed that nationwide in 1996, 0.4% of the identified elder abuse cases were American Indian/Alaska Natives, and American Indians were underrepresented for all forms of elder abuse (National Center on Elder Abuse, 1998). Data on elder maltreatment have also been collected in four separate tribes: two unidentified Plains tribes (Maxwell & Maxwell, 1992) and two unidentified tribes in North Carolina (Hudson, Armachain, Beasley, & Carlson, 1998; Hudson & Carlson, 1999). The North Carolina study is the only one that provides concrete numbers regarding the incidence of elder abuse: 4.3% of the elders stated that they had been abused, and 1.5% of the entire sample stated that they had abused an elderly person at some point in their lives (Hudson et al., 1998).

This study also provides valuable information regarding potential differences between tribes in awareness of elder maltreatment. The researchers interviewed members from two different North Carolina tribes. In one, the East tribe, members were better educated and had higher yearly incomes. Members of the West tribe lived in a more self-contained manner than those of the East tribe, who were more dispersed and intermingled with other cultural groups. Members of the East tribe were significantly more likely to have heard of elder abuse prior to the interview. However, members from the West tribe were significantly more likely to have personal knowledge of an elderly person who was being abused (Hudson et al., 1998).

A study of two unidentified Plains tribes (Maxwell & Maxwell, 1992) also provides valuable information on potential differences between tribes in the incidence of elder maltreatment. Elder abuse, in the form of physical abuse and neglect, was more common in the tribe labeled the "Lone Mountain Reservation." High unemployment, no industry, and geographic isolation characterized this reservation, and the most common type of elder abuse was financial exploitation. The elders on this reservation had a guaranteed income from government pensions, which was barely enough to support themselves. However, because many family members were unemployed and had no consistent source of income, they were dependent upon the elderly for their livelihood. Many of the young people also stole from the elderly to support drug or alcohol habits. Consider the following example from this study: An elder on one reservation was subject to a series of sorrows. First, one of his grandsons shot and killed another one of his grandsons. Then, an automobile accident claimed the life of his daughter. Younger relatives beat the elder and his wife when they wouldn't give them money for alcohol. The elder's wife died of a "broken heart" and currently, the elderly man resides in a nursing home.

In contrast, elder abuse was relatively rare on the reservation labeled the "Abundant Lands Reservation." Physical abuse of the elderly did not occur on this reservation, according to tribal leaders. Neglect was somewhat of a problem in the wintertime because people could not travel through bad terrain covered in snow and ice to elderly not living within the community center. In contrast to the "Lone Mountain Reservation," the "Abundant Lands Reservation" had a thriving industry with lower unemployment rates. Therefore, members of this tribe did not have to depend upon the elderly for subsistence, as members of the tribe either owned or were employed in the businesses that flourished within the town center (Maxwell & Maxwell, 1992). What do these studies suggest concerning the role of the ecosystem in elder maltreatment within Native communities?

These studies illustrate the problems in defining maltreatment in communities with very different lifestyles than the majority culture. Clearly, elders suffer when they are needy and isolated by bad weather and cultural patterns. Is it appropriate to say also that they are maltreated? If so, who is responsible for the maltreatment? The younger generations who are too poor themselves to purchase the means to get through the ice and snow to the needy elders? Or, should the broader society be making better provisions for the impoverished elderly? Are the elderly themselves guilty of self-neglect because they do not pursue services that might provide some relief in bad times?

PREDICTORS, CORRELATES, AND CONSEQUENCES

Child Maltreatment

When reviewing the research on the predictors, correlates, and consequences of child maltreatment in Native populations, we come across the same problem discussed in regard to the incidence of these problems in this community—most of these studies are on reported or suspected cases of maltreatment. Consequently, the association of these behaviors with multiproblem families may be greater than what would be found if population-based research were done (Kunitz et al., 1998; Piasecki et al., 1989). Furthermore, the predictors and correlates of child maltreatment in Native communities have been empirically studied only at the individual and microsystem levels.

Alcohol is the individual variable that has most often been implicated as a major correlate of maltreatment in Native populations. For example, in a study primarily of Pueblo and Apache tribes, alcohol abuse was the strongest determinant of child maltreatment; parental alcohol abuse was found to be associated with 85% of the neglect cases and 63% of the physical abuse cases (Lujan et al., 1989). Similarly, in the late 1970s in the Navajo community, 50% of abuse cases and 85% of neglect cases were alcohol-related (White, 1977). However, because there is also a very high rate of alcohol abuse among families who do not maltreat their children, alcohol may be a necessary, but not a sufficient, cause of child maltreatment (DeBruyn et al., 1992).

Many other individual and microsystem factors related to alcohol abuse have also been implicated as risk factors for child maltreatment. A history of divorce, single-parent families, death of an immediate family member (DeBruyn et al., 1992), being female, being transferred from home to home, being physically or mentally disabled (Lujan et al., 1989), the number of father-figures the child has had, and irregular contact with the biological father (Nelson et al., 1996) have all been linked to child maltreatment within Native communities.

Because the risk factor studies are correlational in nature, it is difficult to know which came first—the risk factor or the maltreatment. For example, is being transferred from home to home (as in foster care situations), or being physically or mentally disabled, a risk factor or a consequence of maltreatment? Consider also the risk factors discussed in the previous chapter that are unique to Native Americans. These include macrosystem stresses that have resulted from the enormous socioeconomic changes Native Americans have experienced over the past 200 years since colonization, including gender role changes, changes in the nature of the extended family, and risks associated with being forced into boarding schools (Beiser, 1974; Graburn, 1987; Hauswald, 1987). How might these macrosystem factors have contributed to individual and microsystem level risk factors

empirically shown to predict child maltreatment in these communities? How might they have directly contributed to child maltreatment?

The greatest and most consistent long-term outcomes for maltreated Native children are alcohol abuse and later involvement in abusive intimate relationships (Kilpatrick et al., 2000; Kunitz et al., 1998; Lujan et al., 1989; Robin et al., 1997). However, results on the relationship between childhood sexual abuse and later alcohol use and involvement in spousal maltreatment are mixed. Some Native adolescents who had been sexually assaulted had an increased risk for substance use or dependence (Kilpatrick et al.), whereas among a Navajo sample, there was no relationship between childhood sexual abuse and later alcohol use/abuse and spousal maltreatment (Kunitz et al.). Other studies show an association between sexual abuse as a child and later sexual abuse perpetration and victimization (Lodico et al., 1996) and alcohol abuse (Robin et al.).

Other problems of maltreated Native children include higher rates of anxiety, sleep problems, developmental difficulties, conduct disorder, and schizophrenia-like symptoms than found in nonmaltreated Native children (Piasecki et al.; 1989). Maltreated Native children also have a greater frequency of running away, being expelled from school (Piasecki et al.), dropping out of school, and having poor academic standings (Beauvais, Chavez, Oetting, Deffenbacher, & Cornell, 1996). Physical abuse has been associated with later depression (Piasecki et al., Roosa, Reinholtz, & Angelini, 1999) and conduct disorders (Kunitz et al., 1998), whereas sexual abuse has been associated with hopelessness, suicidality (Pharris et al., 1997), behavioral problems in adolescence and adulthood, antisocial personality disorder, drug abuse, affective disorders, anxiety disorders, post-traumatic stress disorder (PTSD; Robin et al., 1997), sexual risk taking, and sexually transmitted diseases (Hobfoll et al., 2002).

Although the bulk of these studies have been conducted on Native American Indians in southwestern tribes, sexual abuse and its association with hopelessness and suicidality was studied in a national sample of Native adolescents (Pharris et al., 1997). In addition to these findings of adverse consequences of sexual abuse, the researchers also identified protective factors counteracting the development of these symptoms. For females, the protective factors included family attention, positive feelings towards school, high parental expectations, and demonstrations of caring by family, adults, and tribal leaders. For males, they included enjoyment of school, involvement in traditional tribal activities, strong school performance, and caring exhibited by family, adults, school personnel, and tribal leaders (Pharris et al.).

Spousal Maltreatment

The only variable to receive empirical attention as a predictor of spousal maltreatment in the Native communities is an individual variable: alcohol use. Although there is little reliable evidence establishing a causal relationship between alcohol abuse and spousal maltreatment among Native Americans, several studies show that there is at least a link. According to the DOJ, both Indian and non-Indian victims of intimate violence report a relatively high level of alcohol and drug use by offenders. Overall, approximately half of the persons of all races who were victims of intimate violence reported a drinking offender. However, an estimated three out of four Native victims had perceived the offender to be drinking (Greenfeld & Smith, 1999).

There is also evidence of an alcohol link to Native spousal maltreatment from some more localized studies. On the Pine Ridge reservation in 1979, all incidents of wife abuse took place when the husband was under the influence of either alcohol (77%) or drugs (23%; Powers, 1986). In two Arctic Native communities, alcohol was involved in 80% of the reported wife abuse cases (Durst, 1991). Among Hopi women in counseling for wife abuse, 85% said their husbands drank excessively and 55% stated that physical abuse occurred most often when their husbands were intoxicated (Verlarde-Castillo, 1992). Untangling the association between alcohol use and spousal maltreatment in Native communities is important because Native Americans tend to have the highest rates of alcoholism and alcohol abuse of all ethnic groups in this country (Manson, Shore, Bloom,

Keepers, & Neligh, 1989). Therefore, as mentioned in regard to child maltreatment, alcohol may be a necessary, but not a sufficient, cause of wife abuse.

Alcohol has also been found to be a possible consequence of wife abuse in these communities. For instance, women who reported a history of wife abuse in a screening survey at a health facility in the Rocky Mountain region also reported more problems with alcohol than women with no history of wife abuse (Norton & Manson, 1995). Furthermore, 54.3% of female domestic violence homicide victims in New Mexico, which included 34 Native women, had alcohol in their systems at the time of death (Arbuckle et al., 1996). However, because these two studies are correlational, we do not know which came first, the alcohol use or the wife abuse.

Other consequences of wife abuse found among Native women are physical injuries (Hamby & Skupien, 1998; Robin et al., 1998) and increased depression, stress, suicidality, and PTSD symptomatology (Hamby & Skupien; Norton & Manson, 1995). Anecdotal evidence from people who work with abused Native women show that these women are at risk for many health problems, including suicide, the abuse of other substances, and depression (Bohn, 1993). Sexual abuse by an intimate partner has been found to lead to affective disorders and PTSD in Native women. However, physical abuse was not related to either of these mental health problems (Robin et al.). Finally, the gravest consequence of wife abuse found among Native women is death. In one study comparing the rates of domestic violence deaths in White, Hispanic, and Native women in New Mexico, the rates of domestic violence homicide were significantly greater among Native women than in the other two groups. Specifically, among Native women, the rate of domestic violence homicide was 4.9 per 100,000 women, whereas for Hispanic women it was 1.7 per 100,000, and for White women it was 1.8 per 100,000 women (Arbuckle et al., 1996).

There appears to be little research on the predictors or consequences of abuse against Native American men. One relevant study (Hamby & Skupien, 1998) found that among Apache men, 22.5% had sustained an injury from their wives in the previous year and 30% had sustained an injury in the course of their relationship. Although the rate of severe injury among Apache men was significantly lower than for Apache women, 7.5% of the men had sustained a severe injury in the previous year, and 12.5% had sustained a severe injury over the course of the relationship. Psychologically, Apache men assaulted by their wives may suffer from depression and PTSD symptoms; the higher the rates of physical assaults sustained, the more likely they were to experience these symptoms. Although the relationship between variables only approached significance, the sample size was small and a larger sample may show statistically significant relationships between husband abuse and psychological outcomes (Hamby & Skupien).

Elder Maltreatment

The few studies conducted on elder maltreatment actually provide more information on the predictors of this type of maltreatment than on its incidence. In the Older Navajo Elder-Abuse Survey, respondents viewed elder neglect to be far more prevalent than physical abuse. In addition, three factors were related to possible elder abuse: (a) the suddenness of an elderly person becoming dependent upon family members, (b) the presence of mental problems in the elderly person, and (c) income. The elder's income was related to financial exploitation, in that younger members of the family used the government benefits of the elderly for their own benefit. In addition, low income was frequently related to elder neglect (Brown, 1989). Studies of Plains tribes and North Carolina tribes provide the same picture as the Navajo study: Poverty, social isolation, and unemployment were the most obvious predictors of elder maltreatment (Hudson et al., 1998; Maxwell & Maxwell, 1992).

In addition, service providers in the Navajo community indicated that abuse occurred to women who were very old and socially isolated (Brown, Fernandez, & Griffith, 1990). These women lived with family members, yet became suddenly dependent upon them and were therefore burdens. Mostly, they were in poor physical condition. The service providers also indicated their belief that family members who physically abused or neglected the elderly did not do so intentionally. Verbal abuse and financial exploitation, however, were viewed as intentional; these acts, in contrast to physical abuse and neglect, appeared to be premeditated and intentional. Finally, the service providers furnished a picture of the abusive family members: They were unemployed, felt burdened by their caregiving responsibilities, were very poor, and were often depressed (Brown et al.). Given all these data, at how many levels of the ecological framework can you identify causes of maltreatment in Native communities? Based on this general picture, where would you devote resources to combating the problem?

Summary

This chapter presents the little information there is about family violence in the Native communities. Although some individual studies may contradict this conclusion, there is not enough empirical evidence to suggest that Native American Indians suffer from more or less family violence than other communities in this country. However, more research needs to be done to support this conclusion, and to investigate the extent to which the incidence of different types of family violence may differ by tribe. Considering the extent of risk factors for family violence in these communities, what do you think the ultimate conclusion may be? What possible role has the majority culture played in family violence in these communities? Recall the information you learned in chapter 4. Although not much research has been done on the consequences of different types of family violence in these communities, do you think the historical experiences of Native Americans could exacerbate any possible outcomes they may have if they experience family violence? In what way? Would their cultural values serve as protectors?

One final point needs to be considered before we move on to the next section of this book, on African Americans. Although the focus of this book is on maltreatment within the family and various cultural differences in these definitions of maltreatment, let us take a different perspective at this point. Consider what the European settlers and the U.S. government have done to the Native American Indians since they first settled this land centuries ago. Consider the resulting impact on the lives of Native Americans, specifically alcoholism and family violence, which several researchers argue were relatively nonexistent prior to European domination. How would you define the behaviors of these European settlers and the U.S. government? Would you label them "abusive"? If not, why not?

PART III

AFRICAN AMERICAN CULTURES

6

AFRICAN AMERICAN CULTURAL CONTEXTS

....

Definition of "abuse" within the context of family relationships:

- *"Striking another, verbal abuse, expecting a woman to do all the work, and rape."*
- *Extremely abusive behavior: "Deadbeat man who won't pay."*
- *Moderately abusive behavior: "Just leaves after a date."*
- *Mildly abusive behavior: "No responsibility."*
- *Abusive experience: "Been hit by a two-by-four."*

Abuse within the parent-child relationship:

- *Extremely abusive behavior: "Threaten shooting or stabbing or rape."*
- *Moderately abusive behavior: "Kicking, swearing, punching."*
- *Mildly abusive behavior: "Locking door and not allowing in for some days."*

Abuse within the husband-to-wife relationship:

- *Extremely abusive behavior: "Leaving forever; rape."*
- *Moderately abusive behavior: "Punching or hitting."*
- *Mildly abusive behavior: "No money help."*

Abuse within the wife-to-husband relationship:

- *Extremely abusive behavior: "Killing."*
- *Moderately abusive behavior: "Slight poisoning of food."*
- *Mildly abusive behavior: "Not letting him back in the apartment."* (55-year-old African American female)

We have not selected this woman's conceptions and experiences of intrafamilial abuse because they are somehow representative of the views of all the diverse African and Caribbean Americans living in the United States, but because many elements of her implicit theory are instructive. With regard to her conceptions of parent-child abuse, there would probably be very widespread agreement that the behaviors she mentions are abusive. However, many people might argue that all her examples are fairly extreme, and particularly that locking a child out of the home for several days is more than mildly abusive—depending perhaps on the age of the child. With regard to the spousal relationship, her examples illustrate how contextualized conceptualizations of abuse can be. It is easy to believe that her implicit theory of abuse is derived directly from personal experience and observations, not from textbooks or other media.

When asked whether it is ever necessary for family members to hit one another hard, she said that sometimes a parent has to hit children hard because they "deserve it," or hit a teen hard because there is "no alternative." Sometimes, a husband has to hit a wife hard because "some women are bad," and sometimes, a wife has to hit a husband because "men are the worst that I know." Only in regards to elderly parents does she show no tolerance of aggression—"Don't hit old folks." Particularly in her views on hitting, this woman appears both to expect, and to have considerable tolerance for, at least some violence in family life. Following are several other African American responses to the item: "Sometimes a parent has to hit a child hard," to which participants were asked to indicate their degree of agreement:

> "If they are endangering themselves or others, they need to be physically stopped." (21-year-old Black and White female)

> "Although hitting a child is wrong, I don't have a problem with spankings—the severity of the hitting isn't all that important. Teens should know better . . . hitting is no solution at this age . . ." (24-year-old African American male)

> "I feel there are no instances in which physical violence is needed to express one's intent." (20-year-old Black/African American female)

Even in this small sample of responses, we see major discrepancies in views concerning the extent to which it is appropriate to hit children. As we show in the next two chapters, several published studies have indicated considerable tolerance for family aggression, except against the elderly, in some African American respondents. Other studies provide important evidence about the role of socioeconomic status, stress, and personal experience in the acceptance of violence as a form of conflict resolution and control. In this chapter, we consider many historical and contemporary factors that relate to the range of attitudes toward, and experiences of, family aggression in African American/Black families.

What Is Abuse?

Perspectives on Child Maltreatment

One cannot assess African American perspectives on child maltreatment without confronting the ideological debate introduced in chapter 1: Is physical discipline (corporal punishment) of children a form of maltreatment? There is considerable evidence (e.g., Alvy, 1987; Giovannoni & Becerra, 1979) that within many African American communities, spanking and other forms of harsh physical punishment are considered "appropriate discipline" rather than abuse. However, using disciplinary procedures they consider appropriate may bring African American parents into conflict with legal and social service establishments (largely White) mandated to protect children from abuse. Discrepancies in implicit theories as to what behaviors are abusive are important—not just for theoretical reasons, and not just because they influence estimates of the amount of child abuse in this country, but also because they can influence social service judgments about whether particular parents are abusive. Although many African American parents may find corporal punishment acceptable, many entry-level social service workers do not—and they are the ones who frequently make judgments about potential maltreatment in families. Moreover, the greater the social workers' disapproval of corporal punishment, the more likely they are to judge possible maltreatment as abuse and the more likely they are to report it (Ashton, 2001). This fact may be particularly problematic for African Americans given evidence that the same behavior may be judged as more abusive

Box 6.1   Adapted Version of Bessie's Example of Necessary Physical Discipline

"I had one problem. I was downtown at Kresge's and I took my oldest son there. He was a little fellow, about five, and I went into the store. I just had enough bill money to get back on the bus and buy him a hot dog and a little toy and after that I didn't have any more money to spend. So we're walking around the store and he starts pointing at the other stuff and I say 'you can't have that. You already have a little car.' And I said, 'Omar, we gotta go' and that kid said 'Whaaaaaa!' And I looked around to see who was in there and I said, 'Please, Omar, don't do that.' And he goes, 'Whaaaaaaa.' I had a shopping bag and I set the bag down. I snatched my little child, throwed him on my knee, Pow, Pow, Pow, Shook, Shook, Shook. 'Now we're not going out of here.' After that, I never had any trouble with him."

Discussion Questions

1. When Bessie spanked her five-year-old son (pow, pow, pow, shook, shook, shook) in the store for crying over a toy, was she being abusive?
2. Should a social service agency have the right to evaluate the appropriateness of the kind of behavior Bessie described?
3. Might there have been better ways for Bessie to handle what she saw as undisciplined and troublesome behavior on the part of her son? What is the basis of your views on this question?
4. The incident Bessie described took place before there were social service agencies mandated by law to intervene in cases of child abuse. If the incident she described took place today, should a social service agency intervene? If you believe the answer is yes, do you also believe that there are better forms of intervention than removing Omar from his home? What might those be?

SOURCE: Mosby, Rawls, Meehan, Mays, and Pettinari, 1999.

when performed by a Black parent than by a White parent (Nalepka, O'Toole, & Turbett, 1981).

A good illustration of the dilemma can be found in a report concerning six African American elders who volunteered to participate in an intergenerational mentoring program for "high-risk" African American parents (Mosby, Rawls, Meehan, Mays, & Peettinari, 1999). Because of allegations of child maltreatment, the high-risk parents had been mandated by a midwestern court to participate in an intensive social service intervention program. When the volunteers described their own child-rearing theories, their narratives revealed a strong belief in the importance of physical discipline. From the perspective of these elders, parental cursing and screaming at children cause permanent damage to the child and the parent-child relationship, and are, therefore, abusive. In contrast, they believed that physical discipline protects children from becoming unruly and disobedient, and, therefore, actually prevents child maltreatment. Even after a 14-week training program, the volunteer elders held to their positions on the importance of physical discipline, especially when carried out immediately following a child's transgression and when not excessive (e.g., "shaking a child to death"). Consequently, the social service agency decided not to allow these elders to become mentors. Box 6.1 provides a close paraphrase of one of the elder's examples of a situation in which physical discipline was necessary. Consider her example and the discussion questions that follow.

Based on this elder's example of appropriate discipline, would you recommend that she become a mentor to a high-risk parent? Why or why not? Following their analysis of the African American elder's justifications for the positive benefits of physical discipline, Mosby et al. (1999) concluded,

> One might argue that the right to raise one's family according to traditional beliefs should be as sacred under the constitution as the right to one's religious beliefs. . . . Certainly, the current practice of removing children from any family which does not conform to middle class preferences must be re-examined. (p. 516)

Although most professionals in the field of family violence would agree that social service agencies should be knowledgeable about cultural practices and beliefs, and should avoid ethnic and other biases, there are a number of points of debate about Mosby et al.'s (1999) conclusion. For example, although the U.S. Constitution guarantees freedom to worship as one chooses, several members of the Christian Science religion have been prosecuted because they allowed their ill children to die rather than permitting them to receive mainstream medical treatment (Bottoms, Shaver, Goodman, & Qin, 1995). The kinds of questions that can be and have been asked about the culturally approved practice of spanking include the following: (a) Does it have the positive effects it is sometimes presumed to have? (b) Does it have negative effects that directly contradict its presumed positive effects—for example, does it prevent or lead to increased misbehavior in the future?

Mosby et al. (1999) explicitly connect support for physical disciplinary practices with the "cultural values and traditions" of African Americans. However, it is possible that these "traditions" are more a product of forces such as social class and chronic stress (Crouch & Behl, 2001) than of ethnicity. A number of studies (e.g., Dietz, 2000; Wolfner & Gelles, 1993) have found that lower- and working-class parents use physical discipline more often than middle-class parents. Similarly, there is evidence that low-income parents generally approve of spanking more than middle-income parents do, and that this is truer of White families than of Black families (Heffer & Kelly, 1987).

Contrasting positions on the relationship between physical discipline in African American families and later child behavior problems have been taken by Straus (1994) and McLeod, Kruttschnitt, and Dornfield (1994). Straus investigated the relationships between the self-reported experience of corporal punishment in childhood among Whites, Blacks, and Hispanics, and later problem behavior, such as assaults, delinquency, and drug abuse. Across all ethnicities, corporal punishment in childhood and/or adolescence was significantly associated with increased risk of physically attacking a spouse, physically abusing one's own child, and drug use. Therefore, he concluded, corporal punishment during childhood has negative effects among Whites, Hispanics, and Blacks.

By contrast, McLeod et al. (1994) argued that aggressive behavior leads to rather than is an outcome of corporal punishment. Their analyses of a national sample of White and Black families showed a bidirectional relationship between spanking and antisocial behavior in White families—the more the spanking, the more the antisocial behavior, and vice versa. However, in Black families, children's antisocial behavior appeared to produce spankings, and not vice versa. Do these findings show that corporal punishment is good for Black children? This controversy over the effects of corporal punishment is unlikely to be resolved in the near future.

Research on less controversial forms of potential child maltreatment indicate that stereotypes concerning tolerance for child abuse and neglect in African American communities are not always supported. For example, African American mothers rated "unwholesome circumstances" (e.g., parents getting drunk or using drugs, parents constantly fighting in front of the child, one parent physically abusing the other parent in front of the child) as more serious threats to the well-being of a 6-year-old child than did White mothers (Rose & Meezan, 1995). Furthermore, when parents generated their own examples of behaviors they defined as child abuse and neglect, Whites gave more examples of physical acts of maltreatment than did African Americans, and African American parents gave more examples of neglect and inadequate supervision than did Whites (Korbin, Coulton, Lindstrom-Ufuti, & Spilsbury, 2000).

Perspectives on Child Sexual Abuse

The one study, to our knowledge, that addresses views on child sexual abuse among African Americans utilized a focus group of Latinos and African Americans (Fontes, Cruz, & Tabachnick, 2001). When asked what child sexual abuse means, the older African American women defined it as having sex with a child, fondling a child, abusing a child's innocence, touching a child's body parts, "having him touch you," and showing inappropriate adult films. Several African American men indicated that poor family communication, authoritarian parenting, and corporal punishment made a child more vulnerable to sexual abuse. All groups described the coercive aspect of child sexual abuse, and all viewed it as a significant problem.

Perspectives on Child Neglect

When inner-city African American families are reported for child maltreatment, the complaint is typically one of child neglect. But what do African Americans consider to be neglect? Black women appear to have more conservative definitions of neglect than members of other groups. For example, in one study comparing perceptions of neglect in White, Hispanic, and Black mothers and child welfare workers (Rose & Meezan, 1995), the mothers rated all the categories of child neglect (i.e., physical neglect, emotional neglect, lack of supervision, and sexual orientation of the parents) as more serious than the service workers did. Moreover, Black and Hispanic mothers rated the dimensions of neglect as more serious than the White mothers did. In a later study (Rose, 1999), Black mothers and child welfare workers were asked to judge the potential harm to a six-year-old girl of physical neglect (e.g., not feeding the child for a day), emotional neglect (e.g., not hugging or kissing the child when she's upset), inadequate parental judgment (e.g., leaving the child home alone after dark), sexual orientation (i.e., a parent being gay or lesbian), and exposure to injurious parental behaviors (e.g., a parent becoming drunk or high while taking care of the child alone). Black mothers rated these behaviors as more injurious than the child welfare workers did. What do you think of the sample items? Do they all seem to be good indices of neglect? In what ways can these findings be interpreted?

Perspectives on Spousal Maltreatment

There is only limited, and contradictory, evidence concerning the role of ethnicity in judgments of wife abuse. National survey data from 1968, 1992, and 1994 indicated that Blacks are less likely to approve of a husband slapping his wife than are Whites, and that from 1968 to 1994, the percentage of respondents approving of a husband slapping his wife decreased for Blacks but not for Whites (Straus, Kaufman Kantor, & Moore, 1997). By contrast, findings from community residents in Alabama indicated that several acts of aggression against wives were more frequently identified by White than by Black respondents as always being abusive—that is, cursing, not allowing her to have food, hitting her occasionally with an open hand, hitting her frequently with the hand, hitting her occasionally with a fist, hitting her frequently with a fist, and hitting her occasionally with an object (Johnson & Sigler, 2000).

Studies of the attitudes of college students also produce inconsistent results. In one study, males were more likely than females to endorse the statement, "Sometimes a husband must hit a wife so she'll respect him," but there were no ethnic differences in approval ratings (Finn, 1986). However, among college students at a midwestern university, White respondents judged intimate violence vignettes to be more serious than Black, Latino/Latina, and Asian American respondents did, regardless of the type of violence, the injuries caused, and whether the perpetrators were first-time offenders (Miller & Bukva, 2001).

Some workers in the field of Black family violence argue that it is simply a stereotype that violence is considered more normal among Blacks than among Whites, and view this stereotype as part of the general devaluing of Blacks by Whites (e.g., Hawkins, 1987). On the other hand, one Black feminist noted that Black women's traditional silence about the violence many of them and their children were experiencing from Black males "does not stem from acceptance of violence as a Black cultural norm (a view that the media perpetuates and many Whites believe), but rather from shame, fear, and an understandable, but nonetheless detrimental sense of racial loyalty" (White, 1986, p. 12). The limited data available provide no support for the assumption that acceptance of family violence is pervasive in African American communities.

Perspectives on Elder Maltreatment

"You just don't hit your momma!" This injunction, echoing the words of the woman from the beginning of this chapter, has been identified as a major theme in research on potential elder maltreatment in African American communities, and the available data indicate that whatever other forms of abuse Blacks may commit, physical abuse of mothers (kin or non-kin) is typically not among them (Griffin, 1999a). Studies of African American perspectives on elder maltreatment indicate that they are just as intolerant of elder abuse as other groups, and in some cases, even more intolerant. For example, in one study (Moon & Williams, 1993), Whites, Blacks, and Korean Americans judged whether 13 scenarios describing potential elder maltreatment were abusive, and if so, how abusive they were. Overall, 73% of Blacks perceived all 13 scenarios as abusive, compared to 50% of Korean Americans and 67% of Whites. The ethnic group differences were particularly dramatic in relation to a scenario in which an adult daughter, embarrassed by her depressed and agitated mother's behavior in front of guests, gives her mother tranquilizers, falsely claiming they were prescribed by the doctor. Whereas 63% of the Black respondents regarded this scenario as an example of elder abuse, only 36% of the Korean Americans and 10% of the Whites did.

Similar results were found in a related study (Moon & Benton, 2000) of Black, White, and Korean American elders, who were asked to agree or disagree with 12 statements describing potential elder maltreatment (e.g., "It is okay for an adult child caregiver to tie down a physically or mentally impaired parent in bed" [p. 292]). The African Americans were less tolerant of verbal and financial abuse than the Whites, but did not

differ from them in intolerance for hitting an elderly spouse. With regard to the statement "When adult children feel too much stress in caring for their elderly parents, it is okay to calm the parents with medication" (p. 292), 14% of the African American elders agreed, compared to 5.6% of the White and 21.1% of the Korean American elders. Finally, in focus group discussions with White, Black, Puerto Rican, and Japanese American elders and their caretakers (Anetzberger, Korbin, & Tomita, 1996), African American elders were distinguished by (a) an emphasis on love as the central responsibility of the family, (b) the view that the worst thing family members could do was withhold love through ignoring elders or subjecting them to harsh or profane language, and (c) an emphasis on the importance of context in determining whether an act is abusive. Furthermore, African American caregivers insisted that although some behaviors performed under stress (e.g., yelling at or ignoring a demanding elder) might be understandable, they were not respectable or acceptable.

WHO ARE AFRICAN AMERICANS?

African Americans, like European Americans and other ethnic groups in the United States, are very diverse. For example, among the large proportion of today's African American families whose ancestors were brought to this country before the Civil War, a substantial percentage are the descendants of slaves. However, there are also large numbers of black freemen descendants. In addition, the Black population includes many 20th-century immigrants, some of whom arrived before the Civil Rights movement of the 1960s, and some of whom arrived later. According to Census 2000,

> "Black or African American" refers to people having origins in any of the Black racial groups of Africa. It includes people who indicated their race or races as "Black, African Am, or Negro," or wrote in entries such as African American, Afro American, Nigerian, or Haitian. (McKinnon, 2001, p. 2)

Surely, there must be some differences in culture and experiences among a descendant of slaves, a recent immigrant from Nigeria, and, perhaps, a Haitian who has been in this country 20 years!

With regard to all of the other ethnic minority groups considered in this book, there has been at least some attention to the fact that groups having members with different national origins or different immigration histories may show considerable variety in cultural values, views on family violence, and experiences of abuse. Brice-Baker (1994) noted nearly 10 years ago that because of problems related to language, culture, and fear of deportation, African Caribbean immigrants may differ from other African Americans in access to services that can help women escape spousal violence (e.g., welfare, domestic violence shelters). Furthermore, one more recent study (Durodoye, 1997) comparing African American couples and Nigerian male/African American female couples found that the intermarried couples were more dissatisfied, disagreed more over finances, and had conflicts over child rearing—microsystem conflicts that could contribute to family violence. However, rarely do studies of family violence in African American populations make even these minimal levels of differentiation between groups. Perhaps the general lack of attention to potential differences among Black Americans with different origins reflects an assumption that all people of African descent in the United States share the experience of racism (Abney & Priest, 1995). In this chapter, we describe Black Americans with whatever labels the original authors used and provide any available demographic information.

African American Demographic Profile

According to Census 2000, approximately 34.7 million U.S. residents, or 12% of the total population, identified themselves as only Black or African American. An additional 1.8 million respondents indicated that they were Black or African American in addition to at least one other race. Of this interracial group, 45% were African American and White, 10% were African American and American Indian, and the majority of the remainder reported all three racial classifications. Altogether, there are 35.5 million Blacks in the United States, which is 13% of the total population. The majority (54%) live in the South, and 19% live in the Northeast, 19% in the Midwest, and 8% in the West. Although the majority of Blacks (53%) live in central cities, only 21% of Whites live in comparable urban areas. The age distribution of Blacks and Whites is also quite different, with a larger percentage of the Black population (32% vs. 24%) under the age of 18, and a larger percentage of the White population (14% vs. 8%) over the age of 65—indicating that not as many Blacks as Whites are surviving into the later years. Blacks and Whites also differ in their household composition: Although 83% of White families are married couple families, less than one half (48%) of all Black families are. In addition, whereas 13% of White families are maintained by women with no spouse present, 44% of Black families are. Finally, families are larger in the Black than in the White population (McKinnon, 2001.)

Blacks and Whites also show differences with respect to educational, occupational, and economic indices. For example, level of education is higher for Whites, with the percentage obtaining at least a bachelor's degree (29%) nearly double that of Blacks (17%). White males also have higher rates of civilian workforce participation than Black males (73% vs. 68%), but Black females have somewhat higher rates of civilian workforce participation than White females (62% vs. 60%). Employed White men are much more likely than employed Black men to be in managerial, professional, technical, sales, and administrative support positions, whereas employed Black men are much more likely to work in service occupations. White women are more likely than Black women to be in managerial and professional specialty positions, whereas Black women are more likely to be in service occupations or working as operators, fabricators, and laborers. Among economic indices, the poverty rates for Black and White women are 25% and 9% respectively. Of the 32.9 million families in the United States living below the poverty level, 8.1 million were Black (23% of the Black population) and 15.3 million were White (8% of that population; McKinnon, 2003). These demographic patterns are important because, as discussed repeatedly in this book, many studies have found that poverty, low education, lack of employment opportunities, and larger families are positively related to levels of family violence in the U.S. population as a whole.

CULTURAL VALUES: PROTECTIVE OR RISK FACTORS?

African Americans brought with them to this continent a set of strong cultural beliefs, emphasizing the value of children, centrality of an extended family, a strong role for women, and loyalty to the community. These values, along with a strong religious faith, sustained them through the horrors of slavery and the sustained racism of the postslavery era. However, some of these strengths may also create sources of vulnerability to maltreatment within the family.

Adaptive Family Forms, Kinship Bonds, and the Extended Family

There has been considerable debate about the structure of Black families both in African American families and in the African societies from which Black people were seized and enslaved. However, there seems to be considerable support for two conclusions:

1. Complex extended families were the norm in a wide range of traditional African societies and were an important basis for political and economic interdependence, as well as psychological and social interdependence (Foster, 1983).

2. During and following the long era of slavery in this country, Black families were flexible and communal. For example, on slave ships it was customary for children to call their adult shipmates "aunt" and "uncle," and for adults to view each other's children as their own (Foster, 1983).

Furthermore, since the days of slavery, it has been the practice of Black families to informally adopt and care for children of relatives and friends whenever parents were unable, for any reason, to care for their children

(Littlejohn-Blake & Darling, 1993). In contemporary America, Black families headed by elderly women are about four times as likely to take children under 18 into their homes as White elderly women are (Hill, 1972). Furthermore, maltreated Black children taken from their parents by social service agencies may be placed with grandparents and other relatives who become their surrogate parents (Everett, Chipungu, & Leashore, 1991), continuing a long tradition of protection of children by elderly family members.

A complex African kinship system, rooted in West African culture, enabled African Americans to survive slavery and postslavery oppression (Gray & Nybell, 1990). Because of both communal values and economic pressures, African Americans today continue to be much more likely than Whites to live in extended family households, and this adaptability in family structure has been shown to be a protective factor against family violence. For example, in a study of the Black extended family kinship system in the South, it was found that one of its unique functions was preventing child maltreatment in poor Black families (Shimkin, Louie, & Frate, 1973, as cited in Cazenave & Straus, 1990). Furthermore, impoverished Black women may be able to leave an abusive partner by moving into an alternative family form that Blacks have found useful—the "doubling up" of two single mothers with their children. Over 70% of households of this type involve African American mothers (Jayakody & Chatters, 1997). Similarly, whereas approximately 5% of elderly Whites live in institutions, only 3% of elderly Blacks do so (Griffin, Williams, & Reed, 1998). However, the assumption that family members will always help each other and stick together may also be a risk factor for elder abuse. For example, in Rhode Island, a majority of Black elder abuse cases involved substance-abusing adult children who moved back home because they were unable to support themselves. The most typical form of abuse was financial exploitation, although there were also cases of elderly Black individuals being physically abused by their spouses or grandchildren (Hall, 1999).

Strong kinship bonds are an important cultural strength in African American communities, providing resilience in the face of discrimination (Hill, 1972; Stevenson & Renard, 1993). Indeed, the role of extended families among African Americans is virtually identical to the role of familism in Latinos (McAdoo, 2002; see chapter 9 in this book). These close family relationships appear to be related to a number of positive outcomes for African Americans. Extended family membership has been found to buffer the effects of stress among both African American females (Brown & Gary, 1987; Dressler, 1985) and males (Dressler). Because stress is an important predictor of family violence, these relationships may help militate against the occurrence of family violence (Cazenave & Straus, 1990).

Supportive social networks may be particularly important to young and/or single mothers in Black communities. For example, nearly 50% of the African American single mothers in one sample reported receiving much help from family members (Jayakody & Chatters, 1997). Moreover, the single mothers who coresided with others reported receiving more help than those who lived alone, and assistance from families was significantly associated with family closeness and satisfaction. In another study, younger African American mothers (ages 18 to 24) were more likely than older African American mothers (ages 25 to 45) to rely on their social support network for child-rearing advice (Caldwell & Koski, 1997). This availability of mentors may be particularly useful for the younger group of mothers because youth is a predictor of child abuse in some African American communities (Chaffin, Kelleher, & Hollenberg, 1996).

Views on Children and the Role of the Elderly in Child Rearing

In West Africa, before and after the era of slave hunters, grandparents played an important role both in socializing and protecting children (Foster, 1983). Parental child-rearing tactics were often harsh, but the presence of grandparents provided a check on parental practices and consequently a protective factor against child maltreatment. Children could appeal to their grandparents when they felt they were being treated unfairly. The grandparents' relationships

with their grandchildren were friendly, bordering on social equality. This kind of mediating role was maintained among elderly slaves in the United States (Foster). In addition, a contradictory perspective on Black children can be found in literature on both the slave era (Foster) and 20th-century African American communities (Sudarkasa, 1993). This perspective shows Black children as highly valued and treated with great warmth and affection on the one hand, and as recipients of harsh parental discipline on the other. One major explanation for the linking of great affection with severe discipline in Black communities focuses on the heritage of slavery. For Black parents raising children in those times, a child's disobedience could be a matter of life or death for the child (Straus, 1994). Therefore, a child's disobedience was many times dealt with harshly by the slave parents.

Views on Women

Most American slaves were brought from sub-Saharan West Africa, and the historical record indicates that in precolonial, pre-slave trade days, women occupied important social and political roles in that part of the world (Ucko, 1994). They served as priestesses, warriors, advisors to kings and chiefs, agricultural consultants, and crafts makers. They are described as having separate but cooperative and interdependent roles with men, having control of their own resources, and being productive participants in the support of their children and parents (Lewis, 1982, as cited in Ucko)— thus making their roles not unlike those of women in many Native American Indian communities prior to the invasion of White Europeans. Moreover, although there was probably some belief in male superiority and dominance in some arenas, this heritage apparently did not extend into controlling women's lives, property, or activities, and wife abuse seems to have been neither widespread nor culturally acceptable (Ucko).

Even in the 20th century, the strength of these traditions can be seen in a study of family violence in 90 societies worldwide, which revealed that societies from sub-Saharan Africa, including West Africa, had some of the lowest indices of wife beating of the major areas of the world (Levinson, 1989). However, despite the relative equality of men and women, there is also evidence of at least the emotional abuse of wives during the precolonial period—it was acceptable for men to treat women with ridicule (Ucko, 1994).

The flexible gender roles of precolonial Africans seem to have been brought by the slaves to the United States. From preslavery days through contemporary times, there has been a tradition of Black women playing an important role in providing for family members (Ucko, 1994). This tradition, and the ability of Black women to persevere through eras of hardship and discrimination, are probably sources for the stereotypical image of indomitable Black women. Internalizing this stereotype can lead many battered Black women to sacrifice their own needs to take care of others (Brice-Baker, 1994).

Given the African heritage of relative equality, respect, and interdependence in many African American families, it is puzzling that there appears to be so much spousal violence in some Black communities (Ucko, 1994). According to some researchers (e.g., Ucko), poverty and discrimination can be only part of the answer, and another reason probably lies in the psychological and cultural effects of slavery and the postslavery eras. In this perspective, the rage of Blacks becomes deflected onto those closest to them—their wives, husbands, or lovers.

Religiosity

Black churches have played an important role in helping African Americans deal with the adversity of life in the United States and rear their children by providing, for example, emotional support to overburdened parents and by offering low-cost child care and school programs (Franklin, Boyd-Franklin, & Draper, 2002). However, many African Americans belong to fairly conservative Protestant denominations, and conservative Protestants tend to support corporal punishment and other very punitive child-rearing practices (Gershoff, Miller, & Holden, 1999).

The links between religious affiliation, religious beliefs, race, and support for corporal punishment appear to be quite complex. For example, there is evidence that conservative Protestants are significantly more likely than individuals with comparable backgrounds to believe in a literal interpretation of the bible, the inherent evilness of human nature, and the necessity of punishing sinners—all of which contribute significantly to the belief that sometimes children need a "good hard spanking" (Ellison & Sherkat, 1993). In turn, compared with other ethnic groups, Blacks tend to have relatively pessimistic assessments of human nature, more punitive attitudes toward sinners, and, in relation to these views, stronger support for corporal punishment (Ellison & Sherkat), all of which can lead to family violence. However, in one study, religiosity was related to factors that serve as protectors against child maltreatment: Among low-income Black mothers, the greater their knowledge of the scriptures, the less they ignored their child's needs and wants, and the less they expected unyielding obedience to parental authority (Kelley, Power, & Wimbush, 1992).

Although churches have provided much support to Black families in times of stress, they have also played a role in keeping wives in abusive relationships. According to one Black woman,

> When he started beating me I went to the elders of the church. They said I couldn't leave him because it would be a bad reflection on them. I didn't want to bring shame on the church. The church and my faith are very important to me. (White, 1995, p. 71)

In response to this scenario, White (1995) argued that perhaps it is time to challenge members of the Black clergy who, as members of a male-dominated institution (the church), may contribute to the continued abuse of Black women through their sexist attitudes and/or lack of knowledge about spousal violence.

OPPRESSION, RACISM, AND DISCRIMINATION

It would be difficult to overestimate the enduring negative effects of 200 years of legalized slavery on U.S. society today, but it is also difficult to determine the extent to which that historical legacy, in comparison to current racism, contributes to violence within contemporary African American families. Black men, women, and children, brought to this country in chains under incredibly inhumane conditions to serve White masters, were dehumanized, brutalized, and terrorized to maintain the social order. Many slave owners assumed that Black "savages" were incapable of "normal" familial bonds, and they used Black men and women in part as baby machines to perpetuate the slave system. To keep their slaves in a state of docility and obedience, White slave owners used swift, harsh, and violent punishment, including severe beatings, amputation of limbs, and even violent death. Contemporary Black families, even if unaware of the history underlying their child-rearing practices, may accept and follow these harsh, child-endangering practices originally designed to keep Black children from provoking the rage of powerful Whites (Lassiter, 1987).

Lassiter's (1987) perspective is consistent with the constructs of historical and cumulative trauma (the social transmission of one generation's trauma to subsequent generations) described in chapter 4 in relation to Native American Indians. A somewhat different perspective has been proposed by Cross (1998), who suggests that a trauma legacy model does not apply well to the Black experience with American slavery. His primary argument is that oppressive episodes continuing long past the end of slavery (e.g., the Rodney King beating) have enormous traumatic potentials in their own right and, therefore, are the major macrosystem contributors to violence in the Black community. A second shortcoming of the traumatic legacy construct, Cross argues, is that it neglects the remarkable coping strategies used by Blacks to survive their experiences. For example, he describes the life of plantation slaves as follows: During the day, slaves could be brought to their breaking point; family members could be sold or exchanged; children could be forced prematurely into adult work roles, and deliberate or whimsical violence could be perpetrated on any slave by the slave-owner. Nights held terror for Black women, who might be raped by the owner, his sons, or his White employees, but the slaves were able to use this time, within their own communal areas, to develop functional,

efficacious, and deeply human personal, family, and cultural patterns. In contemporary America, ongoing, institutionalized racism, workplace discrimination, and limited opportunities put these cultural values at risk, and Black hatred of White mistreatment can spill over and poison relationships within the Black community. There is ample evidence, Cross believes, that internalized racism can lead to drug and alcohol abuse, anger and rage, and violence—all of which can play themselves out within the family.

Both perspectives may have some validity. It is clear that brutal treatment of Black people did not cease with the Emancipation Proclamation or the end of the Civil War. Indeed, legalized discrimination in public accommodations, including drinking fountains, public restrooms, and hotels/motels, was widespread until the 1964 Civil Rights Act, and lynchings were accepted practices in the South as late as the early 1960s. Even today, African Americans are frequently excluded from jobs, neighborhoods, and organizations for no reason except skin color. Furthermore, according to Weiss (2001), starting with the Nixon administration, public policy has been directed at excluding and punishing lower-class African Americans, who are considered "devoid of market utility" and a "stagnant surplus population," best housed in the nation's prisons and jails. Overall, whether current family violence in African American communities can be traced back to White colonization and the disruptive and brutalizing effects of slavery or is rooted more in current institutionalized racism, it is clear that macrosystem level attitudes and policies contribute at least indirectly, and probably directly, to that violence.

SUMMARY

Within many African American families, there is considerable acceptance of strong physical punishment of children, but little tolerance for child neglect, psychological abuse, or extreme forms of physical abuse. Similarly, African Americans typically show less tolerance for abuse of wives or older family members than members of majority communities. Despite diversity in countries of origin and length of time in the United States, overall, Black

Box 6.2   Personal Reflections on Substance Abuse and Violence, by Vostina DiNovo, Ph.D.

In almost 10 years of working in a substance abuse treatment program for women, I have seen many cases of horrific violence. In telling their stories, both Black and White women repeatedly excuse their partner's abusive behavior ("He only beat me when he was high," "It almost never happened when we weren't drinking") and admit that their own drinking and drug abuse contributed to the violence ("I would just get stupid when I was drunk, and do crazy things like dare him to hit me"). Not uncommonly, women coerced into prostitution by their partners reported being severely beaten when suspected of "liking it too much"; this outcome almost invariably coincided with cocaine and alcohol use. Conversely, they described their own jealousy and rage about real or suspected infidelity by their partner—violent "fits" heightened by drug abuse.

A substance abuser's partner is often the supplier of the drugs, and substance dependence becomes fused with emotional and physical dependence upon an abusive, controlling partner. Tolerance of unacceptable behavior, including violence, increases incrementally and synergistically with tolerance of the drug. For the typical women with histories of sexual abuse, intoxication is a key to sexual freedom, but simultaneously releases unresolved pain. Additionally, dependence on both the substance and the partner draws these women ever deeper into abuse of all forms, criminality, and self-degradation. Although some racial differences may exist in tendencies toward particular patterns of violence or substance abuse, this ensnaring web does not discriminate. The women I have worked with, Black and White, realize how very much they have in common, in suffering and in strength, as they strive toward freedom from the entrapment of their addictions.

families, in comparison to White families, are more likely to consist of adults with less education and lower employment, to be headed by a single mother, and to have larger numbers of children. However, the great diversity among African American communities is rarely acknowledged or addressed in research. Among the cultural values with implications for levels of family violence are strong kinship networks and bonds, reliance on extended families, strong roles of women, children, and the elderly, and deep religious values. Both a history of enslavement and persistent racism are likely to play a powerful role in family violence in African American families.

In this chapter, we pointed out several consistencies between African American/Black communities and Native American Indian communities in cultural values and in experiences of oppression and racism within the macrosystem. What additional similarities do you see? Do there appear to be major differences in cultural values and experiences as well? Given what you have learned about family violence so far and about the cultural context of African Americans, what do you expect to find when you read the next two chapters, which deal with child and adult maltreatment within African American communities? What are likely to be the main predictors, correlates, and consequences of the two forms of family violence? And how are these predictors related, in turn, to the macrosystem cultural contexts discussed in this chapter? Finally, consider the construct of historical or cumulative trauma, the notion that traumatic events that occurred generations ago can have cumulative traumatic effects influencing descendants of victims today. Does this construct help you understand better self-destructive and other destructive behaviors in oppressed communities today? Does it appear to apply better to one oppressed community (e.g., Native American Indians) than to another (e.g., African Americans/Blacks)?

7

AFRICAN AMERICAN CHILD MALTREATMENT

....

Examples of extreme abuse from a parent to a child:

- *"Abuse is an act of malicious physical violence such as being punched or burned with an iron. Spankings or whippings don't constitute abuse but as disciplinary acts."* (21-year-old African American/Black female college student)
- *"When a parent or family member commit incest."* (60-year-old African American female)
- *"A child accidentally spills his milk and he/she is slammed into a wall and then beaten."* (21-year-old Black and White female)
- *"When a mother punches her child (closed fist) in public for talking too much."* (24-year-old African American male)
- *"Battering which causes permanent injury. Withholding of food, medications, and shelter."* (47-year-old African American male)

When providing examples of extreme abuse from a parent to a child, our African American respondents identified some incontrovertibly abusive behaviors. Not all cases of potential child abuse are this clear-cut, however. Moreover, many of the reported cases of child maltreatment in African American families appear to be much less serious than these, and it is arguable whether the removal of African American children from their homes on the basis of child maltreatment is always in the best interest of the child.

SCOPE OF THE PROBLEM

Reporting Issues in African American Child Maltreatment

A major problem in estimating the relative rate of child maltreatment within African American communities concerns the extent to which there are differential reporting tendencies based on race—that is, the extent to which a particular form of parental discipline or punishment is labeled "abuse" and reported to authorities if it occurs within Black families but not within White families. When mandated reporters respond to child abuse vignettes (such as the ones in Box 1.1 in chapter 1), the race of the hypothetical victim can be a predictor of judgments that an incident should be reported. For example, in a national study of nearly 2,000 mandated reporters, both race and social class influenced judgments about how serious a hypothetical maltreatment case was, whether it was abuse or neglect, whether the law should require a report in the case, and the likelihood that the child and the family would benefit from a maltreatment report (Zellman, 1992). Vignettes portraying physical and sexual abuse were generally judged to be more serious, more likely to be defined as abuse, and more reportable when the hypothetical incidents involved lower socioeconomic status (SES) and Black families, who were considered most likely to benefit from the reporting. Moreover, the respondents indicated they would personally be most likely to report such cases if they saw them in lower SES and Black families.

A reporting bias based on race and SES may be especially pronounced among physicians. In one vignette study, physicians' judgments concerning an abusive situation were affected by three manipulated variables—social class, ethnicity, and level of injury—portrayed in the vignette. However, nurses' judgments were influenced only by the level of the injury (Nalepka, O'Toole, & Turbett, 1981). These findings suggest that physicians may not recognize or report some cases of child abuse in White families, but may be too quick to allege abuse for injuries to children when they occur in Black families.

Evidence on actual reporting patterns provides some support for the vignette data. For example, in one survey, physicians from the East Coast and mid-South acknowledged reporting only 90 out of a total of 229 cases in which they suspected abuse, but suspected and reported proportionately more incidents of child maltreatment among non-White groups than among the White majority (Kim, 1986). Given such problems, it is important not to assume that the number of identified cases of African American child maltreatment identified by reporting agencies is an accurate and unbiased reflection of the actual number of cases occurring in those communities.

Table 7.1 provides an overview of studies providing data on rates of child abuse in Black communities. At the heart of this debate over race bias in the reporting of child abuse cases are the discrepancies among the findings of different studies, particularly the national surveys: the National Family Violence Surveys (NFVS), National Studies of the Incidence of Abuse and Neglect (NIS), and annual surveys of the National Committee on Abuse and Neglect (NCAN).

Physical Maltreatment and Corporal Punishment

The 1975 and 1985 NFVS are valuable because they provide considerable information about the frequency of corporal punishment and child abuse in the population at large. In the 1975 study, Blacks had a rate of child abuse (15.7 per 100 children) that was not significantly different from that of Whites (14.1 per 100 children; Straus & Smith, 1990a). In the 1985 study, however, the abuse rate for White children was lower than in 1975 (10.3/100), whereas the Black rate was about the same as for 1975; consequently, the abuse rate for Blacks became significantly higher than the rate in Whites. Another analysis of the 1985 NFVS data revealed that Black respondents did not differ from White respondents in level of severe violence against children, but they did report higher frequencies of severe violence (Wolfner & Gelles, 1993). Similarly, in a later study of a nationally representative sample of parents, there were no significant differences between Whites and African Americans in the amount of corporal punishment they reported administering. However, the African American rate of severe assaults against children (148/1,000) was significantly higher than the White rate (34/1,000; Straus et al., 1998).

A very different picture of the relative rates of severe child abuse in African American communities compared to the majority community comes from the three NIS, which focus on identified cases of child abuse rather than on representative community samples. The reports from all three waves of the NIS indicate that there were no significant racial differences in the incidence of identified cases of child maltreatment (Sedlak & Broadhurst, 1996). These findings have received much attention because of their inconsistency with other data demonstrating an overrepresentation of children of color in the child welfare system. Moreover, several secondary analyses of the NIS 1, 2, and 3 data sets yield different perspectives on the relative frequencies of identified maltreatment as a function of ethnicity. For example, in one reanalysis of the NIS-1 data, Hampton and Newberger (1985) compared characteristics of children

(Text continues on page 118)

Table 7.1 Child Maltreatment in African American Communities

Study	Sample Description	Definition/Measure of Abuse	Findings
National Studies—Reported Cases			
Second National Incidence Study (Cappelleri, Eckenrode, & Powers, 1993)	Nationwide reports to child protective services plus sentinel reports	• *Sexual abuse*: intrusion, molestation, genital contact, and other unknown sexual abuse • *Physical abuse*: physical injury to child resulting from caretaker's behavior	• Out of 133,619 cases of sexual abuse, Blacks had a rate of 2.02 per 1,000 and Whites (including Hispanic and non-Hispanic Whites) had a rate of 1.99 per 1,000 (not significantly different). • Out of 311,524 cases of physical abuse, Blacks had a rate of 7.68 per 1,000 and Whites (including Hispanic and non-Hispanic Whites) had a rate of 4.32 per 1,000 (significant difference).
First National Incidence Study (Hampton, 1987)	Estimated 4,170 unweighted cases of substantiated maltreatment	Identified and reported cases by hospitals as compared with other reporting agencies	• 74% of cases were White. • 15.8% of cases were Black. • 7.7% of cases were Latino.
First National Incidence Study (Hampton & Newberger, 1985)	Over 77,000 cases of abuse identified by hospitals	Reported cases	• 66.7% of identified cases were White; 25% were Black; 7.6% were Latino. • 60.5% of White cases, 74.3% of Black cases, and 91.2% of Latino cases were reported; Black and Latino cases were overreported as compared with White cases (representation in the population not provided).
National Studies—Self-Report			
Dietz (2000)	Nationally representative sample of 1,000 families with a child under the age of 18: 823 Whites and 121 Blacks analyzed	Parent-Child Conflict Tactics Scale (1998)	• African American parents were two times as likely to report using severe corporal punishment in the year before the study.
Straus, Hamby, Finkelhor, Moore, & Runyan (1998)	Unbiased probability sample of telephone households in continental United States (12% Black)	Parent-Child Conflict Tactics Scale (1995)	• No significant difference between Whites and Blacks in corporal punishment. • Severe assault rate by Blacks (148 per 1,000) was 3 times the White rate (34 per 1,000).

(Continued)

111

Table 7.1 Continued

Study	Sample Description	Definition/Measure of Abuse	Findings
Regional Studies—Reported Cases			
California Children's Service Archive (2002)	115,158 substantiated cases of child maltreatment for the year 2001	Case review	• 16% of cases were Black (percentage of Blacks in California population: 7%).
Feiring, Coates, & Taska (2001)	57 African American, 25 Hispanic (mainly Puerto Rican), and 48 European American sexually abused children from CPS and regional abuse clinics	Structured interviews with children, questionnaires with caregivers, plus information from case records	• 35% of African American children, 23% of European American children, and 52% of Hispanic children had been abused by a family member, usually a parent figure.
Forjuoh (2000)	348 cases of child maltreatment identified from discharge data from all Pennsylvania acute care hospitals reporting child maltreatment cases	Case review	• Overall maltreatment incidence rate: 10.8 per 1,000 children. • Rates significantly highest among Black children (23.2 per 1,000 children).
Shaw, Lewis, Loeb, Rosado, & Rodriguez (2001)	82 Black and 77 Hispanic sexually abused girls and caretakers at the Sexual Abuse Trauma Clinic in Florida	Substantiated cases	• 41% of African Americans were abused just once. • 40% of Hispanics were abused more than 10 times. • Number of incidents of physical abuse and maltreatment were comparable. • Hispanics experienced more abusive episodes and waited longer to disclose abuse; perpetrators were more likely to be fathers or stepfathers. • Blacks were more likely to experience vaginal penetration and were more likely to be abused at a friend's house or another location with a nonrelated male or distant male relative.
Taussig & Talmi (2001)	89 maltreated youth who had participated in the	Substantiated cases	• White and Hispanic youth had higher rates of substantiated maltreatment.

Study	Sample Description	Definition/Measure of Abuse	Findings
	Screening Impact on Services and Costs for Foster Children after entering foster care in a southern California county (May 1990–October 1991): 43% White, 31.5% African American, 20.1% Hispanic, 5.4% Other		• No significant difference between groups on rates of substantiated sexual abuse cases. • Trend for more African Americans to have substantiated incidences of neglect.
Levine, Doueck, Freeman, & Compaan (1996)	270 families referred to CPS for alleged maltreatment in western New York in 1993	Coding of case records from random sample of • 108 substantiated closed cases • 82 substantiated open cases • 103 unsubstantiated closed cases	• Blacks: 47% of cases ($n = 128$). • Whites: 53% of cases ($n = 142$). • 52.4% of Black cases and 55.6% of White cases were reported by mandated reporters. • Allegations of physical abuse substantiated more often in Whites ($n = 30$; 21%) than in Blacks ($n = 14$; 9%), but no overall differences in substantiation rates.
Mennen (1995)	134 females at Southern California sexual abuse clinics (51 Whites, 38 Hispanics, 35 Blacks, 8 Asians, 2 Others)	Substantiated cases	For Black victims: • Average age of onset: 9.08 years; average duration of abuse: 2.23 years; 78.8% experienced penetration; 40% abused by father figure; 77.8% forcibly abused; 48.5% removed from the home. No ethnic differences in • Kind of abuse (e.g., penetration) • Relationship of perpetrator (e.g., father figure) • Removal from home • Average age of onset Trend for Whites to have longer duration of abuse than Hispanics or Blacks.
Sorenson & Peterson (1994)	Case records of 213 child homicide victims from Los Angeles Police Department records 1978–1987	Record review	• Most common victim: Black male child less than 4 years old killed in home with gun or knife by male suspect or family member. • Only 1 in 6 cases known to CPS.

(Continued)

113

Table 7.1 Continued

Study	Sample Description	Definition/Measure of Abuse	Findings
Leventhal, Horwitz, Rude, & Stier (1993)	219 children born to 154 Black, unmarried teen mothers in Yale-New Haven Hospital, October 1979–December 1981	Review of children's medical records (1979–1986)	• Evidence of abuse in 4.4% of cases, of neglect in 6.3% of cases, and of serious abuse in 2.5% of cases.
Saunders, Nelson, & Landsman (1993)	Longitudinal cohort of 182 (out of 445) families referred for neglect to Allegheny County (Pittsburgh), PA, Children and Youth Services Department from October 1986–August 1989	Initial interviews with referred families plus analysis of case files	• African Americans were more likely to be referred for inadequate supervision. • CYS investigators in African American cases reported more problems with chronic neglect and child hygiene.
Powers & Eckenrode (1988)	Representative sample of protective service reports from New York state: victims between 12 and 16	Analyses of initial report, 7-day progress report, and 90-day case determination	• White children were underrepresented and Black children were overrepresented for physical abuse and neglect in relation to their percentage in the population. • No significant differences by ethnic group in substantiation of sexual abuse and neglect in reports involving adolescents. • Among children 0–11 years, sexual abuse and neglect reports significantly less likely to be substantiated in White than in Black and Hispanic children.
Brenner, Fischer, & Mann-Gray (1987)	545 reports from Children's Hospital of Michigan to the Michigan DSS of abused children 18 months and younger, 1980–1985	Reported cases	• 447 Black children and 87 White children in total sample of abused children. • 9% of White babies and 2.7% of Black babies were victims of shaken baby syndrome—a statistically significant difference (representation in the population not provided).
Kercher & McShane (1984)	1,056 Texas residents who hold a driver's license and responded to a mail survey (82% White, 11.2% Hispanic, 5.6% Black)	Sexual interaction between a child and an adult or between 2 minors when the perpetrator is significantly older than the victim or is in a position of power over the victim	• Hispanic females overrepresented as sexual abuse victims (16% of victims). • White females underrepresented (77% of victims). • Black females equal representation (5% of victims).

Study	Sample Description	Definition/Measure of Abuse	Findings
DeJong, Hervada, & Emmett (1983)	566 6-month-old to 16-year-old children presenting at sexual assault crisis centers: 103 males and 463 females; 74.4% Black, 19.6% White, 5.5% Hispanic, and 0.2% Asian	Substantiated cases	• In comparison with the population distribution, Black children were reported 5 to 10 times more frequently than White children. • Hispanics were older than Whites and Blacks when the abuse began. • Hispanic boys were more likely to be sexually abused than boys of other races.
Spearly & Lauderdale (1983)	246 Texas counties' official child maltreatment reports for 1977	Reported cases	• 12.3 reports per 1,000 White families. • 23.3 reports per 1,000 Black families. Significance tests were not reported for these comparisons. • After controlling for social class, Blacks had the greatest risk of maltreatment, followed by Mexican Americans, and then Whites.
Regional Studies—Self-Report			
Cecil & Matson (2001)	249 low-income, African American adolescents from a community-based health program in Milwaukee	Anonymous survey with questions on childhood sexual abuse	• 57 (22.9%) reported childhood sexual abuse. • Of these, 44.3% were intrafamilial and 55.7% were extrafamilial.
DeLillo, Giuffre, Tremblay, & Peterson (2001)	240 high-risk, low-income, low-education women who had physically disciplined child at least once; recruited from federal WIC (Women, Infants, and Children) program	Structured clinical interviews; sex abuse items ranged from being shown private parts to sexual activity with someone at least 3 years older	• Approximately half of each ethnic group reported childhood sexual abuse (not significantly different).
Wyatt, Loeb, Solis, & Carmona (1999)	Stratified probability sample of 182 African American and 156 European American participants	Face-to-face interview; sexual abuse questions limited to bodily contact—e.g., fondling, intercourse	• 29% of African American women and 39% of European American women reported at least one incident of child sexual abuse (rates not significantly different). • 60% of African American and 69% of European American perpetrators were nonfamily (not significantly different).

(Continued)

115

Table 7.1 Continued

Study	Sample Description	Definition/Measure of Abuse	Findings
Brown, Cohen, Johnson, & Salzinger (1998)	Representative sample (91% White, 8% Black) of 644 families in Upstate New York completed surveys 4 times between 1975 and 1992	Self-reports of physical abuse (physical hurt leaving injuries or bruises), sexual abuse (forced sexual activity before 18), and neglect (left alone overnight by caretakers before age 10) from 644 youth over 18 in 1992 and validated maltreatment reports from the New York State Registry for Child Abuse and Neglect	• Non-White ethnicity was 1 of 23 risk factors associated with official reports of neglect, but not with youth self-reported maltreatment. • Ethnicity was not associated with either self-reports or official reports of physical or sexual maltreatment.
Herman-Giddens et al. (1998)	All 734 Black and White mothers of newborns recruited in North Carolina hospitals and health departments, 1985–1987	Participants asked if prior to age 18 they had any sexual experiences where perpetrator was in a caretaker role and they had to give in because perpetrator was bigger, stronger, or older	• 26% of Black and 40% of White mothers reported being sexually abused before age 18 (statistically significant).
Hernandez, Lodico, & Clemente (1993)	5,290 White, 440 African American, and 494 Native American Indian 9th–12th graders in a midwestern state	Answered yes to whether any "adult or older person outside the family ever touched you sexually against your wishes or forced you to touch them sexually," or to whether "any older or stronger member of your family ever touched you sexually or had you touch them sexually," or to "Has anyone in your family hit you so hard or so often that you had marks or were afraid of that person?"	Females: • 11% of Black females and 6% of White females reported incest. • 18% of Black females and 12% of White females reported extrafamilial sexual abuse. • 19% of Black females and 15% of White females reported physical abuse. Males: • 5% of Black males and 1% of White males reported incest. • 25% of Black males and 3% of White males reported extrafamilial sexual abuse. • 20% of Black males and 8% of White males reported physical abuse. No significance tests were reported for these comparisons.

Study	Sample Description	Definition/Measure of Abuse	Findings
Doll et al. (1992)	1,001 homosexual and bisexual men attending STD clinics (73% White, 12% Hispanic, 12% Black, 2% Asian, 2% Native American, <1% Other)	Whether encouraged or forced to have sexual contact prior to age 19 with older or more powerful partner (sexual contact—self-defined)	• 52% of Blacks, 50% of Hispanics, and 32% of Whites were sexually abused. • Hispanics were significantly younger than Whites or Blacks at first episode (8 years vs. 10 years) and were more likely to report >5-year age difference (91% vs.~80%).
Gil (1988)	35 self-reported cases of conservative Protestant child sexual abuse, recruited through social service agencies, therapists, and word of mouth from California, Arizona, and Washington	Case history questionnaires or interviews; questions regarding perpetrators and seriousness of sexual abuse	• Only 3% of respondents were Black—underrepresented for areas. Ratios for Caucasians (74%) and Hispanics (23%) representative of general populations in regions sampled.
Wyatt (1985)	Multistage stratified probability sample of 126 African American and 122 White American women from Los Angeles county, 1984	Face-to-face interview; sexual abuse questions ranging from solicitations to engage in sex to body contact, such as fondling, intercourse	• 57% of African American women and 67% of White women reported at least one incident of childhood sexual abuse (rates not significantly different). • 28% of Black perpetrators and 17% of White perpetrators were family members (rates not significantly different).

NOTE: For information on African American child maltreatment according to the U.S. Department of Health and Human Services (1999, 2000), the Third National Incidence Study (Sedlak & Broadhurst, 1996), the 1990 National Longitudinal Survey of Youth (Giles-Sims et al., 1995), the National Family Violence Surveys of 1975 and 1985 (Cazenave & Straus, 1979; Connelly & Straus, 1992; Straus & Gelles, 1990a; Straus & Smith, 1990a, 1990b; Wolfner & Gelles, 1993), California Children's Services Archive (2002), Rao et al. (1992), Roosa et al. (1999), and Urquiza and Goodlin-Jones (1994), please see Table 3.1. For information on African American child maltreatment according to Lodico et al. (1996), please see Table 5.1. For information on African American child maltreatment according to Hampton (1987), Lindholm and Willey (1986), Moisan et al. (1997), and Torres et al. (2000), please see Table 10.1.

117

reported to CPS agencies by hospitals with characteristics of children referred by other agencies. For hospital personnel, social class and race were the most important perpetrator characteristics distinguishing reported from unreported cases of abuse. Specifically, disproportionate numbers of the unreported cases were White, came from higher-income families, were victims of emotional abuse, and appeared to have been abused by their mothers.

In one attempt to determine why NIS-1 and NIS-2 data show no ethnic differences in frequency of reported cases, Ards and Harrell (1993) analyzed the data on cases reported to CPS agencies compared to cases suspected by the professionals but not reported to the agencies. In contrast with many studies indicating that children of color tend to be overreported to CPS (e.g., Hampton & Newberger, 1985; Newberger, Reed, Daniel, Hyde, & Kotelchuck, 1977), their analysis indicated that race, sex, and income, played *no* significant role in the reporting of suspected cases to CPS agencies. A later analysis of NIS-1 data on 3,000 child abuse cases (2,499 White, 511 Black) revealed that only 28% of Black victims identified by NIS respondents were known to the CPS, compared to 33% of the White victims—suggesting an underreporting of the Black victims in comparison to Whites (Ards, Chung, & Myers, 1998). There was also evidence of differential patterns of over- and underreporting based on type of abuse. Specifically, significantly more of the known Black victims of sexual abuse (68%) were reported to CPS than known White sexual victims (39%), and significantly more White victims of educational maltreatment (10.9%) were reported than Black victims of educational maltreatment (2.65%). These patterns appear to reveal several forms of race bias—perhaps a greater willingness to interfere in Black families when sexual abuse is suspected, but a lack of concern regarding the educational needs of these children.

The NIS data also indicate that lower-class White children were more likely to have been reported to CPS than more economically privileged White children, but nonpoor Black victims were just as likely to be known to CPS as poor Black children (Ards et al., 1998). Again, it is possible that mandated reporters,

perhaps because of a fear of lawsuits, are reluctant to report middle-class White families for abuse, but have fewer reservations with regard to Black families. The reason the NIS studies do not support other findings of a generalized overreporting of Black families to protective services may be that they limit their sample of reporters to professionals. By contrast, CPS agencies receive many of their reports from family, friends, and neighbors, whose referral patterns may be quite different from those of professionals and result in different forms of bias. Therefore, the NIS studies seem to leave ambiguous the question of whether there are racial disparities in child maltreatment (Ards et al.).

Annual reports from state CPS agencies to the U.S. Department of Health and Human Services (DHHS) consistently show a different picture than the NIS data. As discussed in chapter 3, CPS agencies in the 50 states substantiated approximately 826,000 cases of child maltreatment. Victimization rates ranged from a low of 4.4/1,000 for Asian-Pacific Islander victims to a high of 25.2/1,000 for African American victims, with an average victimization rate of 11.8 children for every 1,000 children in the population. Thus, in contrast with NIS findings based on identification of child maltreatment cases by mandated reporters, this report from CPS agencies shows an overrepresentation of African Americans among substantiated cases (including neglect cases). However, the report also indicated that compared to White children, Black children were 17% *less* likely to experience a recurrence of maltreatment (DHHS, 1999).

In general, findings from studies of more localized maltreatment reports (e.g., Levine, Doucek, Freeman, & Compaan, 1996; Powers & Eckenrode, 1988) are consistent with the national data from CPS agencies—indicating an overreporting of African American families. For example, a representative sample of protective service reports in New York State in 1985 revealed that White children appeared to be underrepresented relative to their numbers in the population, whereas Black children tended to be overrepresented in all abuse categories, especially physical abuse and especially at younger ages (Powers & Eckenrode). The overrepresentation of Black children in the reports may indicate that Black children are actually at higher risk for abuse or may reflect the operation of social class or other variables, such as unemployment and poverty, associated with minority group status. Furthermore, Black families may be subjected to higher levels of surveillance than Whites because of greater contact with service providers such as the welfare system (Powers & Eckenrode). What do you think of this speculation? What other hypotheses do you have concerning the overrepresentation of Black children in the child protective service system? Do you think race is the driving factor in the reporting? What roles do social class and poverty play? What about the cultural factors described in the previous chapter?

An analysis of case records in upstate New York in 1993 confirmed that there seems to be an overrepresentation of African American cases in this state. These cases were typically from female-headed families and presumably poorer than the White cases (Levine et al., 1996). In a direct challenge to the argument of Ards et al. (1998), differential referral sources and differential worker attention did not account adequately for this overrepresentation of African Americans in CPS (Levine et al.). Data from California also provides evidence of differential reporting rates for child maltreatment as a function of ethnicity. A report from the California Children's Services Archive (2002) on child abuse referrals indicated that of 548,821 children alleged to be victims of child maltreatment in California in 2001, 16% were Black, 34% were White, 44% were Hispanic, 4% were Asian, and 1% were Native American. Because Black children comprised just 7% of California's child population, they were overrepresented in California's CPS (California Children's Services Archive).

Neglect. One of the limitations of many of the maltreatment studies is that they do not provide incidence information on the ethnicity breakdown for the particular subtypes of maltreatment. In one recent analysis of NIS data, there were substantial differences in types of maltreatment reported by ethnicity, with Whites having a higher rate of abuse reported and

African Americans having a higher rate of neglect reported (Baird, Ereth, & Wagner, 1999). An analysis of the case-level data from states in the NCAN report indicated that a higher percentage of Black children (70%) than of White children (58%) were reported for neglect—the most frequent type of maltreatment reported (Office of Juvenile Justice, 2000). Among low-income, single mothers receiving Aid to Dependent Children in Baltimore (a population that was 55% Black), 67.2% of the mothers who had been reported for child neglect were Black (Zuravin & Starr, 1991).

Childhood Sexual Abuse. Obtaining reliable estimates of rates of child sexual abuse (CSA) in Black communities and potential ethnic differences in rates is difficult because of methodological differences across studies. The NCAN report for 1996, which provides a national sample of caught cases, indicated that there were fewer reported cases of sexual abuse of Black children (7%) than of White children (13%; Office of Juvenile Justice, 2000). In a nationally representative self-report study focusing specifically on CSA, higher rates of self-reported cases of sexual abuse were found in men with an English or Scandinavian heritage (exact rates by ethnicity not provided), but other than that one finding, there were no differences in rates of sexual abuse as a function of race (Finkelhor, Hotaling, Lewis, & Smith, 1990). Thus, the national data are consistent in indicating lower levels of sexual abuse for Black than for White children.

One difficulty in determining relative rates of familial sexual abuse in Black respondents compared with other ethnicities stems from the fact that investigators frequently ask about "childhood sexual abuse" without differentiating between abuse by family members versus abuse by nonfamily members. The available data suggest that this distinction is an important one, particularly for African Americans. In one study of sexually active adolescent African American females, 22.9% reported a history of CSA (Cecil & Matson, 2001), but less than half (44.3%) of the perpetrators were family members. In another study of 68 adolescent girls from an outpatient health service (94% Black), one third reported a history of sexual assault, but only four of the perpetrators were family members and none were parents (Al-Mateen, Hall, Brookman, Best, & Singh, 1999). Sexual assault, primarily by unrelated individuals outside the nuclear family, may be just another form of victimization that poor and marginalized children of color experience.

Ethnic comparisons of CSA dramatize the importance of identifying the relationship of the perpetrator to the victim. Self-reports in a sample of high school students revealed that 15.2% of the African Americans and 9% of the White Americans reported having been sexually abused by someone (either a family or nonfamily member; Lodico et al., 1996). Further analyses indicated that there were no ethnic differences in the prevalence of intrafamilial sexual abuse, but African American teens reported almost twice as much extrafamilial abuse as White teens.

Other studies of community samples confirm the lack of ethnic differences in rates of intrafamilial sexual abuse. In a random sample of African American and White women, 62% (57% of the African American and 67% of the White women, a nonsignificant difference) reported at least one incident of CSA and there was no significant difference between ethnic groups in the relative frequency of abuse by family members (Wyatt, 1985). In a later study, 29% of African American and 39% of White women reported at least one incident of CSA, a statistically significant difference. However, in both ethnicities, the majority of the perpetrators were nonfamily members, and there was no significant difference between ethnic groups in the amount of CSA perpetrated by family members (Wyatt, Loeb, Solis, & Carmona, 1999). In a statewide convenience sample of young women from Arizona, approximately 26% reported some experience of CSA (not necessarily from a family member) and rates of the various forms of CSA were remarkably consistent across ethnic groups (Roosa et al., 1999). Finally, in a study of low-income mothers, the groups identified as sexually abused or nonsexually abused did not differ significantly on race (DeLillo, Giuffre, Tremblay, & Peterson, 2001).

A few studies depart from this general pattern of consistency in rates of intrafamilial sexual abuse across ethnicities, but in some of these, Blacks are overrepresented for sexual abuse, and in other cases, sexual abuse is significantly higher in Whites or in Hispanics. For example, a survey of high school students revealed that in Whites, 1% of the males and 6% of the females reported incest, whereas in Blacks, 5% of the males and 11% of the females reported incest (no test for statistical significance; Hernandez, Lodico, & DeClemente, 1993). Although only 9% of the males in the sample were Black, they represented 27% of the males who had been sexually abused. There are also studies showing underrepresentation of Black children for intrafamilial sexual abuse. In a sample of mostly low-income mothers of newborns recruited from North Carolina hospitals and health departments, significantly more White (40%) than Black (26%) mothers reported having experienced CSA (Herman-Giddens et al., 1998).

Studies of caught cases seem to confirm this last finding of an underrepresentation of Black families for intrafamilial CSA. In a study of incest in conservative Protestant families recruited through social service agencies, Black families constituted only 3% of the total sample despite their high level of contact with the social service agencies (Gil, 1988). Furthermore, in a group of CPS cases involving sexually abused children, Blacks and Whites were both significantly less likely than Hispanics to have been abused by parental figures (Feiring, Coates, & Taska, 2001).

Summary. In summary, there is evidence that (a) Black parents report higher levels of severe physical aggression against their children than White parents do, (b) the incidence of child neglect appears to be somewhat higher in African Americans than in families of other ethnicities, (c) physicians are more likely to report Black families than White families for suspected abuse, (d) Black families, especially impoverished Black families, are more likely to be reported to CPS than White families, especially for sexual abuse, and (e) once reported, Black families are less likely to show a recurrence of child abuse than White families.

Furthermore, the studies indicate that (a) approximately 10% of African American men and 25–30% of African American women

Box 7.1 The Case of Eva Smith

Eva Smith (pseudonym) is a Black woman who was sexually molested first by her great-uncle (ages 3 to 8), and then by her stepfather (ages 9 to 16). She became very fat, which helped to disguise her pregnancy at the age of 15. She got married at 17, while pregnant with her second child, and confessed to her husband that her stepfather was the father of her son. Her husband became increasingly physically and psychologically abusive, and by the age of 20, she was so depressed that she tried to kill herself. To escape from her husband, she turned him in to the military authorities because he was AWOL, and then started her life over. For many years, she went from one brief relationship to another until she met a man with whom she could have an enduring relationship. She says of her early experience: "[When] you go through sexual abuse you almost become a bottomless pit . . . of need. . . . I always enjoyed my sexuality . . . [but] I'd be out of my body and not even aware of it. Tactilely, I was very numb. . . . So when I began to have sex and these scenes would begin to bleed through, it would make me numb out."

SOURCE: Bass and Davis, 1988.

have experienced at least one incident of CSA, (b) CSA is relatively more likely to have been perpetrated by someone other than a member of the immediate family, and (c) generally, the rates of sexual abuse by family members are not significantly different across ethnic groups, although African Americans seem to be somewhat underrepresented for intrafamilial sexual abuse. Now consider the case of Eva Smith in Box 7.1. How are these points reflected in her case? Do any aspects of her case seem directly related to her ethnicity, or could her experiences have happened to any woman?

PREDICTORS AND CORRELATES

There is substantial evidence linking child maltreatment in Black communities to stressors at every level of the ecological model. In general, these stressors appear to be related directly and/or indirectly to an ongoing history of racism, discrimination, and stereotyping that burdens Black families with high levels of poverty, unemployment, anger, and despair.

Macrosystem Level

Although it is difficult to establish a direct empirical link between societal racism and

family violence, there is abundant evidence that various forms of racial discrimination have negative consequences, such as income disparity, poverty, drug abuse, and mental health problems (Belle & Doucet, 2003) that can, in turn, contribute to family violence. Based on the 1985 NFVS data, the profile of the modal severely abused child was an East Coast Black boy, 3 to 6 years old, abused by a mother with less than a high school education, living below the poverty line, with a blue-collar worker for a father, in a family of five children (Wolfner & Gelles, 1993). Consistent with the ecological model,

The responsibility for child maltreatment in Black families resides as much in the larger society as in the relationship among family members. The greater concentration of potential stressors in Black families is one of many consequences of social inequality which impair the quality of life for many Black families and children. (Hampton, 1987, p. 123)

More localized studies also show that poverty or lower socioeconomic status is a predictor of harsh physical aggression in African Americans (Bluestone & Tamis-LeMonde, 1999; Dietz, 2000; Eamon, 2001; Pinderhughes, Dodge, Bates, Peettit, & Zelli, 2000; Saunders,

Nelson, & Landsman, 1993), although in one study (Eamon), the relationship was weaker in African American than in Hispanic or White children. In addition, poverty was related to Black maltreatment cases reported in acute care hospitals (Forjuoh, 2000) and among infants in foster care (Needel & Barth, 1998).

The association of poverty and maltreatment in African American families has been demonstrated in national and local studies of neglect as well. A reanalysis of NIS data (Baird et al., 1999) revealed that neglect cases, which were predominantly African American, were characterized by poverty and the stress of being a single parent. In addition, far more African Americans than Whites had annual incomes less than $15,000 (30.4% vs. 11.6%), single female caretakers (52% vs. 18%), and three or more children in the home (14% vs. 9%)—all of which were risk factors for neglect. In another comparison of substantiated Black, White, and Hispanic maltreatment cases from the NIS files, Black families not only had the highest rate of reported and substantiated neglect, they were also the poorest families, and tended to have younger parents and children, mothers with fewer years of formal education, and households in severe economic adversity (Hampton, 1987). In a more local study, when neglectful mothers were compared with potentially neglectful mothers, the great majority of neglectful mothers, across all ethnicities, suffered high levels of poverty (Giovannoni & Billingsley, 1970). Finally, poverty also appears to play a role in African American CSA cases. In a study of children reported for sexual abuse in Indiana, the caretakers of the abused Black children were significantly more likely than the caretakers of abused White children to be on public assistance (39.7% vs. 17.1%; Tzeng & Schwarzin, 1990).

Exosystem Level

An analysis of the demographic variables associated with both physical child punishment and documented cases of child maltreatment in samples including African Americans provides further evidence of the role of processes derived from macrosystem level racism and inequality and operating at lower levels of the ecological model, such as the exosystem. For example, lower levels of education are predictive of corporal punishment (Dietz, 2000; Stolley & Szinovacz, 1997), and higher levels of education are predictive of using reasoning with children and "letting go" in a situation of potential conflict with a child (Bluestone & Tamis-LeMonde, 1999).

There is also considerable evidence that stress, an important exosystem variable, is associated with harsh discipline and child abuse within African American communities (e.g., Coohey & Braun, 1997; Daniel, Hampton, & Newberger, 1983; Gaines, Sandgrund, Green, & Power, 1978; Pinderhughes et al., 2000), as well as in the broader community. Among the predictors of identified cases of child maltreatment in Black families operating primarily at an exosystem level are inadequate housing (Giovannoni & Billingsley, 1970) and unemployment (Goetting, 1998). In one national longitudinal study, only age and number of people in the household were predictive of later self-reported child physical abuse—that is, abuse serious enough to have resulted in bruises, bed rest, or medical care of the child (Chaffin et al., 1996). However, age, number of people in the household, socioeconomic status (SES), and race at Time 1 were all associated with self-reports of later neglect. Specifically, participants who were younger, unmarried, non-White, from larger households, and lower in SES were more likely than their respective counterparts to acknowledge at least one type of neglect (i.e., leaving very young children alone for long periods of time, inadequately feeding or caring for children, or having a health professional suggest that the children were being neglected) at Time 2.

There are several other localized studies that underscore the role of exosystem variables in African American discipline and child maltreatment. For example, in Pennsylvania, maltreating African American families were more likely to live in dangerous neighborhoods than maltreating Caucasian families (Saunders et al., 1993). Members of the most impoverished minority neighborhoods in Chicago lacked social support networks, were unmarried, and were disconnected from their community (Garbarino & Kostelny, 1992). Also in Chicago, abusive mothers from a largely African

American sample had fewer emotional resources than the comparison sample (Coohey & Braun, 1997). In Boston, abusive Black mothers had significantly less geographic stability and significantly higher social isolation compared with the control sample (Daniel et al., 1983). Finally, in Texas, Black families had the highest county rate of maltreatment, and non-White maltreating families (particularly the Black families) had a higher incidence of poverty, fatherless homes, and working mothers. In addition, the socioeconomic status of counties was significantly related to White maltreatment rates, and degree of urbanization was predictive of maltreatment in the Black and Mexican American populations (Spearly & Lauderdale, 1983).

Microsystem Level

Microsystem factors have been extensively studied as predictors of African American child maltreatment in general, and of African American CSA and neglect in particular. Stressors at the microsystem level that are related to general maltreatment in samples with African Americans include maternal age (younger or older than comparison mothers; Connelly & Straus, 1992; Giovannoni & Billingsley, 1970; Saunders et al., 1993), larger number of children (Connelly & Straus; Needell & Barth, 1998), low-birth-weight babies or babies with abnormalities (Needell & Barth), a physically or psychologically absent parent (Brown, Cohen, Johnson, & Salzinger, 1998; Giovannoni & Billingsley; Rao et al., 1992; Saunders et al.), marital conflict (Eamon, 2001), and lack of a telephone (Goetting, 1988). Furthermore, in Black families, having daily contact with relatives was characteristic of adequate, but not neglectful, mothers (Giovannoni & Billingsley).

Among African American CSA cases, several microsystem variables have been shown to predict abuse. For example, in San Francisco, Black victims, in comparison to White and Hispanic victims, were the least likely to either be living with both parents or to have mothers as primary caretakers (Rao et al., 1992). Among sexually abused adolescent males, Black males were more likely than Latino males to have been abused by an immediate family member, for example, a father or brother (Moisan, Sanders-Phillips, & Moisan, 1997). Finally, among Indiana children reported for sexual abuse, the caretakers of Black children had a higher percentage of new or too many dependents in the home than caretakers of White children did; moreover, caretakers of abused Black female children had a significantly higher percentage of stressors than caretakers of Black male children or White children of either gender (Tzeng & Schwarzin, 1990).

Among neglected children, the microsystem level variable of the presence of a father figure has been shown to partially predict neglect among African Americans. Among five-year-old urban African American children at risk for maltreatment, the mere presence or absence of a father did not contribute significantly to the neglect of the children. However, in families with an identified and interviewed father, the longer he had been involved, the greater his sense of parenting efficacy, and the greater his involvement with household tasks, the lower the child neglect (Dubowitz, Black, Kerr, Starr, & Harrington, 2000).

Individual Level

Although studies of the predictors and correlates of child maltreatment in Black communities often focus on the contexts in which the maltreatment is embedded, there has also been some attention to the individual characteristics of the maltreaters. There is some evidence that within Black families, there is support for classic assumptions of the intergenerational transmission of violence (e.g., Coohey & Braun, 1997; Daniel et al., 1983). In addition, the role of maternal perceptions in mothers' treatment of children has been shown to predict maltreatment among Black mothers: In one study, spanking was more common among Blacks and among mothers who perceived their children as anxious (Stolley & Szinovacz, 1997), and in another study, having a less positive perception of the child mediated the contribution of ethnicity to harsh discipline (Pinderhughes et al., 2000). These parental perceptions can also have important implications for case decisions. In North Carolina, race, income, and education did not contribute significantly to the decision to place maltreated children in foster care, but parental perception of severe physical punishment as acceptable did (Runyan, Gould, Trost, & Loda, 1981).

CONSEQUENCES

Studies on the effects of child maltreatment on members of Black communities consist primarily of local community samples providing information concerning maltreatment, and local samples of individuals who were maltreated in childhood. Although the outcomes studied are exclusively individual level outcomes, experiences leading to problems, such as a tolerance for violence, alcohol/drug abuse, and mental illness, have impacts throughout the human ecosystem.

General Maltreatment Outcomes

Several researchers have examined several short-term effects of childhood maltreatment, including social interaction problems, risk-taking behaviors, and dissociation, in children and adolescents from all-Black or mixed-ethnicity samples. For example, in a case-comparison study of maltreated children (approximately one third African American) engaging in a structured play situation with nonmaltreated peers, the maltreated children were reluctant to "engage their partners"; that is, they showed early signs of social interaction problems (Camras & Rappaport, 1993). Furthermore, in a study of high school students in Minnesota, both physical and sexual abuse moderated the relationship between race and risk-taking behaviors of adolescent males (Hernandez et al., 1993). Specifically, Black adolescent males showed much higher levels of risk taking (e.g., drinking, using drugs, being sexually active, engaging in delinquent acts) than White adolescent males, but when history of sexual and physical abuse were included in the analyses, the race differences decreased substantially. In a case-comparison study of low-SES maltreated children (62% minority; 35% African American), sexually abused, physically abused, and neglected children were judged by their teachers to show

significantly higher levels of dissociation than their nonabused counterparts—levels that were in the psychopathological range (Macfie, Cicchetti, & Toth, 2001).

Studies of adult African American survivors of child maltreatment convey a picture of mental health problems. For example, among African American psychiatric outpatients, more than half of the female patients had experienced physical and/or sexual maltreatment in childhood, primarily from family members (Jenkins, Bell, Taylor, & Walker, 1989). The male patients had also experienced much physical and emotional abuse, but generally not from members of their nuclear families. In addition, among samples containing a sizeable portion of Blacks, child maltreatment has been found to be associated with depression (Meyerson, Long, Miranda, & Marx, 2002; Moisan et al., 1997; Roosa et al., 1999; Stein, Leslie, & Nyamathi, in press) and with alcohol and/or drug abuse (Jantzen, Ball, Leventhal, & Schottenfeld, 1998; Kilpatrick et al., 2000; Schuck & Widom, 2001; Stein et al.). There is also evidence that abuse during childhood is associated with additional victimization later in life (Jantzen et al.). Other negative outcomes that have been linked to child maltreatment in Blacks are problems in cognitive functioning (Mackner, Starr, & Black, 1997), physical health (McNutt, Carlson, Rose, & Robinson, 2002), and sexuality (Lodico et al., 1996; Wyatt & Riederle, 1994).

Neglect Outcomes

Although there have been few studies on the effects of neglect independent of physical child abuse in African American children, two important studies have addressed the issue. Among primarily low-income African American children, aged 3 months to 30 months, four diagnostic groups were identified—Neglect and Failure to Thrive (FTT), Neglect only, FTT only, and No Neglect or FTT (Mackner et al., 1997). Even at this very young age, children in the group characterized by both neglect and FTT were substantially below the other children in their cognitive performance. More recently, among a group of high-risk, predominantly African American urban preschoolers, there was no link between neglect and cognitive development in the three-year-olds, although the intellectual performance of children both at age three and age five was well below normal. Physical and environmental neglect were not related to the children's behavior or development, but psychological neglect was positively associated with internalizing (depressive) and externalizing (aggressive) behavior problems, even after controlling for maternal depression and sociodemographic risk variables related to poverty (Dubowitz, Papas, Black, & Starr, 2002).

Sexual Abuse Outcomes

Several physical and psychological outcomes of CSA, both short-term and long-term, have been studied among African Americans. One major outcome of child sexual assault is trauma. In one study of primarily Black children and adolescents seen at a sexual assault center in Pennsylvania, 25% showed evidence of physical trauma and approximately 2% also showed signs of psychological trauma. Pregnancy was diagnosed in 5 cases and 16 victims tested positively for gonorrhea (DeJong, Hervada, & Emmett, 1983).

Further evidence of psychological effects has been found among African American, sexually abused girls in general and in comparison to sexually abused girls of other ethnicities. For example, low-income, African American adolescent females who had been sexually abused scored significantly lower than their nonabused peers on self-esteem (Cecil & Matson, 2001). Among sexually abused girls in southern California, all of the abused girls, regardless of ethnicity, showed higher than normative rates of depression and anxiety, and lower global self-worth (Mennen, 1994, 1995). Finally, in comparison to Hispanic sexually abused girls, African American sexually abused girls seemed to fare worse, scoring lower on affective involvement, task accomplishment, and values and norms (Shaw, Lewis, Loeb, Rosado, & Rodriguez, 2001).

Consequences of CSA have also been found into the adulthood of these Black survivors. For example, in an African American community sample, adult females with a history of CSA scored significantly lower than their peers on

measures of self-esteem and mastery (Cecil & Matson, 2001). In a prospective study of African American adults originally seen as children in a city hospital emergency room for treatment of sexual abuse, multiple incidents of CSA were an important predictor of heavy alcohol use and binge drinking during adulthood (Jasinski, Williams, & Siegel, 2000). Among women in a Family Rehabilitation Program for mothers of drug-exposed newborns reported to CPS (63% African American), 24% of the women had experienced childhood sexual abuse, 45% had experienced childhood physical abuse, and an additional 18% had experienced both; the perpetrators in most of these cases were family members (Kang, 1999). The women who had been sexually abused were also more likely to be homeless, have extensive criminal involvement, use more cocaine or crack, and have poorer psychological functioning. There is also evidence that CSA is associated with later sexual revictimization (DeLillo et al., 2001; Urquiza & Goodlin-Jones, 1994).

Summary

In sum, outcome studies including African American samples indicate (a) childhood maltreatment appears to have numerous negative consequences, and (b) the consequences of child maltreatment are more similar than different across ethnic groups. Now, given what you have learned about the nature and reporting of child maltreatment in African American communities, and its correlates and outcomes, what would be your recommendations concerning the case in Box 7.2? Are you concerned over whether Shakira will be a "fit mother"? Would you argue that there are reasons the child should have been taken from her? Do you believe she should be allowed to keep and rear her child? Would you recommend any forms of intervention for Shakira and her daughter? What influenced your recommendations?

SUMMARY

It is difficult to determine exact rates of child maltreatment in African American families because of an apparent pattern of overreporting

---

Box 7.2   The Case of Shakira

Shakira, a 24-year-old African American, was born addicted to heroin and was maintained on methadone until the age of 7. She had her first baby when she was 14, and sent him to live with his biological father, a drug dealer, because she wanted to party with her new boyfriend, also a drug dealer. She never saw the child again; he was fatally shot in the cross fire of gang violence when he was 7. After becoming pregnant again at the age of 21, Shakira decided she wanted to keep her baby, so she entered and successfully completed drug treatment. Her daughter, who is now 2, stays in a day care center at the facility where Shakira works. Shakira's current boyfriend is presently in treatment for drug abuse and she's waiting to see how he does before deciding whether she will marry him.

SOURCE: Waters, Roberts, and Morgan, 1997.

---

abuse in these families. Even though, as discussed in chapter 6, African Americans show a greater acceptance of corporal punishment than members of majority cultures, self-report responses generally do not reveal significant ethnic differences in minor physical punishment of children. However, Blacks report higher levels of severe child assault than Whites do. Reports from the National Incidence Studies indicate no overall Black/White differences in child maltreatment, although reanalyses of the data have shown a tendency of medical personnel to overreport African Americans for abuse, and other analyses show patterns of underreporting as well as overreporting of African Americans, depending on the type of abuse suspected. For example, in general, Black and White families seem to have similar rates of intrafamilial sexual abuse, but Black adolescents may be more vulnerable to extrafamilial sexual abuse—perhaps because of microsystem or exosystem factors associated with poverty and a devalued status.

Macrosystem factors, particularly poverty, seem to play a large role in African American child maltreatment, and they also seem to play out in stresses at every level of the ecological model. Among the principal individual factors contributing to child maltreatment are maternal views on the acceptability of severe punishment.

Consequences of maltreatment include psychological and sexual problems, substance abuse, and behavior problems. How do these findings relate to what you learned about family violence in Native American cultures? What similarities and differences do you see? If we want to eliminate child abuse in this country, do you think there are approaches that might work equally well in each set of communities? Are there ways in which we need to approach the problem of family violence differently in the two sets of communities? If so, what might they be?

Given what you have learned about family violence in Native American communities and in the country at large, what do you expect to learn about adult maltreatment in African American communities? Are there commonalities in cultural values that would lead you to expect some commonalities in incidence rates? In predictors and correlates? In outcomes? Or, do you think that macrosystem forces, such as poverty and oppression, and exosystem forces, such as cultural insensitivity in social service agencies, may override cultural differences? What differences, if any, do you think there might be between the macrosystem, exosystem, microsystem, and individual factors associated with spousal and elder maltreatment in African American communities, compared with child maltreatment in those communities?

8

AFRICAN AMERICAN ADULT MALTREATMENT

Extreme abuse from a husband to a wife:

- *"When a man continues to beat on his wife or verbally abuse her."* (63-year-old African American female)
- *"Husband beats wife for not meeting his expectations."* (24-year-old African American male)
- *"Physically beating her and degrading her in public."* (20-year-old black, Caribbean American, African American female)

Extreme abuse from a wife to a husband:

- *"When she disrespect or serve his needs at her own pace."* (63-year-old African American female)
- *"Wife hits husband when he comes in late."* (24-year-old African American male)
- *"Chopping off a man's genitalia with a machete."* (20-year-old black, Caribbean American, African American female)

Extreme abuse from an adult to an elderly parent:

- *"When we become physical or verbal or deny food."* (63-year-old African American female)
- *"Man pushes mother around because she was in his room."* (24-year-old African American male)

These responses are representative of the answers given by self-identified African American/Black respondents asked to describe extreme forms of spousal and elder abuse. What themes do you see in these responses? Do there seem to be any patterns that might be related to the historical and cultural experiences of African Americans? Do you observe any differences between these responses and those of other ethnicities? Any similarities? What experiences of each ethnic group could account for these differences and similarities?

SPOUSAL MALTREATMENT

Scope of the Problem

The media in the United States have given much attention to violence in Black communities, and within the research literature, there is ample evidence that Black violence is primarily intraracial—that is, Black against Black. One of the most compelling questions with regard to African American violence, in general and in the family, is to what extent poverty, unemployment, and other products of racism are the true causal agents of the violence. A related question is to what extent historical macrosystem forces have had an impact on functioning at the individual level. Table 8.1 summarizes studies providing information on the prevalence of spousal violence in African American communities.

Wife Abuse

In general, rates of spousal aggression against Black wives range from around 7% for severe physical aggression (Hampton & Gelles, 1994) to over 70% for verbal/symbolic aggression (Straus & Sweet, 1992). Moreover, there is evidence that Blacks may commit more physical wife abuse than members of other ethnicities. In one nationally representative sample, the rate of male-to-female physical partner violence in Blacks (23%) was significantly higher than the rates for Whites (11.5%) and Hispanics (17%; Caetano, Cunradi, Clark, & Schaefer, 2000). Department of Justice (DOJ) statistics indicate that in 1996, rates of nonlethal intimate violence were highest against Black women, women aged 16 to 24, women in the lowest income categories, and women residing in cities (Chaiken, 1998). However, a simple comparison of prevalence rates neglects the confounding role of social class with ethnicity—in most cases, the ethnic differences diminish or disappear following controls for sociodemographic variables (Cazenave & Straus, 1979; Coker, Smith, McKeown, & King, 2000). Moreover, the higher rates of wife abuse for Blacks may be only for physical violence; rates of verbal/symbolic aggression are high (~75%) in all ethnicities, and unrelated to race and socioeconomic status (Straus & Sweet).

Among the local community studies with convenience samples, a more complex picture of ethnic differences emerges. Some investigators (e.g., Bauer, Rodriguez, & Perez-Stable, 2000) have found no difference between White and African American women in the prevalence of abuse. Other investigators (e.g., Lockhart, 1985) also found no significant ethnic differences, except within the middle class, where Black women reported more husband-to-wife violence than White women. Still others (e.g., Weinbaum et al., 2001) have found that overall, African American women experienced

significantly higher rates of intimate partner violence than White women, but after controlling for ethnicity, variables such as low income, low education, and poor physical and mental health emerged as significant predictors of the intimate violence. Finally, in one study, when controlling for neighborhood-level variables, such as average per capita income and unemployment rates, the risk of partner-perpetrated physical violence was actually significantly higher in White than in Black women (O'Campo et al., 1995). Review the information on measures and samples in Table 8.1. How might methodological and geographical differences across studies, including differences in sample types, contribute to the differences in findings?

Several studies of caught cases of spousal violence also show conflicting data on relative frequency of wife abuse among African Americans versus other ethnicities. For example, there were no significant race differences in levels of self-reported (preincarceration) intimate violence in violent men in Kentucky state correctional facilities (Logan, Walker, Staton, & Luekefeld, 2001). Similarly, the racial distribution of men in Denver, Houston, and Dallas batterer programs was consistent with their respective proportions in the population of those cities. However, in Pittsburgh, batterers who were men of color were disproportionately African American (Gondolf, 1999). Consistent with the Pittsburgh results, Black spousal offenders outnumbered White spousal offenders in the U.S. Army (Newby et al., 2000). Similarly higher relative rates of battering among African Americans were found in studies of battered women in shelters. For example, in a Virginia domestic violence shelter, a disproportionately high number of women and children were Black (Taylor & Hammond, 1987), and among women in Texas shelters, significantly more Black women reported having a weapon used against them (Gondolf, Fisher, & McFerron, 1988).

Husband Abuse

As is true of the majority culture and Native American Indian groups, little information is available on husband abuse in African American communities. However, there is evidence that the rates of husband abuse can be quite high.

(Text continues on page 134)

Table 8.1 Spousal Maltreatment in African American Communities

Study	Sample Description	Definition/Measure of Abuse	Findings
National Studies—Reported Cases			
U.S. Department of Justice Reports on Intimate Partner Homicide (Chaiken, 1998)	All intimate partner homicides between 1976 and 1996	Killed by an intimate partner	Rates of intimate murder declined an annual average of • 8% among Black males • 5% among Black females • 4% among White males • 1% among White females
FBI Supplemental Homicide Reports (Mercy & Saltzman, 1989)	16,595 spousal homicides in United States between 1976 and 1985	Killed by an intimate partner	• Blacks accounted for 45.4% of all spouse homicide victims (representation in population not provided). • Black rate of spousal homicide = 8.4 times the White rate. • White wives were nearly twice as likely to be killed as White husbands. • Black wives were only slightly less likely to be killed than Black husbands.
Regional Studies—Reported Cases			
McFarlane, Campbell, Sharps, & Watson (2002)	437 cases of attempted or completed female homicide and 384 identified abused women as controls from 10 cities	Police and medical examiner records used to identify attempted and completed femicide cases; interviews with attempted femicide victims and proxies for completed femicide victims	Attempted/completed femicides: • 11 Black, 4 White, and 5 Latina women. • Black women more than three times as likely to be attempted/completed femicide victims as White women. Abuse during pregnancy reported by • 7.7% of abused controls • 25.8% of attempted femicides • 22.7% of completed femicides
Rodriguez, McLoughlin, Nah, & Campbell (2001)	375 women victims of interpersonal abuse from hospital outpatient clinics in San Francisco, CA, in 1997; mostly lower class	Computer-assisted phone interviews; abuse questions adapted from Abuse Assessment Screen	• Of this sample, 37% were White, 33% were African American, and 29% were Latina (representation in population not provided).
Newby et al. (2000)	Initial substantiated cases of enlisted U.S. Army spouse abusers, 1989–1997	Substantiated cases listed in Army Central Registry between 1989 and 1997	• 13,677 (40% of cases) White men and 17,910 (52.4% of cases) Black men had substantiated cases of spousal abuse. • 801 (2.3% of cases) White women and 1,812 (5.3% of cases) Black women had substantiated cases of spousal abuse.

(Continued)

Table 8.1 Continued

Study	Sample Description	Definition/Measure of Abuse	Findings
			• Overall race distribution in Army = 61% White, 28% Black. • For each year, the number of Black offenders outnumbered the White offenders. • The highest rates and greatest differences by race were in the youngest age group (18–21). • There were significantly more Black than White offenders in every age group except 42–46. • The only referral source referring significantly more Blacks than Whites was the law enforcement personnel.
McCarroll et al. (1999)	61,827 confirmed cases of spouse abuse in the U.S. Army (1989–1997)	Reports in the U.S. Army Central Registry	• 47% of all victims and 50% of all spousal abuse offenders were Black. • Average % of married Black soldiers during this period was 28%.
Bailey et al. (1997)	Case control study of 123 female in-home suicide victims and 143 female in-home homicide victims in 3 counties (in Tennessee, Washington, and Ohio)	Homicide records	• Homicide victims were disproportionately Black. • 55% were murdered in context of quarrel by husband, lover, or close relative.
O'Keefe (1994)	121 battered women in shelters in both urban and rural areas; 37% Hispanic, 42% White, and 21% Black (geographic location of shelters not given)	Conflict Tactics Scales	• No significant race differences in reported frequency of husband-to-wife and wife-to-husband physical aggression.
Gondolf, Fisher, & McFerron (1988)	5,708 clients in Texas battered women's shelters; 57% White, 15% Black, and 29% Hispanic	Standardized intake interview	• 17% of Whites and 11% of Blacks reported being grabbed, pushed, and/or slapped. • 15% of Whites and 17% of Blacks reported being punched. • 28% of Whites and 24% of Blacks reported being kicked. • No ethnic differences were found in kinds and extent of abuse. • More Black women (48%) reported having a weapon used against them than White and Hispanic women (39%). • Hispanics stayed longer in battering relationships.

Study	Sample Description	Definition/Measure of Abuse	Findings
Roberts (1987)	234 abusive men who came in contact with prosecutor's office and municipal court in Illinois	Files of Domestic Abuse Unit of county prosecutor's office, motor vehicle records, and Computerized Criminal Histories	• 126 (53.9%) men with charges of battering filed against them were White; 104 (44%) were Black (representation in population not provided).
Taylor & Hammond (1987)	2,337 residents in Virginia battered women's shelter, 1984–1985	Shelter records	• Black women and children were 28.1% of the shelter population, but only 19% of the state population.
Regional Studies—Self-Report			
Harrykissoon, Rickert, & Wiemann (2002)	Prospective study of 570 adolescent girls (219 Mexican American, 182 African American, and 169 White) during 24 months postpartum	Abuse Assessment Screen	When controlling for SES and other sociodemographic variables • Minority women were at higher risk for intimate partner violence during first 6 months after delivery. • No significant ethnic group differences were found in intimate partner violence at 12 and 24 months postpartum. • White women were at significantly higher risk at 18 months postpartum.
Campbell, Campbell, King, Parker, & Ryan (2001)	504 low-income African American women aged 14–42 from Detroit, MI, Springfield, MA, Baltimore, MD, and Tampa, FL	Index of Spouse Abuse	• 38% reported physical abuse. • 33% reported psychological abuse.
Logan, Walker, Staton, & Luekefeld (2001)	500 males incarcerated for a variety of crimes at four Kentucky State Correctional facilities; 53% White, 44% African American; classified as low violent, moderate violent, and extreme violent	2-hour face-to-face interview including Conflict Tactics Scales	• No significant ethnic differences were found across violence groups.
Bauer, Rodriguez, & Perez-Stable (2000)	Random sample of 734 women patients, aged 18 to 46, at	Abuse Assessment Screen	• Overall, 15% reported recent intimate partner violence. • Overall lifetime prevalence: 51%.

(Continued)

131

Table 8.1 Continued

Study	Sample Description	Definition/Measure of Abuse	Findings
	three public hospital primary care clinics in San Francisco; 31% White, 31% African American, and 36% Latina		• No difference was found between White and African American women in prevalence of abuse. • Significantly fewer Latinas reported recent abuse.
Beadnell, Baker, Morrison, & Knox (2000)	167 low-income women at risk for HIV and STD; recruited through media campaign targeting areas with concentrations of low-income women and higher STD rates or referred by community agencies and clinics providing services to low-income women	Self-report surveys; were asked if steady partner (a) made them feel bad about themselves, (b) tried to control them, (c) threatened to physically hurt them, or (d) hit, pushed, shoved, kicked, slapped, or hurt in other ways	• African American women: 31% reported no abuse; 51% reported emotional abuse (Items a–c); 19% reported physical abuse (Item d). • White women: 52% reported no abuse; 35% reported emotional abuse; 13% reported physical abuse. • When employment and education variables were controlled for, ethnicity did not predict abuse.
Coker, Smith, McKeown, & King (2000)	1,401 women attending family practice clinics in South Carolina, 1997–1998; 37.2% White, 62.8% Black	Index of Spouse Abuse; Women's Experience With Battering Scale; Abuse Assessment Screen	• 772 (55.5%) had experienced recent partner violence; 20.2% were experiencing it currently. • White race significantly positively associated with increased likelihood of current violence but not sexual abuse. • White race significantly positively associated with battering or emotional abuse without physical or sexual violence in any intimate relationship.
Browne, Miller, & Maguin (1999)	150 women entering maximum security prison population in New York; 49% African American, 25% Hispanic, and 12% White	Conflict Tactics Scales, physical aggression subscale	• 75% reported severe physical abuse in intimate relationships. • No breakdown by race was provided.
McFarlane, Parker, & Soeken (1995)	1,203 White, Black, and Hispanic urbanized, poor pregnant women (ethnically stratified) from urban public health prenatal clinics in Houston and Baltimore	Conflict Tactics Scales, Index of Spouse Abuse, Danger Assessment Scale	• 16% of women experienced physical abuse. • Rates of abuse were lower for Hispanics (14%) relative to Blacks and Whites (20%). • Severity of abuse was less for Hispanics and Blacks relative to Whites.

Study	Sample Description	Definition/Measure of Abuse	Findings
O'Campo et al. (1995)	182 low-income pregnant and 6-months postpartum women from Baltimore (93% African American)	Conflict Tactics Scales	• When neighborhood variables were controlled for, the risk of partner-perpetrated physical violence in the White women was nine times the risk for Black women.
Lockhart (1991)	155 Black women and 152 White women from three socioeconomic classes in Tallahassee, FL, recruited through church and other groups	Conflict Tactics Scales	• 35.48% of Black women and 35.53% of White women reported some husband-to-wife violence. • 3.6 violent incidents reported by Black women and 4.3 incidents reported by White women. • No significant race differences were found, except more Black middle-class women (45.6%) than White middle-class women (29.8%) reported husband-to-wife violence.
Fagan, Stewart, & Hansen (1983)	155 African American and 152 White women	Conflict Tactics Scales	• No significant race differences were found in overall severe violence against wives. • Whites reported greater likelihood of partners' hitting them or using knife or gun on them. • More middle-class Black than White women reported being victims of violence. • Wife-to-husband violence was not analyzed.

NOTE: For information on African American spousal abuse according to the U.S. Department of Justice (Rennison, 2001a, 2001b; Rennison & Welchans, 2000), the National Violence Against Women Survey (Coker et al., 2002; Tjaden & Thoennes, 2000), the National Family Violence Surveys of 1975 and 1985 (Bachman, 1992; Cazenave & Straus, 1979; Hampton & Gelles, 1994; Straus & Gelles, 1986, 1990a; Straus, Gelles, & Steinmetz, 1980; Straus & Smith, 1990b; Straus & Sweet, 1992), the National Comorbidity Survey (Kessler et al., 2001), the 1995 National Study of Couples (Caetano, Cunradi, Clark, & Schaefer, 2000), the 1998 California Women's Health Survey (Weinbaum et al., 2001), and Neff, Holamon, and Schulter (1995), please see Table 3.2. For information on African American spousal abuse according to Torres et al. (2000), please see Table 11.1.

For example, in national community samples, rates of violence against Black husbands ranged from 8% for severe assaults (Cazenave & Straus, 1990) to 30% for overall female-to-male partner violence (Caetano et al., 2001). For most of the specified forms of partner violence, the wives self-reported perpetrating more acts of aggression against their husbands than the husbands reported perpetrating against their wives, independent of ethnicity (Caetano et al., 2001). In addition, there is other evidence that Black husbands may be subject to more physical abuse than White husbands: In one study of adults in South Carolina, 19.8% of the Black men reported intimate partner violence in comparison to 10% of the White men (Coker, Derrick, Lumpkin, Aldrich, & Oldendick, 2000).

Violence against Black husbands can lead to both injuries and death. An analysis of the FBI's Supplemental Homicide Reports from 1976 to 1985 revealed that Black husbands were victims of spousal homicide at a higher rate than Black wives or White spouses of either sex (Mercy & Saltzman, 1989). West (2003) has suggested that Black women may be using aggression against their partners in self-defense or in retaliation for abuse perpetrated against them. Although research specific to husband abuse in African American communities still needs to be done, others (e.g., Hines & Malley-Morrison, 2001) have shown that in the United States overall, self-defense is not the primary motive for the majority of female-perpetrated violence.

Predictors and Correlates

As is typical of research on risk factors for spousal abuse in other cultures, the focus in the African American literature is on macrosystem factors (particularly factors related to racism and discrimination) and individual factors, such as drug use and early exposure to violence. However, a few studies have addressed microsystem and exosystem variables.

Macrosystem Level

Economic Variables. Poverty has been identified as a risk factor for spousal abuse in the nation at large, and appears to be a major risk factor within African American communities

specifically. An indirect approach to the role of poverty in African American spousal violence comes from national self-report studies in which efforts were made to control statistically for the contribution of socioeconomic status to differences among ethnic groups. For the most part, findings from studies with African American respondents are consistent with other studies indicating that relative economic status is an important predictor of spousal violence. In the initial analyses of data from the first National Family Violence Surveys (NFVS), there were higher rates of spousal violence in Blacks than in Whites (Straus, Gelles, & Steinmetz, 1980). However, after controlling for income, Black respondents reported lower levels of spousal slapping than Whites at every income level except the poverty level ($6,000–$11,999; Cazenave & Straus, 1990). Similarly, in the original analysis of the National Violence Against Women Survey (NVAW), African American ethnicity was a significant risk factor for intimate partner violence against women (Tjaden & Thoennes, 2000). However, after controlling for sociodemographic variables, race was no longer a significant predictor of violence (Coker et al., 2002).

A number of investigators examining risk factors for spousal violence in African American and mixed ethnicity samples have identified both race and income as predictors of spousal violence, without determining whether ethnic differences in spousal violence are reduced when controlling for income. For example, an analysis of DOJ statistics showed that nonlethal intimate violence was higher in Blacks than in Whites, and that intimate violence against women was higher for low-income women and women living in urban areas (Chaiken, 1998); this study did not, however, examine the relative contribution of the variables. Similarly, the National Crime Victimization survey showed that between 1993 and 1998, Blacks were victimized by intimate partners at significantly higher rates than persons of any other race; specifically, Black females experienced intimate partner violence at a rate 35% higher than White females, and Black males experienced intimate partner violence at a rate approximately 62% higher than White males (Rennison & Welchans, 2000).

Significant predictors of intimate partner violence included (a) women living in households with low annual household incomes, (b) persons living in rental housing rather than owning homes, and (c) women living in urban areas (Rennison & Welchans). Blacks are over-represented in all of these groups in this country (McKinnon, 2003).

In one analysis of the 1985 NFVS data (Hampton & Gelles, 1994), lower-income families had higher rates (14.4%) of wife battery than upper-income families (5.8%), and low income was the strongest predictor of level of violence in Black families. Furthermore, among Black families, those in which the husband was unemployed had the highest rate of wife abuse, and although there were no ethnic differences in rates of wife assault in families with incomes below $10,000 per year, there were higher rates of wife abuse in Black families with incomes over $10,000. However, like most other investigations of macrosystem contributions to family violence, this study did not consider the role of differences in real income (i.e., income after taking into consideration the effects of inflation on purchasing power) or other economic factors differentiating Black and White families.

Some researchers (e.g., Krieger, Rowley, Herman, Avery, & Phillips, 1993) have argued that there are major problems with the common practice of simply "adjusting" statistically for social class to determine whether observed differences between races can be accounted for by socioeconomic variables. In particular, this practice presumes that the socioeconomic positions of Black and White families within the same social class are roughly comparable. However, as Krieger et al. explained, many studies discount the validity of this assumption. Specifically, (a) within the same occupational categories, Blacks typically earn less and have lower status than Whites, (b) Black professionals generally live in less affluent neighborhoods than White professionals, (c) Black families below the poverty line are much more apt to be concentrated in impoverished neighborhoods than White families below the poverty line, and (d) the Black poor are, on average, much poorer than the White poor. Moreover, wealth is far more unequally distributed in society than is

annual income: Although the average income of White families is two to three times higher than the average income of Black families, the average net worth of White families is 10 times higher—for example, through ownership of real estate and other property, investments, and so forth (Belle & Doucet, 2003). In addition, White families are more likely than Black families to own cars and homes, which are important predictors of well-being and social support, and which, in turn, appear to reduce the likelihood of family violence.

This broader conception of wealth and relative status has important implications for the evaluation of studies purporting to find that socioeconomic variables do not help explain differences between Black and White couples in rates of spousal violence. For example, in their study of spousal abuse cases in the U.S. Army Central Registry, Newby et al. (2000) held that because all of the offenders were in the Army, unemployment and SES were reasonably controlled and, therefore, did not help explain the significantly higher number of Black than White offenders. What is your view of this? Can we assume that in the U.S. Army, all issues of sociodemographic status have been automatically equalized between Blacks and Whites?

Unemployment. Although unemployment may not be a risk factor for spousal violence in active military personnel, it has been identified as a risk factor in several studies of community and clinical samples. Unemployment was, for example, a predictor of intimate violence against women (62% Black) attending family practice clinics in South Carolina (Coker, Smith, et al., 2000), and against the wives of men (44.4% Black) charged with battering in the Marion county prosecutor's office in Indianapolis (Roberts, 1987).

Disparities in Status. Disparities between husbands and wives in education, income, ethnicity (i.e., interracial relationships) and employment status can be considered problems at both macrosystem and microsystem levels. They are macrosystem issues because they reflect the structural forces keeping Black men in low-paying jobs. However, disparities in status between husbands and wives can play themselves

Box 8.1   Possible Risk of Firearms

My husband never actually hit the kids, but he had a gun. He'd leave it lying around and then make comments about how "tragic" it would be if the gun accidentally went off or if one of the kids played with it and accidentally killed himself. I was terrified to leave the house. I didn't want to come home and discover my three-year-old had picked the gun up off the coffee table and blown his brains out.

SOURCE: White (1995).

out in violence within the microsystem. In an analysis of NVAW data, a significant risk factor for violence against women was having a higher education level than their partners (Tjaden & Thoennes, 2000). In a study of African American women participating in the UCLA Women and Family Project, relationship conflict was associated not only with low income, but also with income differentials between the women's income and the total household income (Wyatt, Axelrod, Chin, Carmona, & Loeb, 2000).

Firearms. An important macrosystem variable contributing to severe spousal violence in many African American communities is the ready availability of firearms and cultural resistance to gun control. For example, NVAW (Tjaden & Thoennes, 2000) showed that the use of a weapon was a risk factor for injury to female victims of intimate partner rape and to male victims of intimate physical assault. Furthermore, approximately 25% of the battered Black and White women in one study reported that their partners had used a gun on them (Joseph, 1997).

Firearms may be particularly problematic for members of some Black communities as compared to other ethnic communities. For instance, in a study of battered women's shelters in Texas, the different racial groups reported receiving comparable types of physical, verbal, sexual, and child abuse. However, more Black women (48%) than White and Hispanic women (39%) reported having a weapon used against them (Gondolf et al., 1988). The FBI Supplementary Homicide Reports revealed that among the nearly 52,000 men and women murdered by

an intimate between 1976 and 1996, 65% were killed with a firearm (Chaiken, 1998)—and a disproportionate number of these intimate homicides were of Black men and women (Mercy & Saltzman, 1989). Finally, among the violent deaths to women in their homes in three states (Tennessee, Washington, and Ohio), homicide victims were disproportionately African American, and having one or more guns in the home was a major risk factor (Bailey et al., 1997). Consider the case described in Box 8.1. Does it seem apparent that in this case gun ownership creates a serious risk of injury and death in the family?

Gun ownership is likely to be higher among Black than among White women, possibly because of the Black women's fear of crime and belief that they are responsible for the safety of everyone in their household (Ray & Smith, 1991). Whether in self-defense or from rage during a domestic argument, Black women sometimes use these guns against their male partners. Support for this proposition comes from a study in which Black men were more often threatened with a knife or gun, or assaulted with a knife or gun, by their intimate partners than were White men (Caetano, Cunradi, et al., 2000). However, conflicting results come from a sample of White, Hispanic, and Black abused pregnant women: Almost half of these women reported that their partner owned or had access to a gun, but there were no significant differences in gun access across ethnic groups (McFarlane, Soeken, et al., 1998). Nonetheless, because of the general frequency with which guns are involved in domestic violence cases, the Lautenberg Law (the Domestic Violence Offender Gun Ban) was passed in

1996 to keep guns out of the hands of abusers. According to Eleanor Smeal, president of the Feminist Majority,

> During the first year that this law was in effect, more than 2,000 gun permits were denied because applicants had previous domestic violence convictions. However, we know that 2,000 was just the tip of the iceberg. One half of all 911 calls are related to domestic violence. Allowing convicted abusers to possess guns invites deadly abuse. (Feminist Daily News Wire, 2002, ¶ 3)

Summary. The emphasis on macrosystem contributions to violence with Black communities is not meant to minimize the severity of the problems of spousal violence, which is well recognized and acknowledged within those communities. As one African American woman says,

> When sisters take their shoes off and start talking about what's happening, the first thing we cry about is violence—battering and sexual abuse. The number one issue for most of our sisters is violence. Same thing for their daughters, whether they are twelve or four. We have to look at how violence and sexism go hand in hand. We have to stop it because violence is the training ground for us. (Avery, 1989, as cited in White, 1995, p. xiii)

The point is that a propensity for violence is not inherent in African American biology, cultural heritage, or a generalized personal character. Instead, it is largely influenced by macrosystem forces that subject African Americans disproportionately to such known risk factors as low income, unemployment, inadequate education, and crowding. These macrosystem forces are aggravated by other macrosystem characteristics, such as the ready availability of weapons and alcohol in poor urban neighborhoods (Gyimah-Brempong, 2001). Moreover, consistent with the ecological model, these macrosystem forces interact with and affect processes at the exo- and microsystem levels, and in the developing individual.

Exosystem Level

Neighborhood Variables. One of the most direct tests of an association between characteristics of

neighborhoods (e.g., poverty) and intimate partner violence comes from the Black, White, and Hispanic respondents of the National Alcohol Survey. Among couples residing in census tracts where more than 20% of the population lived below the federal poverty line, residence in an impoverished neighborhood was a significant predictor of both male-to-female and female-to-male intimate violence in Black couples (Caetano, Cunradi, et al., 2000). Similarly, in the National Study of Couples, Black couples living in impoverished neighborhoods were three times more likely than Black couples living in nonimpoverished neighborhoods to be involved in male-to-female partner violence (Caetano et al., 2001). Finally, neighborhood characteristics, such as low median income, frequent changes in residence, and poor education, were all predictive of intentional injuries to women at three hospital emergency departments in Philadelphia (Grisso et al., 1999).

A study designed to bridge the gap between micro- and macrolevel approaches to spousal violence assessed both individual level demographic variables and neighborhood variables among low-income women from the Baltimore area (O'Campo et al., 1995). Not only did several neighborhood-level variables contribute to the risk of violence from partners, but they also modified the relationship between the individual variables and the risk of violence. Neighborhood variables included average per capita income, ratio of home ownerships to rentals, unemployment rates, and per capita crime rates. Living in neighborhoods with the lowest per capita income was associated with four times the risk of partner violence in comparison to neighborhoods with the highest per capita income. Living in a high unemployment neighborhood was also associated with increased risk of partner violence. There was no ethnic difference in risk of abuse when individual variables only were used as predictors. However, when neighborhood-level variables were added to the predictive equation, the risk of partner-perpetrated physical violence was nine times greater for White women than for Black women (O'Campo et al.).

Social Support. Only a few (mostly small) local studies have addressed the role of social support as a protective factor, and lack of social support as a risk factor, for spousal violence in African American communities. Among African Americans associated with a university in North Carolina, having social support from friends was negatively associated with physical abuse in the spousal relationship as reported by Black males, and having persons in whom to confide was negatively correlated with being subjected to spousal psychological abuse in Black females (Huang & Gunn, 2001). Furthermore, social support has been found to reduce the likelihood of abused Black women attempting suicide (Kaslow et al., 2002).

Microsystem Level

Several characteristics of victims have been identified as risk factors for spousal violence in Black couples, including victims' alcohol abuse (Caetano et al., 2001; Mann, 1991), mental health problems such as depression (Hampton & Gelles, 1994; Huang & Gunn, 2001; Rennison & Welchans, 2000), and young age (Cazenave & Straus, 1990; Kessler et al., 2001; Newby et al., 2000; Roberts, 1987; Straus & Sweet, 1992). African American women who were abused by their parents during childhood are at heightened risk for abuse from intimate partners (Wyatt et al., 2000), as are women who grew up in homes where their fathers abused their mothers (Coker, Smith, et al., 2000).

Household composition is another microsystem variable that appears to play a role in the level of spousal violence. For example, the more children and nonnuclear family members in the African American home, the lower the level of spousal slapping (Cazenave & Straus, 1990). One final microsystem variable that may contribute to conflict—with the potential of escalating into spousal violence—involves differences between partners in their views on the role of Black men as providers for the family. As noted in the macrosystem section, historical and institutional factors can play themselves out in the microsystem. Black women have often been able to achieve a higher educational and occupational status than Black men, and higher-status Black women often blame their husbands for not achieving an equal level of success (Dixon, 1998). These women may assume their partners are neither motivated enough nor willing enough to take jobs they see as beneath them, and are too ready to blame their problems on White society—assumptions that can lead to considerable conflict within the household. The presence of conflict is, in turn, a predictor of violence—for example, most Black spousal homicide takes place in the context of an argument (Mercy & Saltzman, 1989).

Individual Level

Substance Abuse. There is substantial evidence that substance abuse is associated with spousal violence within many African American families. Support for this association spans national and local studies with community and clinical samples. For example, there is evidence from a nationally representative sample that drinking during an episode of intimate violence is more frequent in Black partners, independent of gender, than in Hispanic and non-Hispanic Whites (Caetano et al., 2001). Other survey studies with community-based samples (e.g., Kessler et al., 2001) have provided further support for a statistically significant association between substance abuse and perpetration of female partner violence in African American communities. This association has also been found in community samples in Texas (Neff et al., 1995) and North Carolina (Huang & Gunn, 2001), charity hospital patients in Louisiana (Ernst, Nick, Weiss, Houry, & Mills, 1997), family practice clinic patients in South Carolina (Coker, Smith, et al., 2000), battered women's samples (Willson et al., 2000), and emergency room patients in Philadelphia (Grisso et al., 1999). Illicit drug use by anyone in the household has also been associated with (a) the intimate homicide of women who were mostly African American (Bailey et al., 1997), (b) the battering of Black women by identified offenders in North Carolina (Hutchison, 1999) and Indiana (Roberts, 1987), (c) intimate violence by incarcerated men (44% African American) in Kentucky facilities (Logan et al., 2001), and (d) the abuse of women (21% African American) in battered women's shelters in Texas (O'Keefe, 1994).

Although there appears to be little research focusing specifically on the predictors and correlates of Black women's violence against their partners, alcohol use has received some attention. For example, in the Ninth National Alcohol Survey study (Caetano, Cunradi, et al., 2000), nearly 25% of Black women reported drinking during incidents in which they perpetrated violence against their partners, compared to 14.7% of White and 3.8% of Hispanic women. This association between drinking patterns and perpetration of intimate violence was significant in Black, but not White, women. Alcohol use was not related to perpetration of violence against partners by the Black men (Caetano, Cunradi, et al.).

Violence in Family of Origin. Violence in the family of origin is also an important predictor of spousal violence in African American families as well as in the majority culture. The 1975 NFVS (Hampton & Gelles, 1994) revealed that Black respondents who had been hit by their mothers or had observed interparental violence during their teen years had significantly higher rates of husband-to-wife violence. Moreover, respondents who had been hit as a teen by either parent were twice as likely to have been in households where there was severe violence during the previous year. Among both male and female African Americans in North Carolina, the more violence they had observed between their parents while growing up, the greater the likelihood of perpetrating physical aggression in the spousal relationship (Huang & Gunn, 2001). In addition, positive associations between violence in the family of origin and violence in current or past intimate relationships have been found in hospital emergency room patients (Ernst et al., 1997). Finally, in a sample of predominantly African American men in counseling for spousal abuse, a history of childhood trauma (sexual abuse, physical abuse, and observed interparental abuse) was significantly positively associated with dissociative symptoms (e.g., amnesia, multiple personality disorder), which, in turn, were significantly associated with the degree of violence perpetration against wives (Simoneti, Scott, & Murphy, 2000).

Consequences of Spousal Maltreatment

Death

National homicide figures on death—the most severe outcome of any form of

maltreatment—are available from the DOJ. In 1996, for example, the rate of intimate homicide for Black females was 4.51 per 1,000 and the rate for Black males was 2.83—significantly higher than the rates for White females (1.34) and White males (0.36). Black rates of intimate homicide decreased much more dramatically between 1976 and 1996 than did White rates (Chaiken, 1998), greatly reducing the gap between the races in intimate homicide. However, throughout this period, rates of intimate homicide by White husbands were significantly higher than rates of intimate homicide by White wives, whereas the rates of intimate homicides of Black men and women were much less discrepant.

Box 8.2 describes a case of a Black male victim of intimate partner homicide from a study by McClain (1982). When a small number of the female homicide offenders in this study were interviewed about circumstances leading to the homicide, almost half indicated that an argument and subsequent anger were responsible; all held that a woman had the right to take a life if she were being physically abused. To understand the causes of these intimate homicides, is it enough to look at the perpetrator's motives or are there other considerations that should be kept in mind? Overall, how would you explain the causal factors operating in cases like this?

One major risk factor for intimate partner homicide for women is abuse during pregnancy. Among women living in ten different cities across the United States, the risk of becoming an attempted/completed femicide victim was three times greater for women abused during pregnancy and three times higher for Black than for White women (McFarlane, Campbell, Sharps, & Watson, 2002).

Physical and Psychological Injuries

Other, less lethal consequences of intimate maltreatment in African American communities are generally consistent with outcomes in other communities. However, there is evidence from the National Survey of Families and Households that Black spouses may be more at risk for physical injuries than members of other ethnic groups, with Black families reporting the highest rates of physical victimization with injuries

---

Box 8.2   Case of Intimate Partner Homicide

The offender (age 21) and the deceased had been living together for two years. The offender during the last month had caught the deceased three times going out with a former girlfriend. On one occasion the deceased did not come home all night and the defendant, in the early morning, had seen his truck parked in front of his former girlfriend's house and saw him leaving.

One evening the offender went to the parking lot of the deceased's place of employment and asked him to return to her. (The deceased had left her the previous Monday.) The deceased went into his place of employment and when the offender saw him coming back across the parking lot, she took a rifle from her car and fired one shot, fatally wounding the deceased in the head.

SOURCE: McClain, 1982, p. 19.

(1.8%; Zlotnick, Kohn, Peterson, & Pearlstein, 1998). There is also evidence that among Black women, spousal violence is a predictor of physical health problems (Campbell & Soeken, 1999), HIV positivity (Cohen et al., 2000), suicide attempts (Abbott, Johnson, Koziol-McClain, & Lowenstin, 1995; Kaslow et al., 2002), and mental health problems, such as post-traumatic stress disorder (PTSD) (Astin, Ogland-Hand, Coleman, & Foy, 1995; Axelrod, Myers, Durvasula, Wyatt, & Cheng, 1999; Dutton, Goodman, & Bennett, 2001; Hien & Bukszpan, 1999), depression (Axelrod et al.; Campbell & Soeken; Dutton et al.; Zlotnick et al.), and distress (Ingram, Corning, & Schmidt, 1996). Moreover, the experience of intimate partner violence appears to have radiating effects for African American women—the first-order effects being physical injury, depression, fear, low self-esteem, and substance abuse; the second-order effects being changed relationships with family and friends, reduced ability to work or attend school, and trouble obtaining stable housing; and the third-order effects being the impact of the spousal violence on the children and threats by the batterer against other family members (Riger, Raja, & Camacho, 2002).

Although several investigators have identified alcohol/drug use as a predictor of intimate violence, others have viewed drug abuse as an outcome of maltreatment. For example, among a sample of abused pregnant teens (56% African American), drug abuse seemed to be a coping and survival strategy used to deal with violence (Sales & Murphy, 2000). Because such studies are correlational, the causal relationship between variables is difficult to untangle. However, substance abuse may be as much an outcome of family violence as a cause of it. Indeed, there may be a vicious cycle by which the abused child or adolescent turns to substance abuse as a way of coping with the trauma, and then the substance abuse increases the vulnerability of the individual to further victimization (Cohen et al., 2000).

One link in the vicious cycle experienced by many African Americans between maltreatment in childhood and maltreatment in adulthood is homelessness and/or dependence on welfare. Among African American women in Chicago, current and past physical abuse contributed significantly to the probability of being in the welfare system (Nam & Tolman, 2002). In a largely African American sample in New York City (Shinn et al., 1998), spousal violence in adulthood, in addition to abuse and separation from the family of origin in childhood, were important predictors of shelter seeking. In another study of homeless parents in New York City (59% Black), 47% had a history of abuse, 8% had been homeless for a time in childhood, and 13% had been in foster care (Nunez, 2001).

One final consequence of wife abuse is an attempt by abused wives to leave their batterer. There appear to be important differences, including ethnic differences, in rates of attempted fleeing. For example, in one study, abused women who left their batterers were more likely than those who remained in the abusive relationship to be non-White, to be employed, to have been in their relationships for a shorter period of time, and to have tried a greater number of other coping strategies to alleviate the abuse (Strube & Barbour, 1984). Qualitative responses from a predominantly African American sample of abused women revealed several turning points in the abusive relationship that led to women's decisions to leave the relationship—being threatened with death (e.g., when the partner drew a gun on her), being hit during pregnancy, and becoming violent themselves in retaliation (Campbell, Rose, Kub, & Nedd, 1998).

ELDER MALTREATMENT

Scope of the Problem

In contrast to what might be expected given the revered role of grandparents in African American families (discussed in chapter 6), data from the National Elder Abuse Incidence Study (NEAIS; National Center on Elder Abuse, 1998) indicate that African American elders were overrepresented in several categories of abuse and neglect substantiated by Adult Protective Services. Nationwide in 1996, 8.3% of the victims of elder abuse were Black. Although the rate of physical maltreatment of Black elders (9%) was roughly consistent with their representation in the population (8.2%),

Black victims were overrepresented (17.2%) for reported cases of (a) neglect, the most commonly reported form of elder maltreatment, (b) emotional/psychological abuse (14.1%), (c) financial exploitation (15.4%), and (d) abandonment (8.3%). However, they were not overrepresented in the physical abuse category, which is consistent with the proscription in Black families that "you just don't hit your momma!" (Griffin, 1999a). Low income was a major contributor to all forms of elder maltreatment, but the NEAIS did not provide analyses controlling for income or other socioeconomic variables.

In an analysis of substantiated cases of elder mistreatment (48 Black, 59 White victims) from an Illinois Elder Abuse and Neglect Provider Agency (Dimah, 2001), there were no ethnic differences in frequencies of type of abuse except for emotional abuse. In this case, only 18.8% of the Black elders, compared to 52.5% of the White elders, were confirmed cases of emotional abuse. The majority of the perpetrators were children of the victims (approximately 69% of Blacks and 77% of Whites), and most of these perpetrators were living with the victims (72.5% of Blacks and 85.7% of Whites). Consider the case of elder abuse described in Box 8.3. Do you consider this to be a case of financial exploitation? Why or why not?

In general, the available data indicate that rates of elder maltreatment are relatively lower

---

Box 8.3 Jane B: Exploitation, Maltreatment, Intergenerational Cooperation?

Jane B. is a 79-year-old African American woman with three grown children. She has hypertension and arthritis, and has become increasingly forgetful, but is otherwise in good health. Her two daughters are married with children and grandchildren, and live within 50 miles of her. Her only son, Robert, an unemployed Vietnam vet who has never married and has no children, lives with and "looks after" her. "Looking after" her means picking up her monthly checks, helping her pay the bills, going grocery shopping with her, and cleaning the house. He routinely keeps some of the money out of her monthly checks for himself, as well as regularly getting additional spending money from her, which he says he needs for cigarettes. Jane's daughters think that Robert is taking advantage of her generosity and "using" her so that he will not have to work. The situation has been examined by adult protective service workers, who believe that Robert is financially exploiting his mother. Jane denies that she is being abused, and says that the small amounts of money she gives to Robert are worth the peace of mind she gains by having him live with her.

SOURCE: Griffin (1999a).

in African American communities than rates of child and spousal maltreatment. In addition, rates of reported cases of physical abuse are consistent with their representation in the population, and not significantly different from the White rate, although the other ethnic groups are underrepresented in the physical abuse category. Black elders may be somewhat overrepresented in regard to emotional abuse. The NEAIS data indicate that African American elders are overrepresented in the category of financial exploitation, but consider the perspective of Griffin (1999a):

> Poverty fosters frustration and anger about one's circumstances, increasing the likelihood for violence and abuse. It is not surprising that many African American children, who live most of their lives in impoverished conditions, return to the safety of their parent's homes for protection and the security afforded by the elder's fixed income. (p. 34)

Given the substantial correlation of poverty with violence, it may be remarkable that there is not more physical aggression against African American elders. Even the financial exploitation, as is true, for example, among Native American Indians, may be very much in the eyes of the beholder—in this case the adult protective services. What do you think about this possibility?

Correlates, Predictors, and Consequences

There are few published studies of the correlates and predictors of elder abuse in minority communities, and many of the available studies do not analyze their findings separately by ethnicity (e.g., Moody, Voss, & Lengacher, 2000) or are characterized by "ethnic lumping"—that is, combining African Americans with other ethnic groups under umbrella labels such as "minority" or "non-White" (e.g., Lachs, Berkman, Fulmer, & Horwitz, 1994; Lachs, Williams, O'Brien, Hurst, & Horwitz, 1997). Furthermore, to our knowledge, there is little research specifically addressing the consequences of elder abuse in African American communities.

The few studies specifically addressing predictors of African American elder abuse focus primarily on variables at the macrosystem, exosystem, and individual level. The macrosystem and exosystem level variables generally include social support, the availability of medical care, and impoverishment. For example, among confirmed cases of elder abuse by the Texas Department of Human Resources (Hall, 1987), significantly more Black elders (40%) than Hispanic elders (20%) could identify a caregiving person in their lives, and significantly more Black elders than Hispanic elders had an identified source of medical care. When the combined "minority" sample was compared with the White sample, the abused White elders were significantly more likely to have a telephone (a proxy for income) than Black and Hispanic elders. Individual-level variables include the mental health of the abuser. For example, in a study of abused African American elders who sought legal recourse against abusive adult children (Korbin, Anetzberger, Thomasson, & Austin, 1991), the abusive adult offspring were typically male, had a history of mental illness and/or substance abuse, and lived with the victimized elder. In this study, none of the abused elders were dependent or socially isolated; each was relatively independent despite health problems, and had a rich social support network.

SUMMARY

Although the media often dramatize violence in Black communities, the great majority of African American families are not characterized by spousal or elder maltreatment. Almost every large study showing higher rates of maltreatment in Black than in White families also shows higher rates of maltreatment among the poor, the unemployed, and the socially isolated, confirming the role that macrosystem factors related to racism and discrimination play in family violence rates. There is clear evidence that attributes of the communities in which many African Americans live, not always by personal preference, are strong predictors of rates of spousal violence. It is probably also true that rates of adult maltreatment by Black men and women are not substantially different from those of White men and women of comparable real wealth and resources, but there have not yet been adequate empirical tests of this proposition.

Although many of the apparent individual-level risk factors identified in other communities (e.g., alcohol and drug abuse, a childhood history of exposure to violence) also seem to operate in African American communities, the availability of firearms appears to be particularly salient in African American communities and may contribute to the higher levels of intimate homicide found in Black men and women compared to White men and women. It also seems likely that early maltreatment can lead to a vicious cycle in which substance abuse, homelessness, and out-of-family care contribute to the risk of later spousal violence. With regard to elder abuse, social service data indicate that there are somewhat higher percentages of identified cases of elder maltreatment (most commonly neglect) by Black than by White family members. The few studies of risk factors for elder abuse in African American families identify factors such as low income and psychopathology.

You have now learned about family violence in two cultural groups, one of which was driven from its lands by force and one of which was brought here by force. Do there appear to be commonalities in the way historic factors influenced contemporary families in these communities? Do there also appear to be differences? What are the implications of any similarities and differences for combating family violence in these communities and in the country as a whole?

In the next section, we focus on members of communities who have, for the most part, come to this country voluntarily, seeking better employment and other opportunities. The majority of these individuals are light skinned, and have come to be included under the label White—that is, Hispanic White. However, the country they have entered has biases against immigrants, especially in poor economic times. In what ways do you think the experiences of immigrants from South and Central America will be different from those of Native American Indians and African Americans? In what ways do you think the experiences will be similar? Given what you have learned so far, what are your expectations concerning the incidence, predictors, correlates, and consequences of family violence in Hispanic/Latino communities in the United States?

PART IV

HISPANIC/LATINO CULTURES

9

Hispanic/Latino Cultural Contexts

A 5-month-old Mexican American boy presented at a local emergency room with apnea and seizures, and tests revealed that he had subdural hematomas. One or two months prior to this visit, he had rolled off of a bed onto a carpeted floor, and had been vomiting, lethargic, and irritable for the previous month. . . . [Extensive] tests revealed that he had intraretinal and preretinal hemorrhages in both eyes, chronic and acute subdural hematomas in both hemispheres, and two separate parietal skull fractures. A diagnosis of shaken baby syndrome was made, and the baby was taken into state custody. He remained in the hospital for one month to care for the hematomas, and was released with no noticeable residual neurological insult and with a guarded visual prognosis. During that time, his parents revealed that they took the baby to a folk healer four times over the previous 1 to 3 months to treat caida de molerra because they were concerned about his sunken fontanelle. The folk healer, according to the parents, pushed up on the baby's palate with his finger, held the baby upside down with the top of his head in warm water, and gently moved him up and down. (Hansen, 1997)

This medical case shows how certain Latino cultural practices, viewed as helpful by the Latinos themselves, can be perceived as abusive by the majority culture. Hansen (1997) explains that Latinos traditionally use folk remedies to treat depressed fontanels (soft spots on the skull; aka *caida de mollera*) in babies. In Latino culture, *caida de mollera* is thought to result from a trauma and to lead to symptoms such as poor feeding, crying, irritability, diarrhea, vomiting, and fever; restoration of the fontanels is thought to reduce such symptoms. The most commonly used folk remedies are to push on the baby's palate to force everything back into place, hold the baby upside down and shake it up and down, or hold it upside down with the tip of its head in warm water. It is expected that through these procedures, gravity and force should return the fontanels to their appropriate position. If a folk healer performs the traditional therapies correctly, there should be no intracranial bleeding or retinal hemorrhaging, as in the above case. Hansen speculates that Latino parents who shake their babies know they can blame any injuries on folk remedies because of the implicit biases the medical profession has against them.

Although it is arguable whether folk remedies to treat caida de mollera actually lead to injuries in babies, there are other Latino folk

147

remedies seen by the U.S. medical community in forms that may be considered "abusive." For instance, Mexican Americans may use the folk remedy called "cupping" to treat such symptoms as pain, fever, poor appetite, and congestion. Cupping involves soaking a cotton ball in alcohol, placing it on a stick, and putting it in a glass-cupping jar to burn oxygen and create a vacuum. The cotton ball is then removed from the cup, the cup is placed on the skin, and the vacuum draws the skin up. To prepare the skin for cupping, incisions are made to produce bleeding. The cupping itself tends to produce bruising. The theory is that by drawing blood to the skin's surface, congestion can be relieved. However, doctors who see children exposed to this folk remedy may report them as physically abused (Hansen, 1997). What do you think? Should children be referred for maltreatment if the parents tried to help them by using traditional folk remedies? Should standards of physical abuse transcend cultural values?

In addition, many times, Latinos will pray to a saint or the Virgin Mary to help cure a disability; other times, they believe the disability is God's will or God's punishment and must be unquestionably accepted (Zuniga, 1992). However, if a child has a disability that could be treated or cured, praying and passive acceptance may be viewed by outsiders as medical neglect (Kapitanoff, Lutzker, & Bigelow, 2000). If Latino parents truly believe they are helping their children with time-honored methods of responding to physical and mental ailments, and outsiders view the treatments (or lack of treatment) as *mal*treatment, what is the best solution?

WHAT IS ABUSE?

To address such dilemmas, it is important to have a clear picture of Latino conceptions of abuse. Latinos come from the various countries that make up Central and South America and from islands, such as Cuba and Puerto Rico. Some families have been in the United States for generations, whereas others are just arriving. Our own data on implicit theories of abuse show that Latinos' conceptions are as diverse as their communities. When our respondents described what "abuse" meant in the context of family relationships, they gave a wide range of answers—verbal and physical attacks resulting in injury, using verbal or physical punishment for an offense that was not serious, dominating another individual, not giving them their personal space, hurting someone purposely, putting someone down, taking advantage of another person, and sexually abusing someone. There was no consistent pattern based on amount of time in this country, level of acculturation, gender, or age. Their answers were as heterogeneous as the population itself.

Other studies do show some consistent patterns. For example, Latinos' conceptions of child sexual abuse (CSA) in many ways reflect majority culture thinking. In one study, Latinos "emphasized that sexual activities between a child and an adult or older adolescent is abuse even if the child agrees to it because the child may be threatened or brainwashed or simply may not understand what is going on" (Fontes, Cruz, & Tabachnick, 2001, p. 109). Those respondents referred mostly to males sexually abusing both boys and girls. Although they acknowledged that females could also sexually abuse children (particularly boys), they tended to call this seduction rather than abuse. In addition, they identified children's exposure to adults' sexual activities, as could occur in cramped living and sleeping arrangements, as a form of sexual abuse.

In focus groups of primarily Mexican American Latinas (Ramos Lira, Koss, & Russo, 1999), the Latinas displayed a remarkable knowledge about CSA. They recognized that the majority of child sexual abusers were family members and acquaintances. They knew that although females could sexually abuse children, the primary perpetrators tend to be men, and that both boys and girls could be victimized. They also reported that they are more vigilant than their parents were about the threats of CSA by acquaintances on their own children.

Several studies have also examined Latino conceptions of physical abuse. Contrary to popular belief about the violent, hot-blooded nature of Latinos, and the observation that Latinos tend to use an authoritarian parenting style, these studies consistently find that Latinos have more stringent definitions of child abuse than other cultural groups, including Blacks, Whites, and Asians. For example, when judging vignettes for the seriousness of parental behaviors representing forms of child physical and sexual abuse and the use of drugs, Latinos rated them as more serious than any other ethnic group (White, Black, and "other"). Moreover, Spanish-speaking and poorer Latinos were the most conservative in their ratings of abuse (Giovannoni & Becerra, 1979). In comparison to Chinese and White parents, Latino parents presented with twelve vignettes of possible child abuse gave all of the scenarios the highest severity ratings (Hong & Hong, 1991), indicating very stringent implicit theories of child abuse.

However, Latinos do not seem to have such stringent criteria in their implicit theories of behaviors constituting wife abuse. For example, White women, when presented with various abusive scenarios, found more behaviors abusive and were less tolerant of wife abuse than Mexican American women. Although White women found pulling hair, biting, slapping, throwing objects, and pushing, shoving, or grabbing to be abusive, Mexican American women did not. White women also judged physically abusive acts as more serious than did Mexican American women, regardless of whether the acts occurred just once or on a regular basis (Torres, 1991). Such findings suggest that Latinas are less likely to see themselves as victims when abuse occurs and less likely to seek help when assaulted by their husbands (Torres).

Although Latinas seem to have a narrow definition of wife abuse, they acknowledge the existence of wife rape as a form of abuse. In one study, many Latinas recognized that husbands can frequently perform acts against their wives that would be considered rape. Some women said that a husband having sexual intercourse with his wife when she did not want to, or having oral or anal sex or sex during menstruation, could be considered instances of wife rape. Others believed that force was necessary for the behavior to be considered rape. As one woman stated, "Because if they are sharing a life together, they have to be in agreement to have healthy sex, it should not be that if he wants to and the woman does not want to, he forces her" (Ramos Lira et al., 1999, p. 255). Although

these Mexican Americans believed that wife rape occurred and was undeniably the husbands' fault, their typical reaction was silence (Ramos Lira et al.).

Latinos and Whites also differ in their implicit theories of elder abuse. In our study, one respondent, when asked to give examples of elder abuse, stated, "Never experienced any abusive interactions because the elderly are highly respected in our culture. They hold the entire family together." This quote is a good example of how much elders are revered in this community. Another good example can be found in one participant's responses to questions about what is considered extremely abusive adult-elder interactions in his Puerto Rican culture: "putting them in a home," a behavior which is considered acceptable and nonabusive by many people in other cultures. As was found in the Native American communities (see chapter 4), this focus on emotional neglect and disrespect was characteristic of Latino implicit theories of elder abuse, but rarely shown in examples of abuse in other family relationships. These results resonate with the findings of a study comparing Japanese, Puerto Rican, and White responses on various types of elder abuse. Puerto Rican elders and adult caregivers believed that psychological neglect, such as not communicating and isolating, were the worst types of elder abuse (Anetzberger, Korbin, & Tomita, 1996). However, although the majority culture's definition of elder abuse includes financial exploitation, this is not typically true of Latinos (Nerenberg, 1999). Similar to Native Americans, elderly Latinos feel it is their duty to share their resources if necessary, even if it means that they must sacrifice their own needs for food, medication, or other necessities.

In the following sections, we discuss the groups that make up the Hispanic communities, the role of cultural values as risk and protective factors in family violence, and aspects of their histories in this country that may have implications for violence in their relationships. As you read this material, ask yourself two questions: In what ways might implicit theories of family violence and abuse have arisen out of the cultural experiences of Latinos, and to what extent might those experiences have given rise to the implicit theories?

WHO IS HISPANIC/LATINO?

Another definitional problem concerns the terms *Hispanic* and *Latino*. Many immigrants from Central and South America do not like the term *Hispanic* precisely because it was chosen by the U.S. Census Bureau, and still more immigrants are offended by the term because they prefer to dissociate themselves from Spain, which played a colonial role in their history. Consequently, many people who are considered *Hispanic* by the U.S. government prefer the term *Latino*, which is more inclusive. Also, not all people from Latin America come from Spanish-speaking countries, a characteristic implied by the term *Hispanic* (Garcia & Marotta, 1997). In this chapter, we use the term from the particular study being discussed.

The United States has 35.3 million Hispanics, the fifth largest such population in the world. Hispanics are the fastest growing minority group in the United States, and will become the largest minority group by the year 2005, surpassing African Americans. Currently, Hispanics constitute 12.5% of the total U.S. population and 40% of the minority population. Between the years 1990 and 2000, this population grew at a rate of 57.9%, whereas the U.S. population as a whole grew at a rate of only 13.2%. This massive increase in the Hispanic population is due both to increases in immigration and high birth rates (U.S. Bureau of the Census, 2001b).

The highest concentrations of Hispanic Americans are in three states, California, Texas, and New York, which are home to approximately two thirds of the Hispanics in this country. In California and Texas, the predominant Hispanic community is Mexican American, which accounts for approximately 25% of these states' populations. One third of the population in Arizona and New Mexico is Mexican American. In New York, along with neighboring states such as New Jersey and Massachusetts, the predominant Hispanic community is Puerto Rican. In Florida, particularly Miami–Dade County, the main Hispanic community is Cuban; half of the Cuban population in the United States resides in Florida (U.S. Bureau of the Census, 2001b).

Although Mexicans (who comprise 58.5% of the Hispanic population), followed by Puerto Ricans (9.6%) and then Cubans (3.5%), are the largest Hispanic groups in this country, there has recently been a large increase in immigration from other Latin American countries. The U.S. population of other Central and South American Hispanics grew at a rate of 96.9% between 1990 and 2000, from 5.1 million to 10 million people. Immigrants from these Central and South American countries tend to settle in already established Hispanic communities. Even though Central and South American immigration is increasing, the overwhelming majority of research has been done on Mexicans, Puerto Ricans, and Cubans (Garcia & Marotta, 1997; U.S. Bureau of the Census, 2001b; Zea, Diehl, & Porterfield, 1997).

Although the Hispanic population in the United States is mostly young, part of a large household, urbanized, and poor, there is great variation in these variables across Hispanic communities. The most striking variations within the Hispanic community become apparent when we consider socioeconomic status, education, and employment. In comparison to the overall U.S. population, Hispanics are underrepresented in the highest income category and overrepresented in the lowest income categories. Puerto Ricans are particularly overrepresented in the lower income category—31% live below poverty level, compared to 27% of Mexicans and 14% of Cuban Americans, who resemble the U.S. population as a whole. As a group, Hispanics are less educated than the U.S. population; a little more than half of adult Hispanics have completed high school (compared to 83% of the U.S. population), and only 11% have college degrees (compared to 25% of the U.S. population). However, Cubans and Central/South Americans, whose educational status tends to mirror that of the U.S. population, are, on average, better educated than Mexicans or Puerto Ricans. Unemployment is higher among Hispanics than in the U.S. population as a whole, but again, Mexicans and Puerto Ricans account for this difference. Thus, Puerto Ricans have the lowest standard of living among the Hispanic communities, and Cubans have the highest. Mexicans and Central/South Americans fall in between these two groups (DHHS, 2001; U.S. Bureau of the Census, 2001b).

These differences within the various Hispanic communities are, in part, a function of their countries of origin, when and why they immigrated to the United States, how long they have been here, how acculturated they are, and where they live. Furthermore, the sociodemographic variables on which they differ are, in turn, related to both the incidence of family violence and willingness to seek help for it. What should these demographic differences lead you to expect concerning family violence within these different Hispanic communities?

CULTURAL VALUES: PROTECTIVE OR RISK FACTORS?

Despite the heterogeneity among Hispanics in the United States, there are strong similarities in cultural values. A sampling of these cultural values is discussed in this section, with particular attention paid to the definitions of these values and the ways they may act as either protective or risk factors for various issues in family violence.

Familism

Familism is one of the most important cultural values in all Latino groups. Identification with the family is so strong that this unit is the source of its members' self-esteem, self-worth, self-identification, strength, and pride. The family's value and needs are considered more important than the relative value or needs of each individual member, and Latinos rely on the family, more than any other institution, as a source of emotional, structural, and material support. This support system extends not only to the nuclear family, but also to the extended family. Moreover, certain close friends of the family may become honorary members of the unit (i.e., as godparents or *compadrazgo*). The family is considered to be the single most important social institution in the Latino culture (Ho, 1992; Vasquez, 1998; Zayas & Palleja, 1988).

This strong emphasis on the family and the amount of support provided can be a protective factor against family violence. The family can protect the individual members against external physical and emotional stressors, such as poverty, joblessness, oppression, and isolation, which can put families at risk for violence (Vasquez, 1998). Familism as a support and buffer against maltreatment is evident in a study of Mexican Americans, who were more likely than Whites to state that they "can always rely on [their relatives] in times of need" and that "an older person should be cared for by his family" (Keefe, 1984, p. 66). In addition, Cuban, Puerto Ricans, and Mexican Americans were more likely than Whites to say their relatives were a reliable source of support (Sabogal, Marin, & Otero-Sabogal, 1987). Consider the implications of this support for family violence rates: In the general population, parents who physically abuse their children have fewer sources of emotional support from either friends or family members than nonabusive parents (Coohey, 2000; Coohey & Braun, 1997).

This centrality of the family may also serve as a risk factor for maltreatment. Familism has been shown to contribute to the incidence of, and reluctance of the victim to escape from or disclose, three types of maltreatment: CSA, wife abuse, and elder maltreatment. As discussed in the next chapter, Latina girls are more likely than members of other ethnic groups to be sexually abused by family members—perhaps in part because of the very inclusiveness of the family (Moisan, Sanders-Phillips, & Moisan, 1997). Furthermore, by warning that disclosure will disrupt the family's well-being, the abusers may threaten the victim into nondisclosure and continued compliance with the sexual abuse (Comas-Diaz, 1995). Rather than violate the value of familism (Fontes, 1993), a Latino child may submit to a physical violation and not disclose sexual abuse by a family member. Consider the example in Box 9.1 of what can happen when the authority of adults in the family is unquestionably accepted.

Familism has also been shown to play a role in a wife's unwillingness to escape spousal violence. Because Latinos value the family over the individual, many battered Latinas refuse to tear their family apart by leaving an abusive husband. Even when battered Latinas do leave their husbands, they often return because of pressure from their families and for the sake of their children (Torres, 1987). Moreover,

---

Box 9.1   Familism as a Risk Factor in Family Violence

One adult Latina discussed her physical and sexual abuse experiences from her father when she was a child. She was often beaten publicly by her dad, and he sexually abused her in private for many years. When she was old enough, she would run away to a neighbor's house when her father's sexual demands became too intense. Every time she did this, he would find her, beat her, and humiliate her in front of the neighbors. The neighbors and her mother witnessed many of these beatings, but never intervened to stop them. They felt that it was a father's right to punish his child in what he viewed as a just manner. As an adult, this Latina believed that this ideology, coupled with a cultural acceptance of corporal punishment, led to her victimization and her unwillingness to disclose the sexual abuse. She felt that if no one interfered to stop the beatings, why would they intervene to stop the rapes?

SOURCE: Fontes, 1993.

---

because conflicts are supposed to be handled within the family, battered women often do not seek external help (Campbell, Masaki, & Torres, 1997).

There is evidence that familism may also hinder help-seeking by a caretaker who is becoming overwhelmed by responsibilities in caring for an elder (Vazquez & Rosa, 1999). The family member may not seek outside help because of familism; then, when he or she becomes overburdened by the demands of the situation, he or she may maltreat the elder. Moreover, because it is considered essential to care for older family members at home, rather than asking for outside assistance, Mexican American families will accept a certain level of neglect of their elders (Vazquez & Rosa). In turn, maltreated elders may be reluctant to seek help outside the family because to admit that abuse is occurring is to admit that the family, and the value of familism itself, has broken down (Mitchell, Festa, Franco, Juarez, & Lamb, 1999).

Machismo

The concept of *machismo* has both positive and negative connotations. Machismo, in the positive sense, denotes the man as head of the household for an entire extended family, and encompasses the nurturing, caring, and protective role that is necessary to be an effective head (Mayo, 1997). It includes notions of honor, pride, courage, responsibility, and obligation to the family (Panitz, McConchie, Sauber, & Fonseca, 1983; Perilla, 1999). The macho male is gentle and provides well for his family; he is gracious, respectful, and loving, and he is well-respected in the community (Vasquez, 1998). Because he is in charge of the protection and well-being of the family (Comas-Diaz, 1995), this value may protect against any kind of maltreatment of its members.

Machismo also has a negative side, which can be described as a type of hypermasculinity. From this perspective, the macho Latino is supposed to be violent and arbitrarily domineering, a sexually hot-blooded womanizer, drunken, and harsh with children (Mayo, 1997; Panitz et al., 1983; Vasquez, 1998). Many Latino men in the United States have internalized this view (Vasquez), which can affect how they deal with family members. For example, men who subscribe to this stereotype instead of the positive values of machismo, may sexually aggress against their wives because they think it is their right to do so (Perilla, 1999; Wyatt, Strayer, & Lobitz, 1976). These Latino men may believe that their gender provides them with rights and privileges and that their wife's duty is to fulfill their wishes (Abalos, 1986). This situation alone may lead to the maltreatment of women: There is a saying in Latin America that "a man who is manly and macho enough to beat his wife is not really a man if he doesn't do it twice" (Zambrano, 1985). Many Latinas also accept the cultural argument that men who are violent against their wives are conforming to the cultural value of machismo (Campbell et al., 1997); these Latinas may excuse the violence of their husbands because they view it as culturally prescribed.

Another negative consequence of machismo is that Latino men who maltreat their wives or children may not seek external help to end their abusive behavior. Utilization of services could be seen as an admission of weakness and be a blow to the self-confidence of men who are supposed to overcome their problems without the help of others (Mayo, 1997). In addition, the negative notions within the machismo concept may prevent abusive Latinos from noticing that their behavior is problematic. It has been shown that the more Latino men subscribe to machismo notions, the less they use mental health services offered in the community (Mayo).

Marianismo

Marianismo is the female counterpart of machismo. It is the cultural prescription that Latinas will emulate the Virgin Mary's moral integrity and spiritual strength, and it materializes as self-sacrifice for their families (Comas-Diaz, 1995). Marianismo connotes that women are spiritually superior to men and are thereby capable of enduring all the suffering inflicted by men (Stevens, 1973). Therefore, a wife should tolerate her husband's bad habits, comply with his decisions, and support him unwaveringly (Campbell et al., 1997). The concept of marianismo also extends to the woman's role as the family caretaker who is supposed to bear quietly whatever pain may go with her role (Vazquez & Rosa, 1999). Also central to marianismo is the sexual chastity of the Latina. Unmarried women are expected to refrain from sexual behavior prior to marriage. After they are married, they are not to demonstrate any interest in sex (Comas-Diaz). From birth, girls are seen as a burden on the family because the family needs to protect its honor by protecting the girls' virginity (Abalos, 1986).

This concept of marianismo can protect women from family violence in some ways. Because motherhood is the ultimate status of women, it earns them some respect (Mayo & Resnick, 1996). However, although marianismo is romanticized in many ways, it can also lead to various forms of family violence. For instance, it may contribute to the maltreatment of wives and the reluctance of wives to leave an abusive situation. Many Latinas learn early in their lives that wife abuse is to be expected and tolerated as a sometimes unavoidable part of marriage. Young Latinas are often taught that husbands have the right to physically discipline and make demands on wives and still have unquestioning loyalty. Because marianismo prescribes the quiet suffering of women in obedience to husbands, women endure this legacy and do not feel they can or should escape it. Even worse, they pass this legacy on to their daughters, who then pass it on to their children (Mayo & Resnick; Perilla, 1999).

The bigger problem relating to marianismo is the culture's perceptions of sexually abused girls as ruined (Fontes, 1993). Because of marianismo, there is a stigma associated with sexual violation and loss of virginity prior to marriage. Therefore, many Latina girls are unwilling to disclose sexual abuse to their families, even their mothers, because they anticipate lack of support (Rao et al., 1992). Even if the girls are willing to disclose the abuse to family members, the family may not report it to authorities, perhaps because of the shame that would come from others finding out that their daughter lost her virginity (Fontes; Mennen, 1994). Consider this quote from the therapist of a Latina sexual abuse victim:

> And people see a woman's virginity as something so, so valuable, that even though it was abuse—and the fact that this person is not a virgin was not voluntary—it says something about the family's honor. It says something about the person, about the victim, something negative about the victim, even though it wasn't her doing. (Fontes, p. 31)

Marianismo may also negatively affect sexual abuse victims by interfering with psychological adjustment. Latinas who have been sexually abused, particularly the ones who have been penetrated, experience worse psychosocial outcomes than Blacks or Whites (Mennen, 1995; Roosa, Reinholtz, & Angelini, 1999; Shaw et al., 2001). Several researchers have speculated that it is this concept of marianismo that leads to the worsened psychosocial outcomes (Kenny & MacEachern, 2000). These girls know they are considered whores by their cultures, and fear they will never marry. Such a concern is devastating when being a wife is a central component to the Latina identity.

Respeto

Respeto refers principally to the respect that is intrinsically owed to others, particularly those who are older (Brenes Jette & Remien, 1988). It implies obedience, duty, and deference. Older people deserve this respect either because they have worked throughout their lives to achieve power, wealth, and other gains, or because of the hardships they have had to endure, such as poverty, discrimination, and racism (Mitchell et al., 1999). Respeto, then, is considered to be a buffer against elder maltreatment in Latino communities. Because family members are supposed to respect their elders, they must not behave abusively in any way. A violation of this cultural value would be considered a moral offense and form of abuse when the disrespect is directed towards an elder (Vazquez & Rosa, 1999), as indicated in the section "What Is Abuse?"

Respeto can also be a risk factor for nondisclosure of child maltreatment. For many Latinos, feelings of respect for their parents, especially their fathers, become mixed with feelings of fear. The father must be accorded the utmost respect, and if he sees fit to use physical aggression against his children, his wishes should be honored (Perilla, 1999). This notion of respeto may also be used by child sexual abusers to maintain the silence of their victims. If children are sexually abused by parents, elders, teachers, or even older siblings, they may be afraid to disclose the abuse because of respect for and obedience to the abuser, as well as fear of the consequences of violating respeto (Comas-Diaz, 1995; Fontes, 1993).

Catholicism, Cultural Fatalism, and Folk Beliefs

Catholicism is the primary religion of Latinos, and their religious beliefs can serve as a great comfort in times of need (Mitchell et al., 1999). Catholicism preaches that violence in the home is not consonant with God's wish for people to have loving families, for marriage

vows to flourish, for the couple to honor and respect each other, and for parents to give love and understanding to their children. Not only can Catholicism serve as a source of spiritual support, it can also be a source of emotional support. Many churches offer programs that can help people in abusive situations, and many priests will aid members of their congregations in dealing with maltreatment (Zambrano, 1985). Indeed, a higher percentage of Latinas seek assistance from their priests than from community shelters (Torres, 1991). As one Adult Protective Services worker reported, only after seeking advice from a priest did a Latina abused wife realize that she did not deserve to be beaten and leave her husband (Mitchell et al.). However, Catholicism can also be a hindrance for many abused Latinos. For example, the abused Latina may fear the stigma of divorce more than the beatings from her husband (Mitchell et al.). Moreover, the Catholic Church preaches that the maintenance of the family unit should be primary (Campbell et al., 1997), and some priests may encourage the abused wife to try to placate her husband and keep the family together at all costs (Zambrano).

Many Latino Catholics also believe in *cultural fatalism*, the idea that some things are just meant to happen (i.e., are God's will) regardless of any human intervention, and the suffering one must endure is part of one's destiny. Because the suffering on earth is God's will and externally controlled, the devout believe that their earthly suffering will be compensated for in the next life by spiritual reward. The misery they must endure may also be seen as God's way of testing them. It has been theorized that cultural fatalism grew out of a history of domination and political control of Hispanic people in their various countries—it was their way of adapting to a situation they could not control (Campbell et al., 1997; Comas-Diaz, 1995). This means of adapting has negative implications for individuals in a violent family—they may not seek help because they believe it is God's will that they endure suffering in order to gain spiritual rewards later.

In addition, Latino Catholicism tends to be mixed with many indigenous folk beliefs. For example, many Latinos practice *curanderismo*, an Indian folk healing that uses herbs, prayers, and rituals to cure physical, spiritual, and emotional problems. *Santeria*, also common among many Latinos, is an Afro-Cuban belief system involving the worship of both Catholic saints and African tribal deities, principally from the Yoruba tribe of Nigeria (Altarriba & Bauer, 1998; Campbell et al., 1997; Comas-Diaz, 1995). These folk beliefs can have implications for how Latinos interpret and seek help for abusive situations. For example, many abused women practice curanderismo prior to seeking help from outside institutions, and mothers often turn to someone who practices curanderismo for the physical ailments of their children (Campbell et al.). As discussed at the beginning of this chapter, the healing practices of curanderismo may lead to further physical injuries of the child, which then leads to the parents being suspected of child physical abuse (Hansen, 1997). Also, Santeria has been used to interpret the sexual abuse of a child in such a way that the abuser is practically excused from his behavior:

Juan, a 42-year-old male, was accused of sexually molesting a female neighbor. A santero (Santeria priest) diagnosed Juan's problem as not attending to his santo Oshun, who controls money and love by protecting the genitals (Martinez & Wetli, 1982). Therefore, the problem of sexual abuse was seen as part of Juan's punishment for neglecting Oshun. After a series of visits to the santero, Juan was instructed to return to the practice of Santeria. (Comas-Diaz, 1995, pp. 45–46)

Thus, folk beliefs can be both protective and risk factors for maltreatment. Latinas may seek strength in their folk beliefs when dealing with an abusive relationship, but folk practices can lead to suspicions of maltreatment and injury to children. In cases such as Juan's, folk beliefs can excuse the abusive behaviors of a sexual predator and put the abuser back in the community to abuse again.

THE ROLE OF OPPRESSION: ISSUES OF MIGRATION, DISCRIMINATION, AND ACCULTURATION

No discussion of family violence in minority groups is complete without addressing how they came to this country and how their minority status affects their daily lives. In this section, we discuss how matters such as migration history, discrimination, and acculturation can affect issues relating to family violence, such as its prevalence, perpetuation, and disclosure.

Migration History

Think about the Latino family who migrates to the United States—how might this migration affect such cultural values as familism, machismo, and marianismo? Are such values likely to ease the transition to life in the United States or make it more difficult? In addition, what are the implications of migration for family violence and help-seeking behavior? One Puerto Rican child who was sexually abused by a family member in the United States stated that because she was frequently uprooted, she had no strong ties with people to whom she could disclose this abuse (Fontes, 1993). The family members she trusted most were still in Puerto Rico, and she felt isolated in the United States. This child's status as a migrant directly affected her help-seeking behavior; because of her belief in familism, she wanted to disclose her sexual abuse to a family member but the trusted family members were hundreds of miles away.

The cultural values of machismo and marianismo can also become conflicted because of migration experiences. Consider the macho Latino male who comes to this country in search of economic opportunities and faces undue stress because of cultural conflicts. Not only does he lose contact with his extended family, but he also faces a situation in which he is a minority, does not speak the language well, and has limited employment and educational opportunities. His wife, who did not and was not supposed to work in their country of origin, may take the more active role of breadwinner, because there are more job opportunities, such as domestic help and hotel and office housekeeping, for her than there are for him (Mayo, 1997; Padilla, 1996). The new life of this family is inconsistent with the roles prescribed by both machismo and marianismo. This cultural inconsistency can lead to great psychological distress, which can then lead to wife and child maltreatment.

Different Latino groups have had different migration histories and have experienced different levels of receptivity in this country. These migration histories can affect social mobility, geographic mobility, and the level of discrimination they experience, which, in turn, can differentially affect their psychological adjustment and their resulting family violence rates.

Migration History of Mexican Americans

The original group of Mexican Americans did not come to the United States as immigrants. Rather, in 1845, the United States annexed Texas, and in 1849, the United States and Mexico signed the Treaty of Guadalupe Hidalgo, which ended the Mexican American War and gave the United States the rest of the Southwest Territory. The 75,000 Mexicans living in these areas were granted immediate U.S. citizenship, although American anti-Mexican sentiments were still strong. To this day, many of these Mexican Americans do not consider themselves to be immigrants and, in fact, regard the Southwest as still Mexican (Altarriba & Bauer, 1998; Falicov, 1998; Ginorio, Gutierrez, & Acosta, 1995).

Mexican migration to the United States was extremely popular during the 1880s and 1940s. During these times of American economic boom, Mexicans were openly welcomed into low-paying jobs in agriculture, on the railroads, and in industry. However, during periods when unemployment in the United States was high, Mexican immigration was discouraged, made illegal, and punished with deportation. Conflicts between Mexicans and Whites led to discrimination, and Mexicans were relegated to the lowest-paying menial jobs with no hope of regular employment or educational advancement.

Even though Mexicans have been present in the United States for more than 150 years, they have relatively little economic or political power (Altarriba & Bauer, 1998; Falicov, 1998; Ginorio et al., 1995). Their land and people were taken over by the United States in the 1800s; they have continually been the victims of widespread political, economic, and educational discrimination; and they are encouraged to come to this country when menial jobs are available, yet treated harshly when unemployment rates are high. How might this situation affect the incidence of family violence? Are their experiences likely to be associated with stresses shown to be predictive of family violence in the larger society? Would their experiences lead them to the conclusion that they could trust the governmental agencies that are supposed to help them deal with family violence? If victims feared that perpetrators of violence in their families would be dealt with too harshly, would their fears be justified? On the positive side, think about the geographical distance between Mexican immigrants and their families back in Mexico in comparison to other Latino immigrants (e.g., Brazilians). How might proximity affect the ability to see families and use them as a source of social support? Might geographical proximity to the homeland serve as a preventive factor for family violence?

Migration History of Puerto Ricans

The United States acquired Puerto Rico by invading and annexing this Spanish colony in 1898 during the Spanish-American War. In 1917, the U.S. government granted Puerto Ricans full U.S. citizenship, which permitted them unrestricted access and travel throughout the U.S. mainland. Therefore, Puerto Ricans in this country are not technically immigrants (Altarriba & Bauer, 1998). Puerto Rican migration to the mainland peaked in the 1950s and 1960s due to overcrowding and poor economic conditions on the island. At that time, the U.S. government, thinking that industrialization would improve the Puerto Rican economy, transformed Puerto Rico from a plantation economy to an industrial one. However, the United States could not provide enough jobs for unskilled workers on the island, so unemployment has remained quite high and migration has continued for the past 45 years. Many of those who migrated were peasants and workers driven off the island, and most have settled in major Northeast metropolitan areas where they live in barrios, attend the poorest urban schools, and are relatively uneducated and impoverished (Altariba & Bauer; Ginorio et al., 1995; Weis, Centrie, Valentin-Juarbe, & Fine, 2002).

In 1952, Puerto Rico became a commonwealth. Nevertheless, the U.S. government has never been quite sure what to do with inhabitants who mainly speak Spanish. Although they are citizens and subject to military duty, they are not required to pay income tax, are not full beneficiaries of federal social service programs, and cannot vote. Because Puerto Rico is a commonwealth and not a colony, it is autonomous in some ways, but it is subject to federal control to the extent that the inhabitants are limited in their ability to deal with their many sociopolitical problems. Despite limited economic resources and civic rights, Puerto Ricans are immensely proud of their homeland and very involved in island politics, even if they reside on the mainland. Although some Puerto Ricans approve of the United States' involvement in their political affairs, others want full independence (or at least statehood) for the island. This latter group points to the federal government's exploitation and colonialism, which can and does have negative effects on Puerto Ricans' self-esteem and their consequent despair (Falicov, 1998).

U.S. culture has a huge influence on the island, which is, therefore, bicultural; two languages are spoken, two flags are waved, and two national anthems are sung. But mainlanders have also harbored racist sentiments, which have had a negative effect on the way certain inhabitants are viewed. The darkest-skinned Puerto Ricans are often subject to harsh discrimination, even within their home island. Puerto Ricans tend to be the darkest skinned of all Latino immigrants, and it is, therefore, not surprising that they are also the poorest. Similar to the Mexican experience, Puerto Ricans have been wooed during times of economic boom in order to fill the lowest-paying jobs; they are then all but chased back to their island when the economy is bad and jobs are scarce. Although many Puerto Ricans have recognized their cold reception in this country, upwards of 2 million people per year have continued to migrate back and forth. However, they remain the poorest of the Latinos with the fewest economic opportunities (Falicov, 1998).

As you read about levels of family violence in Latino communities in the next two chapters, consider the implications of the destitution of Puerto Ricans for the incidence and perpetuation of family violence. What impact do limited educational and economic opportunities have on family violence? In a country that has dominated, colonized, and discriminated against Puerto Ricans since 1898, what is the likelihood that Puerto Ricans with family violence issues will trust services offered by the U.S. government?

Migration History of Cubans

In comparison to Mexicans and Puerto Ricans, Cubans have had an easy time adjusting to the U.S. economic and political life. Migration began between 1959 and 1965 to Miami, Florida, when the first wave of Cubans fleeing Castro's regime arrived. Those who came first were the ones most affected by a communist regime—members of the upper- and upper-middle class with plenty of educational and economic resources. They were received favorably because they had valued qualities—money, education, white skin, entrepreneurial skills, and an anticommunist, anti-Castro ideology. Due to their refugee status, they were also given financial, economic, and educational resources from the federal government. Although they were a "model" minority (Falicov, 1998; Ginorio et al., 1995) greeted with open arms and generally successful here, they typically have a strong nostalgia for their homeland. They do not wish to return to a country where Castro reigns, but they do long to return to the old Cuba one day—the Cuba they had before Castro took over. Therefore, they try to re-create their traditions and values in their new homes in Miami.

This wish to return home was partially granted in 1980, when Castro opened the doors for Cuban U.S. residents to visit their families in Cuba. However, this decision had its negative repercussions: Thousands of Cuban islanders demanded political asylum in the United States. Therefore, Castro ordered that all U.S. Cubans who came to the island to pick up relatives also transport "undesirables" to the United States. Over 100,000 Cubans came to Miami that year. However, because of Castro's orders, these refugees were unlike the "first wave" of refugees—they were more representative of the broad spectrum of class, skin color, and education of Cuban islanders. Many, like Mexicans and Puerto Ricans, wanted to come to the United States to improve their economic situation or reunite their families. Others were mentally ill people, criminals, and lepers, whom Castro could not wait to get rid of. Approximately 4% were hard-core criminals, and were not well received by U.S. citizens (Altarriba & Bauer, 1998).

These two waves of Cuban immigrants are viewed very differently in the United States. The first wave was the model minority, contributing substantially to the economic and educational system. The second wave was seen as a burden on society. Both groups generally long for a return to pre-Castro Cuba and would seize the chance to return if they could reunite with their culture and their families (Altarriba & Bauer, 1998; Ginorio et al., 1995). Think about this migration history in relation to family violence. How might rates of Cuban family violence compare with the rates in other Latino communities? What differences in family violence rates might there be between the first and second waves? How might the relative ease of reconnection affect familism? Do you think it could affect the disclosure rates of Cuban victims of family violence?

Other Migration Histories

Other Latino immigrants come from Central and South America for many different reasons. Some are political refugees, such as those from El Salvador and Nicaragua. Some are white-collar and professional workers, such as those from Argentina and Uruguay. Modes of entry, refugee status, and educational and economic backgrounds differ greatly. Immigration experiences can be comparable to the first wave of Cuban immigrants, the Puerto Ricans, or somewhere in between (Ginorio et al., 1995), and can have very different impacts on family violence and its disclosure.

Discrimination, Racism, and Classism

Many immigrant groups that have come to the United States started off poor, but by the third generation, their income levels typically mirrored those of the majority culture. However, there is no evidence that the low income level of Latinos is transitory in nature: Third-generation Latinos are just as poor as first-generation Latinos. They show little advancement on educational and economic measures, and in some cases (especially Puerto Ricans) show socioeconomic decline even after

being in this country for generations (Chapa, 1988; Weis et al., 2002). Some may argue that Latinos' inability to improve educationally and economically is a result of discriminatory practices in the United States. How might this perceived discrimination affect Latino families? Several researchers have argued that racism and classism may exacerbate any symptoms generally associated with family violence, such as depression, anxiety, and alcohol and drug abuse. However, discrimination is seldom considered in the assessment of Latinos who suffer from a history of family violence (Vasquez, 1998).

The relatively low income of Latinos has been theorized to affect both the incidence of and disclosure of family violence. Some researchers have speculated that discrimination, underemployment, and poverty lead to wife and child maltreatment because the man is not able to fulfill his duty as a sole provider and must "stoop" to letting his wife help with earning an income (Zambrano, 1985). This economic situation has also been implicated in the sexual abuse of Latino children: Some Latinos who suffered CSA were offered clothes, candy, or toys to gain compliance from them. Furthermore, a few Latino caregivers have accepted such bribes as food and money in exchange for letting others gain sexual access to their children (Fontes, 1993).

Discrimination can also lead some Latino children to not disclose their sexual abuse experiences. They see the discrimination against Latino children in the schools, where they are not given the same opportunities as White children. Therefore, they do not go to the organizations that are supposed to help them (Fontes, 1993). As one Latina victim of CSA states,

> There's so much emphasis put on the White people. I think they would have listened and done something with that if I was White. . . . Maybe I would have gotten more attention, and maybe life at home wouldn't have been so hard. (Fontes, p. 25)

Since the time of the European conquest of Latin America, there has been the implicit assumption that to be White meant power, privilege, and conquest, whereas to be dark implied being conquered, dominated, and intellectually inferior. These dynamics still exist within the United States today. Latinos are heterogeneous when it comes to skin color, and a hierarchy based on color still exists (Falicov, 1998). For instance, Puerto Ricans tend to be the darkest skinned of all the major Latino groups in this country, and are also by far the poorest. Their economic and educational situation has deteriorated continuously since the 1960s (Weis et al., 2002). By contrast, Cubans, the whitest of the Latino groups, are the most advantaged economically.

Racism exists within the Latino community as well as in the larger society. Cubans, the most economically advantaged and the whitest, tend to be considered arrogant by other Latino groups; they, in turn, tend to view other Latino groups in a racist way. Mexicans tend to be prejudiced against the darker skinned Puerto Ricans (Shorris, 1992). The following example is not unusual within the Latino community:

> Teresa [a Mexican American teenager] . . . had fallen in love with Roger, a Puerto Rican youth. When her father discovered a token of love that the young man had given to Teresa, he broke her lip with a slap and told her in no uncertain terms that she had tarnished her family's name. The father objected to Roger's "inferior race" and threatened that he would be the first "to warn" other respectable, interested young men about her past. Teresa had been paradoxically condemned to be "only worthy" of the Puerto Rican boy, and she was no longer allowed to date. (Falicov, 1998, p. 99)

This situation is significant not only because discrimination within the United States led to discrimination among Latinos themselves, but because it also led indirectly to family violence—the father slapped his daughter for dating a boy who was dark.

Racism often also extends into family life. Because Latinos are a mix of Indian, African, and Spanish blood, family members may vary considerably in color. Some Latino parents are grateful when they have a lighter-skinned child (Ho, 1992), and darker children may be subject to harshness within the family itself—which may be even more painful and humiliating than

racism from outsiders (Falicov, 1998). The darker-skinned children often become the scapegoats in the family (Gibson & Vasquez, 1982, as cited in Ho, 1992) and may, therefore, be more at risk for child maltreatment. They may also internalize a view of themselves as a source of shame and become subject to mental illnesses (Falicov), or may believe that any abuse they receive is justified. Further discrimination outside the home can lead to an exacerbation of any symptoms the child may experience as a result of the family violence alone (Vasquez, 1998).

Acculturation

When Latinos first immigrate to this country, they are often faced with a situation in which their values and ways of life are in stark contrast with U.S. values and lifestyles. Acculturation is the process by which immigrants assimilate and accommodate to the majority culture's way of life (Ho, 1992). It tends to be a multigenerational process, in that those who are born outside of this country are less acculturated than their children, who in turn are less acculturated than their own children. Many studies have shown that acculturation for Latinos results in a breakdown of their natural support systems— the more they adjust to the American way of life, the more their support systems disintegrate (Sanchez, 1992). Both machismo (Mayo, 1997) and familism (Sabogal et al., 1987) have been shown to be weaker in acculturated Latinos. However, because these cultural values can have both negative and positive effects on family violence in the Latino population, the effects of this cultural breakdown could be either positive or negative. What do you think is most likely?

With regard to CSA, findings concerning the role of acculturation are mixed. One study (Romero, Wyatt, Loeb, Carmona, & Solis, 1999) found that level of acculturation did not predict the prevalence of CSA among Latina women, whereas another (Siegel, Sorenson, Golding, Burnam, & Stein, 1987) found that acculturated Mexican Americans reported a rate of CSA that was five times higher than that for the less acculturated Mexican Americans. What variables might account for the differences

---

Box 9.2   Reflections on Strength, by Soledad Vera, Ph.D.

"Why do women stay?" (in abusive relationships) is a question all too often posed in popular and academic cultures. The question itself implies a negative appraisal of women, holding us accountable for the endurance of abusive relationships. In my clinical work and research with Latina women, I more often ask myself, "How was she able to do it, despite it all?" An abused Latina must choose to leave her partner despite (a) her loyalty to family unity and to the abusive partner because of his extreme dependence on her; (b) her husband's threats to harm her, her children, and her immediate family if she leaves him; (c) the cultural responsibilities of motherhood; (d) economic hardships; and (e) her migration to the United States and the resultant apprehensions about immigration issues and difficulties in negotiating U.S. institutions and services. However, I have seen many women leave abusive partners in the face of these numerous and dramatic dilemmas, which are confusing because, historically, a Latina's self-sacrifice and loyalty are central for familial and cultural survival. There are also multiple contradictory and ominous challenges, the least of which is confronting the significant loss inherent in terminating relationships, even ones that are so profoundly negative.

It is clear to me that how Latinas enter, remain in, and/or dissolve abusive relationships is a multilevel, complex process: It is gendered, cultural, economic, interpersonal, and intrapsychic. I feel that we must approach understanding and helping Latinas with respect for, and curiosity about (a) how each has contended with the compelling dilemmas of being a Latina woman, (b) what has empowered her politically, interpersonally, and intrapsychically, and (c) what stands in the way of the most constructive choices in her life. The task for us as a society is to abandon our assumptions of abused women having deficits, abandon our bewilderment about their plight, and reorient ourselves toward recognizing their dilemmas and their immense strength.

---

between these two studies? For spousal maltreatment, the picture is a bit clearer. In one study, Mexican Americans born in Mexico had wife abuse rates that were equivalent to Whites (20% vs. 21.6%), but Mexican Americans born in the United States had significantly higher rates (30.9%; Sorenson & Telles, 1991). In another study, for both Mexican Americans and Puerto Ricans, being born in the United States significantly increased the risk of men assaulting their wives (Kaufman Kantor, Jasinski, & Aldarondo, 1994). In a third study, low and high acculturated Latinos had lower rates of both husband and wife abuse than did medium acculturated Latinos (Caetano, Schafer, Clark, Cunradi, & Raspberry, 2000). Although country of birth of these Latinos was not analyzed, it could be presumed that low acculturated Latinos were born in another country, whereas high acculturated Latinos were born here to families that may have been here for generations; furthermore, medium acculturated

Latinos may be either first- or second-generation Latinos, who have been shown to have a high rate of psychological distress (DHHS, 2001). However, it may not be acculturation per se that predicts wife assault; rather, environmental stressors accompanying acculturation in work, school, and economics may be what contributes to maltreatment (Perilla, Bakeman, & Norris, 1994).

Overall, the evidence indicates that acculturation does not decrease the rates of various forms of violence in the family, and may even have an exacerbating effect. Perhaps acculturated Latinos may be more prone to family violence because as they become more acculturated, they may also desire the greater economic and educational opportunities that seem available but are often closed to them. As they come to realize that discrimination blocks their ability to take advantage of opportunities, they may become more frustrated and hostile, factors that could lead to violence in the home (Jasinski,

1996). Low acculturated Latinos may have lower rates of family violence relative to first- and second-generation Latinos because they may use their families back home as a frame of reference and realize how much better their lives are here versus how they would be if they had remained in their homelands. Their children and grandchildren, however, do not have this frame of reference, may recognize their relative deprivation in the United States, and become psychologically distressed—a condition that could lead to family violence (Suarez-Orozco & Suarez-Orozco, 1995). Alternatively, the loss of traditional cultural values may lead directly to family violence. Because there are no longer strict social controls and monitors over their behaviors and activities, an increased sense of freedom could contribute to violence (Sorenson & Golding, 1988).

Although acculturation may lead to an increase in family violence rates, it also leads to more help-seeking behaviors in Latinos experiencing family violence. Among Puerto Rican men, higher levels of acculturation led to more service utilization (Mayo, 1997). Furthermore, among battered women, second- and third-generation Latinas are more familiar with the mental health system as a means to get help for wife assault than are immigrant Latinas (Kanuha, 1994).

Thus, acculturation can have two very different influences on family violence: It can lead to a higher incidence, but also to more help-seeking behavior. Consequently, some researchers argue that a bicultural identity is the best solution to family violence in immigrants. Although strong identification with the American culture can lead to psychological distress, those Latinos who identify with and adopt both an American and a Latino culture seem to have a healthier adjustment. If they are proud of

their Latino heritage, they seem to be protected from the stereotypes and discrimination of the majority culture; they also seem to have a more realistic expectation of what they can hope to achieve. If they also adopt an American cultural orientation, they are able to function better within the United States (Ho, 1992).

SUMMARY

As you read the next two chapters on the prevalence, predictors, and consequences of family violence in the Latino communities, keep in mind the cultural context discussed in this chapter. We have shown how Latinos can have some different ideas as to what constitutes "abuse" in parent-child, spousal, and other family relationships—sometimes, these ideas are more stringent than those of the majority culture, sometimes they are more lax. In addition, some of their methods for dealing with certain childhood illnesses and disabilities can be considered "abusive" by members of the majority culture. How can these differing definitions, ideas, and practices affect their experiences of family violence? Also as you read the next two chapters, recall exactly who the Latino communities are—how they differ from the majority culture and how they differ from each other, especially in their economic, political, and educational backgrounds. Recall their differing migration histories and the degree to which each group was either warmly or coldly received in the United States. How can these differences contribute to the exacerbation or alleviation of family violence? Finally, think about the cultural values that many Latino groups hold in common. What is their role in family violence, and how do these values change as a result of

10

Hispanic/Latino Child Maltreatment

Examples of extreme abuse from a parent to a child:

- *"Constant physical abuse or emotional abuse."* (18-year-old Latino male from Puerto Rico, born to Puerto Rican parents)
- *"Striking with enough force to cause injury. Food deprivation."* (44-year-old Latino male, born in the United States to Puerto Rican parents)
- *"Dehumanizing a child, ex. being locked in a room."* (20-year-old Latina female, born in the United States to Mexican parents)
- *"The parent beats the child so hard, he was hospitalized."* (19-year-old Latina female, born in the United States to Ecuadoran parents)
- *"Father beats his child with a rod whenever the father comes home drunk, which is frequently."* (20-year-old Dominican Latino male, born in the United States)

SCOPE OF THE PROBLEM

Although, as discussed in chapter 9, Latinos may have some definitions of child abuse that differ from those of the majority culture, the studies assessing the incidence of child abuse in the Latino cultures primarily use majority culture definitions. Most of the studies of child maltreatment focusing on Latinos or having a sizeable subsample of Latinos are presented in Table 10.1. A discussion, including strengths and weaknesses of the studies, follows. It is important to realize two points with regard to this summary: (a) Research into physical abuse and neglect of Hispanic children is sorely needed, as not many studies on this issue exist in this population, and (b) child sexual abuse

seems to be the main focus of most of the research on child maltreatment. Therefore, a more thorough discussion of issues surrounding this type of maltreatment with regard to this population is the main focus here.

Two major sources of data on physical abuse and neglect in the Hispanic population are the National Family Violence Resurvey of 1985 (NFVR; Straus & Smith, 1990b) and the U.S. Department of Health and Human Services (DHHS, 1999). Although it provides valuable data with regard to child maltreatment that may not have been reported to the authorities, the NFVR has some limitations to consider when interpreting the results. First, the survey was not offered in Spanish. Therefore, more recent Hispanic immigrants or Hispanics who did not

Table 10.1 Child Maltreatment in Hispanic Communities

Study	Sample Description	Definition/Measure of Abuse	Findings
Regional Studies—Reported Cases			
Moisan, Sanders-Phillips, & Moisan (1997)	30 Black and 30 Hispanic sexually abused boys (majority of Hispanic boys born outside United States—60% in Mexico, 6% in El Salvador, 3% in Guadalajara, and 30% in United States) from residential programs, juvenile camp facilities, and an outpatient treatment program in Southern California; children were referred to facilities by law enforcement, CPA, and social workers	Substantiated cases	Hispanics: • Were more likely to be abused by an extended family member (Blacks were more likely to be abused by an immediate family member). • Were abused for longer periods of time. • Were older at time of first episode. • Had more sexually abusive behaviors performed on them. • Experienced more genital fondling. • Experienced more oral copulation. • Experienced more anal abuse. • Were more likely to be forced to perform sexual behaviors on perpetrators. • Were more likely to have abusers offer bribes and use authority positions to coerce the child.
Mennen (1995)[a]	134 females at Southern California sexual abuse clinics (51 Whites; 38 Hispanics, primarily Mexican American; 35 Blacks; 8 Asians; and 2 Others)	Substantiated cases	For Hispanic victims: • Average age of onset: 9.23 years. • Average duration of abuse: 2.16 years. • 68.6% experienced penetration. • 57.9% were abused by a father figure. • 63.6% were forcibly abused. • 63.2% were removed from the home.
Los Angeles Epidemiologic Catchment Area Study (Stein, Golding, Siegel, Burnam, & Sorenson, 1988)	3,132 Whites and Hispanics; representative sample	• "In your lifetime, has anyone ever tried to pressure or force you to have sexual contact (touching your sexual parts, your touching their sexual parts, or sexual intercourse) prior to age 16?" • Excluded adults who reported any adult sexual abuse, even if they had child sexual abuse	• 8.7% of Whites vs. 3% of Hispanics experienced only child sexual abuse. • Age of first episode did not differ by ethnicity. • For both ethnicities, significantly more females than males reported abuse.

(Continued)

163

Table 10.1 Continued

Study	Sample Description	Definition/Measure of Abuse	Findings
Hampton (1987)	17,645 cases of child abuse (physical and sexual), neglect, educational neglect, and emotional maltreatment at Boston hospitals	Substantiated cases	• Black and Hispanic children were younger than Whites. • Black and Hispanic moms were less educated and younger than White moms. • Hispanics comprised 4.2% of substantiated cases.
Lindholm & Willey (1986)	4,132 child abuse cases reported to Los Angeles County Sheriff's Department (November 1975–November 1982): Blacks, Whites, and Hispanics	Reported cases	• Whites and Hispanics were underrepresented with regard to population distribution (Blacks were overrepresented). • White and Hispanic males were more likely to abuse (Black females were more likely to abuse). • White and Hispanic females were more likely to be victims (Black females and males were equal victims). • Blacks were less likely to have been sexually abused than Whites or Hispanics. • 73% of Hispanic cases involved physical abuse; 27% were sexual abuse.
Lauderdale, Valiunas, & Anderson (1980)	Cases of child abuse reported in Texas, 1975–1977	Reported cases	• In comparison to Blacks and Whites, Mexican Americans had the lowest rates of abuse and abuse with neglect, but had equal rates of neglect.
Regional Studies—Self-Reports			
Mexican American Drug Use and Dropout Study, 1988–1992 (Perez, 2001)	2,466 Mexican American and White high school dropouts versus nondropouts from three communities in the southwestern United States	• *Physical abuse:* Have you ever been "beaten by parents"? • *Sexual abuse:* Have you ever been "raped or sexually assaulted"?	• Significantly more Whites than Hispanics were physically abused (24% vs. 19%). • Significantly more Whites than Hispanics were sexually abused (24% vs. 10%).
Torres et al. (2000)	1,004 women from five general community hospitals in Florida and Massachusetts, as part of a study on low birth weight and abuse: 19% Mexican American,	Abuse Assessment Screen	Between and within ethnic group differences in prevalence of CSA: • 3.2% of Mexican Americans were sexually abused, whereas 4.3% of Cuban Americans, 8.4% of Puerto Ricans, and 2.2% of Central Americans were sexually abused.

Study	Sample Description	Definition/Measure of Abuse	Findings
	19% Puerto Rican, 19% African American, 20% White, 14% Cuban American, and 9% Central American		• 11.3% of Whites and 17.2% of Blacks were sexually abused. • Being Mexican American served as a protective factor against sexual abuse, as did speaking Spanish or both Spanish and English (vs. speaking only English).
Romero, Wyatt, Loeb, Carmona, & Solis (1999)	905 Los Angeles women between 18 and 50 years of age: 305 Black, 300 Hispanic, 300 White; stratified probability sample; only Hispanics analyzed for this article	Sexual body contact prior to age 18 by someone of any age and relationship to respondent; perpetrator must be more than 5 years older; if less than 5 years older, only counted if contact was not desired or involved coercion	• 33% of Hispanic females were sexually abused. • >80% of cases occurred prior to age 7. • More than one third of victims were revictimized. • The majority of experiences were in a private location by young males known to the victims. • Four women were forced to marry perpetrators. • 56% of cases experienced very severe abuse. • 26% of cases experienced rape. • 48% of cases had a family member as the perpetrator. • The mean age at first episode was 11 years.
Arroyo, Simpson, & Aragon (1997)	263 Hispanic and White college women in New Mexico	Childhood Sexual Experiences Survey	• 27.1% of Hispanics reported CSA (no ethnic differences). • For Hispanics, CSA was more serious in that it occurred at a younger age and was more physically intrusive. • Hispanics were more likely to have an extended family member as the perpetrator.

NOTE: For information on Latino child maltreatment according to the U.S. Department of Health and Human Services (1999, 2000), the Third National Incidence Study (Sedlak & Broadhurst, 1996), the 1990 National Longitudinal Survey of Youth (Giles-Sims et al., 1995), the National Family Violence Surveys of 1975 and 1985 (Cazenave & Straus, 1979; Connelly & Straus, 1992; Straus & Gelles, 1990a; Straus & Smith, 1990a, 1990b; Wolfner & Gelles, 1993), California Children's Services Archive (2002), Rao et al. (1992), Roosa et al. (1999), and Urquiza and Goodlin-Jones (1994), please see Table 3.1. For information on Latino child maltreatment according to the First National Incidence Study (Hampton, 1987; Hampton & Newberger, 1985), Delong et al. (1983), Doll et al. (1992), Kercher and McShane (1984), Shaw et al. (2001), Spearly and Lauderdale (1983), and Taussig and Talmi (2001), please see Table 7.1.

a. For ethnic comparisons, please see Table 7.1.

feel comfortable speaking English were excluded from the sample. Second, the country of origin was not assessed. Consequently, possible differences among Puerto Ricans, Cubans, and Mexicans are lost. Third, the survey was conducted over the telephone; thus, the poorest Hispanics, many of whom may commit acts of child maltreatment due to social stresses, were probably not represented in the sample because they lacked a telephone.

Despite these limitations, the results of the survey are quite informative. The NFVR (Straus & Smith, 1990b) revealed that 4.8/100 Hispanic children were the victims of child abuse, defined as severe violence excluding hitting or attempting to hit with a belt or stick, in 1985 (Definition 1). With a broadening of the definition of child abuse to include hitting or attempting to hit with a belt or stick (Definition 2), the rate jumped to 13.4/100 Hispanic children. These estimates translate into approximately 288,000 (Definition 1) or 804,000 (Definition 2) Hispanic children nationwide who were the victims of abuse by their parents in 1985. These rates are significantly greater than the rates found for White children, even after controlling for other sociodemographic variables correlated with child abuse.

These results stand in stark contrast to the number of reported cases of physical and sexual abuse, neglect, medical neglect, psychological maltreatment, and other abuse reported to Child Protective Services (CPS) nationwide in 1999. According to DHHS (1999), 12.6 per 1,000 Hispanic children were the victims of child maltreatment during that year, a rate comparable to the U.S. population as a whole. Of course, the cases reported to the NFVR may never have been reported to CPS. However, in partial support of the CPS results, both Whites and Hispanics are underrepresented with regard to their population distribution in child abuse cases reported to the L.A. County's Sheriff's Department (Lindholm & Willey, 1986). To further complicate matters, there are studies showing that Hispanics commit less physical abuse and physical abuse with neglect than Whites or Blacks (e.g., Lauderdale, Valiunas, & Anderson, 1980; Perez, 2001). Overall, then, it is difficult to say what the exact rate of child physical abuse and neglect is in Hispanic

communities. It is possible that the rate may differ with respect to the social class, acculturation level, and country of origin of the Hispanics being studied. It seems, though, that rates of physical abuse and neglect are probably not that much different than the rates for the U.S. population as a whole.

A few studies also show some differences in the dynamics of child abuse and neglect between the Hispanic community and other communities in the United States. For example, within the Los Angeles community, White and Hispanic males are more likely to be the abusers (for Blacks, females are more likely) and females are more likely to be victims (for Blacks, both sexes are equally likely to be victimized; Lindholm & Willey, 1986). In addition, in hospital cases in Boston, Black and Hispanic abuse victims tended to be younger than White abuse victims and their mothers tended to be younger and less educated than White mothers (Hampton, 1987).

As mentioned previously, child sexual abuse (CSA) seems to be the major focus in studies of child maltreatment in the Hispanic community. Studies directed at establishing rates of CSA find that in comparison to Whites, Hispanics are at greater risk for CSA (e.g., Doll et al., 1992; Kercher & McShane, 1984), lower risk (Stein, Golding, Siegel, Burnam, & Sorenson, 1988; Urquiza & Goodlin-Jones, 1994), or equal risk (Arroyo, Simpson, & Aragon, 1997; Roosa et al., 1999). Depending on the study, the rate of Hispanic victimization of CSA ranged between 3% (community sample of Los Angeles Hispanics; Stein et al.) and 33% (Los Angeles and Arizona women respectively; Romero et al., 1999; Roosa et al.), and as high as 50% (homosexual and bisexual Hispanic men; Doll et al.). As can be seen in Table 10.1, variations in the definitions of CSA, in the population being studied, and the year in which the studies took place could account for these differences.

The study by Torres et al. (2000) explicitly shows that the differences in the population under study can greatly influence the rates of CSA. They found that Puerto Ricans had by far the highest rate of CSA of all the Hispanic subgroups: A full 18.4% experienced CSA, the highest of all ethnic groups and Hispanic subgroups. Furthermore, the level of acculturation, as measured by language preference, also predicted CSA: The more acculturated the Hispanics, the more likely they were to have experienced CSA, with a full 16% of the English-only speakers experiencing CSA, in comparison to 9.5% of the bilingual speakers and 3.7% of the Spanish-only speakers.

These studies of CSA also illuminate some important similarities and differences in the nature of the sexual abuse itself. For all ethnicities, females are at higher risk for CSA than males (Stein et al., 1988). Therefore, a discussion of research on female victims is presented first. The studies reviewed here have samples including any combination of Hispanic with Black, Asian, and/or White participants. Many studies report that the average age at first CSA episode does not differ by ethnicity (e.g., Mennen, 1995; Stein et al.). However, one study found that Hispanic females tend to be younger than Whites or Blacks (Arroyo et al., 1997) and another found that Hispanics and Whites tend to be older than Blacks at the age of onset (DeJong et al., 1983). In general, the average age of the first CSA episode for Hispanic girls is somewhere between 9.23 years (Mennen) and 11 years (Romero et al., 1999), and 16% of cases seem to occur prior to the age of 7 (Romero et al.). Although the majority of cases were one-time episodes, more than one third of Hispanic girls were revictimized (Romero et al.), and the average duration of the abuse was 2.16 years (Mennen).

The majority of Hispanic girls are victimized in a private location by young males who are known to the victim (Romero et al., 1999). It appears that Hispanic girls are more likely than Whites to be victimized by a male relative (Arroyo et al., 1997; Rao et al., 1992): A full 48% of Latina CSA cases in one study were perpetrated by family members (Romero et al.). Moreover, Hispanic girls are more likely than Blacks to be victimized by a father figure (Shaw et al., 2001). Indeed, 57.9% of Hispanic girls in therapy for sexual abuse were abused by a father figure (Mennen, 1995). In addition, Hispanics and Blacks were more likely than Whites or Asians to experience vaginal intercourse during their CSA (Rao et al.), and reports from college women indicate that the Hispanic women's episodes of CSA are more intrusive physically

than those of White college women (Arroyo et al.). Furthermore, 68.6% of Latina girls in therapy for CSA were victims of penetration (Mennen), and 56% of the CSA cases in a community sample of Hispanic girls were characterized as "very severe abuse," whereas 26% of them were characterized as "rape" (Romero et al.).

Sexually abused Hispanic girls also experience more abusive episodes and take longer to disclose the abuse than sexually abused Black girls (Shaw et al., 2001). Most shockingly, in one study, four Hispanic girls were forced to marry the perpetrator of their CSA (Romero et al., 1999). Recall some of the cultural values of Latino communities presented in chapter 9. What do you think are some of the reasons that Latina sexual abuse victims may be reluctant to disclose their abuse? Why may they be forced to marry their abusers? Consider the case study of CSA presented in Box 10.1. What are some of the similarities of this case to cases you have seen from other cultures? What aspects of the abuse seem to be unique to the Hispanic cultures? According to the information in chapter 9, why may they be unique?

Although boys are much less likely to be victimized by CSA, there are two studies that focus specifically on Hispanic boys as victims. In a study of homosexual and bisexual men who were seeking treatment at clinics for sexually transmitted diseases in several U.S. cities, Black and Hispanic males were much more likely to have been victimized by CSA than White males (50% vs. 32%). Moreover, Hispanic males were younger than White or Black males at age of onset of the CSA (8 years vs. 10 years) and were more likely to report a greater than 5-year difference between themselves and the perpetrators (Doll et al., 1992). Other differences between Hispanic and Black boy victims of CSA included the following: Hispanics were more likely to be abused by an extended family member, were abused for longer periods of time, had more sexually abusive behaviors performed on them, experienced more genital fondling, were more likely to have experienced oral copulation, experienced more anal abuse, and were more likely to be forced to perform sexual behaviors on the perpetrators; in addition, more of their abusers offered bribes or used their authority positions to coerce the

---

Box 10.1   Account of Child Abuse in the Hispanic Communities

---

"Being Latina is real precious to me. However, part of the culture that I hate is the silence. . . . There was no talk of sex in the house ever. It was all out on the streets. And how can you go to a woman you haven't been able to talk to about your damn period and tell her that her husband is raping you? I think this kind of silence might be common, but I think it's especially true because my people feel so powerless in this culture, fearing authorities outside the family. We had to stick together and protect each other from the system, and from the white people who control it. . . . Admitting any problem would reflect badly on our whole culture. . . ." (p. 374)

This quote is from Soledad, a Latina woman who suffered frequent physical and sexual abuse from her father. The physical abuse consisted of intense beatings at least every other day for years. The sexual abuse started the day she was brought home from the hospital as an infant. At that time, her father no longer slept with her mother—he slept with Soledad. The abuse began as fondling, and when she was 8 years old, he raped her for the first time. After that, he raped her three times a week, in many different locations. His favorite spot was in the car at night, a place where he also raped many neighborhood girls. Many times, he raped Soledad from behind, and each time, he threatened to slit her throat or cut out her tongue.

SOURCE: Bass and Davis, 1988.

---

victims (Moisan et al., 1997). These two studies provide preliminary evidence that Hispanic boys victimized by CSA may experience much more severe and lasting CSA than boys of other ethnic groups. Again, recall the material you read in chapter 9 on Latino cultural values. What cultural reasons may there be for the greater severity and duration of CSA against Latino boys?

PREDICTORS AND CORRELATES

Studies assessing predictors and correlates of child maltreatment in Latino communities have found four major predictors for childhood physical abuse: (a) macrosystem level economic stressors, (b) exosystem level lack of social support, (c) exosystem level neighborhood problems, and (d) individual level dysfunctional childhood of abusers. Interestingly, to our knowledge, no studies assessing Latino CSA have looked at these types of predictor variables. Instead, they seem to focus on the dynamics of the abusive situation (e.g., who the abuser is in relation to the child, how old the child is at the first incident, what types of sexual behaviors

are performed on the child, the duration of the abuse) and the consequences of the abuse, which are discussed in the next major section. Our discussion of the predictors and correlates of child maltreatment focuses specifically on the ones that relate to childhood physical abuse.

Macrosystem Level

Economic stressors seem to characterize abusive Latino families. In many studies that have found ethnic differences in the rates of child physical abuse, the ethnic differences disappear when controlling for income (e.g., Hampton, 1987), and lower income is related to child abuse for all ethnicities. However, it is certainly not the case that all people with low income abuse their children. Therefore, it is important to consider which variables that are related to low income characterize those parents who abuse their children.

Exosystem Level

Social Support

A second major predictor of child abuse in the Latino community is a familiar exosystem variable—lack of social support for the parents. In one study, both U.S.-born and Mexican-born Mexican American child abusers experienced a high degree of alienation from their relatives, having either a strained relationship with them or none at all (Navarro & Miranda, 1985). In a detailed study of social support and its relation to child abuse among Latinas, it was not the number of social supports available that predicted child abuse, but the use of the existing social supports. During childhood, there were no differences between future child abusers and nonabusers in the desire to talk with family, friends, or community leaders, or the availability of these sources of support, but nonabusers were significantly more likely to actually make use of these sources. This pattern continued into adulthood; there were no differences in the number of relatives or friends available to support them, but abusers were significantly less likely to seek help from these relatives and friends. Therefore, there was probably some sort of interference in childhood attachment caused by physical abuse of these Latinas, which translated into a reluctance and/or inability to seek help when it was needed both in childhood and adulthood (Mitchell, 1990).

Lack of social support can aggravate many individual-level problems for abusive Latino caregivers. For instance, abusive Latina mothers, in comparison to nonabusive mothers, have significantly greater feelings of rejection, anxiety, loneliness, and self-blame. They are more withdrawn, less open, and less aware of people's needs, including their own children's (Mitchell, 1990). Perhaps these feelings are related to a skewed perception that abusive parents have of their children and their children's abilities. In one study, abusive Mexican American parents expected their children to provide them with an unrealistically high degree of affection, and to act like mini-adults (Navarro & Miranda, 1985). In addition, one risk factor for physical abuse and neglect is the parents' unrealistic expectations of the child (Wood, 1997). Perhaps if these abusers were able to take advantage of social supports, they would have more realistic information as to the capabilities of children and would not be so harsh when their children did not live up to their expectations.

Neighborhood Problems

In an interesting investigation of exosystem influences on child abuse, Garbarino and Kostelny (1992) studied communities in poor Black and Hispanic Chicago areas. Variations in child maltreatment were linked to nine demographic and socioeconomic factors. Taken together, these factors accounted for 79% of the variance in child maltreatment: higher percentage living in poverty, higher percentage unemployed, percentage of female-headed households (lower for Hispanics but higher for Blacks), higher percentage living in overcrowded households, higher percentage of Black households, higher percentage of Hispanic households, lower percentage of affluent people, lower median educational attainment, and higher percentage of people living in their residence for less than five years.

Garbarino and Kostelny (1992) also spotlighted the differences between two low-income Chicago neighborhoods: an African American community with high rates of child abuse and a Hispanic community with low rates of child abuse. The differences in rates of child abuse were striking: Deaths due to child maltreatment were twice as high in the African American community. Dramatic differences between these two communities in exosystem-level stressors were observed. Specifically, in the African American community, the residents had nothing good to say about the community, crime was very evident, and the mood was dark and depressed. By contrast, in the Hispanic community, the residents acknowledged that they were poor and had problems, but they described their community as a decent place to live. The residents in the African American community did not know about community services and there was little evidence of support networks. In contrast, residents of the Hispanic community knew about support services, had good formal and informal support networks, and had faith in the political leaders of their community. Finally, in the African American community, there was a weak sense of community, especially because the residents felt that a local gang controlled it. It is important to note that Garbarino and Kostelny addressed rates of child maltreatment at the community level; they did not interview families about the level of physical abuse within individual homes. How do you think these characteristics of the exosystems, as described by the residents, might have contributed to the different levels of child maltreatment reported?

Individual Level

As has been found with most populations of abusers, Hispanics who experience abuse in childhood are significantly more likely to abuse their own children than Hispanic parents not abused as children (Straus & Smith, 1990b; Wood, 1997). In addition, Hispanic parents who severely abuse their children report that they had experienced severe childhood abuse (Mitchell, 1990). Mexican American child abusers have reported that their relationships with their parents were not happy and that their parents demanded strict, unquestioned obedience to their rules (Navarro & Miranda, 1985). Furthermore, in comparison to those who did not abuse their children, Hispanic child abusers spent shorter periods of time in their families of origin; they were separated from their parents because of family problems or rejection by their parents; and they experienced a greater variety and frequency of threats of abandonment, separation, and physical punishment (Mitchell). Indeed, child abusers experienced very dysfunctional childhoods themselves. The frequency of physical punishment during the mother's childhood, the number of her childhood separations from her own parents, and the mothers' perceptions of their own self-reliance accounted for 93% of the variance in their current abusive behaviors against their own children (Mitchell).

CONSEQUENCES

In contrast to the studies of predictors and correlates of child maltreatment, the majority of studies assessing the consequences of child maltreatment in Hispanic communities focus on CSA. Very few studies assessed the consequences of physical abuse or neglect, and those that did look at physical abuse or neglect combined them with sexual abuse. Therefore, it is difficult to tease apart the relative effects of the different types of abuse in these studies.

To our knowledge, three studies with at least a Hispanic subsample combined all types of abuse and assessed the consequences. In a study comparing abused White and Mexican Americans to nonabused adolescents, there were higher rates of property damage and sexual offenses among adolescents with a history of physical and/or sexual abuse (Perez, 2001). This delinquent behavior may be more common among abused Hispanic adolescents than among adolescents in other minority groups. In a comparison of substantiated cases of abused White, Black, and Hispanic children in foster care on their subsequent engagement in four types of risk behaviors as teenagers (sexual, substance use, self-destructive, and delinquent), Hispanic teenagers had the highest rates of engagement in risk behaviors. For Whites and Hispanics, higher self-esteem and more parental involvement were associated with a lower incidence of risk behaviors, whereas a greater commitment to negative peer groups and more trauma symptoms were linked to greater risk behaviors (Taussig & Talmi, 2001).

Other psychological consequences of physical and/or sexual abuse were found among Mexican American abuse victims. In comparison to nonabused children, abused Mexican American children had significantly higher negative moods, ineffectiveness, anxiety, worry, physiological symptoms of anxiety, dissociation, and externalizing and internalizing behaviors. Moreover, many abused children scored above the clinical cutoff for depression (27%), anxiety (26.7%), internalizing symptoms (58.1%), and externalizing symptoms (54.8%), and 19.4% scored above the mean on dissociation reported for children suffering from dissociative identity disorder (Mennen, 2000).

The outcome studies focusing specifically on sexual abuse show that this type of abuse can have dramatic and long-lasting effects on Latino children. Take, for example, the case of Soledad introduced in Box 10.1. Now read Box 10.2, a description of the long-term consequences of Soledad's abusive childhood. What were the psychological and physical consequences of her repeated abuse as a child? Is there any reason to think her case is different from other Hispanic women who were sexually abused as children?

When Hispanic children are compared to other groups on psychological outcomes of

---

Box 10.2   Consequences of Childhood Sexual Abuse

Soledad went to school and got a good job, but things were okay only on the surface. She often came home from work and just lay alone in her dark apartment, not answering the door if someone came by and not answering the phone when someone called. She would have a bottle of Coke for dinner, or on better days, a pint of ice cream. She didn't care if anybody cared enough about her to check in on her—she just wanted to be left alone.

Because she didn't care about others, she ate and drank a lot to comfort herself. She gained a lot of weight, and one night, she drank shot after shot of tequila. If her girlfriend hadn't found her passed out on the floor and gotten help, Soledad would have probably died. Soledad describes her relationships with others as follows:

> I never really believed that anyone loved me, so I felt kind of orphaned. I was self-sufficient. If I hadn't been, that would have been the end of me. It's prevented me from ever wanting anyone to take care of me. I will take care of myself and that's it. And if anyone needs to be taken care of, I will take care of them, but I will never let them take care of me. And that's kind of hard, 'cause I get sick too and I'll grow old.

SOURCE: Bass and Davis, 1988, p. 376.

---

sexual abuse, they seem to suffer the more adverse consequences (Russell, 1986; Sanders-Phillips, Moisan, Wadlington, Morgan, & English, 1995). A community survey of ethnically mixed adult females showed that approximately 56% of those who were sexually abused as a child reported lasting effects of the CSA (Romero et al., 1999). One result of CSA is that female victims appear to be at risk for further sexual abuse, even rape, as adults. For Hispanic college women, 40% of CSA victims had already experienced rape as adults, as compared to 10.3% of non-CSA women. Perhaps these CSA victims are at a higher risk for rape as adults because of the adverse psychological consequences of their CSA (Arroyo et al., 1997).

Some common symptoms experienced by Hispanic children who experienced CSA are sexual acting out (13.8%), anger (20%), suicidal ideation and/or attempts (10%), and urinary symptoms (6.3%; Rao et al., 1992). The most common symptoms among all ethnicities seem to be depression and anxiety (Mennen, 1994, 1995; Moisan et al., 1997; Roosa et al., 1999; Shaw et al., 2001; Stein et al., 1988). These reactions may be more severe in Latina victims of CSA. In one study of sexually abused girls, Hispanic females were more likely than Blacks to display anxiety and depression (Shaw et al.). In comparison to Hispanic females who were not penetrated and members of other ethnicities who were either penetrated or not, Hispanic females who were penetrated had the highest rates of anxiety and depression (Mennen, 1995; Shaw et al.). Moreover, the severity of CSA seems to be the strongest predictor of depression in Hispanic females, but not necessarily females of other ethnicities (Roosa et al.). That is, the higher rates of depression and anxiety among Hispanic females seem to be accounted for by those girls who were penetrated. As you think back to the previous chapter's discussion of cultural values, what do you think are some reasons why the Hispanic girls who were penetrated have the most severe psychological problems? How many of these negative outcomes can you identify in Soledad's story?

Many studies of minority populations attempt to identify ethnic differences that may occur in other psychological responses to CSA. Overall, the evidence indicates that the severity of consequences is based on the severity of the abuse, the closeness of the perpetrator (e.g., family member vs. close friend vs. stranger), the duration of the abuse, the age at which the abuse began, and the age difference between the perpetrator and the victim (Doll et al., 1992;

Mennen, 1995; Roosa et al., 1999). However, there is some evidence that ethnic groups differ in the extent and types of reactions they display. In addition to the higher rates of depression and anxiety among the Hispanic girls, Hispanic girls, relative to Black sexually abused girls, are more likely to display aggression, somatization, and internalizing and externalizing behaviors. They are also more likely to see their families as dysfunctional (Shaw et al., 2001). Hispanic sexually abused girls, relative to Black girls, are more likely to display hopelessness, self-dislike, a poor self-image, and loneliness, whereas Blacks are more likely to display crying, somatization, and anger. For Hispanic girls, the experience of anal abuse leads to a significant increase in anger, and the number of individuals living in their homes at the time of the abuse leads to an increase in both depression and anger (Moisan et al., 1997). Why might this microsystem variable aggravate the negative consequences of abuse?

The most comprehensive study of ethnic differences in the reactions to CSA is a study of Los Angeles White and Hispanic residents. Because this was a community survey, in which only 8.7% of Whites and 3% of Hispanics reported having experienced CSA, there was not enough statistical power in many of the comparisons to detect all potentially significant differences in psychological outcomes. Therefore, most of these differences are only trends; any differences found to be statistically significant are so labeled. Hispanic males and females who experienced CSA displayed, over the course of a lifetime, more of the following symptoms than did Whites who experienced CSA: fearfulness (60.3% vs. 26%), behavioral restrictions (34.2% vs. 23%), less sexual interest (57.4% vs. 16.3%, significant), less sexual pleasure (40.4% vs. 23.5%), depression (60% vs. 39.3%), anger (67% vs. 32.8%), appetite disturbances (24.3% vs. 5.3%), and fear of being alone (29.2% vs. 11.7%). Whites were more likely to feel guilty (50% vs. 36.6%) and to abuse substances (5.5% vs. 0%). In addition, over the course of a lifetime, sexually abused Hispanics were more likely than nonsexually abused Hispanics to be given some type of diagnosis and more likely to evidence substance use disorders, specifically drug abuse/dependence; affective disorders,

specifically major depressive disorder and dysthymia; and anxiety disorders, specifically phobias (Stein et al., 1988).

Overall, child abuse has short-term and long-term adverse effects on the Hispanic children who experience it. They experience the full range of psychological symptoms and disorders in response to the abuse, and in many cases these psychological consequences follow them into adulthood. There also seem to be some ethnic differences in psychological reactions to sexual abuse, with Hispanics showing more severe reactions than other ethnic groups in many domains, especially depression.

SUMMARY

In sum, it appears that there is not enough evidence to suggest that Latinos differ in the prevalence of child abuse, although there may be some differences in the nature of child sexual abuse. The abuse of children seems to be predicted by four major factors in Latino families—economic stressors, the dysfunctional childhood of the parent, lack of social support, and neighborhood stressors. The consequences of child abuse in Latino cultures seem to mirror those of the majority culture, although Latina victims of CSA may experience more severe outcomes.

Based on the information in this chapter and in chapter 9, what do we still need to know about the different forms of child abuse in these communities? For instance, do we know whether the rates, predictors, and/or consequences differ as a function of the specific community to which the Latino belongs? Do we have reason to believe, based on the information in chapter 9, that Mexicans, Puerto Ricans, Cubans, and other Latinos may differ in these areas? Why or why not? Could acculturation level make a difference in these factors? In what way? Furthermore, preliminary results show that Latinas suffer more severe consequences of CSA in comparison to other groups. What are likely reasons for this? Could this result perhaps differ by the specific community studied? By the level of acculturation? What are your predictions based on what you now know about the Latino culture?

11

HISPANIC/LATINO ADULT MALTREATMENT

Extreme forms of wife abuse:

- *"Carrying on an open relationship with someone else than spouse; rape, hitting, alcoholic."* (18-year-old Latino male from Puerto Rico)
- *"Rape wife."* (19-year-old Hispanic female from the United States with Spanish and Cuban parents)
- *"Physical contact, i.e., hitting, shoving, choking. Forcible sex, not allowing a person to go out on their own."* (44-year-old Latino male from the United States with Puerto Rican parents)

Extreme forms of husband abuse:

- *"Sabotaging other's day or plans, always asking for too much, stressing out partner, no sex."* (18-year-old Latino male from Puerto Rico)
- *"Punching her husband."* (19-year-old Hispanic female from the United States with Spanish and Cuban parents)
- *"Physical contact, i.e., slapping, hitting; not allowing a person to go out on their own."* (44-year-old Latino male from the United States with Puerto Rican parents)

Extreme forms of elder abuse:

- *"Putting in a home. Never visiting; a family feud; spreading rumors or intimate details."* (18-year-old Latino male from Puerto Rico)
- *"Refuse to take care of."* (19-year-old Hispanic female from the United States with Spanish and Cuban parents)
- *"Physical contact, i.e., slapping, punching; food deprivation, theft of savings."* (44-year-old Latino male from the United States with Puerto Rican parents)

As discussed in Chapter 9 and as the above quotes illustrate, Latinos may have differing conceptions from the majority culture as to what constitutes "abuse" in adult relationships. Furthermore, they may differ among themselves in their definitions, depending upon what specific Latino community they belong to, how long they have lived in this country, and their own personal experiences. In addition, as can be seen from the above quotes, what is considered "abusive" may depend upon the relationship being discussed. Latinos, in our sample and in the studies presented in Chapter 9, seem to have more stringent criteria for what constitutes "abuse" when an elder is the victim than when a spouse is the victim.

The majority culture has been studying the incidence and dynamics of abusive adult family relationships in Latino communities for approximately 20 years. As the Latino population has grown, so has attention to spousal and elder maltreatment in the Latino community. As you read about adult maltreatment in Latino communities, keep in mind what you have learned about the cultural contexts of those communities, and consider the role of culture in the incidence, predictors, and consequences of violence in Latino families.

SPOUSAL MALTREATMENT

Scope of the Problem

Table 11.1 contains several studies from the past 20 years on the incidence and descriptions of both wife and husband abuse in Hispanic communities.

Wife Physical Abuse

The government agencies that have previously been described have collected information on the incidence of wife abuse by Hispanic versus non-Hispanic perpetrators. The U.S. Department of Justice (DOJ) found that overall, between 1993 and 1998, there were no differences in reported rates of wife abuse between Hispanics and non-Hispanics. However, other statistics show that between 1993 and 1999, non-Hispanic women age 20 to 34 were victimized by significantly more intimate partner violence than were Hispanic women of comparable ages; moreover, intimate partner violence victimization rates for Hispanic females peaked at lower ages and were spread over a wider range of ages than rates for non-Hispanic females. Hispanic females experienced their highest rates of intimate partner violence in the age range between 16 and 34 (12 per 1,000 Hispanic females; Rennison, 2001a; Rennison & Welchans, 2000; see Table 3.2 in this book).

In contrast to the DOJ statistics, the National Family Violence Resurvey (NFVR) of 1985 (Straus & Smith, 1990b), which had an oversampling of Hispanics, showed that the incidence of wife abuse in this population was 17.3% (or 519,000 Hispanic wives nationwide) and that the incidence of severe abuse was 7.3% (or 219,000 Hispanic wives nationwide). These rates were significantly greater than those for the White community, and, contrary to expectations, these differences held regardless of income, occupation, or employment status. Hispanic families in the Northeast (where Puerto Ricans are the major Hispanic group) had the highest rates of wife abuse. Because the NFVR results are based on a sample that is more representative of the population at large and not restricted to reported cases, it may give the best estimates of abuse in this community, but these data also have some shortcomings. The NFVR did not assess the nation of origin for the Hispanics, nor did the sample include any Hispanics who did not speak English. It is likely that newer immigrants were not included in this survey, and according to other surveys (Coalition for Immigrant and Refugee Rights and Service [CIRRS], 1990; Hass, Dutton, & Orloff, 2000), newer immigrants may have a much higher incidence of wife abuse.

To address at least one of these issues, the National Violence Against Women Survey (NVAW) was offered in both English and Spanish, with results somewhat discrepant from the National Family Violence Surveys (NFVS). In the NVAW study, a higher percentage of Hispanic women (21.2%) reported a physical assault by their husband, which, when compared to 22.1% of non-Hispanic women who were abused, was not significantly different (Tjaden & Thoennes, 2000). However, this survey also has its drawbacks. For non-Hispanics, NVAW combined Whites, Blacks, Asians, and Native Americans, as long as they did not report that they originated from a Spanish-speaking country. This type of "ethnic lumping," as discussed in previous chapters, does not allow for meaningful comparisons across major ethnic groups, and each of these groups may have vastly different rates of spousal abuse. NVAW also did not ask for the country of origin of their Hispanic respondents; therefore, comparisons within the Hispanic communities are not possible.

(Text continues on page 181)

Table 11.1 Spousal Maltreatment in Hispanic Communities

Study	Sample Description	Definition/Measure of Abuse	Findings
National Studies—Self-Report			
1992 National Alcohol and Family Violence Survey (Jasinski, Asdigian, & Kaufman Kantor, 1997)	1,970 families: nationally representative; oversample of Hispanic families; 812 Whites; 702 Latinos	Conflict Tactics Scale	• 12.3% of Hispanics reported wife assault in the previous year, vs. 10.5% of Whites. • No significant ethnic differences in these rates.
1992 National Alcohol and Family Violence Survey (Kaufman Kantor, Jasinski, & Aldarondo, 1994)	1,025 Whites and 743 Hispanics representing Puerto Ricans, Cubans, and Mexican Americans nationwide; respondents must be living as a couple	Conflict Tactics Scale	• 9.9% of White males abused their wives. • 20.4% of Puerto Rican males abused their wives. • 10.5% of Mexican American males abused their wives. • 2.5% of Cuban males abused their wives. • Hispanics did not differ from Whites in rates of wife abuse when norms regarding violence approval, age, and economic stressors held constant.
Regional Studies—Reported Cases			
Krishnan, Hilbert, & VanLeeuwen (2001)	102 rural battered women in shelters (72% Mexican American) in New Mexico	Substantiated cases	No ethnic differences in types of abuse except the following: • 62% of Mexican Americans vs. 40% of others were sexually abused. • 37% of Mexican Americans vs. 48% of others were harassed. • 24% of Mexican Americans vs. 10% of others experienced all types of abuse measured (physical, verbal, emotional, sexual, abuse with weapon, harassment, and stalking). • Mexican Americans remained in abusive relationships longer.
Krishnan, Hilbert, VanLeeuwen, & Kolia (1997)	242 battered women in rural southern New Mexico shelters: 107 Hispanic, 103 White, 9 Native American	New Mexico Coalition Against Domestic Violence Survey	• More than one half of Hispanics, but less than one half of Whites, were abused on a weekly basis. • Fewer Hispanics than Whites experienced violence in their previous relationship. • Hispanics experienced more violence in current relationships and more violence during pregnancy. • No ethnic differences were found regarding length of stay at the shelter or whether the women went back to the abusers. • More White than Hispanic battered women used drugs or alcohol.

(Continued)

Table 11.1 Continued

Study	Sample Description	Definition/Measure of Abuse	Findings
Torres (1991)	25 White battered women and 25 Mexican American battered women (born in United States, but parents born in Mexico) in two urban-area shelters and one rural shelter; matched on age and SES; geographic location of shelters not given	Conflict Tactics Scales and Battered Women Interview Schedule	• No differences were found in the nature or severity of abuse. • Mexican Americans remained in abusive relationships longer. Sources of conflict were the same for both groups (e.g., dominance, jealousy, drinking). • More Whites than Mexican Americans were battered for more than 2 hours.
Torres (1987)	25 White battered women and 25 Mexican American battered women (born in United States, but parents born in Mexico) in two urban area shelters and one rural shelter; matched on age and SES; geographic location of shelters not given	Substantiated cases	• Hispanics stayed in abusive relationships for the children and because of threats to family members. • Whites stayed in abusive relationships because of love or because they had nowhere to go. • Hispanic women's most frequent reason to go back to the abuser was the children. • Hispanic women stayed longer in abusive relationships because of children and pressure from family members. • Hispanics were hit more frequently than Whites in front of family members. • Hispanics left abusive relationships and came back more frequently.
Torres (1986)	25 White battered women and 25 Mexican American battered women (born in United States, but parents born in Mexico) in two urban area shelters and one rural shelter; matched on age and SES; geographic location of shelters not given	Substantiated cases	• Whites experienced more frequent abuse and were hit harder. • Mexican Americans remained with the abusive partner longer. • One fourth of both ethnicities had siblings in abusive relationships. • Mexican American men took the initiative more often than White men to make up.

Study	Sample Description	Definition/Measure of Abuse	Findings
Regional Studies—Self-Report			
Lown & Vega (2001)	3,012 Mexican American men and women living in Fresno County, CA; multistage, randomized household survey	*Physical abuse:* "Has your current spouse/partner ever pushed you, hit you with a fist, used a knife or gun, tried to choke or burn you?" *Sexual abuse:* "Has your current spouse/partner ever forced you to have sex against your will?"	• 10.8% of women reported either physical or sexual abuse by their spouse/partner within the previous 12 months. • 4% of women reported sexual abuse victimization. • 9.5% of women reported physical abuse victimization. • Two thirds of sexually abused women also reported physical abuse. • One third of physically abused women also reported sexual abuse.
Hass, Dutton, & Orloff (2000)	280 undocumented and recently documented immigrant Latinas from El Salvador, Guatemala, the Dominican Republic, and Honduras; recruited through fliers at schools, health clinics, churches, and other locations, and through word of mouth in the Washington, D.C., area	CIRRS[a] Survey results; coded according to Conflict Tactics Scales categories for minor and severe physical abuse	• 49.3% were physically abused; 42.1% were severe. • 11.4% were sexually abused. • 60% were victimized by dominance/isolation and were emotionally abused. • 40.7% experienced other emotional and verbal abuse.
Van Hightower, Gorton, & DeMoss (2000)	1,001 migrant farm workers (patients at 11 migrant farm worker health clinics): 80% Latina; all women	Migrant Clinician's Network Domestic Violence Assessment Form	• 19% were physically or sexually abused. • One fourth of these were both physically and sexually abused. • The average number of incidents was 13.5 (max. = 70).
Suarez-Al-Adam, Raffaelli, & O'Leary (2000)	46 Latinas recruited from two community-based social service agencies in New Jersey as part of an HIV/AIDS prevention study	Psychological Maltreatment of Women Inventory; physical violence subscale of the Conflict Tactics Scales	• 80.4% reported dominance/isolation victimization in the previous year (mean number of acts was 6.3); 84.8% reported emotional/verbal abuse (mean number of acts was 7.4). • 72% reported both types of psychological maltreatment. • 58.7% reported physical violence victimization in the previous year (mean number of acts was 3.13).

(Continued)

Table 11.1 Continued

Study	Sample Description	Definition/Measure of Abuse	Findings
			• 71.7% reported physical violence at some point in the relationship.
			• Most common physical acts were pushing, grabbing, and shoving.
			• For severe violence at some point in the relationship, 23.9% reported being beaten up, 15.2% reported being hit on the head, and 8.7% reported being threatened with death.
Torres et al. (2000)	1,004 women from five general community hospitals in Florida and Massachusetts, as part of a study on low birth weight and abuse: 19% Mexican American, 19% Puerto Rican, 19% African American, 20% White, 14% Cuban American, 9% Central American	Index of Spouse Abuse; Abuse Assessment Screen	Physical abuse: • Variable rates of physical abuse were reported, depending upon the subgroup of Hispanics. • 14.7% of Mexican Americans were ever physically abused, whereas 7.2% of Cuban Americans, 23% of Puerto Ricans, and 5.7% of Central Americans were ever physically abused. • 11.8% of Whites and 26.3% of African Americans were ever physically abused; African Americans and Puerto Ricans had significantly higher rates than all other groups, and Cuban and Central Americans had significantly lower rates. Physical abuse during pregnancy: • Variable rates were reported, depending upon the subgroup of Hispanics. • 5.3% of Mexican Americans were abused during pregnancy, whereas 1.4% of Cuban Americans, 8.6% of Puerto Ricans, and 2.2% of Central Americans were abused during pregnancy. • 3.6% of Whites and 7.5% of African Americans were physically abused during pregnancy; African Americans and Puerto Ricans had significantly higher rates, and Cuban and Central Americans had significantly lower rates. Sexual abuse: • No significant differences were found between ethnic groups in sexual abuse. • 6.3% of Mexican Americans, 0.7% of Cuban Americans, 3.0% of Puerto Ricans, and 2.3% of Central Americans experienced sexual abuse.

Study	Sample Description	Definition/Measure of Abuse	Findings
			Emotional abuse: • No significant ethnic group differences were found in the rates of emotional abuse. • 8.4% of Mexican Americans, 7.1% of Cuban Americans, 14.7% of Puerto Ricans, and 11.4% of Central Americans experienced emotional abuse.
Van Hightower & Gorton (1998)	155 low-income female patients at two rural healthcare clinics in Texas (76.1% Hispanic)	Migrant Clinician's Network Domestic Violence Assessment Form	• 19% reported physical abuse. • One third of them also reported sexual abuse. • The average number of incidents was 4 (max. = 6).
McFarlane, Wiist, & Watson (1998)	329 pregnant Hispanic women (aged 15–42 years) identified during prenatal screening as physically abused; all subjects were from three prenatal clinics of a public health department of a large city in the Southwestern United States	Severity of Violence Against Women Scale	• 32% reported sexual abuse by their husbands during the previous 12 months. • Sexually and physically abused women reported more threats of abuse and physical abuse than women who were physically abused only.
Wiist & McFarlane (1998)	329 pregnant Hispanic women (aged 15–42 years) identified during prenatal screening as physically abused; all subjects were from three prenatal clinics of a public health department of a large city in the Southwestern United States	Severity of Violence Against Women Scale	• 30% were threatened with death. • 18% were threatened with a knife or gun. • 80% were shaken or roughly handled. • 71% were pushed or shoved. • 64% were slapped on face and head.
Sorenson & Telles (1991)	1,243 Mexican Americans and 1,149 Whites in Los Angeles	• *Physical abuse:* "Have you ever hit or thrown things at your spouse/partner?"	• 12.8% of Mexico-born Mexican Americans perpetrated physical abuse. • 30.9% of U.S.-born Mexican Americans perpetrated physical abuse.

(Continued)

Table 11.1 Continued

Study	Sample Description	Definition/Measure of Abuse	Findings
		• *Sexual abuse:* "Has anyone ever tried to pressure or force you to have sexual contact (i.e., touching sexual parts, touching their sexual parts, sexual intercourse)?"	• 21.6% of Whites perpetrated physical abuse. • 2.2% of Mexico-born Mexican Americans were sexually abused. • 2.5% of U.S.-born Mexican Americans were sexually abused. • 3.5% of Whites were sexually abused. • Gender did not predict physical abuse of spouse.
CIRRS (1990)	Immigrant Latinas in California	CIRRS Survey	• 34% experienced wife abuse. • 48% said the level of violence increased since immigration. • 52% were still with batterer.

NOTE: For information on Hispanic American spousal maltreatment according to the U.S. Department of Justice (Rennison, 2001a, 2001b; Rennison & Welchans, 2000), the National Violence Against Women Survey (Coker et al., 2002; Tjaden & Thoennes, 2000), the National Family Violence Surveys of 1975 and 1985 (Bachman, 1992; Cazenave & Straus, 1979; Hampton & Gelles, 1994; Straus & Gelles, 1986, 1990a; Straus, Gelles, & Steinmetz, 1980; Straus & Smith, 1990b; Straus & Sweet, 1992), the National Comorbidity Survey (Kessler et al., 2001), the 1995 National Study of Couples (Caetano, Cunradi, et al., 2000), the 1998 California Women's Health Survey (Lund, 2002; Weinbaum et al., 2001), or Neff et al. (1995), please see Table 3.2. For information on Hispanic American spousal maltreatment according to Bauer et al. (2000), Gondolf et al. (1988), Harrykissoon et al. (2002), McFarlane et al. (1995, 2002), O'Keefe (1994), or Rodriguez et al. (2001), please see Table 8.1.

a. CIRRS = Coalition for Immigrant and Refugee Rights and Service.

Perhaps more helpful are surveys that offer respondents the opportunity to participate in either English or Spanish and to indicate their countries of origin. In one such study of Los Angeles residents, 20.1% of Mexican Americans and 21.6% of Whites in Los Angeles reported perpetrating spousal abuse, a non-significant difference. What is very interesting about this study, though, is the difference between Mexican-born Mexican Americans and U.S.-born Mexican Americans: 12.8% of the Mexican-born Mexican Americans reported spousal abuse perpetration, whereas 30.9% of U.S.-born Mexican Americans reported spousal abuse perpetration, a significant difference. Moreover, U.S.-born Mexican Americans were significantly more likely than Whites to report abusing their spouse, and Whites were significantly more likely than Mexican-born Mexican Americans to report spousal abuse perpetration (Sorenson & Telles, 1991). What are some of the possible reasons for this difference? Recall from Chapter 9 the discussion on acculturation issues. Could these issues be operating in this study? In what way? However, how would acculturation issues account for the fact that, as previously mentioned, newer immigrants may actually have higher rates of wife abuse (CIRRS, 1990; Hass et al., 2000)? What issues other than acculturation may be operating here? How can we resolve these seemingly contradictory findings—that newer immigrants have the highest rates of wife abuse, but that Latinos low in acculturation have the lowest rates?

Possibly the best nationwide survey to assess incidence of wife abuse in Hispanic communities comes from the same group who did the NFVR. A representative sample of Whites and Hispanics completed the *Conflict Tactics Scales* in either English or Spanish. The Hispanic sample consisted of members of each of the three major Hispanic communities in the United States—Puerto Rican, Cuban, and Mexican. Overall, Hispanics did not differ from Whites in the rates of wife abuse when norms regarding violence approval, age, and economic stressors were held constant. However, within the Hispanic communities themselves, some meaningful differences were observed: 20.4% of Puerto Ricans, 10.5% of Mexican Americans, and 2.5% of Cubans reported abusive tactics with wives (the rate for Whites was 9.9%; Kaufman Kantor, Jasinski, & Aldarondo, 1994). Consider these results from the NFVR. In what part of the country did the greatest percentage of Hispanics abuse their wives? Which Hispanic group is most represented in that part of the country? Furthermore, compare these results to the following results from an ethnically diverse group of pregnant women. Significantly greater percentages of Puerto Ricans reported being physically abused, whereas significantly lower percentages of Cuban and Central Americans did; Mexican Americans fell in between these groups (Torres et al., 2000). Recall from Chapter 9 that Mexican Americans, Puerto Ricans, and Cubans have vastly different migration experiences to the United States and, consequently, very different economic, political, and educational opportunities. Do you think that these differing experiences may have relevance for the findings of this study? In what way?

Studies of selected populations (e.g., pregnant women, migrant workers) parallel the findings from the community samples. That is, sometimes Hispanics commit less abuse (e.g., in pregnant women; McFarlane et al., 1995), sometimes their abuse rates mirror that of the general population (e.g., in migrant workers; Van Hightower & Gorton, 1998; Van Hightower, Gorton, & DeMoss, 2000), and sometimes they commit more abuse (e.g., among immigrants; CIRRS, 1990; Hass et al., 2000). Furthermore, among recent Latina immigrants, disturbingly high rates of wife abuse have been observed (CIRRS; Hass et al.), confirming that the Latina immigrant, particularly the undocumented one, is probably the most abused, but least reported, woman in the United States (Rasche, 1988). Perhaps the principal conclusions that can be drawn from all of these studies is that (a) overall, rates for wife abuse in Hispanic communities probably mirror those for the majority population, and (b) it is likely that there are differences among specific Hispanic communities and between earlier and more recent immigrants.

The final source of data on wife abuse comes from battered women's shelters. These studies reveal both similarities and differences between Whites and Hispanics (and sometimes Blacks) in the experience of being battered. Consider the

---

Box 11.1   Wife Abuse Experiences Hispanics Share with White Women

---

"After high school we moved in together. . . . It seemed like everything was great. After about two months he started again, started hitting me. This time I was going to do something, so I told Yolanda, my best friend. She said, and I'll never forget it, 'So what, you think my boyfriend doesn't hit me? That's how men are.' It was like I was wrong or weak because I wanted to do something about it. Last time he got mad he threatened me with a knife. That really scared me." (Magdalena, 19 years old, p. 140).

"One time the neighbors called the police. They heard screaming and yelling. He had been hitting me and throwing things around the house. A police officer came to the door and asked if everything was all right. You know, he stood right behind me and I had to say that everything was fine. I was afraid he'd do something if I didn't." (Cati, single mom of 2, p. 144).

SOURCE: Zambrano (1985)

---

cases presented in Box 11.1. They seem to indicate that the experiences of battered Hispanic women mirror those of White majority women. Similarly, the studies on battered women presented in Table 11.1 indicate that for the most part, there are no ethnic differences in the nature, severity, or extent of abuse (Gondolf et al., 1988; O'Keefe, 1994; Sorenson, 1996; Torres, 1991). However, some studies have found that White battered women may experience more frequent and severe abuse than both Hispanic and Black battered women (McFarlane et al., 1995; Torres, 1986).

Other similarities found between White and Hispanic battered women are the sources of conflict (Torres, 1991), the length of stay at battered women's shelters, and the percentages of women who return to their abusers (Krishnan, Hilbert, VanLeeuwen, & Kolia, 1997). However, even though the ethnic distribution of women using battered women's shelters tends to mirror that of the community in which the shelter provides assistance (Brisson, 1981; Krishnan et al.; Kuhl, 1982; Walker, 1983), Hispanic women are one of the least likely minority groups to utilize these services (Ginorio, Gutierrez, & Acosta, 1995). Therefore, any similarities found between White and Hispanic battered women may be more a reflection of the battered Hispanic and White women who choose to use shelters for assistance than a true similarity between ethnic groups.

As Box 11.2 shows, Hispanic women also have experiences that are unique to their communities. As illustrated in these two accounts, battered Hispanic women often have issues to consider that never even occur to battered White women: How will leaving my batterer affect my immigration status? To whom can I turn when my family lives in the "old" country? What will happen to my status in this country if I ever need to call the police for assistance? Several studies (Gondolf et al., 1988; Krishnan, Hilbert, & Van Leeuwen, 2001; Torres, 1986, 1987, 1991) confirm that battered Hispanic women tend to stay with their abusers much longer than battered White women. Besides fear of deportation and unavailability of family support, might cultural considerations, such as extreme sanctions against divorce or the cultural values of familism and marianismo, play a role in this situation?

Other differences found between battered Hispanic and White women relate to the reasons why battered women stay in, or return to, abusive relationships. Hispanic women tend to leave and return to abusive relationships more often than White women, most frequently because of the children and because the abuser has threatened their family members. In addition, pressure from family members contributes to their staying and returning. That is, Hispanic women's considerations when thinking about leaving an abusive relationship generally revolve around their families, especially their

---

Box 11.2   Wife Abuse Experiences Unique to Hispanics

"The first time I went to the hospital Manuel had broken my nose and cut my head open. He hit me on the head with a wooden clothes hanger and I got seventeen stitches over my ear. I can't hear well on that side since that happened. The other time, I was pregnant with my third boy, Panchito. Manuel hit me and kicked me so that I almost miscarried in my sixth month. You know, Panchito has always been a slow learner and I think it's because of the beating before he was born. . . . Manuel has been promising that he will immigrate me. I've never seen any papers, but he says that he has someone working on it. If I ask him about it he gets mad and says that I don't deserve it because I don't trust him." (Pilar, 35 years old, p. 142-143).

"Well, what can I say. I'm very ashamed to be in this position. I have a cousin who I could talk to, but he lives in Chicago, I think. I don't know, I sometimes think about going back to Mexico. But life is very hard there and I don't think I could support myself and the kids. I haven't told my family anything about Felipe. You see, my mother has a very weak heart and I don't want anything to upset her. Besides, what can they do so far away? I have never called the police here because Felipe told me that they will deport us if I do. I've thought about learning some English, but between work and the kids there is hardly any time. So I've never really asked anybody for help. . . . I'm very sad because the last time Felipe beat me my two little ones started hitting me too. They were saying 'You're a bad mommy, you're a bad mommy.'" (Esperanza, mother of 2, p. 143).

SOURCE: Zambrano (1985)

---

children. White women have very different considerations. Their most cited reasons for staying with an abuser are for love and because they have no place else to go—reasons that do not center on their family (Torres, 1987).

Wife Psychological and Sexual Abuse

Similar to women from the other ethnic groups under consideration, Latinas have also been subjected to verbal, emotional, and sexual abuse. Among undocumented and recently documented Latinas, 60% experienced dominance and isolation from their spouses, and 40.7% experienced other types of emotional and verbal abuse (Hass et al., 2000). Higher rates were found among a sample of Latinas using social service agencies in New Jersey: Specifically, 80.4% reported dominance and isolation, 84.8% reported emotional and verbal abuse, and 72% reported all types of psychological maltreatment. Still higher rates of emotional abuse were observed among battered women: 94.2% experienced verbal/emotional abuse, and there were no ethnic differences in this rate (Krishnan et al., 1997, 2001).

As with physical abuse, emotional abuse may also vary depending upon the subgroup of Hispanics studied. In a study of an ethnically diverse group of pregnant women, being Cuban American or having a Mexican or Central American partner served as protective factors against emotional abuse (Torres et al., 2000). Overall, although emotional and verbal abuse seem to be occurring at high rates in the Hispanic communities, these rates may not differ from those of other communities, but they may differ within the Hispanic subgroups themselves.

However, it appears that Hispanic women may be at a greater risk for sexual abuse by their significant others. In the only nationwide study addressing this question, the NVAW survey indicated that a significantly greater percentage of Hispanics than non-Hispanics reported rape by an intimate partner (7.9% vs. 5.7%; Tjaden & Thoennes, 2000). Similar results were found on a more local level among a group of battered women: 62% of Mexican American battered women reported sexual abuse as compared with 40% of battered women from other ethnic groups (Krishnan et al., 2001). However, others have found that Whites may be more at risk for sexual abuse. Specifically, over the course of a lifetime, 2.2% of Mexican-born Mexican Americans and 2.5% of U.S.-born Mexican Americans in Los Angeles experienced sexual abuse by an intimate, as compared with 3.5% of Whites (Sorenson & Telles, 1991). Thus, although Hispanic women as a whole may experience more sexual abuse than other ethnic groups, prevalence rates appear to vary among particular Hispanic communities and in some cases are lower than in the majority community. Among battered women, it seems to be the Mexican American women who are at greater risk of sexual abuse by their intimates.

Overall, it can be concluded that a substantial minority of Hispanic women are subject to physical, emotional, and sexual abuse. The exact extent is open to debate, more research is needed, and it is difficult to reach definitive conclusions about the amount of abuse they experience relative to other communities, such as Whites. In addition, although there may be similarities between Hispanics and other ethnic groups in the nature of the abuse they experience, there are important differences, too. Finally, there appear to be substantial differences in the rate of wife abuse within the various Hispanic communities themselves.

Husband Abuse

Only a small subset of the studies that researched wife abuse also gave attention to husband abuse, and to our knowledge, there are no studies that focus specifically on husband abuse within Latino communities. However, it does seem to be a problem. The DOJ reports that between 1993 and 1998, there were approximately 1.5/1,000 male Hispanic victims of intimate violence, a rate that was no different than that of non-Hispanics (Rennison & Welchans, 2000). Again, these are "caught cases" of husband abuse, and for reasons discussed in Chapter 3, husbands may be generally reluctant to report abuse by their wives. Considering the Latino cultural values presented in Chapter 9, do you think that Latino men may differ from other groups in their willingness to report husband abuse? Why? Fortunately, we do not

need to rely solely on official reports of husband abuse in this community. Three other nationally representative studies (Caetano, Schaefer, Clark, Cunradi, & Raspberry, 2000; Straus & Smith, 1990b; Tjaden & Thoennes, 2000) and two regional studies (Neff et al., 1995; Sorenson & Telles, 1991) also show that many Latino husbands suffer aggression from their wives.

The NFVR showed that Hispanic women were significantly more likely than White women to physically abuse their husbands (16.8% vs. 11.5%) and to inflict severe physical violence (7.8% vs. 4%). Nationwide, these numbers project to 504,000 physically abused and 234,000 severely physically abused Hispanic husbands (Straus & Smith, 1990b). Although the rate of husband abuse among Hispanic men in the 1995 National Study of Couples (NSC; 21%) was higher than in the NFVR, it was still lower than the rate in Black men (30%) and higher than the rate in White men (15%; Caetano et al., 2001). On the NVAW survey, 6.5% of Hispanic men reported a physical assault from their wives, a rate similar to the severe abuse found in the NFVR. However, unlike the NFVR and the NSC, there were no significant ethnic differences in the rate of husband abuse in the NVAW (Tjaden & Thoennes, 2000).

More localized studies considering the role of gender provide some basis for inferences about rates of husband abuse. For example, there were no gender differences in the amount of physical abuse of spouses perpetrated among Mexican American residents of Los Angeles. Therefore, the same conclusions drawn from this study for wife abuse can be drawn for husband abuse: Mexican-born Mexican Americans had the lowest rate of husband abuse, whereas U.S.-born Mexican Americans had the highest. Whites fell somewhere in between those two groups (Sorenson & Telles, 1991). Finally, among San Antonio residents, 19% of White males and 20.4% of Mexican American males reported being physically abused by their significant others; 26.3% of White females and 26.5% of Mexican American females reported physically abusing their significant others. Thus, there were no ethnic differences in the reported rates of either husbands being abused or wives abusing their husbands (Neff et al., 1995).

These studies lead to three competing conclusions: (a) Hispanic women abuse their husbands more often than White women do, (b) there are no ethnic differences in the rates of husband abuse, and (c) there are ethnic differences in these rates depending on the country of origin of the Hispanics being studied; Hispanics born in the United States have higher rates, whereas those born in Mexico have lower rates. Considering the cultural contexts of Latinos (Chapter 9), specifically the discussion on acculturation, do any of these conclusions seem more likely than the others? Why? Can we make any definitive conclusions at this point about Latina violence against husbands? Why or why not?

Predictors and Correlates

Macrosystem Level

Economic Variables. One of the most consistent predictors of both husband and wife abuse among the Latino communities is low income. This association has been found in nationally representative surveys of spousal abuse (Cunradi, Caetano, Clark, & Schafer, 2000; Straus & Smith, 1990b) and in large regional self-report studies (Neff et al., 1995). A variable somewhat related to low income, high financial strain, has also been shown to predict wife abuse (Neff et al.). Furthermore, when compared to White battered women, Latina battered women are more likely to experience impoverishment (West, Kaufman Kantor, & Jasinski, 1998). Conversely, income can act as a protective variable for spousal abuse: Among a national probability sample of Hispanics, family income between $20,000 and $29,999 or above $40,000 protected Hispanics from spousal abuse (Caetano, Schafer, et al., 2000).

One interesting economic variable assessed as a predictor of wife abuse among Latinos is the extent to which the wife contributes to the family income. Consider the information presented in Chapter 9 about the cultural values of Latinos. According to the concepts of machismo and marianismo, in what way do you think the wife's economic contribution would contribute to the incidence of wife abuse? If she contributed substantially, would her chances of

being abused increase or decrease? Perhaps it is no surprise that the more a wife contributed to the family income in a Latino family, the more physical abuse she experienced from her husband (Perilla, Bakeman, & Norris, 1994).

Employment and Education. The husband's level of employment has been a common variable of interest among spousal abuse researchers in the Latino communities. Consistent with research in the population as a whole, unemployed Latino husbands commit more wife abuse than employed husbands (Cunradi et al., 2000; Kaufman Kantor et al., 1994). Interestingly, when Whites were separated from Hispanics in the National Alcohol and Family Violence Survey, the direct relationship between unemployment and wife abuse was significant for only Hispanics, not Whites. Furthermore, experiencing trouble with the boss at work also contributed indirectly to wife abuse for Latinos. That is, experiencing trouble with the boss led to heavy drinking, which in turn led to wife abusive behavior (Jasinski, Asdigian, & Kaufman Kantor, 1997).

In Latino communities, although the husband's unemployment may predict wife abuse, the husband's employment does predict husband abuse (Straus & Smith, 1990b). Furthermore, wives who were employed, in comparison to wives who were retired, were more likely to abuse their husbands (Cunradi et al., 2000). In addition, even though the Latino husband's level of education did not predict wife or husband abuse (Sorenson & Telles, 1991), the more educated a Latina was, the more abusive she was towards her husband (Cunradi et al.). What do you think accounts for these findings? Why would employed, highly educated Latinas be more inclined to abuse their husbands? Why would they be more likely to abuse their *employed* husbands? Can you think of any cultural values that may account for these findings?

Attitudes. Although having attitudes consistent with sex role traditionalism has failed to predict either wife or husband abuse among Latinos (Neff et al., 1995; Perilla et al., 1994), other variables representing male dominance over females have been shown to predict wife abuse in Hispanic communities. For instance, in comparison to White battered women, Latina battered women are significantly more likely to come from male-dominated marriages (West et al., 1998). Furthermore, Latino husbands who endorse norms sanctioning wife assaults (Cunradi et al., 2000; Kaufman Kantor et al., 1994), view violence as manly, have calloused sex attitudes, and view danger as exciting (Suarez-Al-Adam, Raffaelli, & O'Leary, 2000) commit more wife abuse than their counterparts.

Exosystem Level

The only exosystem level variables that have been assessed in Latino communities are neighborhood variables. For instance, living in an urban environment predicted both wife and husband abuse among Hispanics in the NFVR (Straus & Smith, 1990b). In a more extensive analysis of exosystem predictors of spousal abuse, several neighborhood variables were assessed, including neighborhood poverty, and neighborhood percentages of high school diplomas, unemployment, and blue-collar workers. Among Hispanics, and consistent with the NFVR, the only predictor of husband abuse was neighborhood impoverishment. There were no neighborhood predictors for wife abuse (Caetano, Schafer, & Cunradi, 2002).

Microsystem Level

Victim Characteristics. Several characteristics of the victim have been implicated as predictors of both wife and husband abuse among Latinos. For instance, younger Latinos are victimized by more husband (Straus & Smith, 1990b) and wife (Cunradi et al., 2000; Kaufman Kantor et al., 1994; Straus & Smith; Torres, 1986) abuse than older Latinos. In addition, being over 40 years of age serves as a protective factor for both husband and wife abuse (Caetano, Schafer, et al., 2000), and abused Latinas are significantly younger than abused White women (West et al., 1998).

Another consistent risk factor for spousal abuse (both wife and husband) victimization among Latinos is the experience of abuse in one's family of origin (Caetano, Schafer, et al., 2000; Gilbert, El-Bassel, Schilling, &

Friedman, 1997; Krishnan et al., 1997; Perilla, 1999; Straus & Smith, 1990b; Torres, 1986, 1991). In one study, 85% of Latina battered women had witnessed their fathers beating their mothers (Perilla). In another, Latina women who were physically abused before the age of 16 and/or sexually abused before the age of 13 were more likely to be physically or sexually abused in their current relationships (Gilbert et al.). A study comparing battered Hispanic and White women found that although White battered women were significantly more likely to report child abuse, a substantial percentage of Hispanic battered women (41.2%) were also the victims of child abuse (Krishnan et al.).

Other risk factors for spousal abuse victimization among Latinos include impulsivity, mental disorders, being formerly married, and alcohol use. The more impulsive Latino wives or husbands are, the more likely they are to be victimized by abuse (Caetano, Schafer, et al., 2000; Cunradi et al., 2000). Furthermore, having a mental disorder or being formerly married leads to increased victimization rates for husband physical abuse and wife sexual abuse (Sorenson & Telles, 1991). Finally, wives and husbands who drink more are also more likely to be victimized by abuse (Caetano, Schafer, et al., 2000). Moreover, even though some data indicate that White battered women are significantly more likely than Hispanic battered women to use drugs and alcohol, a substantial percentage (32.1%) of Hispanic battered women also use them (Krishnan et al., 1997). Also, the higher the quantity of alcohol consumption by the woman, the greater her chances of being beaten, an association that is stronger in Mexican Americans than in Whites (Neff et al., 1995).

Pregnancy may be another victim-level risk factor for Hispanic women, although the data are mixed. Some studies show pregnant Hispanic women at lower risk for experiencing abuse than women of other ethnic groups (e.g., McFarlane, Parker, & Soeken, 1995) and pregnant Hispanic women to be at less of a risk for experiencing abuse than nonpregnant Hispanic women (e.g., Van Hightower et al., 2000). Still others find that once sociodemographic factors are controlled for, Hispanic women are no less likely to be abused during pregnancy than any other ethnic group (e.g., Torres et al., 2000)—another reminder of the power of SES variables.

The risk for physical abuse during pregnancy may be different for different subgroups of Hispanic women. For instance, among White, Black, Mexican American, Cuban American, Puerto Rican, and Central American women who had just given birth, African Americans and Puerto Ricans had the highest rates of abuse during pregnancy (7.5% and 8.6%, respectively), whereas Cuban Americans and Central Americans had the lowest rates (1.4% and 2.2%, respectively), even after controlling for several sociodemographic variables. Furthermore, having a Central American partner was a protective factor against being abused during pregnancy (Torres et al., 2000). How do these rates compare to the rates of physical abuse in general among these differing cultural groups?

Although differing groups of Hispanics may experience differing levels of maltreatment, abuse during pregnancy is a serious concern. Several studies among Hispanics show that abuse during pregnancy is associated with increased sexual abuse (McFarlane, Wiist, & Watson, 1998), increased severity of abuse overall (Wiist & McFarlane, 1998), and increased chances of being killed at some point by their partners (Campbell, Soeken, McFarlane, & Parker, 1998; McFarlane et al., 1995). It is important to note, though, that in nationally representative studies, there is no evidence that pregnancy predicts wife abuse. For example, in the 1992 National Alcohol and Family Violence Survey, even though pregnancy was associated with minor assaults among Hispanic women and severe assaults among White women, after controlling for several sociodemographic variables (i.e., SES, stressful life events, age), pregnancy did not increase one's chances of being abused (Jasinski & Kaufman Kantor, 2001).

Relationship Characteristics. Characteristics of the marital relationship have also been implicated as microsystem predictors of spousal abuse. For instance, marital status itself has been shown to predict wife abuse among Latinos. Latinas who are either separated or divorced (Sorenson & Telles, 1991) or cohabitating (Caetano, Schafer, et al., 2000; Cunradi et al., 2000; Jasinski, 2001) are significantly more

likely to experience abuse than their married counterparts. Furthermore, lower levels of mutuality in the marital relationship are also correlated with higher levels of wife abuse (Perilla et al., 1994).

One of the strongest predictors of wife or husband abuse found in the population at large, and also found among Latinos, is abuse by the other partner. Wives who hit husbands are likely to be victimized by wife abuse, and husbands who hit wives are likely to be hit in return (Neff et al., 1995). Moreover, Hispanic couples in which both partners reported experiencing child abuse are significantly less likely to experience husband abuse than those couples in which neither reported experiencing child abuse (Caetano, Schafer, et al., 2000). Finally, Hispanic couples who report joint alcohol problems have the highest rates of wife assault: They are eight times more likely to report wife abuse than couples not reporting joint alcohol problems (Cunradi et al., 2000).

Individual Level

Alcohol. The most widely studied predictor of spousal abuse in the Latino community is alcohol use and abuse, and the studies consistently show that alcohol use and abuse by the perpetrator predicts both wife abuse (e.g., Caetano, Cunradi, Clark, & Schafer, 2000; Krishnan et al., 1997; O'Keefe, 1994; Perilla et al., 1994; Van Hightower & Gorton, 1998; Van Hightower et al., 2000) and husband abuse (Caetano, Schafer, et al., 2000; Neff et al., 1995).

The National Alcohol Survey is particularly informative because it assessed the incidence of spousal maltreatment and the extent of alcohol involvement in the abusive episodes in a nationally representative multiethnic sample. Rates of both wife and husband abuse were highest among Black couples (23% and 30%), followed by Hispanic couples (17% and 21%) and White couples (12% and 16%). In addition, drinking during the violent incident was less common among Hispanics and Whites than among Blacks. Specifically, over 25% each of White and Hispanic male perpetrators reported drinking during the incidents compared to two fifths of the Black male perpetrators, and significantly fewer of the White (14.7%) or

Hispanic (3.8%) female perpetrators reported drinking during the incidents than the Black female perpetrators (nearly 25%; Caetano, Cunradi, et al., 2000).

Alcohol abuse by the perpetrator has been identified as a serious problem by battered Hispanic women (O'Keefe, 1994). In a study of Hispanic migrant farm workers, drug or alcohol use by the woman's partner increased her odds of being beaten by that partner sixfold (Van Hightower et al., 2000). In addition, in one study, as many as 92.3% of battered women's partners used drugs or alcohol (Krishnan et al., 1997). Furthermore, the strongest predictor of injury among White and Hispanic women reporting to an emergency room for spousal abuse was a history of alcohol abuse by the male partners (Kyriacou, McCabe, Anglin, Lapesarde, & Winer, 1998). Finally, the association between being battered and having an alcoholic husband may be stronger in battered Hispanic women than in battered White women: Battered Hispanic women are more likely to report that their husbands are heavy drinkers (West et al., 1998).

The association between alcohol use and spousal maltreatment may be partially mediated by a macrosystem level variable—that is, acculturation. In one study, wife abuse was associated with high levels of alcohol consumption among highly acculturated husbands only. Moreover, husband abuse was associated with high levels of alcohol consumption among wives at either medium or high levels of acculturation. There was no association between level of alcohol consumption and either wife or husband abuse among low-acculturated Hispanics (Caetano, Schafer, et al., 2000).

Family-of-Origin Abuse. Another strong predictor of either husband or wife abuse among Latinos is the perpetrators' experiences of violence in their own homes as children (Krishnan et al., 1997; Perilla, 1999; Rouse, 1988; Straus & Smith, 1990b; Torres, 1986). In one study, 92% of Latino male batterers had witnessed their fathers beating their mothers (Perilla), and among nationally representative samples of Hispanics, the experience of violence in the family of origin has been associated with the perpetration of both husband and wife abuse (Caetano, Schafer, et al., 2000; Straus & Smith).

Mental Disorders and Age. Among Los Angeles-area Mexican Americans, being diagnosed with a DSM-III mental disorder was predictive of perpetrating both husband and wife abuse. In addition, being older than 45 years predicted a Latina's perpetration of husband abuse (Sorenson & Telles, 1991). Other studies have found that younger wives are at greater risk for abusing their husbands (Cunradi et al., 2000).

Consequences

Few studies have addressed the consequences of wife abuse in Hispanic communities. Even with regard to spousal homicide, few studies exist, partly because Hispanic origin is not identified in FBI homicide files (Sorenson, 1996). One study that assessed intrafamily homicide rates among Hispanics was a five-state analysis of homicide records in states reporting Hispanic ethnicity information for murders (Arizona, California, Oklahoma, Oregon, and Texas). In these states, 3 of every 100,000 Hispanic females were murdered in 1999, in comparison to 2 and 8.1 per 100,000 for White and Black women, respectively. Hispanic women were much more likely than Hispanic men to be murdered by a family member or intimate partner than a stranger: 117 victims were killed by a male they knew versus 7 who were killed by a male stranger. More than 60% of the Hispanic women who knew their offenders were killed by a husband, common-law husband, ex-husband, or boyfriend. In 78% of the murders, the Hispanic women were killed by the male during an argument, and in 52% of the murders, the woman was shot and killed with a gun during the argument (Violence Policy Center, 2001).

Injury rates in Hispanic women are also difficult to obtain. In one study of battered women, the most frequent injuries for Mexican American women were burns, broken bones, and broken teeth (Torres, 1991). Other common physical problems in physically and sexually abused Mexican American women include poor overall health, poor physical health, heart problems, persistent health problems, and gastrointestinal, cardiopulmonary, neurological, sexual, and reproductive somatic complaints (Lown & Vega, 2001). Psychological problems include poor mental health (Lown & Vega), poor eating habits (Sanders-Phillips, 1994), depression, and low self-esteem (Perilla et al., 1994). However, because these symptoms have been identified in cross-sectional correlational studies, there is insufficient evidence to suggest that they are actually psychological consequences of wife abuse.

ELDER MALTREATMENT

There is a dearth of studies on the incidence, predictors, correlates, and consequences of elder maltreatment in Latino communities. Overall, Hispanic elders do not seem to be abused at a different rate than either the majority or other minority communities in the United States. In addition, they have the same representation in the official reports to Adult Protective Services (APS) as they do in the population at large (National Center on Elder Abuse, 1998; see Table 3.2). However, most cases of elder abuse do not get reported to APS (see Chapter 3). Consistent with cultural values, elder Hispanics are less inclined than other groups in the United States to report abusive acts to governmental authorities; they prefer to keep family problems within the family. Therefore, these numbers of abused Hispanic elderly are probably a serious underestimate.

The available literature indicates that elderly Hispanics suffer from many of the majority culture risk factors for elder abuse (e.g., poverty, crowded living conditions, and lack of social support), which may also be due to their unique migration experiences. In one study that compared elder maltreatment in minority families (Black and Hispanic) to White families, there were no striking differences between the two groups (e.g., the majority of elderly in both groups lived in poverty). However, the Hispanic elders had a less developed social support network than either the Black or White elders; 79% of the Hispanic elders did not have a caregiver and 41% had no known source of medical care (Hall, 1987).

Even though the extent of the problem has not been well-researched, elder abuse may be a growing problem in the Hispanic community. For example, Puerto Rican elderly in New York City reach higher levels of disability at

younger ages than their White or other minority counterparts. In addition, nursing home placement for disabled elders is seen as a last resort for these Puerto Rican families, and because these families tend to be poor, the extent to which they possess the materials, time, and energy to care for disabled elderly is a concern. All these factors put the Puerto Rican elder at a high risk for abuse (Espino, Neufeld, Mulvihill, & Libow, 1988).

There does appear to be some recognition of the problem of elder maltreatment within Hispanic communities. For instance, of Mexican American elderly living in Carson City, NV, and Detroit, MI, 33% were aware of at least one incident of elder abuse (self-defined) in their community. The most common type of abuse, according to these Hispanic elders, was denial of shelter (40.3%); neglect (22.6%), financial abuse (12.9%), and physical abuse (11.3%) were the next most common types of maltreatment (Sanchez, 1999). Similarly, the most common types of Hispanic elder abuse reported to APS in Texas are physical neglect, emotional abuse, and financial exploitation (Mitchell, Festa, Franco, Juarez, & Lamb, 1999).

These few studies of elder abuse in the Hispanic community show that the dynamics of elder abuse may not be much different within this community than they are in others. However, there may be some aspects that are unique to the Hispanic culture. Consider the case of Mr. Ortiz in Box 11.3. From what types of abuse did Mr. Ortiz suffer? Do any aspects of his situation seem to be unique to his ethnic group? If so, what might account for this uniqueness?

Overall, the few studies on elder maltreatment in Hispanic communities show that it is a problem deserving much more rigorous research. We do not know its prevalence among Hispanics because the only incidence data we have are the official reports to APS.

SUMMARY

Among the different types of adult maltreatment in Hispanic communities, wife abuse is the most researched. Based on the incidence studies, there is not enough evidence to conclude that Latinas are abused at a different rate than

---

Box 11.3   Case Example of Elder Abuse in the Hispanic Community

---

Juan Ortiz is an 87-year-old Mexican-American man currently having problems with his nephew, who has been living with him for two years. Recently, the nephew asked his substance-abusing girlfriend to move into the home without asking Mr. Ortiz's permission. Even though Mr. Ortiz pays all of the household expenses because neither the nephew nor his girlfriend work, gradually the girlfriend takes over the home: she refuses to allow Mr. Ortiz into "her" kitchen, and eventually, she even bars him from leaving his bedroom. Furthermore, the nephew tells Ortiz's family members not to visit, and he intercepts phone calls for Mr. Ortiz, telling Ortiz's family and friends that Ortiz does not want company. A neighbor and close friend of Mr. Ortiz had recently been bringing Ortiz a meal everyday. The nephew tells this neighbor not to come around anymore because the girlfriend was cooking all the meals now. Suspicious, the neighbor calls APS and Ortiz's family. The family members meet to discuss the situation and decide that the nephew and his girlfriend must move out of Mr. Ortiz's home. Mr. Ortiz, however, refuses to talk with APS because the situation is a family matter, and initially, he refuses to force his nephew and the girlfriend to leave. However, Mr. Ortiz finally agrees with his family and APS, and the APS worker sets a deadline for the nephew and his girlfriend to leave.

On the day of the eviction, Mr. Ortiz changes his mind. He states that he will not make a member of his own family homeless. For several months thereafter, Mr. Ortiz continues to suffer financial exploitation and verbal abuse from his nephew and the girlfriend. Eventually, the nephew and girlfriend move out, but they take with them all of Mr. Ortiz's cash, his car (they forged the title transfer), and some heirloom jewelry. Ortiz refused to call the police or press charges. He died 6 months later, still expressing guilt over making his nephew move.

SOURCE: Mitchell et al. (1999)

---

women from other cultures, that there are different predictors of wife abuse in the Latino communities, or that there are differing consequences of the abuse. Considering the cultural contexts discussed in Chapter 9, what would your hypothesis be? Is there reason to believe, for instance, that Latinas may suffer more from wife abuse than White women? Why or why not? What cultural influences are you implicating in your hypotheses? Furthermore, incidence studies show that there may be differing rates of wife abuse in different cultural groups (e.g., Cuban, Mexican, Puerto Rican) and at different levels of acculturation. If these results prove to be reliable and valid, what cultural contexts could be implicated in these differences?

Although more work certainly needs to be done on wife abuse in the Latino communities, there is a greater dearth of research on both husband and elder abuse. The reasons behind this lack of research may be different for the different types of abuse. We know that Latino husbands are abused and we know some correlates of this abuse, but why is it not researched in this community? Do any cultural values specific to the Latino community potentially cause this topic to be "off-limits"? If so, which ones and why? We also know that the Latino elderly can be the victims of abuse, but our only data come from APS reports. To our knowledge, there are no nationally representative or regionally representative surveys of Latino elderly to assess the incidence and nature of this problem. Why do you think that is? Do cultural values come into play here at all? Which ones and how?

PART V

ASIAN AMERICAN CULTURES

12

Asian American Cultural Contexts

When I have the headache, my mom do her finger for the massage, the temple, my eyes, the temples there, and she move the finger up to the Center, the forehead . . . and she continue to do up and down, up and down, couple time. Then she touch my skin like this. . . . Until I have the red in here. The red stay a couple days. My headache go away. I think she do that because of the blood run to help my headache. . . . And to let the nerve inside your head work faster, look much stronger, and that help your headache. (Davis, 2000, p. 91)

The procedure being described by this respondent is *cao gio*, which involves using the smooth edge of a metal object such as a coin or spoon to press a special ointment (Tiger or Monkey balm, an external analgesic) into the skin (Davis, 2000). It is an ancient remedy known to Southeast Asians, used to bring bad blood to the surface so that bad wind can be released. As we saw with the Hispanic use of *caida de mollera*, the reddening of the skin caused by *cao gio* has sometimes led medical practitioners to suspect abuse. As another Southeast Asian noted: "The first time I came here [to the United States] I did that, and I go to see a doctor and the doctor yelled at me, 'Don't do that, don't do that!' I'm afraid because I get yelled at again." Still another explained:

See, in America, you do that [*cao gio*], you take your kid in your house and you do that, you're in trouble. I had to explain to the doctor what happened for my first child. When my baby is have a

fever and sick, and we call that flu because hot and cold, you can do that. And so, I called the doctor and I gave the medicine, but still she had the fever . . . and I took her in and he [doctor] checked the whole thing and he said, "What happened to the back?" And I told him what I did. (Davis, 2000, p. 92)

Although it is common in Vietnam for mothers and daughters to use *cao gio* to relieve a variety of common symptoms, many of them learn that the effects of the procedure are viewed with suspicion by majority culture medical practitioners. One woman explained: "My mother, a lot of time she call me first and ask me, and I don't do it [*cao gio*]. I say just in case something else happen and it looks like you get abuse or something" (Davis, 2000, p. 92).

Such cases raise important issues. If *cao gio* produces no effects worse than a redness lasting a couple of days, should it ever be considered abusive? Some of the assumptions underlying *cao gio* seem similar to the ones underlying the

Mexican American folk procedure of "cupping," but are less invasive. Does that mean one folk procedure is abusive and the other is not? What if *cao gio* in some way provides real benefits to the patient? If medical authorities warn patients not to use the procedure, are they then guilty of some sort of institutional neglect?

WHAT IS ABUSE?

- *"Not following family roles; not taking care of children or family to raise them properly; misrepresenting the family; violence."* (29-year-old Japanese American Buddhist male)
- *"Abuse in my book is physical violence, or an unhealthy power dynamic in a relationship. Even taking advantage of a person's neediness can be considered abuse."* (28-year-old Asian Indian Hindu male)
- *"Abuse is when any member of the family strikes another member with the intention of hurting the member. Example: If the father hits his wife during an argument, or if the daughter strikes her mother when the daughter is angry."* (20-year-old Roman Catholic Singaporean American female)
- *"Abuse is being physically or verbally assaulted for no reason. A parent beating you because he or she had a bad day and you did nothing wrong."* (20-year-old Chinese American Buddhist male)
- *"Abuse in the family is when punishment goes to an extreme (above spanking), or verbal attack is overly copious, any punishment that is worse than the crime."* (21-year-old Korean American Episcopalian male)
- *"When it's physical because in my background emotion is not a concern, thus, emotional abuse is never concerned."* (21-year-old Chinese American female)
- *"Physical, mental, verbal—example: hitting someone."* (22-year-old Pakistani Muslim female)

Qualitative analysis of hundreds of Asian American responses to our survey revealed several strong themes—for example, that spanking children is not abusive. Abuse was frequently defined in terms of harm done or malicious intent, and most respondents did not view "ordinary" spanking as harmful—only when hitting is done constantly or maliciously did they consider it abusive. Moreover, terms like "fairness" and "deserved" occurred frequently in the responses. That is, respondents indicated that physical aggression becomes abuse when it is "unfair," "undeserved," done for "no good reason" and "excessive," and when "the punishment does not fit the crime." A related theme was that physical aggression is abusive when the perpetrator has lost control. Although many participants did not include verbal or psychological maltreatment in their definitions, some respondents noted explicitly that verbal/psychological aggression was not considered abusive in their culture, and others indicated that verbal/psychological aggression could be abusive when it caused permanent damage.

Research on judgments of the abusiveness of various behaviors has revealed several differences between Asian Americans and other ethnic groups (e.g., Whites, Blacks), as well as within the Asian American groups themselves. In a vignette study (Hong & Hong, 1991) of Whites, Hispanics, and Chinese Americans, the Chinese judged four cases of potential child maltreatment (specifically, beating a 12-year-old girl with a cane and burning a mark into her arm for stealing; dressing a girl as a boy and telling her they really wanted a boy; beating a child for not doing homework; and leaving red marks on the neck and back of an 8-year-old girl by scratching her with a spoon to make her feel better) to be significantly less serious than did the Hispanics and Whites. The Chinese also judged several scenarios as significantly less serious than Hispanics did, including leaving a 9-year-old boy alone to feed and take care of himself at night, refusing to take a withdrawn 8-year-old girl to a counselor, and frequently using drugs in front of an 8-year-old girl. In another study (Yick, 2000), over 40% of a community sample of Chinese American adults said that spanking was an effective way to discipline a child, and over 30% indicated that the use of physical punishment teaches children self-control.

There is an old Vietnamese saying about child rearing: "When you hate them, give them sweetness; and when you love them, give them punishment" (Gray & Cosgrove, 1985, p. 393). Some Vietnamese Americans view physical punishment as a way for parents to show love to their children, as long as it is not done in anger and the child understands the reason for it (Gray & Cosgrove)—a perspective quite similar to the one held by many of our Vietnamese and other Asian American participants. Similarly, hitting a child on the hand is considered to be an "acceptable" form of punishment by Vietnamese immigrants (Segal, 2000).

Asian American professionals concerned with the prevention of child abuse are often keenly aware of practices that may be common in their cultural communities but viewed as harmful in majority community agencies (Gray & Cosgrove, 1985). Among Japanese Americans, such practices include expecting Japanese American children to use nearly all their free time to study, giving the children little say in their own lives until they grow up and leave home, and intentionally not praising children. One Filipino American practice that might be misconstrued as emotionally abusive is overprotectiveness, such as never allowing children to climb trees or stairs. Finally, Samoan Americans appear to be particularly tolerant of practices considered abusive by the majority culture. For example, beatings that fall just short of requiring medical attention are considered acceptable and appropriate by Samoan Americans. Moreover, Samoans also approve of a style of interaction with children that includes much emotional abuse and an absence of an open display of affection (Gray & Cosgrove).

Asian American groups also differ among themselves and from the majority culture in their degree of acceptance of certain behavioral practices that may be considered forms of sexual abuse in the majority culture. Filipino Americans are quite comfortable seeing their 1- and 2-year-old children go naked around the house, and find the majority culture's view of young children as sexual beings very odd (Gray & Cosgrove, 1985). Furthermore, except for the Vietnamese proscription against mothers (because they are "impure") bathing with their sons, some Asian groups (Cambodians, Koreans, and Vietnamese) consistently favor parent-child co-bathing for a longer period than do Caucasians, African Americans, and Hispanics (Ahn & Gilbert, 1992). Similarly, mothers from these three Asian groups generally approve of

parent–child co-sleeping arrangements until a later age than do White, African American, and Hispanic mothers. When asked to judge the acceptability of a grandfather touching his 3-year-old grandson's genitals with pride, approximately half of the Vietnamese and Korean mothers, and 28% of the Cambodian mothers, found it acceptable, whereas between 88% and 98% of the respondents from the other groups found it unacceptable. The high degree of tolerance for this behavior shown by the Koreans and Vietnamese reflects what they view as a harmless custom of a grandfather showing affection and pride for a male child. A different pattern of responses was shown regarding parents kissing in front of a 12-year-old son. Over 90% of the Whites, African Americans, and Hispanics were quite comfortable with this demonstration of affection, whereas 90% of the Cambodians, 73% of the Vietnamese, and 32% of the Koreans disapproved (Ahn & Gilbert).

To summarize, Asian Americans tend to be quite accepting of corporal punishment, and there is evidence that Chinese and Samoan Americans view even some very harsh practices (e.g., burning, beating) as nonabusive in some circumstances. In addition, several practices that would be seen as potential signs of sexual abuse by the majority community (e.g., child nudity, caressing a child's genitals, and co-bathing) are also seen as acceptable.

With regard to spousal abuse, there are again important differences in perspectives between Asian American and other ethnicities, as well as among different Asian American groups. In one study, Asian Pacific Americans were less likely than European Americans to define a husband's shoving his wife or smacking her in the face as spousal violence (Family Violence Prevention Fund, 1993). Furthermore, in many Asian languages, there is not even a term for "domestic violence" (Lemberg, 2002), and in some Asian cultures, psychological abuse may not be included as a type of spousal violence. For example, a sample of Chinese Americans generally defined spousal violence in physical and sexual, but not psychological, terms (Yick, 2000). In contrast, 90% of a sample of Asian Indian American women defined abuse to include not just physical, but also mental, verbal, emotional, and economic maltreatment (Mehrotra, 1999).

Perspectives on the extent to which there are particular circumstances justifying spousal assault also vary among Asian Americans. For example, about half of a small sample of Chinese Americans thought that hitting a spouse was justifiable in cases of self-defense and defense of a child (Yick & Agbayani-Siewert, 1997). Moreover, the older Chinese American respondents showed tolerance of spousal violence perpetrated in response to an extramarital affair. In contrast, a sample of Filipino American students tended to view physical violence as unjustifiable under any circumstances, although Filipino males were more likely than Filipino females to endorse physical violence if the woman was flirting or unfaithful (Agbayani-Siewert & Yick Flanagan, 2001). In another study, few differences were observed among Asian, Hispanic, and U.S. college students in attitudes toward abuse, except that the Asian students (Japanese and Korean) showed significantly greater acceptance of a man mutilating his wife/partner if she abused him, and for a man hitting his wife/partner if she verbally abused him (Gabler, Stern, & Miserandino, 1998). As shown in other ethnic communities, the gender of the aggressor appears to have some influence on Asian American judgments of abuse. Only 5% of a sample of Chinese American respondents agreed that it is acceptable for a man to hit his wife/partner, compared to 11% who indicated that it is acceptable for a woman to hit her husband/partner (Yick, 2000).

In one other comparative study, two groups with Southeast Asian origins (Cambodians and Vietnamese) were more likely than Chinese and Koreans to endorse male privilege (e.g., "A husband is entitled to have sex with his wife whenever he wants it.") and less likely to endorse alternatives to living with violence (e.g., "Wife beating is grounds for divorce."). Of all groups, the Korean Americans were the least likely to view violence as justified in the specified situations (e.g., when the wife has sex with another man; Yoshioka, DiNoia, & Ullah, 2001).

Although samples are small, local, and perhaps unrepresentative, and few of the studies reviewed consider more than two or three different Asian American groups, there appear to be some differences among Asian Americans whose origins are Asian Pacific (e.g., Chinese, Japanese, and Korean Americans), Asian Indian, Southeast Asian (e.g., Cambodian, Vietnamese), and Pacific Islander (e.g., Filipino). Although more research needs to be done to confirm this pattern, it appears that while in general, Asian Americans are more tolerant than European Americans, and sometimes other ethnic groups, of a husband's right to discipline or punish his wife, Southeast Asians may be the most tolerant of this right, and Pacific Islanders may be the least tolerant. Overall, Asian communities differ among themselves not only in characteristics such as language and religion, but also in attitudes toward wife abuse. Consequently, studies in which Asians with different heritages are combined in a single "Asian American" sample must be viewed with caution (Yoshioka, DiNoia, & Ullah, 2001).

Although the popular image of treatment of the elderly in Asian countries emphasizes honor and respect, these outward expressions may mask much aggression toward the elderly in some Asian countries (e.g., Koyano, 1989; Malley-Morrison, You, & Mills, 2000), as well as in the United States. To address this issue, Moon and Williams (1993) used 13 scenarios portraying situations of elder maltreatment (e.g., a daughter-in-law drugging her mother-in-law when guests visited to avoid being embarrassed by her) to compare perceptions of elder abuse and help-seeking in White, African American, and Korean American elderly women. Overall, fewer Korean American than White and African American women viewed the hypothetical situations as abusive. Moreover, Asian American women were much less likely than Whites and African Americans to say they would seek help if they were in situations like the ones in the scenarios. Compared to White and African American elderly, Korean American elderly appear to be the most tolerant of possible elder abuse, the most likely to blame the victims for the occurrence of elder abuse, and the most negative toward outside involvement in families in which elder abuse was taking place (Moon & Benton, 2000).

This tendency for Korean Americans to be more tolerant of abuse also applies when they are compared to other Asian American groups. For example, in a small study of elder Asian American women from Honolulu, nine tenths of the Filipino American women, compared to five tenths of the Korean American women, thought it was abusive for a son, who generally took adequate care of his mother, to verbally abuse her when he was drunk (Pablo, 1998). Furthermore, compared to the Chinese and Japanese Americans, Korean and Taiwanese Americans were more likely to disapprove of a caregiver who ties a physically or mentally impaired adult in bed or yells at elderly parents. Financial exploitation was most tolerated by the Korean Americans. Taiwanese Americans were least tolerant of leaving bedridden elderly parents alone occasionally for a few hours. Korean Americans were more likely (43%) than Taiwanese Americans (11%) and Chinese and Japanese Americans (6% each) to agree that if elderly people are mistreated, they deserve it (Moon, Tomita, & Jung-Kamei, 2001).

WHO IS ASIAN AMERICAN?

Census 2000 showed that 11.9 million people in the United States (4.2% of the U.S. population) identified themselves as Asian—an increase of over 50% from 1990. Within this broad category, respondents identified more than 24 specific group affiliations. Although Chinese (except Taiwanese) and Filipino were the most common (with over 200,000 in each group), there were also combined over a million self-identified Asian Indians, Japanese, Koreans, and Vietnamese, with much smaller numbers of Singaporeans, Thais, Laotians, and other groups. The majority of Asian Americans live in just three states—California, New York, and Hawaii (U.S. Bureau of the Census, 2002).

On average, according to many economic indicators, Asians and Pacific Islanders (API) were nearly as well-off as non-Hispanic Whites in 2000. However, there are enormous economic disparities within the Asian American population. For example, Asian Americans have both a higher median income and a higher poverty rate than non-Hispanic Whites (Council of Economic Advisors [CEA], 1998). Overall, the average income of Asian Americans, like the income of non-Hispanic Whites, is nearly twice that of Blacks and Hispanics. At the same time, the Asian American poverty rate is more than twice as high as the non-Hispanic White rate (CEA, 1998). Although many reports do not disaggregate different Asian American groups, the 1990 census revealed that the median income of Japanese Americans exceeded that of non-Hispanic Whites, whereas the income of Cambodian Americans, perhaps because they are much newer arrivals in the United States, was lower than that of Black families. Although one third of Asian American families have incomes of $75,000 or more, 20% have incomes below $25,000 (Foo, 2002). Similarly, although Census 2000 reports a poverty rate of 10.7% for Asian Americans overall, some Asian American groups have had poverty rates of over 60% (Foo).

As a group, Asian Americans have the highest average educational level of all the major ethnic groups within the United States, including the majority population of non-Hispanic Whites (CEA, 1998). In 1997, more than 75% of both Asians and non-Hispanic Whites had at least a high school degree or its equivalent. However, 15% of Asian Americans had master's, doctoral, or professional degrees compared to 9% of non-Hispanic Whites. Similar to non-Hispanic Whites, Asian Americans are much more likely than Blacks, Hispanics, and Native Americans to work in professional and managerial occupations, and much less likely to have blue-collar positions. Asian Americans have a very high proportion of dual-income families, and as with the men, Asian American women tend to be employed in white-collar positions.

Each Asian American group has a distinct culture and a different migration history. The first major wave of Chinese to the United States were single men coming to help build the railroads to take gold-seekers and other pioneers West (Lee, 1997). Prejudice against these workers led to the Chinese Exclusion Act of 1882, which excluded family members and additional workers from entering the United States. Typically, any Chinese or Japanese women brought to the United States in the 19th century were sold into sexual slavery; their forced role as prostitutes was then used to prove the

---

Box 12.1   The Story of Mrs. L., Age 52

Age 6. Mother starved to death at home in China during war with Japan.

Age 9. Younger brother died of untreated high fever.

Age 10. Father remarried; step-mother became physically abusive.

Age 13. Was given responsibility to take care of her new step-brother.

Age 15. Many of her relatives, including her father, were tortured when Communists overran her village.

Age 17. Was married off to a man she had never met and went to live with him and his family in a different village.

Age 24. Three-year-old son died of a fever after she followed the advice of others who urged her to feed him "holy ashes." Was left with her mother-in-law when her husband emigrated to the United States to join his father, who had immigrated years before.

Age 27. Observed the public beheading of her mother-in-law who had been found guilty of adultery.

Age 34. Joined husband in United States. Was forced to have sex during her period, take fertility drugs, and have operations because husband wanted a son.

Age 36. Gave birth to a daughter, who became very acculturated to American values as she grew up, and resented her parents' dependency on her as a translator and negotiator for them.

Age 52. Was referred to an outpatient mental health clinic in Chinatown because of shortness of breath, dizziness, insomnia, fear of ghosts, and acute anxiety attacks.

SOURCE: Lee (1977).

---

depravity and inferiority of Asians and justify further discrimination (Root, 1995). Not until 1930 did immigration laws become flexible enough to allow Chinese wives of Chinese American citizens to join their husbands in the United States, and not until 1965 did Chinese immigrants begin to come to this country in family units. In recent decades, there has been a tremendous influx of ethnic Chinese from China, Hong Kong, Taiwan, and Vietnam, as well as substantial numbers from Laos and Cambodia. All of these groups are heavily influenced by Confucian values emphasizing interdependence, patriarchy, emotional control, obligations, and duties. The kinds of experiences these refugees may have had with family violence and the exosystem can be seen in Box 12.1.

What are the probable causes of the symptoms Mrs. L. had at the age of 52? In addition to the terrible experiences she underwent in China because of political turmoil, did she experience any forms of family maltreatment? What kinds? How likely is it that Mrs. L. will view her experiences within the family as forms of maltreatment?

Similar to the Chinese, Filipino immigrants, who came to the United States in the greatest concentrations in the 20th century, were typically single men recruited to work as laborers on farms in Hawaii and on the West Coast (Sustento-Seneriches, 1997). They were not allowed to own property or marry interracially, and were subjected to racial discrimination. However, for many reasons—including their Catholic heritage and higher level of education, as well as exosystem efforts to wipe out prostitution—Filipina immigrants tended not to be sold into prostitution like their Japanese and Chinese predecessors (Root, 1996). Most Filipinos in the United States today are recent immigrants who fled economic catastrophe and political oppression during the Marcos dictatorship. They are typically Catholic, belong to extremely broad kinship networks, emphasize respect and harmony among family members, and have a long tradition of granting considerable economic and educational equality to women.

The major wave of East Indians into the United States came after the Immigration and Naturalization Act of 1965 put an end to racial discrimination in immigration policy, mandating that entry into the United States be determined by skills rather than race (Prathikanti, 1997). During and following U.S. involvement in the Vietnam War, which increased the country's need for physicians, engineers, and other technical specialists, a substantial number of young, well-educated, English-speaking East Indian professionals entered the country, generally gained considerable economic success, and became U.S. citizens. Despite the enormous cultural diversity characteristic of India, Hindu values are pervasive in these immigrants. This influence is reflected both in the tendency of families to encompass several households that assist each other with key life issues, as well as a privileged status for males, expectations of obedience to elders, and arranged marriages in which women become members of their husband's family.

The peak period for Japanese immigration to the United States was 1880 to 1920, when they were brought as alternatives to the Chinese workers; many of these men had wives who, without ever having met the men they were to marry, came to the United States as "picture brides" (Homma-True, 1997). As with the Chinese, Japanese immigrants were subjected to poverty and harsh working conditions, prohibited from bringing Japanese wives with them or marrying White women, and faced with enormous discrimination—which culminated in the internment of many Japanese Americans during World War II. Since the war, the immigration of Japanese has dropped to a trickle in comparison to many other Asian groups. In part because many of the wives are in the labor market, the median family income in contemporary Japanese American families is the highest of all the Asian groups, and even higher than the median for the United States as a whole (Homma-True). Although the earlier generations of Japanese in this country were, like the Chinese, strongly influenced by Confucian values, there has been considerable acculturation since World War II to the Judeo-Christian values of the majority culture.

Korean immigration into the United States is a 20th-century phenomenon, and in recent decades has taken place primarily for the family reunification of Korean women and elderly with family members already in this country (Kim, 1997). Underemployment is a major problem for Korean immigrants, who are often unable to continue the white-collar occupations they held in Korea. Traditionally, Koreans were heavily influenced by Confucian principles emphasizing a patriarchal system in which a husband was the breadwinner and decision maker who exercised authority over his wives and children, who in turn were expected to respect and obey him. The formerly strict role relationships have changed somewhat in the United States, partly because of the economic necessity for wives to work. Moreover, although only 25% of the population in Korea is Christian, a sizeable majority of the new generation of Korean Americans attend ethnic Korean Christian churches, which often serve as extended families for recent immigrants.

Other Asian Americans include, among many other groups, the following:

Laotians, who suffered terribly as a result of the Indochinese war, have fled to the United States primarily since the fall of Saigon in 1975. Among them are many tribal people, such as the Hmong, who are often influenced by Hindu and Buddhist traditions.

Vietnamese, who also fled war-torn Indochina, typically embrace a Chinese Confucianism that includes ancestor worship. The Vietnamese have traditionally also granted somewhat greater economic equality to women than the Chinese have.

Cambodians, who were tortured, traumatized, imprisoned, and forced into work camps during the Pol Pot regime from 1975 to 1979, escaped to Thailand where they awaited repatriation for years. They generally follow a form of Buddhism that includes Brahmanistic beliefs in animistic, ancestral, and demonic spirits (Boehnlein, Leung, & Kinzie, 1997).

Pakistanis, who are typically Muslim, include a large number of legal or illegal refugees from the Indian-Pakistan conflict over Kashmir.

As with the respondents to our survey, the characteristics of these different groups illustrate an important point about Asian Americans—they differ not only in their own or their ancestors' country of origin, but also in religious affiliation. Although the vast majority of Hispanic Americans (regardless of country of origin) are Catholic and the vast majority of African Americans (except for some of the newest immigrants) are Protestant or Catholic, Asian Americans represent a very broad and diverse set of religions—Christian, Hindu, Buddhist, Jain, and Muslim, among others. Although it is beyond the scope of this book to analyze the contribution of religion to implicit theories concerning family abuse, there are clearly some variations across the major religions in assumptions concerning men, women, and children, and their relationships with each other. Moreover, there are also strong subcultural differences in the interpretation of religious texts (e.g., the Bible or the Qu'ran) dealing with the treatment of women and children.

There are other sources of diversity among Asian Americans. In our sample, participants who identified themselves as ethnic "Chinese" listed origins in China, Taiwan, or Hong Kong—areas with very different historical and cultural experiences. Moreover, U.S. residents who identify themselves as "Asian" or "Asian American," or some variant such as "Japanese" or "Filipino," may vary considerably among themselves based on whether they are relatively new immigrants or descendants of ancestors who have lived in this country for generations. Such differences are likely to be associated not only with degree of acculturation, but also with knowledge concerning U.S. laws and practices. In addition, in our sample, as well as in a few other studies, some participants identify themselves as Amerasian—that is, part Asian and part White. These participants often have Asian mothers married to White fathers. Thus, as is the case for the other minority groups in this book, programs geared toward intervening in or preventing family violence in Asian American families need to recognize the tremendous diversity underlying the general ethnic label.

CULTURAL VALUES: RISK OR PROTECTIVE FACTORS?

Patriarchy

Much of the blame for family violence in Asian American communities has been placed on histories of patriarchal values that devalue women and girls. For example, according to Chinese Confucian cultural norms, girls must obey their fathers, wives must obey their husbands, and widows must obey their eldest son (Hsu, 1967, as cited in Chin, 1994). In Chinese, the word for husband literally means "supporter," whereas the word for wife means "subordinate" (Chen, 1971, as cited in Chin, 1994). In Korea, wives call husbands *uri chip ju in* ("the master of our house") and husbands call their wife *chip saram* ("house person"). In Vietnam, there are popular sayings such as "A hundred girls aren't worth a single testicle" (Tran & Des Jardins, 2000). On the other hand, the first consonant of the ancient Philippine Tagalog word *Bathala*, meaning God, refers to woman (Mananzan, 1985, as cited in Agbayani-Siewert & Yick Flanagan, 2001).

Many scholars have made a direct connection between patriarchal values and wife abuse in Asian American communities. According to Tran and Des Jardins (2000), "Although Vietnamese and Korean cultural and social values do not explicitly encourage men to mistreat or abuse their partners, the fact that they are rooted in a patriarchal perspective influences and supports the subjugation and abuse of women" (p. 82). A 33-year-old Vietnamese woman said,

> He told me he hits me because I talk too much; I didn't stay quiet when he ordered me to. He thought that he could just continue to beat me and control me like he did in Vietnam, like most Vietnamese men control their wives. (Tran, 1997, p. 18)

A community-based sample of Japanese American women (Yoshihama, 2000) also emphasized the role of male domination in domestic violence; a 40-year-old, third-generation, U.S.-born Japanese American woman said,

"Being a Japanese woman, I sometimes feel a sense of subservience. . . . [Being] Japanese makes me believe that a woman has a certain role. . . . As a result, it causes me to just quietly take the abuse" (Yoshihama, p. 216). Similarly, physical and psychological battering of Korean American women may be deeply rooted in a philosophy of male domination (Song-Kim, 1992).

A focus group with Chinese American, Filipina, Japanese American, Samoan, South Asian, Vietnamese, and Amerasian representatives agreed that the major causes of wife abuse against Asian American women are a legacy of patriarchy and sexism, acceptance of the violence within the community, socialization of Asian Americans in cultural values tolerating men's violence against women, and lack of accountability for the batterers within the community (Warrier, 2000). However, the Filipino heritage, according to Agbayani-Siewert and Yick Flanagan (2001), is one of indigenous egalitarian values—reflected, for example, in the Tagalog term *pakikipagkapwa*, meaning "self and others," and representing the treatment of others as equals—overriding the patriarchal values brought to the Philippines by Spanish colonizers.

With regard to African American wife abuse, we saw that a number of feminist workers made a strong argument that African American men should not be able to excuse their violence by blaming it on the stresses of racism (see Chapter 10). Similarly, Asian American feminists argue that violence against Asian American women should not be excused on the grounds that it is culturally acceptable. A case in point is that of Dong Lu Chen, a Chinese man who beat his wife to death with a hammer because he thought she was having an extramarital affair (Agtuca, 1995). Mr. Chen was allowed to plead guilty to manslaughter and was sentenced to five years probation because, according to the judge, the defendant was driven to violence by traditional Chinese values regarding adultery and loss of manhood. According to Agtuca,

> Women of every race are killed every year by their husbands, but in these and other recent cases involving Asian men such behavior was viewed as cultural. Murder, rape, and physical violence against women by men is no more cultural than it is for European men. Horrible acts of domestic violence are inflicted on women by members of every ethnic group and such arguments by defense attorneys and the acceptance of them by prosecutors and judges only perpetuates a racial stereotype that such behavior is condoned in Filipino and other Asian cultures. (p. 49)

Suffering/Endurance/Fatalism

Another cultural value that may be associated with tolerance for family violence in many Asian American societies is suffering, which is seen as a path to maturity and a stronger, better character (Masaki & Wong, 1997). Indeed, the assumption that life is inherently full of suffering is one of the Buddhist Four Noble Truths (Tomita, 1994). Battered Japanese American women have explained their response to their husbands' violence by saying such things as, "[I was] taught to bear it, don't complain, make the best of things" (age 47, third-generation, U.S.-born), and "As a Japanese, I 'gaman'—just like a habit, I endure" (age 48, Japan-born; Yoshihama, 2000, p. 216). A related cultural value is fatalism, conveyed in Japanese by the term *shikata ga nai*, which means "It cannot be helped." Japanese American women and older adults suffering maltreatment at the hands of husbands, children, or other relatives may not view their maltreatment as abuse, but as suffering they must *gaman* because *shikata ga nai* (Tomita). Similarly, Filipinos are often characterized by an attitude of *bahalana* ("Leave it to God," or "Come what may"; Sustento-Sneriches, 1997), which may contribute to a reluctance to seek help in cases of family violence. Buddhist ideals also emphasize suffering as an expected part of life, and elderly Korean Americans may tolerate suffering in order to maintain harmonious interpersonal relationships (Rittman, Kuzmeskus, & Flum, 1999). All Asian American groups have faced violence, repression, and, in some cases, colonization in their countries of origin, and have faced racism and discrimination in the United States. Their stoicism and an assumption that suffering will lead to better things in this life or the next may have helped them survive considerable pain and loss (consider the case in Box 12.1). However, their acceptance of suffering and fatalism may also interfere with the seeking of help for current family problems.

Family Harmony/Conflict Avoidance

Family harmony and avoidance of conflict are important values in many Asian and Asian American communities. East Indians, for example, have been characterized as avoiding open expressions of conflict within the family, and viewing direct displays of anger as symptoms of a shameful lack of patience and self-control (Prathikanti, 1997). Confucian values discouraged the expression of feelings because Confucius viewed such displays as individualistic infringements on the harmony of others (Tang, 1997). In hierarchically organized Japanese households, influenced by Confucian traditions, family members tend to avoid conflict for the sake of saving face (Kozu, 1999). Although on the surface, this pattern may allow families to maintain an image of harmony, such suppression of feelings could lead to deepseated resentment and conflict, which could explode in reactive rage and lead to family violence (Kozu, p. 51).

Although maintaining an image of family harmony may be overwhelming in the midst of such stresses as economic and acculturation pressures, generational differences in values, difficulties in conversing in multiple languages, and coping with a variety of discriminatory practices, families are typically a source of support and comfort for Asian Americans. One implicit theory of the dilemma for these families is as follows:

> The Pacific Asian family has been the traditional source of support and nurturance to its members. The emotional and economic security that the individual finds within the bosom of her family are seen to compensate for the harsh restrictions and de-emphasis on individuality. . . . Nevertheless, this system, which is propped up by traditional sex roles, that is, male dominance, results in a power imbalance. Wherever that imbalance exists—especially without the mediating presence of elders—there is always at least the potential for violence. (Rimonte, 1989, p. 330)

Saving Face/Avoiding Shame

A related cultural characteristic serving as a barrier to help-seeking in some Asian American communities is the concern with avoiding any behavior that could bring shame to the family (Rasche, 1988). According to Singelis, Triandis, Bhawuk, and Gelfand (1995), "East Asians avoid confrontation and would rather tell a lie than cause anyone to lose face" (p. 244). A deep sense of family loyalty and honor, and an abhorrence of "losing face," may also keep maltreated Asian Pacific women from reporting abuse; they are likely to feel more shame than anger, and are likely to avoid talking about the incidents to anyone (Lai, 1986).

Collectivism

In general, Asian American communities, like Native, Hispanic, and African American communities, are much more collectivistic in orientation than the individualistic majority culture. Battered Asian American women may be more concerned with their partners and families than themselves, and may act to protect their abusive partners—particularly if they are socially isolated within a racist community (Lum, 1998). A 44-year-old Japanese American explained, "Even if you are abused, you think that the children need both parents. Only for that reason alone, I stayed married. I wish I had time to think only about myself" (Yoshihama, 2000, p. 218). When conflicts occur in Japanese culture, the most important goal is to maintain the relationship, not protect the individual (Wah, 1998). According to Wah,

> In many ways there is a lot to be said for the Japanese perspective of not humiliating someone to the point that they feel isolated or in danger of having their integrity questioned in public. The term "losing face" is about humiliation and disgrace. (p. 132)

However, as with the other factors, the desire to avoid losing face can result in maltreated family members not seeking help.

Filial Piety

Many Asian cultures honor the values of filial piety, derived from Buddhist and Confucian teachings, and obligating younger generations to respect, obey, and care for elderly parents. In Korea, filial piety is particularly the obligation of elder sons, who can in turn expect to inherit all the family's money and resources when their parents die (Rittman, Kuzmeskus, & Flum, 1999). There is considerable evidence that among Asian American communities in the United States, filial piety is breaking down. Because so many immigrant Asian elderly have limited financial resources to offer their children, they are often expected to be little more than household servants, and to provide their adult children with whatever money they may receive from social security or similar sources (Moon, 1999)—which can lead to exploitation.

THE U.S. MACROSYSTEM: EXPLOITATION, DISCRIMINATION, AND OPPRESSION

Although many family violence researchers have identified historical and cultural features of Asian Americans' countries of origin as risk factors for family violence, others have emphasized experiences of Asian American immigrants within the United States. Lai (1986) attributed violence in Asian Pacific communities to frustration and misdirected anger stemming from the poverty, discrimination, powerlessness, and oppression generated by a racist, capitalistic society. She pointed out that since the 19th century, the United States has forced China and Japan to concede favorable trade rights, and has annexed, occupied, or otherwise dominated Hawaii, the Philippines, Guam, Samoa, Palau, the Marshall Islands, Micronesia, Korea, Vietnam, and Laos. The legacy of this domination is a White American attitude of self-righteousness and superiority towards Asian and Pacific peoples still seen as representing gooks and a "Yellow Peril." In response to those attitudes and the institutionalized racism of American society, Asian Pacific people not only become angry, but also develop hatred of themselves and their own people—a

self-hatred that plays itself out in violence against women and girls (Lai). Other social scientists have noted that although hated and discriminated against, Asian Americans have also been seen as the "model minority"—hardworking, successful, well educated, uncomplaining, passive, and well behaved (e.g., Lee, 1998; Tong, 1998). In what ways might this new stereotype serve as an additional barrier to the reporting of family maltreatment within Asian American communities?

Focusing primarily on Chinese Americans, Tong (1998) argued that the etiological roots of physical, emotional, and sexual abuse of partners could be found in (a) problems of adaptation to mainstream culture, (b) cross-cultural clashes, (c) racist oppression by White America, and (d) a repressive heritage in which Confucian values were distorted into a justification for cruel and autocratic power by a small male minority. In his view, virtually every Asian American group has undergone at least one major experience of what he calls "collective racist trauma" at the hands of White America. Tong stated,

> For Philipino America, it was the brutal colonial subjugation of the Philippine Islands at the turn of the century; for Japanese America, the concentration camps of World War II. For Korean wives of White American servicemen, it was the alienation and abuse of dysfunctional post-Korean War interracial marriages. For Vietnamese America, it was the intervention of the United States in a civil war between the Vietnamese. And for Chinese America, it was the infamous Anti-Chinese Movement. (p. 121)

SUMMARY

Unlike the majority of African Americans, the ancestors of Asian Americans were not brought to this country in chains. Like Hispanic Americans, early Asian American immigrants were brought here as low-paid labor, but unlike Hispanic Americans, the early immigrants were not allowed to bring wives and families, and were not allowed to intermarry with White Americans. Similar to all of the ethnic minorities considered in this book, they have been

---

Box 12.2   Vulnerability, by Dr. Anita Raj

I grew up in an Asian Indian immigrant community in Mississippi, where I saw the vulnerability of immigrants in this country firsthand. I became interested in domestic violence specifically when I saw a few women in my community brutalized by their husbands. The community was at a loss as to how to respond to this problem. As in all populations, sexism kept the women at risk, but I soon realized that sexism was compounded among these Asian Indian immigrant women by the racism and xenophobia of the society surrounding us. These experiences led to my commitment to addressing this issue among Asian Americans as a both a researcher and an advocate. I have conducted two community-based research studies focusing on South Asian women's health, using samples of women from the greater Boston area. These studies investigated the prevalence and incidence of domestic violence in this community and how experiences of intimate partner violence related to health and legal immigration concerns for these women. I am also a Core Member of Saheli, a local community-based organization that focuses on supporting South Asian women in crisis. Many of these women turn to the organization for assistance related to intimate partner violence, and I have served as a lay advocate for them and as a community health educator building awareness of this issue among South Asians.

---

subjected to racism and discrimination at the macrosystem level, and have often maintained a rigid hierarchical paternalistic family organization that has been a source of both support and violence within the family. Moreover, as is also the case with all the other ethnic minority groups considered, Asian Americans constitute a diverse set of communities. Among the cultural values and traditions embraced by many, but not all, of these communities are patriarchy, an acceptance of suffering and valuing of endurance, a fatalistic outlook on life, a desire for family harmony and avoidance of conflict, an emphasis on the importance of not losing face or causing shame, and a collectivism in which the well-being of the family is valued over that of the individual. All of these characteristics may have played some role in the survival of Asian Americans in the face of what has often been hostile discrimination and racism within the majority culture, but all of them may also contribute to the occurrence of family violence and reluctance of family members to seek help. Which of these values seem similar to ones identified in other cultural groups? Given similarities and differences between Asian Americans and the other ethnic minority groups discussed in this book, what do you expect to learn in the next chapter about family violence in Asian American communities? Do you think child, spousal, and elder maltreatment will be over- or underreported? Why? What do you expect will be the most likely outcomes of family violence in these communities? Why?

13

Asian American Family Violence

Examples of severe child abuse:

- *"Physical abuse causing death. Beating."* (21-year-old Catholic Filipino female)
- *"Drunk father hitting drunk son."* (20-year-old Chinese American male)
- *"Father beating son for some minor disagreement; power."* (22-year-old Muslim Pakistani male)

Examples of severe husband-to-wife abuse:

- *"Husband repeatedly hurting her physically & mentally."* (21-year-old Catholic Filipino female)
- *"Husband beating, raping wife for not having dinner ready."* (20-year-old Chinese American male)
- *"Husband beating wife out of anger as a form of maintaining power."* (22-year-old Muslim Pakistani male)

Examples of severe wife-to-husband abuse:

- *"Wife in total control of her husband."* (21-year-old Catholic Filipino female)
- *[Respondent could not think of an example.]* (20-year-old Chinese American male)
- *"Hitting & verbal abuse out of retribution and anger."* (22-year-old Muslim Pakistani male)

Examples of severe elder abuse:

- *"Adult hitting parent."* (21-year-old Catholic Filipino female)
- *"Beating an elderly person for her wallet."* (20-year-old Chinese American male)
- *"Becoming angry and striking the elderly out of frustration."* (22-year-old Muslim Pakistani male)

As with the other ethnic minority groups considered in this book, Asian Americans have varying perspectives and examples of abuse, depending on who is maltreating whom. In general, when our participants gave examples of severe forms of abuse, the behaviors attributed to women abusing their husbands were much less physically violent than the behaviors attributed to husbands abusing their wives. Indeed, a number of respondents either did not respond to the item on severe abuse by wives, or indicated that they had "never heard of such a thing." Examples of moderate or mild abuse by wives generally focused on issues such as nagging, screaming or yelling, failing to fulfill duties, failing to obey husband, and discrediting his abilities or making fun of him. Examples of elder abuse often focused on behaviors such as neglect, shouting, and disrespect. Only rarely did respondents give the same answer for more than one relationship. How do these patterns fit with what you learned in the preceding chapter? Do you see any consistencies in themes and definitions across cultural groups?

As is true of other minority groups, it is difficult to determine the exact rate of family violence in Asian American communities because of ethnic lumping—perhaps due in part to the relatively small percentage of Asian Americans in the population at large and perhaps due also to the stereotype of Asian Americans as a "model minority." Typically, in studies of family violence in community samples, Asian Americans are included either in an inclusive "minority" category contrasted with Whites, or an "other" category contrasted with Whites, Blacks, and sometimes Hispanics. Such ethnic lumping may lead to serious distortions in profiles of abusing families. For example, Wolfner and Gelles (1993) reported that among the risk factors for severe child abuse in the first National Family Violence Survey was "race," categorized as Native American, Asian, and "others." Such lumping seems questionable in light of evidence indicating major overreporting of Native American Indians and underreporting of Asian Americans for child abuse.

Studies providing incidence data specific to Asian Americans typically focus on officially reported cases. For example, in the annual reports of state CPS agencies to the federal government, incidence rates for Asian Americans are indicated. However, reports of family violence in specific Asian American communities (e.g., Vietnamese, Filipino) are generally limited to refugee/immigrant samples, and there are very few studies providing comparative data from more than one Asian American/Pacific Islander (API) group.

Scope of the Problem

Child Maltreatment

Physical Maltreatment

Table 13.1 summarizes the studies on child maltreatment in Asian American communities.

If we consider the reported cases in the country at large, as well as in selected states (e.g., Hawaii, California) and cities (e.g., San Francisco) with published data, the rate of child maltreatment in Asian American families seems relatively low compared to other ethnic groups and compared to their proportion in the population. For example, although the proportion of Asian Americans in the country overall is over 4%, the proportion reported for child abuse and neglect is under 2% (DHHS, 2002). Moreover, nationwide, being Asian American is associated with a decreased likelihood of recurrence of reported child maltreatment (Fluke, Yuan, & Edwards, 1999).

The small studies of community and refugee/immigrant samples present a somewhat different picture—typically of a relatively high rate of child maltreatment. For example, in a Vietnamese refugee sample in St. Louis, more than half the children had been hit, threatened with hitting, scolded, and condemned (Segal, 2000), and a sample of Korean immigrant mothers also reported considerable physical aggression against their children (Park, 2001). On the other hand, in a study of Caucasian and Asian American college students in southern California, there were no significant ethnic group differences in retrospective reports of childhood physical and sexual abuse (Foo & Margolin, 1995).

The few studies providing comparative data on reported cases from different Asian American communities indicate significant variation in the use of aggression against children. For example, in Hawaii, Japanese Americans are underrepresented in reported cases of child abuse, whereas Polynesian Americans (including Samoans) are overrepresented (Dubanoski & Snyder, 1980; Hartz, 1995). Moreover, among API child maltreatment cases in San Diego, the percentages of Vietnamese (36%) and Cambodian (23.6%) cases were disproportionately high in relation to their proportion in the population (23% and 6%, respectively) whereas Hmong (from Laos), Koreans, and Filipinos were underrepresented (Ima & Hohm, 1991).

Research with community samples also provides evidence of differences across different Asian American groups in the experience of parental physical aggression. In a sample of

Table 13.1   Child Maltreatment in Asian American Communities

Study	Sample Description	Definition/Measure of Abuse	Findings
National Studies—Reported Cases			
Fluke, Yuan, & Edwards (1999)	Substantiated cases of child maltreatment from 10 states, 1994 and 1995	Child Protective Services reports in NCANDS[a]	• For all states except Vermont and North Carolina, Asian/Pacific Islander families had the lowest rate of child abuse recurrence.
Regional Studies—Reported Cases			
Hawaii Department of Social Services and Housing (Hartz, 1995)	Confirmed child abuse cases in Hawaii, 1978–1979	Hawaii Department of Social Service records	• Percentage of groups in Hawaii population: 27.7% European American, 26.6% Japanese American, 18.2% Polynesian American, 10.2% Filipino American, and 9.2% Mixed. • European Americans comprised 24.8% of abuse cases. • Japanese Americans comprised 4.2% of abuse cases. • Polynesian Americans comprised 33.6 % of abuse cases. • Filipino Americans comprised 9.6% of abuse cases. • Mixed ethnicity comprised 5.6% of abuse cases. • Japanese Americans were underrepresented; Polynesian Americans were overrepresented.
Rao, DiClemente, & Ponton (1992)	69 Asian cases of sexual abuse at the Child & Adolescent Sexual Abuse Resource Center at San Francisco's General Hospital, 1986–1988	Substantiated cases	Ethnic distribution of Asian American cases: • 30.4% Filipino • 15.9% Vietnamese • 15.9% Pacific Islander • 11.6% Chinese • 5.8% Fiji Islander • 5.8% Cambodian • Remainder: Laotian, Thai, multi-Asian, and other Asian.
Ima & Hohm (1991)	158 Union of Pan Asian & Pacific Islander child maltreatment cases in San Diego (4.9% of total reported cases)	Case reports; categorization of maltreatment cases: 53% physical abuse, 4.9% sexual abuse, 6% emotional abuse, and 36% neglect	• Physical abuse rate was higher and sexual abuse rate was lower than rate in population of country as a whole. • Rates were disproportionately high in Vietnamese and Cambodians. • Over 83% of Samoan and 72% of Vietnamese victims were physically abused.

(Continued)

Table 13.1 Continued

Study	Sample Description	Definition/Measure of Abuse	Findings
Dubanoski & Snyder (1980)	Confirmed child abuse cases in Hawaii, 1976–1977; percentage of groups in Hawaii population: 27% Japanese American, and <1% Samoan American	Hawaii Statistical Report on Child Abuse and Neglect, 1976–1977	• Japanese Americans: 3.45% of abuse perpetration cases; 4.65% of neglect perpetration cases. • Samoan Americans: 6.65% of abuse perpetration cases; 2.6% of neglect perpetration cases. • Japanese Americans were underrepresented; Samoans were overrepresented.
Regional Studies—Self-Report			
Park (2001)	144 Korean immigrant mothers who came to United States after age 16 and had at least one child under 18	Conflict Tactics Scale parent-to-child physical aggression items	• Conflict Tactics Scale physical aggression scores (on scale ranging from 0 to 20): $M = 5.6$, $SD = 4.4$.
Segal (2000)	28 Vietnamese refugees in St. Louis area: 41–65 years of age, at least one child age 8 to 18	Parent-child Conflict Tactics Scale and Child Abuse Potential Inventory (CAPI) with parents; interview with children	• CAPI scores were elevated in 68% of sample. Parent reports of Conflict Tactics Scale frequencies: • Threatening to hit: 64% • Hitting: 57% • Name-calling: 43% • Threatening to put out of house: 39.3% Child report: • Scolding or condemning: 52% • Spanking or hitting: 22%
McKelvey & Webb (1995)	102 Vietnamese Amerasians at Philippines Refugee Processing Center: 68 males and 34 females, age 18 to 25	Self-administered questionnaire regarding physical and sexual abuse	• Females: 6 (18%) reported abuse—3 were physically abused and 3 were sexually abused; all abusers were close family members. • Males: 15 (22%) reported being abused—7 reported physical abuse, 4 reported sexual abuse, and 4 reported both; 1 was abused by a foster mother, 4 by friends, 3 by spouses, and 7 by unidentified perpetrators.

NOTE: For information on Asian American child maltreatment according to the U.S. Department of Health and Human Services (1999, 2000), the Third National Incidence Study (Sedlak & Broadhurst, 1996), California Children's Services Archive (2002), and Urquiza and Goodlin-Jones (1994), please see Table 3.1.

a. NCANDS = National Child Abuse and Neglect Data System.

Asian American adults recruited from ethnic community fairs in northeast urban areas, a higher portion of Korean Americans than Chinese Americans reported being hit by a parent while growing up (Yoshioka, DiNoia, & Ullah, 2001). Moreover, significantly more Cambodians than Chinese reported witnessing interparental violence during childhood. Although all of these studies have limitations—for example, being restricted to small, unrepresentative samples—they highlight the importance of examining different Asian American groups separately.

Sexual Abuse

Very few studies of Asian American participants have provided evidence concerning sexual abuse, either alone or in combination with physical abuse. McKelvey and Webb (1995) found that 18% of a sample of young Vietnamese Amerasian women (i.e., women with Vietnamese mothers and White American fathers, typically servicemen in the Vietnam War) had experienced childhood physical or sexual abuse from a close family member. In a study of California community college students with a population that was 16% Asian American, 21.1% of the women reported having experienced child sexual abuse (Urquiza & Goodlin-Jones, 1994).

Spousal Maltreatment

Wife Physical Abuse

Table 13.2 summarizes studies providing information on the occurrence of wife abuse in Asian American communities. Large-scale studies consistently show that Asian American women experience less spousal abuse than women of other groups. For example, data from the National Violence Against Women Survey (NVAW; Tjaden & Thoennes, 2000) indicate that API women experienced significantly less lifetime victimization and physical assaults than women from other racial groups. Similarly, a study of California women (Lund, 2002) revealed that Asian women reported experiencing significantly less physical violence than Black women.

In contrast, state and local community and refugee samples reveal a considerable amount of spousal violence in Asian American communities. Although definitions of violence vary across studies, the self-report evidence indicates that violence from partners has been experienced by 20% to 80% of Asian American women, depending upon their country of origin. Specifically, physical abuse has been reported by 80% of Japanese American women (Yoshihama, 2000; Yoshihama & Horrocks, 2002), 20% to 60% of Korean American women (Kim & Sung, 2000; Song, 1996, respectively), 40% of South Asian American women (Raj & Silverman, 2002), and 50% of Vietnamese women (Bui & Morash, 1999). A study of Vietnamese women recruited both from a domestic violence center and from a civic organization illustrates well the pervasiveness of partner violence against some Vietnamese women—nearly all of the women from the community sample, in addition to the battered sample, experienced physical and/or verbal abuse (Tran & Des Jardins, 2000). Such findings support the views of several workers in the field (e.g., Yoshihama), who believe that the actual magnitude of physical violence against Asian American women is much higher than the reported cases indicate.

A number of factors appear to contribute to the underreporting of wife abuse in Asian American communities—and many are similar to factors operating in Hispanic and Native American Indian communities. These factors include language barriers (Lai, 1986; Warrier, 2000), experiences of institutional racism and discrimination (Yoshihama, 2000), lack of information about available services (Song, 1996), the view that wife-beating is a private matter (Bui & Morash, 1999), unwillingness of victims to initiate discussion of abuse with medical personnel (Rodriguez, Bauer, Flores-Ortiz, & Szkupinski-Quiroga, 1998), fear of "losing face" (Rasche, 1988), and fear of deportation (Anderson, 1993; Lee, 2000). Consider the case of Geeta in Box 13.1. She went to medical school in India, and then came to the United States to join her husband, Ramesh. Ramesh had emigrated to the United States as a student, returned to India to get a green card and find a wife, and was introduced to Geeta by friends of

Table 13.2 Spousal Maltreatment in Asian American Communities

Study	Sample Description	Definition/Measure of Abuse	Findings
Regional Studies—Self-Report			
Raj & Silverman (2002)	160 South Asian women in the Boston area	Conflict Tactics Scales	• 40% of women were victims of intimate partner violence. • Two thirds of physical abuse victims also reported being sexually abused.
Yoshioka, Dang, Shewmangal, Chan, & Tan (2000)	Community sample of 607 Asian Americans (57% women, 43% men): Chinese, Korean, Vietnamese, Cambodian, and South Asian from Boston and Lowell, MA	Interview (conducted in five languages); source and specific wording of questions not identified	• Nearly 50% reported knowing a woman who was being abused by her partner (ranging from 5% of South Asians to 47% of Cambodians). • 12% reported knowing a man being abused by his partner (ranging from 3% of Koreans to 37% of Cambodians).
Yoshihama (2000); Yoshihama & Horrocks (2002)	Community-based random sample of 211 Japanese American women from Los Angeles, age 18–49	Expanded version of CTS, including additional emotional abuse items	• 80% reported at least one incident of partner violence, including slapping, kicking, choking, and refusing to use contraceptives. • 45% were abused by husbands. • 46% were abused by boyfriends.
Kim & Sung (2000)	Random sample of 256 Korean American families from Chicago and New York City areas	Telephone interviews, including CTS	Female victims: • Any violence: 18% • Severe violence: 6.3% • Rates of severe violence by husbands were four times greater than in U.S. population as a whole (based on National Family Violence Survey 1). Males victims: • Any violence: 8.2% • Severe violence: 0.8%
Segal (2000)	28 Vietnamese refugees in St. Louis area: 41–65 years of age, at least one child age 8 to 18	Semistructured interview, including original CTS	• Every form of psychological aggression was reported by at least 25% of the sample. • 40% reported threatening to throw something at spouse. • Wife-to-husband violence rates were slightly higher than husband-to-wife rates.

Study	Sample Description	Definition/Measure of Abuse	Findings
Tran & Des Jardins (2000)	65 Vietnamese women recruited from New England–area Asian domestic violence agency and a Vietnamese American civic association	CTS	• 51 out of the 65 reported maltreatment within the previous year. • Of those, 92% reported physical abuse; 80% reported verbal abuse. • 55% reported being punched, 45% being slapped, 24% being choked, and 33% being threatened with knife or gun.
Bui & Morash (1999)	Purposive sample of 10 Vietnamese women in shelters and 10 nonabused women from urban areas in South and Midwest, age 28 to 62	In-depth interview in Vietnamese, including CTS1 and psychological aggression items from Sullivan, Parisian, & Davidson (1991) emotional abuse measure	• 10% reported using physical aggression against partners. • 80% reported undergoing psychological abuse.
Song (1996)	150 Korean women immigrants in Chicago aged 21–56.	Measure based upon the CTS	• 60% of women reported battering. • Of those, 57% were hit with closed fist, 42% slapped, 24% choked, and 20% threatened with knife or gun. • 70% were battered severely enough to at least leave bruises.

NOTE: For information on Asian American spousal abuse according to the U.S. Department of Justice (Rennison, 2001a, 2001b; Rennison & Welchans, 2000), the National Violence Against Women Survey (Tjaden & Thoennes, 2000), and the 1998 California Women's Health Survey (Lund, 2000; Weinbaum et al., 2001), please see Table 3.2.

Box 13.1 Geeta's Case

[He] asks me, "When are you going to pass the exam, they [his family] want to come to States?" . . . . Then he threw me on the bed and he started stamping his feet all over my body. When he started boiling oil on the stove and he said he would pour it on me, I screamed and went to the bathroom and called my friends. I was screaming, the neighbors heard me screaming and they called the police I think. The police came and my friend's husband came at the same time. . . . The police said that they have to talk to me. My friend's husband said, that it is nothing, only a wife and husband matter. . . . My friend's husband told me in my language to tell them it is nothing, and I said it is nothing. . . and they left. The friends took me to their house. They started talking like it was my fault the police came. . . . Once he threw me out of the apartment. . . [He] would take the telephone with him so that I could not make any telephone calls. He threw away all my clothes. . . . For every small thing he would pick a fight. I told my uncle. He said it was usual between wife and husband.

SOURCE: Abraham, 2000, p. 232.

the family. Approximately 4 to 5 months after Geeta's arrival in the United States, Ramesh began battering her in an effort to force her to speed up her preparation for medical exams so that she could support his family back home and sponsor their emigration to the United States. What forces made it difficult for Geeta to leave her abusive husband? What similarities do you see between these factors and the factors observed in battered women from other minority groups?

Wife Psychological Abuse

Most of the research on maltreatment of wives in Asian American communities has focused on physical abuse, but there has been some attention to psychological maltreatment as well, and these studies show that emotional abuse may also be a widespread problem for Asian American women. For example, 80% of a sample of Vietnamese immigrant women reported at least some emotional abuse from their husbands (Bui & Morash, 1999). Among Japanese American women in Los Angeles, 48% reported emotional abuse (Yoshihama, 1999), and among a sample of "out of town" mail-order brides, psychological abuse was probably the most prevalent form of maltreatment experienced (Chin, 1994). In addition,

Chinese American males who worry about their wives' fidelity may use tactics that can be considered psychologically abusive, such as prohibiting their wives from working, learning English, leaving the home, calling or writing their families in China, and holding onto their wives' legal documents and threatening them with divorce or interference with their immigration status (Chin).

Wife Sexual Abuse

Several factors make Asian American women vulnerable to sexual abuse from intimate partners, including socialized reluctance to discuss sexual matters, denigration of sexual activity in unmarried females, distrust of governmental agencies, and traditional norms assuring sexual access to women by their husbands. Abraham (1999) views sexual abuse by South Asian men as a way of obtaining and keeping a dominant role within a patriarchal system, and describes it as a frequent form of maltreatment of South Asian women. Among the South Asian immigrant women she interviewed, approximately 60% reported being forced to have sex with their husbands against their will. Several told stories of husbands who forcibly impregnated them or forced them to have an abortion, supporting Abraham's implicit theory that many

South Asian husbands feel entitled to control their wives' reproductivity as part of their patriarchal rights. Sexual abuse of wives by Japanese American men seems more rare, although approximately 5% of Yoshihama's (1999) sample reported some sexual maltreatment, such as being forced to have sex or experiencing unwanted touching.

Husband Abuse

As is true of the other ethnic minorities under consideration, there has been much less research on violence against men than on violence against women in Asian American communities. However, some studies that investigated wife abuse have also included husband abuse in their analyses, and these studies show that although husband abuse occurs much less frequently than wife abuse in Asian American families, it does occur to some extent. For example, on a national level, the NVAW survey revealed a similar pattern for Asian American men as for Asian American women: relatively low rates of violence, both in comparison to their proportion in the population and to other ethnic groups (Tjaden & Thoennes, 2000).

In local studies with nonrepresentative samples, some aggression was shown by wives against husbands in 8% of a Korean American sample (Kim & Sung, 2000). However, fewer than 1% of the sample reported severe physical aggression of wives against husbands. In a community sample of Vietnamese American couples, physical aggression was reported relatively infrequently, but women reported somewhat more aggression against their partners than men did (Segal, 2000). In addition, overall reported rates of psychological maltreatment were very similar across gender, although wives tended to shout and husbands tended to swear.

Elder Maltreatment

Although there have been several studies of attitudes toward elder maltreatment in Asian American communities (see Chapter 12) and a few qualitative studies of Asian American elder abuse, empirical evidence on the incidence of elder abuse is extremely limited. Data from the National Elder Abuse Incidence Study (NEAIS)

reveal that this form of maltreatment is underrepresented in Asian Americans. Although their percentage in the population is just over 4%, only 2.1% of the elder maltreatment cases reported to adult protective servies (APS) in 1996 were API. The figures for specific types of reported maltreatment were even lower: 0.3% of neglect cases, 0.4% of emotional abuse cases, 0.4% of physical abuse cases, 0.2% of financial abuse cases, and none of the abandonment cases were API. For the sentinel reports of the NEAIS of 1996, API were combined with Blacks, Hispanics, Native Americans, and other groups in a minority category, which was compared with the Whites. Cases reported by the sentinel agencies were overwhelmingly White (National Center on Elder Abuse, 1998).

Similar to incidence studies of reported cases, community studies of elder maltreatment in Asian American communities are quite rare. In a community study of 20 elderly Vietnamese Americans, no cases of physical abuse were reported (Le, 1997). However, there was one case of financial abuse, and more than half of the respondents gave examples of psychological abuse—for example, being coerced to stay in the house, insulted, harassed, and given the silent treatment. When asked to provide examples of incidents they had encountered that they considered to be abuse, 34 of 100 elderly Koreans in Los Angeles County described at least one such incident, for a total of 46 incidents (Chang & Moon, 1997). The most frequently mentioned types of elder abuse were forms of financial exploitation (typically by sons) and psychological abuse (typically by daughters-in-law).

Among elderly Chinese Americans referred to a health and social service agency in San Francisco, many types of maltreatment were also identified (Fang, 1998). Specifically, 60% of these Chinese American maltreatment cases were neglect, 10% were financial abuse, 10% were physical abuse, and 20% were psychological abuse and abandonment. A typical case was Mrs. W., who was invited to the United States by her niece because her niece needed someone to take care of her three children and clean house. Six years later, when the children were in school, Mrs. W. was deemed a useless burden; consequently, her niece hid her green card and

> **Box 13.2**   The Case of Mrs. Park
>
> Mrs. Park was 61 when she came to live with her 27-year-old son Sung in the United States. Sung had trouble holding a job, and talked his mother into loaning him enough money to start his own restaurant business. After the business went bankrupt, Mrs. Park became dependent on Supplemental Security Income (SSI) and moved into government-subsidized senior housing. Sung, who began to drink heavily, picked up his mother the first day of every month and took her to the bank to cash her SSI check. He kept most of the money, giving her only $50 to live on for the month. Although her neighbors occasionally fed her, they did not want to get involved in family problems. Consequently, no one intervened by notifying social services of her plight. Mrs. Park became weaker and weaker until she died in the street at the age of 71, on her way to pick up a package of free food.
>
> SOURCE: Moon, 1999.

social security card, and gave her a one-way ticket to China where there was nobody with whom she could live. Consider also the case described in Box 13.2. What forms of maltreatment are occurring? What would you identify as the major causal factors leading up to Mrs. Park's death? Which factors, if any, reflect Korean culture? Which, if any, reflect broader macrosystem processes?

PREDICTORS AND CORRELATES

Child Maltreatment

Although research on predictors and correlates of child maltreatment in Asian American communities is relatively limited, there are studies of factors at every ecological level.

Macrosystem Level

Based on case records and related research, Ima and Hohm (1991) suggested that one of the causes of child maltreatment among Cambodian and Vietnamese refugees in this country was trauma experienced by the abuser in the countries of origin, a macrosystem level variable. Other macrosystem variables implicated in Asian American child maltreatment cases include economic and employment variables. For instance, unskilled Asian American workers are at increased risk for abusing their children (Dubanoski, 1982). Cambodians are relatively

overrepresented among Asian American child maltreatment cases seen at a pan-Asian social service agency in part because they are poorer and more dependent on pubic welfare bureaucracies (macrosystem), and, therefore, are simply more visible to authorities in the exosystem (Ima & Hohm).

Exosystem Level

In addition to being more visible to authorities in the exosystem when dependent on public welfare, Asian Americans may actually be at some risk for maltreating their children because of exosystem factors such as stress. Among Korean immigrants in Texas, parents reporting stress due to their immigration status and/or perceived discrimination were more likely to use physical aggression with their children during times of conflict (Park, 2001).

Microsystem Level

Consistent with research on other cultural minority groups, some emphasis has been given to the microsystem level. A study of European and Hawaiian (mostly Asian) Americans revealed that broken families were at risk for maltreating their children (Dubanoski, 1982). Risk factors for child maltreatment among Korean immigrant mothers include having younger children and experiencing high familial conflict regarding issues of acculturation (Park,

2001). A microsystem predictive factor for child sexual abuse in Asian American families is residence of the child with a father, the most frequent abuser in those families (Rao et al., 1992).

Individual Level

At the individual level, both sociocognitive and experiential factors appear to play a role in Asian American child maltreatment. Among Samoan Americans in Hawaii, the greatest risk factor for child maltreatment was the mother's childhood experience of abuse (Dubanoski & Snyder, 1980). In comparison to Japanese Americans, these Samoan Americans were significantly more likely to see their abusive practices as normal discipline—even though these practices resulted not just in cuts, bruises, and welts, but also brain damage in several cases. In addition, alcohol dependence was blamed for child maltreatment in a significant number of both the Samoan American and Japanese American child maltreatment cases (Dubanoski & Snyder). Among recent Korean immigrants, mothers who emphasized traditional Korean valuing of children were more tolerant of abusive practices than mothers emphasizing this valuing less—suggesting that the more acculturated mothers were less accepting of abusive practices.

Spousal Maltreatment

Macrosystem Level

Much of the responsibility for abuse of Asian American women has been placed on values and traditions embedded in a patriarchal heritage (Tran & Des Jardins, 2000; Yoshihama, 2000). Consistent with these views, the physical and emotional abuse of Vietnamese women by their husbands was shown to be positively correlated with the husbands' dominance in decision making, belief in patriarchal values, and conflicts with wives on changing norms and values (Bui & Morash, 1999). Among immigrant Korean women, the battered women were more traditional than the nonbattered women in their norms for the family, and more rigid in their sex roles (Song, 1996). Interestingly, Korean

American women in either husband-dominant or wife-dominant marriages appear to experience higher levels of husband assault than Korean American women in egalitarian marriages (Kim & Sung, 2000).

Several researchers have noted that not just male power and dominance, but a generational hierarchy in which in-laws contribute to the abuse of women, can be found in the following immigrants to the United States: Vietnamese women (e.g., Tran & Des Jardins, 2000), Asian Indian women (Mehrotra, 1999), and other Asian American women (Sorenson, 1986; Warrier, 2000). Among abused South Asian immigrant women from India, Pakistan, and Bangladesh, the power given to men by the macrosystem seemed to be a key factor in the maltreatment of those women (Abraham, 2000). To solidify their superior position, the batterers often used their power to isolate their wives within the microsystem and the exosystem. As one woman recounted,

> He gave me no money for household expenses. . . . He used to do all the shopping and spending. He never took me for grocery. He told me not to go, because it wasn't a good neighborhood. . . . I had no slippers to wear at home, so I asked him for one. He bought me one that was one size bigger. So I was in a state, that I couldn't even go out to buy a pair of slippers. (Abraham, 2000, p. 229)

The collusion of in-laws in such abuse is described by another one of Abraham's (2000) respondents:

> Since I came here I have been working but my husband took the money . . . and then they [husband and in-laws] would give me 20 dollars a week. With this I had to pay my gas and for all my lunches. Things kept getting hard because when you go out and all, you have to contribute to other things. . . . I started saying that I need some more. Then the father-in-law started interfering. Then the brother-in-law started interfering. . . . If I go for grocery, why did I spend so much. They would open my groceries and go through everything. How much I spent on it. Whatever I do at home is wrong. (p. 231)

Another variable implicated as a risk factor for wife abuse among Asian Americans is language; for example, among Korean immigrant women, wife abuse is associated with language difficulties (Song, 1996). Macrosystem cultural variables also seem to contribute to the abuse of Asian American husbands. In one study of Korean Americans, wives' physical aggression against husbands was negatively correlated with the husbands' dominance in family decision making and contribution to housework (Bui & Morash, 1999). Other macrosystem factors associated with spousal abuse among Asian Americans include educational, occupational, and economic variables. Abused Vietnamese immigrant women tend to be less educated than their nonabused counterparts, and their husbands tend to be less satisfied with their occupations (Tran & Des Jardins, 2000). Also, immigrant Korean men who experienced a lowering of either occupational or economic status after moving to the United States were more likely to beat their wives than men who did not experience such a loss of status (Song; Song-Kim, 1992).

Exosystem Level

An important exosystem level factor associated with spousal abuse is social isolation. Among Korean (Song, 1996) and South Asian (Abraham, 1999; Mehrotra, 1999) battered immigrant women, social isolation was found to contribute to abuse. In another community sample of Korean American couples, nearly 39% of husbands with high exosystem stress (e.g., becoming a lot worse off financially, having trouble with a boss, getting fired, getting arrested, having difficulty speaking English) were much more physically aggressive against their wives than men with low exosystem stress (Kim & Sung, 2000).

Microsystem Level

Specific stressors at the microsystem level have also been identified as predictors of wife abuse. Among Vietnamese immigrants, predictors of wife abuse include marital separation (Tran & Des Jardins, 2000), husband's dominance

in family decision making, and conflicts with wives about changing norms and values (Bui & Morash, 1999). Predictors of wife abuse in Korean American families also include conflicts and sex role dynamics. For example, Korean immigrant battered women reported that just prior to being abused, they had an argument with their husbands about in-law problems, money, employment, his drinking, or chores and responsibilities (Song, 1996). Among battered Asian Indian women, physical abuse was generally associated with the husbands' demands for total subservience from their wives; when the wives challenged their husbands' authority by arguing or demonstrating attempts at greater independence, the violence escalated, even during pregnancy (Dasgupta & Warrier, 1996).

Individual Level

As shown consistently in studies of other ethnic groups, a major individual variable predictive of Asian American spousal abuse is alcohol use. Among Vietnamese women, almost half of the battered women in one study attributed their beatings to their partner's alcohol abuse, drug abuse, or gambling (Tran, 1997). One of the participants explained,

> He began hitting me after he started using cocaine. He never had enough money, always demanded money from my mother or I. I was always scared because I never knew what kind of mood he would be in. He sometimes used his gun to threaten my mom and I so we would give him more money. (Tran & Des Jardins, 2000, p. 85)

In another Vietnamese sample, physical abuse of wives was positively associated with husbands' patriarchal beliefs and negatively associated with husbands' educational attainment (Bui & Morash, 1999). Would you expect those individual factors to operate in other Asian American men as well? Why or why not?

Elder Maltreatment

There have been several conceptual analyses, but very little empirical research, on the predictors and correlates of elder abuse in Asian

American communities. Among Vietnamese immigrants, risk factors have been pinpointed primarily at the individual level of the abuser (e.g., impatience with the elderly parent, rejection of old norms) and at the microsystem level, in that elderly women living with sons and daughters-in-law were at heightened risk of abuse, particularly from their daughters-in-law (Le, 1997).

OUTCOMES

Child Maltreatment

Some of the findings concerning the outcomes of child maltreatment among Asian Americans are quite consistent with what has been found in other groups, although there are some differences in patterns. For example, support for the intergenerational transmission of aggression was shown in a study of European and Asian American high school students in Hawaii (Hartz, 1995). Specifically, in each ethnicity, students' aggression toward parents was significantly positively correlated with parents' aggression toward them—a correlation that was stronger for the European American teens than for the Asian American teens (Hartz).

The extent to which the experience of childhood maltreatment has short- and long-term negative effects on Asian American children is mixed. In a sample of young adult Vietnamese Amerasians, abused male Amerasians had significantly higher levels of psychological distress than nonabused male Amerasians, but there were no significant differences in symptomatology between abused and nonabused female Amerasians (McKelvey & Webb, 1995). In a sample of working-class API adolescents, harsh parental discipline was associated with temper tantrums and feeling worthless, but not with delinquent behavior (DeBaryshe, Yuen, & Stern, 2001). Finally, in a retrospective chart review of Black, White, Hispanic, and Asian American victims of child sexual abuse, the Asian American children were more likely to express suicidality and less likely to display anger and sexual acting out than non-Asians (Rao, DiClemente, & Ponton, 1992). Although

this study suggests that Asian American children might have more negative outcomes than children of other ethnicities, another study showed that higher rates of rape in adulthood were associated with a prior history of child sexual abuse in White, African American, and Latina, but not in Asian American women (Urquiza & Goodlin-Jones, 1994). In a community-based random sample of Japanese American women, childhood abuse was significantly correlated with current post-traumatic stress disorder [PTSD] symptoms (Yoshihama & Horrocks, 2002).

We know of no studies linking childhood experiences of abuse to later substance abuse or sexual acting out in Asian Americans. Overall, the evidence seems to indicate that the effects of child abuse in Asian Americans are more likely to be expressed in psychological symptoms, such as anxiety, depression, and suicidality, than in more behavioral symptoms, such as the substance abuse, aggression, and sexual acting out seen in other ethnicities.

Spousal Maltreatment

Although in some of the ethnic communities we have studied (e.g., African American), terminating the relationship is one outcome of abuse, this alternative is rarely considered viable to Asian Americans because of their emphasis on the sanctity of the family and fear of community ostracism (Dasgupta & Warrier, 1996; Huisman, 1996). The limited research available on the outcomes of spousal abuse in Asian American communities indicates that abused Korean immigrant wives suffer from a number of stress-related symptoms, such as difficulty sleeping, headaches, and loss of appetite (Song, 1996). Among Japanese American women, ratings of the partner's violence were positively associated with the number of PTSD symptoms experienced during the previous year (Yoshihama & Horrocks, 2002). Japanese women who had been injured by their partners and/or feared for their lives reported higher levels of reexperiencing and avoidance symptoms. There was also a positive correlation between forced sex and avoidance symptoms. Satisfaction with social support mitigated symptoms in these abused women (Yoshihama & Horrocks).

Elder Maltreatment

There has been little systematic research on the effects of elder maltreatment in Asian American communities, although case studies confirm that extreme neglect can lead to the most serious outcome—death (Moon, 1999). In a small sample of maltreated Vietnamese elders in California, interviews revealed that almost all of the respondents were depressed, and most were stressed, anxious, lonely, and fearful (Le, 1997). Because of reticence and a concern with face saving, the effects of maltreatment in many elderly Asian Americans may be difficult to detect; they may be expressed, for example, in physical discomforts, such as fatigue, backache, headache, or insomnia (Le).

SUMMARY

Frequent ethnic lumping of Asian Americans into broad "minority" or "other" categories makes it difficult to establish the exact incidence of family violence in those communities. Although physically and psychologically aggressive behaviors seem quite common and accepted within many Asian American communities, reported rates of child abuse are low compared to other ethnic communities. However, within the Asian American population, there are wide variations, with rates of child abuse probably being somewhat higher among Polynesian, Vietnamese, and Cambodians than among Southeast Asians, Filipinos, and Chinese. The limited data on child sexual abuse indicate that it does occur in at least some of these communities. As with child abuse, the national studies of reported cases show underreporting of spousal abuse in Asian American families, but more localized studies indicate that it can be a fairly serious problem in some communities, with 40% or more women of Japanese, Korean, Southeast Asian, and Vietnamese descent reporting physical abuse, and greater numbers reporting psychological maltreatment. Although wife sexual abuse may be quite high among South Asian women, it seems considerably lower in Japanese American women. Elder maltreatment in these communities is underreported, and seems to consist primarily of neglect, psychological maltreatment, and financial exploitation.

Predictors and correlates of maltreatment in Asian American communities include classic factors related to stress at every level of the ecological hierarchy as well as traditional attitudes condoning violence. Outcomes are generally psychological and physical symptoms rather than behavioral problems. However, as has been the case of many of the subgroups considered in this book, the available data are typically from small and unrepresentative samples; thus, firm conclusions cannot yet be made.

Given what you have learned concerning cultural values in different Asian American communities, do some of these findings appear more solid than others? Do you believe that future research will unearth patterns of sexual acting out, substance abuse, or delinquency in abused children from different Asian American communities? Why or why not? With greater acculturation, are abused spouses and elderly from these communities more likely to seek help? If they do, what are the likely implications for family dynamics?

The final two chapters of this book address the problem of combating family violence in the United States. The focus is on available resources and ongoing needs for prevention and intervention programs in the various ethnic communities. To what extent do you expect the needs to be consistent across ethnic groups? What kinds of resources might be more important for one group (e.g., African Americans) than for another group (e.g., Asian Americans)? Why?

PART VI

CONCLUSION: PREVENTION
AND INTERVENTION

14

PREVENTION AND INTERVENTION IN CHILD MALTREATMENT

An ecological approach to combating family violence in the many different communities of the United States requires identifying (a) the levels of the ecological system in which there are, or should be, structures and programs to prevent family violence, (b) the ecological level at which those efforts are targeted, (c) whether the primary focus of the efforts is the perpetrator or the victim, and (d) the extent to which the operations or outcomes of programs are influenced by or targeted toward perpetrators and/or victims in minority cultural groups.

A defining characteristic of the ecological model is its attention to ways in which processes at every level are intimately and intricately interwoven with processes at other levels. For example, interpretations of macrosystem federal laws (e.g., in the form of welfare reform) have effects within the exosystem (e.g., state regulations directed at unemployed mothers), the family microsystem (e.g., the time and energy a parent has to spend with a child), and the individual level (e.g., the well-being of the stressed mother or the developing child).

An ecological analysis of prevention and intervention efforts should ask what needs to be changed (at what ecological level) and by whom (at what ecological level). There have been legislative efforts at the macro- and exosystem levels intended to reduce or prevent family violence at microsystem and individual levels.

However, many of the causes of family violence are rooted in institutionalized biases and practices at the macro- and exosystem levels, and it is essential to address these biases and practices if family violence is to be ended. Efforts to make such changes in the macrosystem can be initiated at the individual level (e.g., by courageous reformers and scholars), at the exosystem level (e.g., by professional organizations concerned with family violence), or at the macrosystem level itself (e.g., in federal courts or in Congress).

In this and the next chapter, we consider intervention and prevention programs that have been developed and further steps that need to be taken at each of the major ecological levels in order to reduce violence within American families. We pay particular attention to programs tailored toward or with differential impacts on the cultural groups discussed in this book. A fairly typical pattern is for organizations operating at an exosystem level (e.g., local CPS agencies, battered women's shelters) with at least partial funding and directives from the macrosystem level (e.g., the federal government) to intervene at the level of either the microsystem (e.g., to remove children from an abusive home, or help battered women obtain resources to leave) or the individual (e.g., by arresting an abuser or providing counseling or substance abuse treatment).

In general, members of minority communities, particularly African Americans, are overrepresented in the coercive interventions in this country, and underrepresented in other forms of intervention such as mental health services (Hawkins, 1987). Methods of prevention and intervention in the United States approach child maltreatment largely as microsystem parental aggression against children. By contrast, issues such as poverty, child hunger, inadequate housing and health care, overcrowded and underfunded schools, and dangerous neighborhoods are viewed as forms of child maltreatment in other nations, where the concept of children's basic human needs dominates considerations of maltreatment (Finkelhor & Korbin, 1988; Fontes, 2002). In our view, prevention and intervention efforts in this country need a broader view of child maltreatment so that predictors at all levels of the ecological model can be addressed.

MACROSYSTEM EFFORTS

Child Abuse Laws and CPS Procedures

In 1962, the U.S. Children's Bureau adopted the first laws requiring physicians to report known cases of child abuse to social service agencies. The logic was as follows: Because children are often not able to speak for, or defend, themselves, professionals who deal with children have the obligation to protect them from abuse by reporting their cases to authorities so that appropriate services and protection can be offered to the children and their families. Within five years, all states had passed child abuse reporting laws for physicians, with provisions that any professionals reporting such cases would be exempt from civil or criminal liability (Davidson, 1988; Paulsen, Parker, & Adelman, 1966; Zellman & Fair, 2002).

As research into child abuse expanded, increased understanding led to a broader definition of acts constituting child abuse, and by the 1970s, sexual abuse, emotional maltreatment, and neglect were included in definitions. It also became evident that other professionals might be in a position to detect child maltreatment, and by 1986, virtually every state required that nurses, social workers, other mental health professionals, teachers, school staff, and physicians

be mandated reporters of child abuse (Fraser, 1986; Zellman & Fair, 2002).

Perhaps the most influential child abuse law ever passed in this country was the 1974 Child Abuse Prevention and Treatment Act (CAPTA), which freed millions of federal dollars to support state child protection agencies. To receive this funding, states had to conform their child abuse reporting laws to federal standards. They also had to create policies and procedures for reporting and investigating alleged child abuse, and offer treatment services for these families. CAPTA also gave states the power to remove children from homes if the child was deemed to be in danger (Myers, 2002; Pleck, 1987; Zellman & Fair, 2002).

In 1980, the federal government passed the Adoption Assistance and Child Welfare Act, requiring that states do everything possible (reasonable effort) to prevent removal of children from their families and to reunite families in the event of a removal. In 1997, the government further defined the "reasonable effort" phrase in the Adoption and Safe Families Act: "in making reasonable efforts, the child's health and safety shall be of paramount concern" (42 U.S. Code § 671[a][15][A]; Myers, 2002). In January 2002, President Bush signed into law the 2001 amendments to the Promoting Safe and Stable Families program, extending it until 2006, and providing funds for states to ensure the safety of abused children by facilitating quick adoption into safe, stable homes if efforts to keep the family together failed. Furthermore, the funds provide for education and training vouchers for youth who age out of foster care and mentoring programs for children with parents in prison (Child Welfare League of America, 2002).

Under federal regulations, the job of child protective services (CPS) is to receive calls of potential child abuse cases, investigate these cases, decide if abuse has occurred, and take appropriate action. CPS workers often collaborate with local law enforcement and other child professionals in medicine, mental health, education, and law, to determine an appropriate action. Most cases do not go to court unless the abuse is very serious, probably because, as the U.S. Supreme Court noted in the 1987 *Pennsylvania v. Ritchie* case, "child abuse is one of the most difficult crimes to detect and prosecute, in large part because there often are no witnesses except the victim." The majority of cases are referred for tertiary intervention (Myers, 2002, p. 313).

Unfortunately, the system is very flawed. When the laws were first enacted in the 1960s, it was assumed that child abuse was very rare, and that prevention would be a low-cost venture (Nelson, 1984). Today, the vast numbers of child abuse referrals are overwhelming CPS agencies short on funds, staff, and time. In reaction to unmanageable caseloads, agencies have been forced to narrow their definitions of abuse so that usually only the most serious cases get attention. Unfortunately, this means that many families needing services fall through the cracks; their abuse cases are just not severe enough to receive CPS attention (Zellman & Fair, 2002).

Because CPS is so overwhelmed, many "mandated" reporters have chosen not to report certain cases of child abuse—as evident in the Third National Incidence Study of Child Abuse and Neglect (NIS-3) data collected from CPS agencies and professionals. In 1993, only 28% of abused children under the Harm Standard and 33% of abused children under the Endangerment Standard received CPS attention. Even more alarming is that only 25% of children who were seriously harmed or injured by abuse or neglect received CPS attention. In addition, these percentages represented a decrease from the previous NIS study, indicating that as time went on, fewer and fewer cases were reported to the designated authorities (Sedlak & Broadhurst, 1996). An investigation showed that 40% of mandated reporters decided not to report a case of suspected child abuse at some point in their career (Zellman & Fair, 2002). Child psychiatrists were the professionals least likely to report suspected child abuse, primarily because they believed reporting would not help the child or family or stop the maltreatment. Some professionals also feared that a report would disrupt treatment of their client or family, and some believed they could help the family better than the CPS agency. Many respondents believed that in some cases, reports to CPS agencies would hurt matters, not help them, especially in milder cases of abuse that might just be screened out by CPS agencies anyway. Moreover, reporting such cases would carry a risk that the family would terminate

treatment, and then even the child professional would not be able to monitor the child's safety.

This study adds to the considerable evidence that CPS is overburdened and unable to carry out the goals imposed by law. One implication of failure to report is that appropriate statistics on the problem cannot be obtained and funding could be cut (e.g., Finkelhor, 1993). However, overreporting of abuse can also be a problem (e.g., Besharov, 1993). Requiring professionals and encouraging laypeople to report "suspected" cases of abuse may contribute to overburdening the system; too much time may be spent investigating cases of unfounded maltreatment, and victims who truly need help may be ignored because there are simply not enough resources to find and help them. What do you think? Is it likely that overreporting is what interferes most with protecting children from abuse, or is underreporting the more likely problem? Or could both be problems? What kinds of solutions are needed? Consider some cultural and societal influences on maltreatment in this country—for example, the acceptance of violence in general, the acceptance of physical aggression as appropriate child discipline, and the belief that parents should be able to raise their children as they see fit. Consider also your solutions to problems in the CPS system. Would they be readily accepted in this country?

Foster Care

The most common intervention into cases of presumed child abuse in African American families, derived from macrosystem laws and values, involves intervention into the microsystem by removing African American children from their homes and placing them into foster care (Rosner & Markowitz, 1997). Nationally, by 1994, 46% of the children in the U.S. child welfare system were White, 41% were Black, and the rest were Hispanic or "other." Given that only 15% of the children in the country were Black, this shows a dramatic reversal of an earlier pattern of excluding Black children from facilities and programs for maltreated children to their overrepresentation in the child welfare system (Roberts, 2001). What role may each of the following forces have played in this dramatic change: Racism? Changing perspectives

---

Box 14.1 The Case of Rilya Shenise Wilson

Rilya Shenise Wilson was removed from her drug-addicted mother, Gloria Wilson, six weeks after birth (September 29, 1996) and placed in foster care in the home of Pamela Kendrick. Kendrick, the foster mother, was herself investigated on charges of child abuse in 1998, but the charges were dropped. Rilya was removed from Kendrick's home in April of 2000, and placed in the home of two sisters, Pamela and Geralyn Graham. Meanwhile, the Wilson family formally lost custody of Rilya in 1999 because of parental drug problems; Rilya's reported father, Manville Cash, had never been involved with her. Deborah Muskelly, the social worker who was assigned to Rilya's case, was supposed to meet with the Graham sisters once a month, but did not do so, although she falsified records that she presented to court indicating that she had seen Rilya and the girl was well cared for. Geralyn Graham, one of Rilya's guardians, told authorities that she turned Rilya over to someone she thought was a Florida caseworker on January, 18, 2001, and never saw her again. Rilya was not originally reported missing because the Grahams were given assurances by Muskelly, who reported to the family court that Rilya was in the care of her guardians and in day care. When it was determined that Rilya was no longer in the Graham home, social workers dithered back and forth before notifying the police. An internal memo dated September 4, 2001, suggests that the child welfare agency wasn't sure where Rilya was but nobody informed the police until seven months later. When the case finally reached the news media, Rilya had been missing for 16 months. According to newspaper reports, the Graham sisters were given polygraph tests that they didn't pass (Wilson, n.d.). As if Rilya's story wasn't bad enough, it became apparent that there were hundreds of children officially in the custody of the state of Florida that could not be accounted for. As of the writing of this chapter, Rilya is still missing.

SOURCE: Compiled from numerous newspaper accounts.

---

on child maltreatment? Assumptions about the relationship between government and families?

Compared to Hispanic or White children, African American children are placed in foster care more often and stay in foster care longer (Morton, 1999). Moreover, compared to White children, both African American and Hispanic children in foster care are more likely to come from households with economic problems, large urban areas, and neighborhoods with crime and safety problems. Even when families have the same characteristics and are free of problems such as extreme poverty, parental substance abuse, and dangerous neighborhoods, Black children have still been more likely than White children to be placed in foster care (Morton).

Given the frequency with which children are put into foster care to protect them from child abuse, the outcomes of such placements are important. One of the tragedies of the overloaded foster care system is that children get lost—sometimes literally—in today's child welfare system. Consider the case of Rilya Shenise Wilson, a 5-year-old African American girl from Miami. She was in the custody of the Florida Department of Children and Families, but ended up missing. The basic facts of Rilya's case are summarized in Box 14.1. What are the implications of Rilya's story? Is the child welfare system hopelessly incompetent? Would Rilya have been better off left in the custody of a drug-addicted mother? Are there other alternatives?

Studies on the outcomes of foster care placement for children provide a mixed picture. There is some evidence (e.g., Runyan & Gould, 1985) that children with multiple foster care placements are at risk for delinquency. Among children investigated for maltreatment, Black children had the highest rate of entry into the California Youth Authority (CYA) for serious and violent delinquency. However, their rate of entry *declined* following in-home or foster care placement. This pattern differed from that of Whites or children of other ethnicities, who had higher rates of CYA entry *following* foster care (Jonson-Reid & Barth, 2000).

Another important question about the foster care system is whether removing African American children from homes with substantiated maltreatment reports protects them from further abuse. The answer is "Not always." For example, of 443 reports of maltreatment within foster homes in Baltimore for the years 1984–1988, the rate of reported maltreatment of the foster children (80% of whom were African American) was three times greater in foster families than in nonfoster families, especially for physical abuse (Benedict, Zuravin, Brandt, & Abbey, 1994).

Problems and Needs

Programs to Combat Poverty and Its Effects

Given that poverty has been identified as a risk factor for abuse, federal antipoverty programs (e.g., welfare, food stamps, public housing, tax credits) and related programs (e.g., Head Start; Women, Infants, and Children) might be expected to have an indirect effect of reducing child maltreatment and other forms of family violence. The prevailing opinion within the family violence community is that federal programs are woefully inadequate, poverty continues to be a lethal form of violence, and impoverished families are routinely subjected to structural violence—that is, violence imposed primarily on the poor as a direct result of (macro) societal influences (Brown, 2002). Melton (2002), who has served on U.S. Advisory Boards on Child Abuse and Neglect, shared an important conclusion from the 1990 meeting of the Board:

> The most serious shortcoming of the nation's system of intervention on behalf of children is that it depends upon a reporting and response process that has punitive connotations, and requires massive resources dedicated to the investigation of allegations. . . . [It] has become far easier to pick up the telephone to report one's neighbor for child abuse than it is for that neighbor to pick up the telephone to request and receive help before the abuse

happens. If the nation ultimately is to reduce the dollars and personnel needed for investigating reports, more resources must be allocated to establishing voluntary, nonpunitive access to help. (U.S. Advisory Board on Child Abuse and Neglect, 1990, p. 80, as cited in Melton, 2002, p. 571).

Growing alienation, disconnection, and distrust evident among Americans adds to the catastrophic failures of systems designed to protect individuals from family violence (Melton, 2002) and the propensity to engage in other forms of violence. It can be argued that to create a fair society, we need to develop new jobs, ensure employment, raise the minimum wage, provide realistic income credits for the poor, guarantee adequate health insurance for all families, and provide quality day care centers for all children (Geiger & Fischer, 1999). Based on what you have learned, do you think such steps can reduce family violence? If so, do you think Americans are ready to make the commitment?

A Special Case: The Native Macrosystem

The macrosystem in which Native communities are embedded is, in important ways, different now than in earlier times, and Native American Indians in today's world are different from other minority communities in their relationship with the U.S. government. Tribes recognized by the federal government have sovereignty; that is, basic governmental powers have been allocated to them. They are free to establish their own legislative bodies, tribal courts, and laws pertaining to the protection of children and families, and on many reservations, states have little or no jurisdiction (Wichlacz & Wechsler, 1983). Therefore, efforts to combat family violence have come largely from within the Native communities themselves.

Most of the prevention and intervention efforts of tribal governments have followed the Indian Self-Determination and Education Assistance Act of 1975, in which reservation tribes were given the freedom to design their own services, including mental health services (LaFromboise, 1988). Since then, services have become more integrated and accessible to the communities, there has been a strong emphasis on employing Native professionals from the local community as service providers, and there has been an inclusion of traditional Native practices (Johnson, Gibson, & Luckey, 1990). The number of Native American Indians earning master's or doctoral degrees in psychology continues to increase (Stapp, Tucker, & VandenBos, 1985), and funds for the Indian Health Services (IHS), the largest provider of mental health services for Native American Indians, have grown steadily (Nelson, McCoy, Stetter, & Vanderwagen, 1992). However, the ratio of psychologists to the population is still well below the national average (Stapp et al.), and available funding for mental health services provides for less than 50% of the minimal services needed (Nelson et al.).

There are several barriers to providing adequate mental health programs in Native communities. First, the salary for IHS mental health workers is far below the private sector level, and the salary for mental health workers in tribal programs is even lower. Moreover, the geographic isolation and harsh climate in some tribal reservations is not attractive to many non-Native mental health professionals. Finally, high demands, coupled with the complexity and seriousness of the health needs and the lack of support from other personnel or tribal members, lead to a high degree of burnout and turnover (Nelson et al., 1992). Given these problems, limited services are available for most Native Americans, and especially for special populations, such as children. Moreover, although Natives are eligible for state and local programs, many cannot use these programs because they are too far away, too expensive, or the staff is too insensitive (Nelson et al.). Even when programs are available, many Native Americans do not utilize them. In the Native Americans for Community Action Family Health Center in Northern Arizona, only 48% of the clients found the mental health services useful and continued to use them. Native Americans who stopped using the services did so because their family criticized them (20%), they felt judged by the mental health professional (16%), they received referrals for costly services (8%), and they felt

that the professional lacked appropriate skills (8%). Of those who never used the services in the first place, 20% had no information regarding the services, 17% believed one should talk about these issues only with one's family, and 16% said the services cost too much (Chester, Mahalish, & Davis, 1999).

Other barriers to utilization of mental health services include mistrust (Dukepoo, 1980; LaFromboise & Dixon, 1981), feeling that the services are unresponsive to their needs (Barter & Barter, 1974), and differing cultural views, particularly of the healing process (Heinrich, Corbine, & Thomas, 1990; Trimble & Hayes, 1984). Native Americans have complained that Western psychology simply cannot help them with their problems because it does not consider their worldview. Specifically, Native Americans have traditionally believed that mental illness is the outcome of human weakness; of not maintaining cultural values; of an imbalance between the spirit, mind, and body or between the spirit and other spirits in the environment; of offending a natural spirit; of breaking a taboo; or of an enemy casting an evil spell on the community (Kahn, 1982; LaFromboise, 1988; Martin, 1981). Whatever the ultimate cause, the problem resides in the community, not just the afflicted individual. The treatment, usually involving confessions, atonements, restorations into the good graces of the family and tribe, and intercessions with the spiritual world, involves the person's significant others and community members, not just the healer and afflicted person. This approach runs counter to the Western tradition in which perceptions of the community are considered unimportant and the focus of treatment is the relationship between the therapist and the client (LaFromboise). Whereas Western psychologists try to strengthen the client's individuality, Native American Indians believe the self is embedded in the community, and wish to transcend the individual (Katz & Rolde, 1981; LaFromboise). Because of this clash between Western psychology and Native values, many communities have incorporated traditional healers and healing ceremonies into their mental health services (Nelson et al., 1992).

Therapists in Native communities also need to consider the impact cumulative trauma can have on individual clients (Robin, Chester, & Goldman, 1996). As discussed in Chapter 4, Native American Indians have a long history of prolonged and repeated trauma. The impact of any one traumatic event, such as an incident of family violence, should be considered within the context of multigenerational and community trauma. When a traumatic event happens to an individual or set of individuals, the entire community is often collectively affected (Robin et al.). Recall from Chapter 4 that many children who went to boarding schools were both physically and sexually abused. Also recall that the boarding school era was decades long and was then followed by the Indian Adoption Project. How do you think these repeated historical traumas might affect a Native American who suffers further personal trauma? Also consider the fact that Native Americans suffered the loss of the vast majority of their population at the hands of the European settlers. When you add this trauma to their current traumas, what kind of impact might it have on mental health?

The incorporation of rituals, ceremonies, and appreciation of the history and culture of Native American Indians into mental health services seems to be necessary for community members to trust these services (Nelson et al., 1992). Therefore, in many communities, the use of traditional healers and helpers has been made a priority over other types of clinical treatment (LaFromboise, 1988). However, in the Family Health Center in Northern Arizona, only 1% of the respondents of a mental health needs assessment survey reported utilizing the traditional healers offered at the center (Chester et al., 1999). If Native Americans do not seem to utilize such programs when they are offered, should there still be a push to include them? Perhaps the problem with utilization lies in the level of acculturation of Native Americans who present at IHS and tribal mental health services. Native Americans who do not even know such services exist are probably more traditional in worldview and more strongly committed to tribal culture. Indeed, the more traditional Native Americans are, the less favorable their attitudes are toward mental health counseling, the less they recognize a personal need for counseling, the less confident they are in mental

health professionals, and the less interpersonal openness they show regarding their problems. Native Americans who are either fully acculturated into the majority White culture or who identify with and are committed to both their traditional and the majority culture do not seem to have these negative attitudes toward mental health services and professionals (Price & McNeill, 1992). These are probably the ones who utilize the mental health clinics offered by the IHS, and they probably do not seek traditional means of healing when they go there.

Issues Specific to Native Child Maltreatment

The Indian Child Welfare Act (ICWA; see Table 4.1) was passed by Congress in 1968 in reaction to reports that Native children were placed in out-of-home care at 12 to 18 times the rate of children at large and that 85% of these placements were to non-Native homes. The ICWA set minimum standards for removal of Native children from their families, and gave tribal governments jurisdiction over the placement of their children into foster and adoptive homes. Tribes were given the authority to develop their own child welfare and family services, and they were to give preference to Native families and environments when a child was placed in out-of-home care (Cross, 1986; MacEachron, Gustavsson, Cross, & Lewis, 1996).

Since passage of the ICWA, many tribes (a) offer a full range of child welfare and family services, including foster care, protective services, prevention of child abuse, and counseling; (b) offer parent training classes to reestablish the high standards and expectations of care valued by many Native tribes; and (c) provide family advocacy services, which work with state agencies to make sure children have appropriate services. These services draw on the strengths and traditions of the Native culture, relying on natural helping mechanisms such as the extended family. When a child is placed in out-of-home care, priority is given to the child's extended family members, followed by Native foster families not related to the child (Cross, 1986). In less than a decade after its passage, tribes gained substantial control over foster care and adoptive services for their children, and the number of Native children placed in non-Native homes was down 15% (MacEachron et al., 1996). However, despite the ICWA, the number of Native children placed in out-of-home care rose from 7,200 in the early 1980s to 9,005 in 1986, a 25% increase. This increase parallels the increase in the United States as a whole, but Native children were still placed in substitute care at 3.6 times the rate of non-Native children (Plantz, Hubbell, Barrett, & Dobrec, 1988). By 1996, the situation had not changed much— 12.5/100,000 Native children were placed in out-of-home care versus 6.9/100,000 of all other children in the country (Cross, Earle, & Simmons, 2000).

The funding provided by tribal authorities is inadequate for even 25% of the needed services (Cross et al., 2000). In addition, many service workers in Native communities do not have a college degree, many are not adequately trained, and many who are trained did not find the training helpful (Wares, Wedel, Rosenthal, & Dobrec, 1994). In 1990, the Indian Child Protection and Family Violence Prevention Act (see Table 4.1) authorized funding for tribal child abuse prevention and treatment programs. Congress, however, never appropriated more than a token amount to these programs (Cross et al.).

Tribes have also found it difficult to carry out the mandate not to remove children from their homes unless efforts have been made to provide placement prevention services. Fewer than half the cases in the ten years after passage of the ICWA provide documentation of this effort. The most common preventive step was counseling of the family by the caseworker, followed by referrals to mental health services and substance abuse programs. The emphasis was on protecting children by placing them in protective services, but placement was not always possible (Plantz et al., 1988). Moreover, the adults who spent much of their childhood in substitute care themselves were now the ones in the troubled families having their children removed to substitute care (Mannes, 1993). Because of such problems, in 1988, a family preservation initiative was directed toward tribal and Indian nonprofit organizations to provide family and children's services. Many placement prevention services were then developed and funded, including the Minnesota Indian Woman's Resource Center and the Fairbanks Native Association Inc., which have seen success in family preservation (Mannes).

EXOSYSTEM EFFORTS

Governmental Programs

As discussed previously, the Child Abuse Prevention and Treatment Act (CAPTA), revised in 1996, provides funding to states and local agencies developing and administering programs for ending child abuse and neglect. Thus, although the legislation was enacted on a macrosystem basis, much of its operation takes place at the exosystem level. Included in its provisions are directives that (a) abuse and neglect prevention, assessment, investigation, and treatment should take place at the neighborhood level; (b) support staff should be properly trained and have specialized knowledge to carry out their child protection duties; and (c) programs should be sensitive to ethnic and cultural diversity. CAPTA also includes community-based family resource and support grants intended to (a) support state efforts to develop, operate, expand, and enhance community-based, prevention-focused, family resource and support programs for coordinating resources divided among current human service programs (e.g., Head Start, child abuse and neglect prevention, juvenile justice, domestic violence prevention and intervention, and housing); and (b) foster an understanding, appreciation, and knowledge of diverse populations in order to be effective in preventing and treating child abuse and neglect.

Primary Prevention Programs

Exosystem efforts in the form of primary prevention programs for child abuse were popular in the 1970s and 1980s, and came in the form of public service announcements on television and radio, and news coverage of the most egregious cases of child abuse (Daro & Connelly,

2002). Although often viewed as a "soft" approach to preventing child abuse, research has shown that many parents who view child abuse prevention advertisements have changed their behavior, attitudes, and beliefs about child rearing (Daro, 1988, 1991). In addition, even though these programs may not alter the behavior, attitudes, and beliefs of the most abusive parents, they have been found valuable in changing the behavior of mildly to moderately abusive parents and in preventing the negative psychological outcomes these practices may cause in their children. Furthermore, by providing information on how to get help, they educate adults as to how they can help children who are severely abused in their neighborhood.

In the area of child sexual abuse (CSA), the most widely used, and most controversial, programs are primary prevention programs targeting children. These programs tend to have the following goals:

Educating children about what sexual abuse is; broadening their awareness of possible abusers to include people they know and like; teaching that each child has the right to control access to his or her body; describing a variety of "touches" that a child can experience; stressing actions that a child can take in a potentially abusive situation, such as saying no or running away; teaching that some secrets should not be kept and that a child is never at fault for sexual abuse; and stressing that the child should tell a trusted adult if touched in an inappropriate manner until something is done to protect the child. (Reppucci & Haugaard, 1993, p. 312)

The controversy over these programs stems from their being modeled on sexual assault programs designed to empower women by educating them about sexual assault and ways of protecting themselves (Berrick & Gilbert, 1991). The programs for elementary school students aim at similar types of empowerment (Reppucci & Haugaard, 1993). The problem is this: Are all children developmentally mature enough to understand "good" versus "bad" touches and by whom and when they can be touched in private places? For example, can a 4-year-old understand the following:

A good touch is when someone close to you gives you a hug. A bad touch is when someone touches you in a private place. Someone close to you can touch you in a private place and it may not be bad, such as when they are touching you there to clean you. However, someone close to you can touch you in a private place and it can be bad even if it is in the context of bathing.

Furthermore, if we find that some children, particularly older ones, are capable of understanding the intricacies of sexual abuse, as some (but not all) have been shown to be, should we give them the responsibility of protecting themselves? A potential problem with placing responsibility for preventing sexual abuse directly on children is that if they subsequently become victims of sexual abuse, the normal self-blame reaction that tends to follow an abusive experience may be compounded by their perception that they were supposed to have protected themselves.

Despite these criticisms, such programs appear to have had some positive influence on the prevention of CSA. Millions of people, including adults, have become educated as to the extent and nature of the CSA problem, and children are now more willing to come forth and disclose experiences of sexual abuse (Plummer, 1993). However, it is probably more appropriate to call such programs "disclosure programs" instead of "prevention programs" (Finkelhor & Strapko, 1992), and, as the primary protectors of their children, parents should probably be brought into them (Plummer; Reppucci & Haugaard, 1993). Unfortunately, as research has shown, parents do not attend such programs (Reppucci & Haugaard).

A point of caution is that majority culture prevention programs may not prove effective for minority children. For example, Millan and Rabiner (1992) suggest that the cultural values of Hispanics are counter to the lessons being taught in majority culture programs, and offer suggestions for a culturally sensitive CSA prevention program for Hispanic children. In the Hispanic cultures, children are taught not to question authority (*respeto*), but it is usually an adult or authority figure who sexually abuses the child. In order to address this problem, Millan and Rabiner recommend that materials be in the form of *novellas* (soap operas) or *cuentos* (story telling), that the materials and the program itself be accepted and trusted by Hispanic communities, and that community members and resources be utilized to relay the information to the children. Children who learn this information about sexual abuse, and how to deal with it, may be less likely to shy away from saying no to a predator or reporting the experience. They will realize the differences between obeying an authority figure who means well, versus obeying one who means to hurt them (Millan & Rabiner).

Information and Support Services

Social service agencies dealing with African American, Asian American, Latino, or Native American families are often seen at best as culturally insensitive and at worst as racist agents of additional victimization. For example, among Asian Pacific and Filipino clients, the following problems were observed: (a) Some child protective workers do not let the children they have placed in foster care speak to their parents in their parents' language because of fear of negative influences; (b) mothers of child abuse victims who do not communicate in English may face punitive reactions (e.g., extension of out-of-home placement, denial of visitation rights) from criminal, judicial, and child welfare personnel; and (c) children have been placed for permanent adoption because immigrant parents have been unable to communicate with agents of the system due to language and cultural differences (Okamura, Heras, & Wong-Kerberg, 1995).

Governmental and private organizations in Hispanic communities have also been criticized for cultural insensitivity (Padilla, Ruiz, & Alvarez, 1989). Take, for example, the case of "Maria," who had her two children removed from her home because of alleged physical abuse. If you were Maria, how would you view the social service agencies our country offers?

Maria had two preschool age children removed from her home resulting from alleged physical abuse. During a supervised visit held at the county social services department between Maria and her children, she was forbidden from speaking in Spanish because (1) the worker could not

understand what was being said, and (2) "the children need to learn to speak English." The worker further informed Maria that should she continue to speak Spanish to the children, future mother-children visitation would be jeopardized. (Herrerias, 1988, p. 106)

Many governmental and private agencies attempt to treat Hispanics merely by translating majority-culture treatment programs into Spanish, but this approach seems to ignore the subtle and not-so-subtle differences between White and Hispanic cultures (Mennen, 2000), and among the various Hispanic cultures themselves—for example, in beliefs with regard to child-rearing practices, disciplinary practices, expectations of normal childhood behavior, the causes of disabilities, and the meanings of disabilities (Fontes, 1997). Consequently, not only are Hispanics less likely to utilize child abuse prevention and intervention resources, they are also less likely to report child abuse to the appropriate authorities (Buriel, Loya, Gonda, & Klessen, 1979).

In response to these observed problems, several minority community organizations have mobilized efforts to offer culturally sensitive services. As a result, currently in this country, there are a number of resources that provide valuable information concerning the prevention of family violence in minority families and a variety of intervention services for these communities. For Blacks, these resources include:

- The African American Family Services in Minneapolis, Minnesota, which provides (a) information on community-based, culturally specific health, mental health, and family preservation services; (b) on-site training; and (c) information, publications, and videos through its African American Resource Center (http://www.aafs.net).
- The Institute on Domestic Violence in the African American Community (2003), located in the University of Minnesota School of Social Work, which provides (a) an interdisciplinary forum for scholars, practitioners, and observers of family violence in the African American community; (b) research, publications, resources, training, and technical assistance; and (c) examples of appropriate and

effective responses to prevent/reduce family violence in the African American community (http://www.dvinstitute.org).

- The National Black Child Development Institute (2003), located in Washington, DC, which offers programs, training conferences, and publications to improve and protect the well-being of African American children (http://www.nbcdi.org).
- The Center for Child Protection and Family Support of the People of Color Leadership Institute in Washington, DC, which provides training in the areas of child abuse and neglect, attitude competency, domestic violence, substance abuse, and family support preservation. It also has developed a self-assessment tool for family welfare agencies that allows them to assess their level of cultural competence (http://www.centerchildprotection.org).

There have also been significant efforts to design programs that will encourage Hispanics to participate in child abuse prevention and intervention. It is recognized that (a) because the family is so important in the Latino culture (*familism*), the family should be the focus of any prevention or intervention efforts; (b) because many Hispanics do not reside only within a nuclear family, intervention efforts need to be directed at the extended family as well; and (c) prevention and intervention efforts should be more personal because Hispanics value sincere personal interactions (Keefe & Padilla, 1987). In response to these suggestions and concerns, the following programs have been set up in Hispanic communities to prevent child maltreatment:

- *Festiva Educativa* is a parent-training program for Hispanic parents with developmentally disabled children, and is tailored specifically to the cultural values of the Hispanic family. The program is offered in Spanish, and the entire family is involved in the intervention efforts, which are designed to be less formal (and perceived as less cold) than the social service organizations that many Latinos are accustomed to using in this country (Rueda & Martinez, 1992).
- The *MADRE* parent education program is designed for Hispanic women who are deemed to be at high risk for abusing or neglecting

their children. It is a 20-week program with twenty lessons (in both English and Spanish) that considers Latino cultural values. The mothers receive a one-hour, in-home lesson each week, supplemented by a two-hour, weekly group session at the local Latino outreach service center. The main issues addressed are the misconception that parental skills are instinctual, lack of participation in the community, lack of utilization of community resources, feelings of hopelessness and low self-esteem, maternal overprotectiveness, and cultural conflicts around parenting. The goal is to provide mothers with more effective parenting skills within a culturally sensitive framework. Based on preliminary data, the *MADRE* program seems to be working: By the 12th week of the program, mothers who initially scolded or spanked their children were more likely to coax gently or use diversionary tactics when their children misbehaved (Herrerias, 1988).

- The National Coalition of Hispanic Health and Human Services Organization (COSSMHO; n.d.) made physical and sexual child abuse prevention efforts a priority in the 1990s. COSSMHO is the only national Hispanic Health Organization, and members include practitioners and officials in the fields of public health, medicine, nursing, social work, psychology, and youth services. They sponsor research programs and education in various health-related areas, but one of their primary concerns is child physical and sexual abuse.

There are also a number of resources available for combating child abuse within Asian American communities:

- The Union of Pan Asian Communities (www.upacsd.com), a program for Asian Pacific and Filipino American communities, offers a range of services for child abuse victims and their families, employs a bilingual/bicultural staff, includes a multicultural team of mental health professionals and paraprofessionals, and has collaborative relationships with lawyers, teachers, physicians, law enforcement agencies, and child protective service agencies (Okamura et al., 1995).

- The Coalition for Asian American Children & Families (1999), in New York City, advocates for better child care, health care, after-school programs, and child abuse and prevention services for Asian American families. Available online from their Web site are a fact sheet on child abuse and neglect in Asian American families and a report on Asian American families in the child welfare system (www.cacf.org).
- Khmer Health Advocates in Rhode Island is a Cambodian organization with mental health services for Cambodian children and families. To protect children from victimization while treating parents who survived massacres in Cambodia, they use a contextual therapy model emphasizing the family as the greatest resource for healing and incorporating genograms and storytelling into the healing process (Scully, Kuoch, & Miller, 1995).

MICROSYSTEM EFFORTS

Secondary Prevention

A common type of microsystem-level prevention program consists of secondary prevention programs aimed at parents deemed to be at high risk for abusing their children, often pregnant women or women with young children whose circumstances match those of parents who have abused their own children. The most popular type of secondary prevention program is home visitation. These programs began in 1993, and the six most common ones serve 550,000 children each year (Daro & Connelly, 2002; Gomby, Culross, & Behrman, 1999). The most widely cited home visitation project, conducted by Olds et al. (1997) in Elmira, New York, was designed to investigate the effectiveness of intensive nurse home visitation in preventing abuse by poor, unmarried teenagers recruited before the birth of their first child. Early reports showed that only 4% of the high-risk mothers in the intensive nurse home visitation program abused their children, compared to 19% of the other high-risk mothers. These short-term benefits persisted; 15 years later, the mothers who had received the home visitation still had lower rates of child abuse (Olds et al.).

Home visitation programs are thought to work because they prevent the problem of maltreatment before it has the chance to occur. In addition, mothers who are pregnant or just starting out are less likely to be offended by someone coming in and educating them in child care than mothers who have been reported for abuse. Moreover, by coming into the home, the service provider is able to evaluate and make changes in the home environment and work with parents in the privacy of their homes. Finally, they are able to educate the parents about appropriate child-rearing techniques and child development on a flexible schedule (Daro & Connelly, 2002).

Other home visitation programs have shown similar successes. For instance, the Healthy Start Program in Hawaii recruited several high-risk mothers for their program, and in 99% of the cases, child abuse was not reported, a rate significantly different from that of the high-risk families not enrolled in the program. Moreover, at two years of age, the children in the program had more positive developmental outcomes and improved health status in comparison to the controls (Wallach & Lister, 1995). The success of this program led to the development of a national program disseminated by the National Committee to Prevent Child Abuse and Neglect (Wallach & Lister). An analysis of 29 evaluations of this program showed that

> Healthy Families America (HFA) home visitation programs documented notable change among participant families, particularly in the area of parent-child interaction and parental capacity. Most families receiving these services appear better able to care for their children; access and effectively use health care services; resolve many of the personal and familial problems common among low-income, single parent families; and avoid the most intrusive intervention into their parenting, namely, being reported for child abuse and neglect. (Daro & Connelly, 2002, p. 436)

Not all participating parents improve in parenting skills, as some program "graduates" are reported for abusive behaviors, and some children do not fare well psychologically (Daro & Connelly, 2002; Gomby et al., 1999).

An evaluation of the Good Start Project, a home- and clinic-based program designed to improve parenting skills, indicated that families at moderate risk for abuse were most responsive to the services offered, including developmental assessments, counseling, medical care, social advocacy, and parent-child enrichment sessions (Kowal et al., 1989; Willett, Ayoub, & Robinson, 1991).

Tertiary Prevention

Tertiary services, directed at preventing re-abuse in families already substantiated for abuse, are the most common type of prevention service at the microsystem level. According to the DHHS (1999), approximately 1,563,000 children received tertiary prevention services in 1999, a count that is probably an underestimate. This figure represents only 55.8% of child victims substantiated by CPS. Thus, a sizeable minority of child abuse victims do not receive tertiary services, even though their cases were substantiated.

It is not quite clear how policies within each state's social service agencies influence which children get the needed care (Kolko, Seleyo, & Brown, 1999), but several factors have been identified by DHHS (1999). Victims who had multiple forms of maltreatment, had a prior history of maltreatment, were non-White, and were over the age of 3 were more likely to receive services than their counterparts. Many of these families have long histories of multiple forms of abuse, and dysfunctional methods of dealing with stress have been firmly established within the family relationships (Browne & Herbert, 1997). Moreover, many of these families are also characterized by severe depression, substance abuse, and spousal violence (Daro & Cohn, 1988). What are the implications of these findings? How do you think their situations affect their willingness and ability to get help?

Because the substantiated cases are generally from the most violent families with the most dysfunction, these families are the least likely to show improvements no matter how much treatment they receive (Ayoub, Willett, & Robinson, 1992; Willett et al., 1991). Indeed, approximately one third of families receiving tertiary services and half of service completers

have a recurrence of abuse (Malinosky-Rummell et al., 1991, as cited in Kolko, 2002). In addition, tertiary programs are characterized by problems with initial engagement and compliance, and high dropout rates (Cohn & Daro, 1987). Up to 66% of those families receiving these services drop out before completion (Warner et al., 1990, as cited in Kolko).

Two programs that appear useful are Homebuilders, which offers intensive counseling, casework, and concrete services to abusive families, and Project SafeCare, which addresses behavioral deficiencies of abusive parents. Both programs have shown improvements in family functioning and parental skills, although in the absence of comparison data, it is difficult to evaluate them fully (Kolko, 2002; Lutzker, Bigelow, Doctor, Gershater, & Greene, 1998; Whittaker, Kinney, Tracy, & Booth, 1990). However, their apparent success indicates that perhaps the best way of treating abusive parents is through a combination of therapeutic techniques and parenting instruction. That way, they can receive the support that they need from the group setting, but still benefit from the individualized attention that addresses their psychological needs (Daro & Connelly, 2002; Gambrill, 1983).

Kinship Care

Although CPS interventions in the microsystem can involve coercive removal from the home, there have been several initiatives, including kinship care, designed to be less disruptive for children judged to be at risk for continuing maltreatment. As of January 1, 1999, there were more than one half million American children living in foster care; of these, 29% were living in a kinship family home (Administration for Children and Families, 1999). Kinship care (i.e., caring for the children of relatives who are unable to provide adequate care for their children) has a long tradition in African American and many other ethnic communities. In recent decades, more formalized kinship care programs have proliferated as a possible solution to problems associated with foster care by nonrelatives. The most common kinship family appears to be African

American (Keller et al., 2001), and most often, the chief caregiver is a grandmother (Kelley, Whitley, Sipe, & Yorker, 2000).

Among the major advantages of kinship care in comparison to traditional foster care are the greater moral responsibility kin caregivers often feel for the children and the children's greater access to their biological parents. However, the time children spend in kinship care, as was historically true of traditional foster care, can extend almost indefinitely (Smith, Rudolph, & Swords, 2002), and there can be a strong resistance to adoption among the fostering relatives because of loyalty to the biological parents.

In part because child welfare agencies are not required to keep records of type of child placements into out-of-home care, there is little research available on the effects of kinship care, and the available findings are often inconsistent. For example, in one study of children in the Casey Family Program (which provides long-term, out-of-home care services for children and youth in 14 states), children in the kinship foster sample (42% Black) scored within the normal range on competence and problem behavior scales, whereas the nonrelative, foster care sample children were significantly more likely to score in the clinical range on almost every problem behavior scale. Overall, children of color showed fewer behavior problems than White children (Keller et al., 2001). However, in a study of teacher reports from the Casey Family Program, children in kinship care scored significantly higher on a delinquent behavior scale than youths in nonkinship care, and African American youth scored higher than White youth on an externalizing problems scale (Shore, Sim, Le Prohn, & Keller, 2002).

It appears that some of the inconsistencies in reports on African American children's wellbeing are related both to the source of the reports (e.g., teacher vs. child caregiver) and sampling issues. For the most part, studies of the Casey Family Program youth and others (e.g., Scannapieco, 1999) indicate that African American youth in kinship care do just as well or better than children in nonrelative foster care. More support for the relative benefits of kinship

care come from an examination of the records of children (87% Black) in Baltimore (Benedict, Zuravin, & Stallings, 1996), which revealed that behavior problems (e.g., aggressiveness) and mental health problems (e.g., anxiety) were reported more frequently among the children placed with nonrelatives than among the children in kinship care. Follow-up interviews revealed few differences between the kinship care and traditional foster care youth in adult functioning.

INDIVIDUAL EFFORTS

Programs for Victims

Recently, researchers and clinicians began to focus on the individual level of the ecological model to address the needs of abused children. Although the ultimate policy goal has always been to keep the family together, an abused child will most likely have therapeutic needs following abusive episodes. Two types of programs have been shown to help. Therapeutic day programs, which offer developmentally appropriate and therapeutic activities, have led to improved intellectual and language abilities in abused children at a one-year follow-up (Oates & Bross, 1995). Also, an intensive, group-based treatment program for abused children, designed to offer supportive peer relationships to abused children and help them recognize their feelings through play, speech, and physical therapy, led to increased cognitive functioning, peer acceptance, maternal acceptance, and developmental skills (Culp, Little, Letts, & Lawrence, 1991).

Although such programs have proven valuable, not all treatment approaches are appropriate for all children. Treatments need to be individualized, and more treatment alternatives are necessary (Bartholet, 1999). In addition, as discussed previously, not all suspected cases of abuse are reported or even investigated, and over 40% of substantiated cases of child abuse are not referred for services. Therefore, a large majority of abused children and their families do not receive any services at all (Kaplan, Pelcovitz, & Lubruna, 1999). What is the likely impact of lack of services on the future of these children and of child maltreatment in this country?

Among minority children, sexual abuse programs aimed at the individual needs of the child have been the focus of much attention. For example, there have been a number of suggestions for making child sexual abuse assessments and therapy culturally sensitive for Asian Americans. Sexually abused Asian Pacific and Filipino American children are likely to take longer to work through issues of disclosure, expression of feelings, and integration than majority culture children typically do. It seems likely that counselors should not pressure these children to express deep, conflictual feelings about family members, and that they should use projective techniques in both assessment and treatment. Interventions with the nonoffending Asian Pacific or Filipino parent may involve helping a mother assume the unusual role of head of the family, dealing with her ambivalence and conflicting loyalties to the perpetrator/spouse versus the victimized child, and educating her about the legal and child protection systems. Interventions with the perpetrators may involve addressing any cultural excuses for violence and tendencies to minimize the trauma of sexual abuse. If therapists pressure Asian Pacific and Filipino perpetrators to discuss their remorse at every session, the outcome may be a sense of shame that destroys the client's ego resources. Moreover, to behave in a culturally syntonic way, therapists should subdue their own expressions of empathy (Okamura et al., 1995).

Key features of a program designed specifically for another group of sexually abused Asian Americans, Cambodian refugee children, include (a) always trying to treat children with their families, which may involve asking family members to cook special food for or "make massage" for the child following a difficult therapy session; (b) having all female Khmer-speaking staff members; (c) attempting to enlist the help of extended family members to care for a child who is experiencing ongoing abuse rather than separating the child from all family; (d) never pushing people to face their trauma stories until they are ready; and (e) encouraging clients to seek the help of traditional healers (Scully et al., 1995).

Programs for Perpetrators

Individual services in child maltreatment aimed at perpetrators tend to focus mostly on sexual abusers, because, as mentioned previously, programs for physically abusive or neglectful parents are often aimed at the microsystem level of improving parent-child or familial relations. A sexual abuse intervention program in Memphis, Tennessee, which includes intake interviews specifically designed to assess the extent to which the offender devalues African American children, takes an Afrocentric perspective in its efforts both to change faulty cognitions enabling offenders to abuse children and to replace erroneous sexual knowledge with more precise information (Abney & Priest, 1995).

SUMMARY

Efforts to combat child maltreatment include federal laws mandating and supporting programs and policies at the state and local (exosystem) level that lead primarily to interventions at the microsystem level. Children of color tend to be overrepresented in the more coercive programs such as involuntary removal to foster care. Although members of many ethnic minority communities find many programs and personnel to be culturally insensitive, programs are being developed to address these problems; nevertheless, there are many barriers facing families of color experiencing problems of child maltreatment. According to what you have learned about each minority community in this country (i.e., their culture, their history, and their issues in family violence), what kinds of prevention and intervention services would you suggest to combat child maltreatment? Would the services be the same or different for each community? Can there be an "all-encompassing" service delivery system for child maltreatment? Or, do we have to develop unique ones to focus on the unique experiences of each group? Would unique systems even be practical in a country as large as and as diverse as the United States? How can we solve this problem of child maltreatment among all communities in this country?

15

PREVENTION AND INTERVENTION IN ADULT MALTREATMENT

Efforts to confront the maltreatment of adult family members, which have intensified in recent decades, have focused primarily on macro- and exosystem level interventions designed to change the microsystem by getting victims away from perpetrators. Recommendations for improvement are generally directed at (a) addressing problems related to poverty, and (b) promoting cognitive-affective change, particularly for combating pervasive racist, sexist, and patriarchal values that increase risk in the more vulnerable members of families.

SPOUSAL MALTREATMENT

Macrosystem Level

Efforts

When wife battering came to the public's attention in the 1970s, the criminal justice system was criticized for not responding to "domestic disputes" quickly enough or in a way that prevented future violence. Since then, all states have enacted legislation modifying police and court responses to wife (but not always husband) abuse (Bergen, 1996; Buzawa & Buzawa, 1996). Most police precincts have adopted mandatory arrest policies in domestic

violence cases, and prosecutors do not necessarily need the victim's consent to press charges against the batterer. Although these policies may deter some victims from reporting incidents of battering (i.e., when they do not want their spouses to be arrested and prosecuted), the criminal justice system, and police in particular, appear to be more helpful in domestic violence cases than they were 30 years ago (Buzawa & Buzawa). Criminalizing wife rape took longer than criminalizing battering. Until July 5, 1993, men in some states could still legally rape their wives. Resistance to criminalizing sexual assault on wives came, in part, from several legislators who argued that the criminal justice system would be overwhelmed by cases of so-called "wife rape" (Bergen). However, recent statistics confirm that rape by a husband is the least likely form of rape to be reported to authorities. According to Department of Justice reports for the years 1992 through 2000, 77% of rapes committed by an intimate went unreported, compared to 54% of rapes by a stranger (Rennison, 2002). Many laypeople are still unaware that wife rape is against the law, and some do not believe it can or should be a crime. Moreover, many states still have exemptions from prosecution for a husband raping his wife—for instance, when he does not have to use force to make her have sex (e.g., if she is physically or mentally impaired and unable to give consent).

The primary federal laws pertaining to wife abuse are the Violence Against Women Act (VAWA) of 1996, its modifications in 2000, the Trafficking Victims Protection Act of 2000, and the revised Gun Control Act of 1994 and 1996 (making it a federal crime in certain situations for wife abusers to possess guns). The National Advisory Council on Violence Against Women, in conjunction with the Violence Against Women office, has developed a Toolkit To End Violence Against Women for intervention and prevention programs. The Violence Against Women Act of 2000 (a) allows battered immigrant women to obtain lawful permanent residence without the aid of their husbands; (b) secures for them all protections established under VAWA, regardless of how they entered the country; and (c) creates a new type of visa allowing victims of serious crimes to attain lawful permanent residence (Office on Violence Against Women, 2000).

Laws have also been enacted in Native American Indian tribal communities to combat spousal abuse. The Spouse Abuse Code developed by the Cangleska Domestic Violence Program of the Oglala Sioux criminalizes assault of an intimate partner, and provides for mandatory arrest, no bond until arraignment, and mandatory sentencing for offenders (Oglala Sioux Tribe Social Services, 1999). Similarly, the Native American Women's Health Education Resource Center of the Yankton Sioux Tribe in South Dakota drafted a tribal code dealing with the rights of domestic abuse victims, arrest procedures for police officers, and penalties for perpetrators and violations of protection orders. This code, approved as law in 1995, suggested strict penalties for perpetrators of spousal violence, along with strict enforcement by police officers (Chanda, 1995). Also in 1995, the U.S. Department of Justice began funding STOP Violence Against Women Grants in Native American Indian communities, which led to the funding of 98 programs in 1998 alone (Centers for Disease Control, 2001). It also provided grants for (a) developing a Tribal Court Bench Book (Northwest Tribal Court Judges Association, 1999), with recommendations to tribal courts for dealing with domestic violence

cases (Tribal Court Clearinghouse, 2001), (b) developing the Violence Against Indian Women sample tribal code, and (c) evaluating the existing 40 tribal codes. None of these prevailing codes met all of the standards set forth in the model code, but five (Jicarilla Apache, White Mountain Apache, Northern Cheyenne, Confederated Tribes of Siletz Indians, and Cangleska) met many of the criteria set forth (National American Indian Court Judges Association, 2001).

Problems and Needs

Within many communities of color, macrosystem level concerns focus primarily on racist, sexist, and patriarchal implicit theories within the United States at large, and within the specific communities themselves. For example, within African American communities, the prevention of family violence has been hampered by a long-standing devaluation of Black lives and the generalized cultural assumption that violence among Blacks is normal (Hawkins, 1987). Historically, Black women have been afforded significantly less protection from spousal abuse than White women. Moreover, unless macrosystem values and practices change, there is a danger that most prevention efforts will be of more benefit to the White middle class than to women and children of color (Campbell, Masaki, &Torres, 1997).

To address issues of wife abuse in communities of color, practitioners need to differentiate between culture and violence. It has been argued that oppressive practices exist in many very different cultures. However, that does not make those practices cultural (e.g., Almeida & Dolan-Delvecchio, 1999). Violence against women, like dowries, wife burning, female infanticide, mandatory veiling of women, and foot-binding, is not culture; these practices are all simply traditional patriarchal customs tolerated in various societies for generations.

Barriers to Utilization of Services

Distrust of the Criminal Justice System. Maltreatment of their batterers by members of the criminal justice system, especially police, keeps many women of color from filing criminal reports (Richie & Kanuha, 1993). In some jurisdictions, when men of color have been subject to mandatory arrests, they return with more bruises from the police than they inflicted on their partners (Kanuha, 1994). Unequal treatment by police and judicial officials may reflect the devalued status of Black (Bachman & Coker, 1995), Asian American (Abraham, 2000; Ho, 1990), and other immigrant victims of violence, while at the same time contributing to further violence. Moreover, because Hispanic men already have a reputation in the majority culture of being hypermasculine (violent, sexual, and drunken), their wives may fear that reporting their husbands to the police will reinforce stereotypes and betray their ethnic group (Kanuha)—a fear shared by many Black women (White, 1986). Perhaps because of distrust of the majority culture criminal justice system, battered women of color are less likely to seek restraining orders or housing in domestic violence shelters than their White counterparts.

Distrust of the criminal justice system may be intensified for Latinas (Gonzalez, 2002) and immigrant Asian women (Warrier, 2000) if the government and police in their countries of origin were oppressive. Furthermore, many battered immigrant Vietnamese women, whose husbands suffered in communist reeducation camps before they came to the United States, do not want to be blamed by their community for having their husbands arrested in their new country (Bui & Morash, 1999).

Issues Specific to Immigrants. Hispanics, in particular, may be the least likely major ethnic group to utilize services at every ecological level (Ginorio et al., 1995). However, experiences of discrimination can make all women of color more cautious and possibly more reluctant to take advantage of whatever limited services are available (Sorenson, 1996; Walker, 1995). Macrosystem practical and cultural barriers for Latina (Gonzalez, 2002) and Asian American (Thomas, 2000; Tran & Des Jardins, 2000; Yick & Agbayani-Siewert, 1997) women include language barriers, lack of transportation, and lack of knowledge of existing services. Fear of deportation may also be a barrier for battered immigrant Latinas and Asian American women if they are dependent on husbands who

are U.S. citizens or legal permanent residents for their residency status in this country. Battering husbands often utilize this power over their wives to keep them subservient, even threatening to contact the INS if the wives try to call the police or leave them (Chin, 1994; Endabuse, 2002; Gonzalez). As one battered woman stated, "He is always saying that he is going to report me and I do get scared, so I never call the police on him" (Gonzalez, p. 5).

To address such macrosystem barriers to help seeking among immigrant Latinos and Asians, more resources are needed (Tran & Des Jardins, 2000). Such services include a national hotline to provide crisis intervention in all languages, safe homes across the nation, and more sensitive legal and judicial systems, with personnel who speak the woman's language and do not collude with her partner to pressure her to drop charges. Immigrant women who seek shelters to escape violence should receive ongoing services, such as transitional and affordable housing, job training and placement, ESL classes, and child care (Warrier, 2000).

Added to practical barriers to help seeking among battered immigrant women are cultural barriers. These include differing perceptions as to what constitutes "abuse" and greater tolerance of violence against wives in the original culture than in the U.S. majority culture (Chin, 1994; Ho, 1990; Rasche, 1988). When one Latina told her mother-in-law about her husband's physical abuse, she was told the following:

> It is not a beating if he slapped me or broke my lip. . . . She would say, "To beat is to drag someone through the house—that is a beating. When he does that to you, then you tell me." So I never told her when he did beat me after she told me that. (Gonzalez, 2002, p. 4)

Exosystem Efforts

Battered Women's Shelters

Programs at the exosystem level focus primarily on helping battered women escape further abuse rather than on combating the causes of spousal violence. There are currently over 2,000 shelters in the United States for battered women and their children. Many of these shelters are part of the National Coalition Against Domestic Violence (2002), which was formally organized in 1978 and is the only national organization of shelter and service programs for women. One example is the Center for Domestic Violence Prevention (www.cdvp.org) in Northern California, which offers a 24-hour support line, support and therapy groups, counseling, legal assistance, shelter services for women and children, a 52-week batterer program for the male batterer, and transitional housing for up to 1 year for completers of the shelter program.

Are these shelters effective, though, for the women who use them? For example, do women leave their batterers as a result of these programs? The evidence is mixed. Some studies find that 25% to 50% of shelter women eventually return to their violent homes (Gondolf, 1988; Strube, 1988). Those who do not return tend to have higher economic status and husbands who do not seek help for their battering problems (Gondolf & Fisher, 1988). For those who do return, contact with postshelter advocates may decrease the chances of further abuse (Sullivan, Tan, Basta, Rumptz, & Davidson, 1992). However, judging the effectiveness of shelters on the basis of whether women return to their abusers is problematic, because leaving abusive partners can increase the likelihood of being battered and killed, and the women may not be psychologically or financially ready to leave (Hamby, 1998). Moreover, women who use shelters without engaging other legal or social support systems may actually be at an increased risk for spousal violence in the form of retaliation. Women who combine the use of shelters with other services seem to fare better, at least for the first 6 weeks after seeking help (Berk, Newton, & Berk, 1986).

Research on whether women perceive services received from shelters as helpful is quite limited. Some women have reported that shelters are somewhat more helpful than other service agencies (Donato & Bowker, 1984), but many battered women, especially those who have been raped as well as battered, are disappointed (Bergen, 1996). Battered rape victims who call shelters for help are often referred to rape crisis centers, where they are referred back to shelters. Critics argue that both types of

centers need policies to aid victims of wife rape and validate their experiences. In one shelter, when a weekly support group was announced for battered women who had also been sexually assaulted, nearly every woman attended (Russell, 1990).

VAWA 2000 enacted provisions for furnishing social and legal services, such as domestic violence shelters and education and training for personnel working with battered women, at the state or community level. VAWA also includes specific provisions for providing services to "underserved populations," including ethnic minorities. To facilitate this process, a report produced by the Health Resources and Services Administration (2002) profiled nine major domestic violence projects across the country— six served Whites, six served Blacks, seven served Hispanics, two served Native American Indians, four served East and South Asians, and two served Pacific Islanders. All nine programs indicated that they respond to sexual assault and offer mental health and substance abuse assessment, treatment, and referrals. Only three reported partnerships with local housing organizations, and only one had linkages with employment or educational services for abused individuals and their families. Thus, most of the programs were ill-equipped to deal with major needs of battered women of color—that is, jobs, education, and financial independence (O'Campo, McDonnell, Gielen, Burke, & Yi-hua Chen, 2002).

Wife Abuse Programs Specific to Each Minority Community

As in the majority culture, shelter programs in minority communities are primarily grassroots efforts. The first domestic violence shelter for Native American Indian women, begun in 1977, was the White Buffalo Calf Women's Society of the Rosebud Reservation, South Dakota. Subsequently, many other reservations have established shelters and domestic violence programs (DeBruyn, Wikens, & Artichoker, 1990). Another resource available to abused Native American Indian women is Mending the Sacred Hoop (2001), a program designed to improve tribal response to Indian women victimized by spousal violence and sexual assault and to restore their safety and integrity. It sponsors conferences and publishes a newsletter on issues of family violence. Also, the End Violence Against American Indian, Alaska Native, and First Nation's Women Web site (http://home.earthlink.net/~deers/native.html) addresses violence in the lives of these women.

An excellent guide to exosystem resources for maltreated African American women is White's (1995) book *Chain, Chain, Change: For Black Women in Abusive Relationships*. Topics include considerations in the decision to leave a batterer, protecting oneself, using the legal system, getting help from community organizations, and abuse in lesbian relationships. A comprehensive and readable book for Latinas is *Mejor Sola Que Mal Acompañada (For the Latina in an Abusive Relationship)* by Zambrano (1985). This book, written in both English and Spanish, provides the Latina with definitions and examples of abusive situations, reasons for abuse, reasons to stay or flee from an abusive situation, and practical and legal advice on divorce, child custody, orders of protection, arresting an abusive husband, and finding a lawyer. It also suggests sources of both formal and informal support—friends and relatives, churches, support groups, counselors, and shelters. Finally, it offers advice specific to recent immigrants, including undocumented ones, Latinas with no money, and Latinas who do not speak English.

Several resources offer culturally specific programs for Latinas. In 1995, W.O.M.A.N., Inc. (2002) established a domestic violence program in which Latinas can receive counseling, support-group services, advocacy, and information regarding spousal abuse, education, and outreach programs. Assessments of community needs (e.g., Elliot, Quinless, & Parietti, 2000) led to the establishment of *LA VIDA*, a community-based program for preventing wife abuse among Latina women in Detroit (Maciak, Guzman, Santiago, Villalobos, & Israel, 1999). The most comprehensive Web site for abused Latinas, supported by Alianza (www.dvalianza.org), the National Latino Alliance for the Elimination of Domestic Violence, provides information on (a) symposia such as the National Symposium on La Violencia Domestica; (b) current initiatives,

such as the Alianza Training and Technical Assistance Division, which offers culturally relevant training in dealing with wife abuse, technical assistance, and national resource materials; (c) facts about Latinos and wife abuse; and (d) case examples and helpful video resources for Spanish-speaking victims.

Endabuse (2002) offers material specific to battered immigrant or refugee women, whether Latina, Asian, or of other nationalities. This Web site provides valuable information on the definition of wife abuse, what the battered immigrant can do, whether or not she should leave her home or call the police, what protection orders are and whether they can be obtained by non-U.S. citizens, how a battered immigrant can gain lawful permanent status without her husband's help, how to keep her children, how to support herself and her children without her husband, eligibility for Medicaid and welfare, deportation issues, and hiring an attorney.

Problems and Recommendations

Although the primary exosystem interventions in this country are battered women's shelters, these shelters do not always adequately fulfill federal mandates to assist "underserved" minority populations—often because of cultural insensitivity or racism. Typically, the extent to which cultural and practical barriers impede battered minority women from seeking services depends on how long they have been in this country and their level of acculturation.

Racism in Service Delivery. In both medical and social service settings, racism of service providers has been implicated as a barrier to help-seeking. Former Surgeon General C. Everett Koop, who declared domestic violence a public health problem, noted the apparent bias against women of color in medical settings (Walker, 1995). In addition, there are inequities in service delivery based on ethnicity (Padgett, Patrick, Burns, & Schlesinger, 1994), and within the African American (Campbell & Gary, 1998) and other ethnic minority communities, public services are often in short supply.

Differing Methods of Dealing With Abuse. Among many ethnic minority women, a primary motivation for not using shelters is a different philosophy on dealing with family violence. In a 1997 survey by the American Indian Community Housing Organization in Duluth, Minnesota, 78% of Native women indicated that tribal women did not want to use existing shelters ("Dabinoo'Igan: A Place of New Beginnings," 1999). A strong belief that wife abuse should be dealt with at the microsystem level (i.e., by the woman's family) is prevalent among Native American Indians (Wolk, 1982), South Asian immigrants (Abraham, 2000), and other Asian Americans (Ho, 1990). Women who seek help outside their immediate community—for example, from the police, shelter, or justice system—may be ostracized by their own and their husbands' families, and may suffer retribution from their husbands' families. If a woman's immediate network cannot help, she may have to face leaving her families, friends, and community to escape the abuse. Fear of isolation, relocation, and poverty are often enough to keep her in the abusive situation (Wolk).

Cultural Barriers. Cultural values emphasizing the importance of family integrity and the responsibility of women to keep the family together often keep Hispanic (Torres, 1987) and Asian American (Ho, 1990) women from seeking help or from staying in treatment (Ginorio et al., 1995; Kanuha, 1994; Vasquez, 1998). This high dropout rate appears to be due primarily to a cultural clash between what the women need from support services and what is offered, as the majority culture tends to offer mental health treatments based on a medical model that is perceived as impersonal. Latinas, for example, tend to value an emotional interchange and may prefer folk remedies that are rarely available in Western psychology (Ginorio et al.; Kanuha; Vasquez). Vietnamese, Korean, and other Asian immigrant women may prefer interventions that mobilize members of their community to provide help, or intersperse talk therapy with other forms of intervention such as meditation (Tran & Des Jardins, 2000).

Disagreements With the Feminist Philosophy of Wife Abuse. Several components of the feminist program in many battered women's shelters appear to alienate ethnic minority battered women. Such components include emphasizing empowerment as the best way to end abuse, promoting assertiveness and independence, and emphasizing career training and advancement as keys to empowerment—all of which may seem to interfere with the women's commitment to raising their children (Kanuha, 1994). In addition, domestic violence workers have sometimes reproduced the subordination and marginalization of women of color by adopting strategies of empowerment that disregard the needs of those women (Crenshaw, 1994). Consequently, when many battered ethnic minority women make the decision to use a battered women's shelter for support and help, they feel ostracized by the shelter community itself as well as further isolated and abandoned (Bohn, 1993; Braveheart-Jordan & DeBruyn, 1995). Moreover, feminist values, many women of color believe, betray their men, who are also oppressed (Thomas, 2000).

Partly in response to feminist philosophies, many ethnic minority women have felt conflicted about services designed to help them, finding the philosophies culturally insensitive and oppressive. For example, Latinos feel that wife abuse affects not only the victimized woman, but also the whole family. Therefore, the North American method of dealing with wife assault, often involving putting the husband in jail at least temporarily, and/or placing the wife in a shelter and removing the children from the home, is anathema for Latinas and other ethnic minorities. The approach is seen as an "antimale" means of breaking up the family, the most vital social structure in their communities. They prefer an integrated and comprehensive approach focusing not only on the batterer but also on the family and the entire community (Alianza, 2002; Ginorio et al., 1995; Ho, 1990; Kanuha, 1994; Kim & Sung, 2000; Vasquez, 1998).

However, several domestic violence advocates from ethnic, minority communities have seen value in a modified feminist perspective. Some have argued that battered African American women need to understand the role of racism, sexism, and classism in their lives, which can be achieved through incorporating a feminist perspective into clinical practice (Taylor, 2000). Among Asian Americans, some suggest that traditional Western methods of empowerment need to be tailored specifically for Vietnamese, Korean, and other women raised with rigid patriarchal values (Tran & Des Jardins, 2000). In addition, because isolation is a strategy widely used by immigrant male batterers to control their wives—a problem exacerbated when the wives lack English language skills—educating these immigrant women about their rights and available services is an important part of the empowering process (Lee, 2000).

What Is Being Done Among Native American Indians? Efforts among Native American Indians to create more culturally sensitive services for battered women include conducting counseling in their homes. In group counseling, the inclusion of Native traditions such as sharing food before sharing problems has been found helpful. This practice is reminiscent of the traditional Talking Circle, in which members express their feelings as long as they want without interruptions or contradictions. In addition, because confidentiality is a major concern, especially among women in small tribes who do not want their problems broadcast on the "tribal telegraph," assuring confidentiality is essential (Norton & Manson, 1997).

Battered women's programs on reservations include the Dabinoo'Igan shelter in Duluth, Minnesota, which offer traditional ceremonies, sweat lodges and healers, a well-known and respected tribal elder to work with the women, and opportunities for women and children to participate in talking circles and naming ceremonies ("Dabinoo'Igan: A Place of New Beginnings," 1999). The Cangleska Domestic Violence Program's battered women's shelter, which opened in 1997, has helped over 650 Oglala Sioux women and children escape violence in their homes, while helping abusers learn traditional Indian ways and grow spiritually (Oglala Sioux Tribe Social Services, 1999).

What Is Being Done in Other Minority Communities? A number of recommendations have been made for assisting battered African American women in need of services. Education programs are seen as valuable not only to educate practitioners working with ethnic minorities, but also to challenge implicit theories of people of color concerning male-female relationships. For example, because Black women hold certain stereotypic images of Black men, both the men and women may benefit from education about the roots of those stereotypes and the destructive role they play in relationships (Gillum, 2002). Such education could take place in forums such as schools, churches, magazines, and television stations with predominantly Black clients.

Furthermore, shelters should increase their outreach to battered minority women and recognize that these women may need to stay longer in shelters than White women because of the institutionalized racism that can interfere with their finding housing or work. Moreover, social service agencies should not be staffed with White personnel who patronize, ignore, or behave hostilely toward African American (Asbury, 1999; Sullivan & Rumptz, 1994), or other minority clients. A model shelter would provide appropriate food and grooming aids (e.g., wide-toothed combs for African Americans), and material and financial support (Lee, Thompson, & Mechanic, 2002; Sorenson, 1996). To assist non-English-speaking immigrant women, facilities need to provide translators and to appreciate the terrible isolation from their families and homes these women may be experiencing; values clarification training for therapists who intend to work with minority women has also been recommended (Brice-Baker, 1994).

To reduce wife abuse in Asian American communities, community education and prevention programs might discuss how cultural values can discourage abused women and their families from seeking help (Tran & Des Jardins, 2000). Community education of Chinese men, informing them that spousal abuse is a criminal act with legal consequences, is likely to be an important first step in deterring them from abusing their wives (Lee, 2000). Furthermore, it is important to help battered Asian American women see themselves as victims, recognize they can choose not to be victims, find out about their rights and obligations, and decide among alternatives (Rimonte, 1989). An essential goal of therapy is reducing the powerful role that shame plays in keeping Asian American women silent about their abuse (Crites, 1991).

The most common approach to improving services for Hispanics has been to offer bilingual services. In many cities with large Hispanic populations, shelters now provide programs in both Spanish and English (e.g., Wallace and Vannucci Shelter; Yololink, 2002). Although many researchers (e.g., Brice-Baker, 1994; Lee et al., 2002; Sorenson, 1996; Williams & Becker, 1994) have argued that simply supplying bilingual services is not enough, others (e.g., Rosenthal, 2000; Wohl, 1989) have replied that there is no research supporting the argument that Western psychological principles do not work for a Latino population. Furthermore, they argue, researchers who call for "culturally sensitive" methods of therapy do not satisfactorily specify the particular forms these methods should take, or what makes them "culturally sensitive."

Available research indicates that simply providing a bilingual staff is, in fact, a helpful program modification. For example, when non-English-speaking Latinos are offered a bilingual therapist, their dropout rates are lower, they stay in treatment longer, and they improve psychosocially. Furthermore, there are no differences between Whites and non-English-speaking Latinos on these treatment-outcome variables, and English-speaking Latinos show similar benefits to Whites when they use English-speaking therapists (Sue, Fujino, Hu, Takeuchi, & Zane, 1991). It appears that merely offering either a bilingual therapist or a bilingual therapy program that services mostly Latinos within a Latino community is an effective means of providing services to this community (O'Sullivan & Lasso, 1992; Takeuchi, Sue, & Yeh, 1995).

Are Minority Groups Even Aware of Shelters? The goal of providing bilingual or bicultural services to minority communities does not fully address the problem of underutilization of programs. For example, in one survey of Native American Indians, 87% said that Native women stay in abusive relationships because they do not think they have a safe place to go ("Dabinoo'Igan: A Place of New Beginnings," 1999). Even though Latinos seem to benefit from Western mental health programs, they do not use them at a rate comparable to their representation in the community (Sue et al., 1991)—perhaps because recent immigrants frequently do not know about the services available to them. Lack of knowledge of available services has also been shown among Asian Americans—for example, among a sample of Korean women, 60% of whom had been physically abused, 70% were unaware that there were services available to them (Song, 1996). What might be done to educate recent immigrants about available services and to facilitate their use of programs if they need them?

Churches

Although it may appear rare for battered minority women to seek help, many of them do reach out—but to family members or the Church rather than "official" support systems. Although many clergymen emphasize values of nonviolence and respect, and offer support for the battered woman, some battered women have the same experience Piedad did with her priest:

> He told me I should try harder to understand my husband and make him happy. He told me that I had a lot to thank him for: my children never went hungry or dirty and I was not in need of anything. After that I never mentioned it again. (Zambrano, 1985, p. 146)

Many African Americans and Asian Americans also find it easier to share their problems with clergy than to go to a counselor. For instance, outreach and education to Asian American ministers, church elders, and parishioners are ways of promoting discussion of and reducing spousal violence within these communities. Furthermore, it may lead to less "pathologizing" of Asian American batterers (Tran & Des Jardins, 2000).

Microsystem Efforts

Couples Therapy

One controversial means of intervening in violent relationships is couples therapy, which usually takes a cognitive-behavioral approach and addresses such issues as communication skills. These interventions tend to focus on building up protective factors, rather than getting rid of risk factors (Hamby, 1998). They also tend to adopt a no-blame or shared-blame approach, which has put them under fire from workers believing that batterers should take full blame for their actions. Furthermore, by treating the couple together, they may make the woman less likely to speak about certain issues for fear of the possibly violent repercussions (Bograd, 1984).

Although these are valid concerns, many mental health professionals use couples therapy with some violent relationships. For instance, Holtzworth-Munroe et al. (1995) developed a couples therapy program for engaged couples to teach appropriate conflict resolution skills and to prevent severe violence from occurring. This program is a combination of two cognitive-behavioral marital therapy programs and includes exercises and lectures on understanding the negative consequences of physical aggression, reducing the spouses' tolerance for violence in the relationship, and helping couples examine their risk for using violence. Discussions on conflict resolution, anger management, jealousy, and alcohol use are included, and stressors as influences on violence are addressed. Although couples therapy may not be appropriate for severely violent couples, it may help couples in which the violence is just beginning or is at a low level, such as those found in community surveys of spousal abuse.

Although controversial in the majority culture, this microsystem approach seems to work for some men and women of color. Because most minority communities dislike the feminist approach, many practitioners within communities of color support approaches that can keep the family together while simultaneously ensuring that the women not be battered. For example, within Asian American communities, couples therapy is seen as a viable alternative for Chinese couples when (a) the woman requests couples treatment; (b) the violence in the relationship has stopped; and (c) the man is willing to take responsibility for his abusive behavior. Furthermore, family counseling sessions, in which respected members of the family put pressure on the abuser to stop his violence, can be an effective approach to stopping wife abuse (Lee, 2000). If a battered Asian American

woman has left her batterer to spend time in a shelter, and then returns to her husband, counseling may be useful for both of them (Rimonte, 1989).

Similarly, many leading members of the Latino community have initiated spousal violence programs that encompass the entire family. For example, Julia Perilla (2000) designed a program, which includes women's, men's, and children's groups that meet concurrently at a local Latino Catholic mission, that incorporates the religious beliefs of many Latinos. These groups focus on power imbalances in relationships and patriarchal cultural traditions that can perpetuate wife abuse through the generations. Furthermore, the men's group has a substance abuse component addressing the high correlation between substance abuse and wife abuse. Preliminary evidence indicates that the men stop using violence within 1 or 2 weeks and are still violence-free 6 months after completing the program. Wife abuse recidivism is less than 2%. Many men stop or considerably reduce the use of alcohol and other drugs, and many stay in the program after their court mandate runs out. Many women continue to use the group as a source of support.

Individual Efforts

Programs for Male Batterers

Rather than simply incarcerating men of color who physically abuse their wives and sending battered wives to shelters, communities may benefit from integrating discussions of spousal violence into community settings, such as schools, churches, and social service agencies (Mederos, 1999). One form of intervention designed to avoid incarceration is batterer programs, which started in 1977 and have proliferated across the country. The goals of these programs tend to be ensuring victims' safety, changing perpetrators' attitudes towards violence, getting perpetrators to assume responsibility for their violence, and teaching nonviolent methods of resolving conflicts. Their popularity has become so widespread that judges often order batterers to enter a program as part of their sentence. Consequently, most clients are court-mandated, and tend to be severely violent

(Austin & Dankwort, 1998; Hamby, 1998). Many states have developed standards for batterer programs, requiring periodic evaluations, participation in a coordinated community response to wife abuse, reporting threats of violence to the authorities, maintaining staff with certain levels of training and experience, providing group intervention, avoiding individual and couples interventions, and considering issues of power and control. Such state mandates have been challenged by many mental health professionals, who believe the mandates interfere with their rights to treat patients as they see fit and argue that ordering certain practices (e.g., no individual or couples therapy) without evidence that these practices work (Hamby), is problematic and indefensible (Austin & Dankwort).

In African American, Latino, and Asian American communities, few culturally and racially specific models exist for counseling minority men who batter. Of the available programs, most focus either on power and control (approximately one fifth of the programs) or on anger management (approximately one fourth of the programs). Programs focusing on power and control grew out of the shelter movement and are organized around the feminist notion that battering is a social problem stemming from the patriarchal organization of society. The male batterer is seen as intentionally committing violence to maintain a patriarchal structure in which he is superior. To address this macrosystem value orientation, the programs emphasize getting men to admit and take responsibility for what they have done, without resorting to denial, minimization, or victim blaming (Hamby, 1998). The previously mentioned state mandates for batterer programs seem to be influenced by these types of programs.

Programs with an anger management focus are organized around the notion that batterers anger easily, dwell on their anger, escalate in anger during confrontations, and spend much of their time in an angry state of mind. These programs emphasize that men should take time-outs to cool themselves down when a conflict occurs and use positive self-talk during arguments (e.g., "This isn't worth going to jail over."). They also tend to emphasize treating

concurrent substance abuse problems and teach assertive communication skills, emotional expressiveness, and stress reduction and relaxation techniques. Thus, in contrast to the "power and control" method, which focuses on societal level risk factors, the "anger management" method focuses on individual risk factors (Hamby, 1998).

Barriers to program evaluations include many problems inherent in the programs themselves. For instance, dropout rates are incredibly high. In one study, of 200 initial phone calls requesting information about a program, only 27% of the men showed up for an initial assessment, only 14% ever went to a program session, and only 1% actually completed the 32-week treatment program (Gondolf & Foster, 1991). Official "success rates" are usually determined by following up the 1% who actually completed treatment; therefore, any statements of success are flawed at best, particularly because treatment completers tend to be better educated, less severely violent, less likely to be unemployed, and less likely to have substance abuse problems or a criminal history than dropouts (Rooney & Hanson, 2001). It may seem contradictory that dropout rates are so high when treatment is usually court mandated, but most jurisdictions do not assess the progress of men ordered into treatment, nor are penalties imposed for not attending (Gondolf, 1990; Harrell, 1991). Moreover, most programs have no discharge criteria other than attendance. Batterers can come to a program, not participate, not make any efforts to change, and still be discharged—which is in stark contrast to treatment methods for people with mental health problems, who are discharged from treatment only after clinical judgments as to their progress. If a batterer is discharged from a program just because he attended it, he may be just as violent as when he began (Gondolf, 1995).

Overall, reviews of the research on batterer programs show no evidence that men who complete treatment are any different in future rates of violence than men who do not, and no evidence is shown that one type of treatment is better than another. There is evidence that in community samples of less violent men, use of violence tends to decline naturally over time—which may occur in severely violent men as well (Hamby, 1998). What are the implications of these findings? Consider again that many states mandate that batterers enter treatment programs and that the programs have certain treatment methods. What are your views now on these mandates?

Native American Indian communities have also designed programs for men who abuse their wives. One example is the Violent Partner Project, part of the Division of Indian Works Family Violence Program in Minneapolis. This program, which has been in operation since 1981 and holds meetings twice a week for groups of 6 to 7 men, has worked with approximately 90 men per year. The men, primarily from the Ojibwa and Lakota tribes, are typically court ordered into the program, although many come straight from a 28-day alcohol detox treatment program. Issues addressed include the role of alcohol in their violence, inability to communicate emotions, problems with low self-esteem, childhood experiences in abusive homes or foster care, and exposure to more general forms of violence on the reservation (Warters, 1989). Because of a high dropout rate, and a belief that group sessions inhibited discussions of personal experiences of victimization, the Violent Partner Project has recently instituted individual sessions. These individual sessions allow the men to explore childhood experiences and to consider a heritage in which family members were killed because of their color, grew up in alcoholic homes, or were beaten in foster homes for using their native language. The program has helped many men deal with their own violence, but has not helped end violence in the community, perhaps because violence may be a problem for all Native American Indians, not just these men (Warters).

If batterer programs are to be effective for African American men, practitioners need to deal up front with the role of racism in their lives. Practitioners who minimize the role of racism, confuse social problems with inadequacies in people of color, or insist on being "color-blind" and treating every batterer the exact same way are unlikely to be successful. Culturally sensitive practitioners understand (a) the need to build trust with minority clients, (b) how clients' past experiences with majority culture institutions may lead them to resist treatment,

and (c) how for some Black men, battering may be a response to the hostility they receive in the broader culture. The successful practitioner not only confronts the African American man concerning abusive behaviors and sexist attitudes, but also acknowledges positive behaviors (Williams, 1992).

A national survey of partner abuse programs showed that to attain cultural competence, programs need primarily to network with minority communities, recruit consultants experienced in working with minority clients, obtain information concerning service delivery to minority clients, and have at least one bilingual counselor (Williams & Becker, 1994). Such steps were followed in the development, with a largely African American sample, of a manualized couples' treatment for spousal violence (Stith, Rosen, & McCollum, 2002). This program was designed for males who perpetrate mild-to-moderate violence and partners who want to remain together. Evaluations of program success revealed that abusers significantly reduced their levels of physical and psychological abuse during treatment and reported positive changes in attitudes concerning violence against women. At a 3-month follow-up evaluation, female partners reported being significantly less afraid of being abused than they were prior to treatment.

Batterer programs have also been created for Latinos and Asian Americans. To help Latino batterers change their behavior and become better role models for future generations, Carillo and Goubaud-Reyna (1998) developed a culturally specific treatment program that (a) incorporates many traditional Latino beliefs, including the real definition of *machismo*; (b) uses stories from ancient times, prayer, and healing circles; and (c) offers batterers a clearer perspective on the causes of their violence, its relation to their history, and its consequences. Another approach that addresses the role of culture in family violence, particularly among Asian Americans, is the Cultural Context Model (CCM; Almeida & Dolan-Delvecchio, 1999). This treatment approach emphasizes responsibility-taking in the batterers and particular forms of empowerment not only of the victims, but also of the men. Most of the CCM therapeutic work takes place in same-sex group sessions called "culture circles." In these groups, men may be challenged to apply their understanding of racism to the ways they use sexism to justify their misuse of power within their marital relationships. Finally, several researchers urge batterer programs to focus on ways to help immigrant men take responsibility for their violence; in particular, they should not be allowed to use their cultural traditions as excuses for abusive behavior (e.g., Tran & Des Jardins, 2000).

Programs for Male Victims of Spousal Abuse

The dearth of resources for victims of husband abuse has been attributed to the feminist view of power relationships. According to feminist theory, men cannot be victimized by women in a society in which males are dominant. Shelters and batterer programs growing out of the feminist movement are inherently unlikely to offer services to victims of husband abuse. Recently, given the growing recognition that women can and do perpetrate intimate aggression, and not solely in self-defense, treatment programs, hotlines, and Web sites have begun to address this problem (e.g., Stacey, Hazlewood, & Shupe, 1994). For example, Stop Abuse for Everyone is a program that offers services for all victims of family violence and is particularly sympathetic to male victims. On its Web site (www.safe4all.org), it lists services that are available and responsive to male victims and provides training to law enforcement, health care providers, social services, and crisis lines on how to recognize husband abuse. Furthermore, it offers a brochure on issues of husband abuse.

The first hotline in the United States specific to abused husbands—the Battered Men's Helpline (www.noexcuse4abuse.org)—offers a 24-hour hotline, referrals to sympathetic mental health professionals, support groups, and advocacy assistance. In response to several requests for shelter assistance, the personnel are setting up a shelter in Maine specifically for battered men (J. Brown, personal communication, September 9, 2002). Valley Oasis in Lancaster, California, offers shelter services for both men and women. The state of Michigan required in 1996 that because the laws for domestic violence are gender-neutral, shelters receiving state funds must offer services to battered men. Since then, about one fourth of the shelters have provided shelter to at least one abused man, with many others arranging for men to be housed elsewhere. However, even though some abused men are now being served by these traditionally female-oriented programs, many do not even know about the help that is available. Furthermore, to our knowledge, there are no culturally specific programs specifically for male victims of domestic violence.

Although some resources exist for male victims of spousal violence, there seem to be no resources for female abusers. Consider this woman who remarked on the recovery of her battering husband by stating,

> [Now] he tries to understand my side of the argument. He talks to me rather than hits me. I still hit him, however. I would like to enroll in a class in anger management, but the [local] shelter for battered women does not help women with this problem. (Stacey, Hazlewood, & Shupe, 1994, p. 63)

ELDER MALTREATMENT

Macrosystem Efforts

At the macrosystem level, the federal government has not developed programs for victims of elder maltreatment comparable to the ones for maltreated children or wives. The federal Older Americans Act of 1965, revised in 2000, provided definitions of elder maltreatment, authorized a National Center on Elder Abuse, and provided for the use of federal funds for specified elder abuse education and administrative activities in states and local communities. It did not authorize funding for adult protective services (APS) or shelters for abused older persons, and had no specific mandate for addressing elder abuse in communities of color.

Efforts to combat elder abuse in Native American Indian communities, which have also lagged behind those for child and spousal abuse, have been limited largely to laws and codes acknowledging elder abuse as a problem and providing clear behavioral norms. For instance, Resolution 88–14 of the National Indian Health

Board states that elder abuse is a significant health problem that must be investigated and remedied (U.S. Senate Hearing 100–981, 1988). A more recent law passed by the Navajo Tribal Council acknowledges elder abuse as a problem and offers ways to deal with it, such as providing care for elders when abusers are removed from the situation. The Blackfeet Tribe of Montana has also developed an elder abuse code, and it appears likely that other tribes have codes as well (BigFoot, 2000). However, as recently as 1999, there were few corrective programs or laws for dealing with elder abuse in this population (Brown, 1999), and a continuing problem of lack of resources and trained personnel.

Exosystem Efforts

Currently, every state has an intervention agency, usually APS, which handles cases of elder abuse. However, there is little to no uniformity in the laws, definitions, or provisions for elder abuse across the states. For instance, 46 states have mandatory reporting laws requiring professionals who care for elders to report suspected cases of abuse; failure to do so is usually some kind of misdemeanor. The other four states (Colorado, New York, Wisconsin, and Illinois) have voluntary reporting. Of the states with mandatory reporting, 15 require mandatory reporting not only from professionals, but also from anyone suspecting elder abuse. In addition, domestic violence laws (for cases of spousal elder abuse) or guardianship laws (for cases in which a frail elder needs to be removed from an abusive home) can be relied upon in certain cases of elder abuse (Griffin, 1999b; Jones, 1994; Williams & Griffin, 1996).

Even though most elders see a doctor regularly, some investigators have found that in states in which physicians are mandated to report elder abuse, fewer than 10% of referrals to APS are made by health care professionals (National Institute of Justice, 2002). Some researchers surmise that physicians' reluctance to report results from a conflict between doctor-patient confidentiality and the law. Furthermore, an elder patient is an adult with certain rights, such as the right to self-determination. If an elder understands that he or she is being abused but wishes to remain in the situation, a physician may believe there is little that can be done, or that a nursing home is the most appropriate solution (Gottlich, 1994; Macolini, 1995). Moreover, physicians are not the only ones with a poor record of reporting elder abuse to APS. As mentioned in Chapter 3, the National Elder Abuse Incidence Study (NEAIS) shows that most suspected cases do not get reported, and many elder abuse victims do not get needed services. One recommended solution is the use of multidisciplinary investigatory teams, including a doctor, nurse, social worker, and APS specialist, and possibly a police officer, sheriff, district attorney, forensic pathologist, DNA expert, neurologist, psychiatrist, and a member of the clergy (National Institute of Justice).

Outreach

Advocates argue that to deal effectively with elder abuse, we must educate the public, increase the availability of respite care and supports for families caring for elders, and encourage treatment for problems contributing to elder abuse (American Psychological Association, 2002). There is also a strong consensus about the need for outreach efforts to communities of color to inform them about elder abuse laws and available services. For instance, social service agencies need to engage in public educational efforts to inform Asian Americans about the meaning of elder abuse in this country, including its legal implications, reporting requirements, and types, causes, and consequences. These elders also need to know about alternatives to suffering silently, and to understand how available services can help perpetrators as well as victims (Moon, 1999).

An ethnic-specific approach to public outreach and education is likely to be more effective than a more general approach. For example, within the African American community, education about elder abuse should be provided to informal and formal networks, a nonjudgmental attitude toward both victims and perpetrators should be promoted, and the use of available private and public agencies by Blacks should be encouraged (Griffin & Williams, 1992). In addition, informational posters and fliers placed around the neighborhood, and workshops, speakers, and lectures at church functions, might lead Black elder abuse victims to seek help (Brown, 2001). In Korean American communities, attention to the consequences of victim-blaming practices would be useful, along with explaining how third-party intervention can help victims of elder abuse. This process would be most effective when framed within an appropriate cultural context—for example, by emphasizing how changes could help restore harmony in the family (Moon & Williams, 1993). To address elder abuse in the Vietnamese community, several recommendations have been made, including (a) addressing problems of PTSD; (b) providing respite care and in-home services to relieve family members caring for an elder; (c) providing emergency shelters with other Vietnamese families; (d) addressing isolation issues; (e) hiring bilingual staff; (f) encouraging seniors to take responsibility; and (g) alleviating fear of reporting (Le, 1997). For recent immigrants, outreach programs should be implemented to educate immigrants, particularly those from countries with no elder abuse laws, concerning the American legal and social service systems related to elder abuse (Moon & Benton, 2000).

As with child and spousal abuse, there is a great need to educate the practitioners who work with elderly minority clients. Such practitioners need to learn that (a) a hesitation to answer direct questions about abuse may reflect an elder's culturally conditioned commitment to the family rather than resistance or denial; (b) "abuse" is not a familiar term to many immigrant elders, who might be better able to discuss their experiences if asked about issues like "sacrifice" and "suffering"; and (c) making tentative, nonaccusatory statements (e.g., "If that happened to me, I would be frightened") about abusive behaviors that elders have experienced may preserve the elders' dignity while letting them know that such behavior is not considered acceptable in this country (Tomita, 2000). Other useful tactics for practitioners include (a) allowing clients to express feelings in their own words, (b) making clients aware of their right to self-determination, (c) working with the entire family with the client's approval, and (d) discussing the role of family versus government in preventing and treating elder abuse (Hall, 1999).

Although some of these suggestions have helped with the problem of elder abuse in Asian and African American communities, the services available to the abused Hispanic elder are underutilized and many attempts to help these elders are doomed to fail. An excellent example of the gravity of Hispanic underutilization of elder abuse services can be found in a community in San Francisco. After a particularly successful conference on elder abuse in 1985 with the Asian community in San Francisco, staff members began to set up a similar conference with Central and South American, Mexican, Puerto Rican, and Cuban families in the Mission District. They met with community representatives to discuss the status of the elderly and factors that might hinder or help elders in getting services for abuse they might be experiencing. The conference was well attended and well received, but did not lead to any long-lasting services or outreach programs for the elderly in this Hispanic community (Nerenberg, 1999). Staff members found that abuse victims were unwilling to do anything to better their situation.

The primary dilemma in providing elder abuse services to the Hispanic community is the same one discussed in regard to child and spousal maltreatment—that is, the Hispanic community members do not seem to view the services as helpful. The majority culture's ideas appear to be regarded as overly simplistic, divisive of families, and insensitive to a primary value of the Hispanic culture (familism). Another complaint is that service providers seem to ignore the fact that elder abuse does not occur in isolation from other problems, such as poverty, drug and alcohol abuse, and unemployment. Therefore, the treatment of elder abuse requires a more holistic approach than what is currently being offered (Nerenberg, 1999).

Other potential systemic barriers to elder abuse prevention and intervention in ethnic minority communities are distrust of the service network for the elderly, fear that service agencies will discriminate against people of color, fear that agencies will report undocumented people to the INS, and perceived anti-immigrant and racist sentiments (Nerenberg, 1999). Benton (1999), who focused particularly on African Americans, noted that in minority communities, there is a justified distrust and dislike of programs that seem to reinforce negative stereotypes relating to poor family relationships, violence, and criminal behavior. Superficially favorable biases about ethnic groups also lead to distrust, as when majority-group service providers assume all Hispanic families are extended in nature and, therefore, always have someone available to care for elderly members (Nerenberg). Often, this is not the case.

Perhaps because of their mistrust of majority-culture services and because of a strong cultural value of the family, many abused older adults from ethnic minority communities want to have problems addressed within the family, not by outside authorities (Mitchell et al., 1999; Rittman, Kuzmeskus, & Flum, 1999)—although this preference appears to be stronger in some Hispanic and Asian American communities than in some Black communities. For example, in one sample of elderly women, nearly 56% of Korean Americans and 30% of Whites, compared to less than 18% of African Americas, said that if they had experienced the kinds of maltreatment portrayed in a set of elder abuse scenarios, they would turn to family members for help (Moon & Williams, 1993). Asian American elderly women, particularly Korean Americans, may be particularly anxious to avoid the "family shame" involved in letting others know about abuse in the family, and may also want to avoid conflict among their children and relatives because of disclosures (Moon & Williams). Similarly, in a focus group discussion of elder abuse with Mexican American elders, over 76% of the participants said they would discuss problems of elder abuse with family members prior to contacting any authority (Sanchez, 1999). In addition, many elderly Hispanics see their family as the only means of escaping impoverishment, and, therefore, any outside individual who threatens family cohesiveness is not likely to be well-received (Rittman et al., 1999). This reluctance to utilize outside help and the reliance solely on family members may be a large hindrance in resolving the problem of elder abuse. Strong familial cultural values, coupled with economic need and the poor health of an aging relative, prompt many impoverished Hispanics to share housing with elders with the good intention of helping

them (Rittman et al.). This difficult situation often puts the elderly at further risk for abuse.

To help develop services that minority elders may use, researchers (e.g., Nerenberg, 1999) have made many suggestions that address these cultural, systemic, and practical barriers. The first suggestion is to reframe the problem, such that seeking help is reframed from a form of weakness to an indicator of strength, with emphasis on the idea that elders will be helping their abusers get the services they need to address their problems. Second, religious institutions should be involved in any elder abuse prevention and intervention services. Churches have traditionally been the foundation of both the family and the community among Hispanics, African Americans, and Asian Americans, and after seeking help within the family, without success, many of these elders turn to their church for assistance (Robison, Bubb, Beach, Brown, & Sutton, 1998). Unfortunately, churches in minority communities are inundated with requests for all types of social services and may be limited in their ability to help (Benton, 1998). Finally, programs need to personalize services. In the majority culture, it is generally seen as unprofessional for service providers to divulge personal experiences or get too emotionally involved with a recipient of the services, but many minority cultures value a personal touch. They may view mainstream service workers as cold, aloof, and suspect, and, therefore, may not develop any rapport or trust with the service provider. Moreover, the service provider must develop a rapport with the family as a whole rather than with specific individuals, or else the provider will risk arousing further suspicion that will hinder the help that the family needs (Nerenberg).

Individual Efforts

Interventions at the individual level seem to concentrate mostly on the type of elder abuse in which a middle-aged adult caregiver abuses a frail elder. As mentioned in Chapter 3, this type of elder abuse is most widely known, and, consequently, is the focus of most intervention efforts, but may not be the only, or even the most prevalent, form of elder abuse. In a study of intervention programs for elder abuse, the most accepted strategies for victims provided nursing, other medical care, and homemaking assistance, and the programs most accepted and successful for abusers provided supportive counseling to reduce anxiety, stress, and depression, along with education and training (Nahmiash & Reis, 2000). Furthermore, education and anger management intervention programs for people who maltreat the elderly proved successful in reducing strain, depression, and anxiety in the abuser. Abusive caretakers reported declines in their use of physical aggression, which were maintained at follow-up (Campbell Reay & Browne, 2002).

Few shelters have been established for elderly victims of abuse and the few that are available receive little funding. Moreover, elders appear reluctant to use them (National Institute of Justice, 2002). One team of advocates in Wisconsin found that the younger older women who were physically abused by their spouses or adult children were least likely to accept services for elder abuse. By teaming up with domestic violence advocates, this group hoped to find ways to help these women help themselves (Raymond, 2002). In addition to these efforts, strategies fostering empowerment of the elder victim, such as support groups, information about rights and resources, and volunteer buddy/advocates have been the most successful victim-oriented strategies, whereas referrals to community activities and programs have been the least successful (Nahmiash & Reis, 2000). Finally, intervention programs to prevent financial exploitation have begun to appear. These programs, which are sometimes run by social service agencies, assist elders in writing checks for monthly expenses and in preparing budgets. Furthermore, they offer the elders a safe place to hold their valuables and cash their checks (Baron & Welty, 1996).

Additional recommendations for helping abused minority elders include cognitive reframing and providing social support. For example, if abused elders cite family loyalty as a reason for not attempting to end their maltreatment, the counselor might emphasize the elders' obligation to report the abuse in order to get help for the perpetrator and reduce the tension experienced in the family because of the abuse. Practitioners can help victims of elder abuse grasp that they, too, are powerful (e.g., by having a monthly income from Social Security, attaining alliances through community services, or understanding how to use protective service and law enforcement agencies), and can help minimize the perpetrator's power, which may have been expressed in the form of abuse (Tomita, 2000).

SUMMARY

Combating spousal and elder maltreatment in communities of color requires efforts at every level of the ecological system. Such efforts must include addressing issues of poverty and racism; moving beyond conceptions of maltreatment and program orientations that are individualistic and feminist; mounting community education programs for immigrant and other ethnic minority families; incorporating informal sources of support and assistance in prevention and intervention efforts; and helping individuals, couples, and families develop nonviolent ways of dealing with anger, frustration, and fear.

Although some professionals might argue that progress has been made in combating maltreatment in families of all colors, we believe that the system is still in need of the changes recommended by Gil (1979) 25 years ago in regard to protecting children: (a) reconceptualizing childhood, children's rights, and child rearing; (b) rejecting force as a means of achieving societal ends; (c) eliminating mental illness (including substance abuse); and (d) eliminating poverty.

REFERENCES

Abalos, D. T. (1986). *Latinos in the United States: The sacred and the political.* Notre Dame, IN: University of Notre Dame Press.

Abbott, J., Johnson, R., Koziol-McClain, J., & Lowenstein, S. R. (1995). Domestic violence against women: Incidence and prevalence in an emergency department population. *Journal of the American Medical Association, 273,* 1763–1767.

Abney, V. D., & Priest, R. (1995). African Americans and sexual child abuse. In L. A. Fontes (Ed.), *Sexual abuse in nine North American cultures* (pp. 11–30). Thousand Oaks, CA: Sage.

Abraham, M. (1999). Sexual abuse in South Asian immigrant marriages. *Violence Against Women, 5,* 591–618.

Abraham, M. (2000). Isolation as a form of marital violence: The South Asian immigrant experience. *Journal of Social Distress and the Homeless, 9,* 221–236.

Administration for Children and Families. (1999). *The AFCARS report.* Retrieved February 17, 2003, from http://www.acf.dhhs.gov/programs/cb/publications/afcars/rpt0199/ar0199.htm

Agbayani-Siewert, P., & Flanagan, A. (2001). Filipino American dating violence: Definitions, contextual justifications, and experiences of dating violence. *Journal of Human Behavior in the Social Environment, 3,* 115–133.

Agtuca, J. R. (1995). *A community secret: For the Filipina in an abusive relationship.* Seattle, WA: Seal Press.

Ahn, H. N., & Gilbert, N. (1992). Cultural diversity and sexual abuse prevention. *Social Service Review, 66,* 410–427.

Al-Mateen, C. S., Hall, P. D., Brookman, R. R., Best, A. M., & Singh, N. H. (1999). Sexual abuse and premenstrual symptoms in adolescent girls. *Journal of Interpersonal Violence, 14,* 1211–1224.

Almeida, R. V., & Dolan-Delvecchio, K. (1999). Addressing culture in batterers intervention: The Asian Indian community as an illustrative example. *Violence Against Women, 5,* 654–683.

Altarriba, J., & Bauer, L. M. (1998). Counseling the Hispanic client: Cuban Americans, Mexican Americans, and Puerto Ricans. *Journal of Counseling and Development, 76,* 389–395.

Alvy, K. T. (1987). *Black parenting.* New York: Irvington.

American Humane Association. (2002). *The story of Mary Ellen.* Retrieved February 15, 2003, from http://www.americanhumane.org/site/PageServer?pagename=wh_mission_maryellen

American Professional Society on the Abuse of Children. (1995). *Guidelines for the psychosocial evaluation of suspected psychological maltreatment in children and adolescents.* Chicago: Author.

American Psychological Association. (2002). *Elder abuse and neglect: In search of solutions.* Retrieved October 1, 2002, from http://www.apa.org/pi/aging/eldabuse.html

Anderson, M. J. (1993). A license to abuse: The impact of conditional status on female immigrants. *Yale Law Journal, 102,* 1401–1430.

Anetzberger, G. J., Korbin, J. E., & Tomita, S. K. (1996). Defining elder mistreatment in four ethnic groups across two generations. *Journal of Cross-Cultural Gerontology, 11,* 187–212.

Arbuckle, J., Olson, L., Howard, M., Brillman, J., Anctil, C., & Sklar, D. (1996). Safe at home? Domestic violence and other homicides among women in New Mexico. *Annals of Emergency Medicine, 27*, 210–215.

Ards, S., Chung, C., & Myers, S. L., Jr. (1998). The effects of sample selection bias on racial differences in child abuse reporting. *Child Abuse and Neglect, 22*, 103–115.

Ards, S., & Harrell, A. (1993). Reporting of child maltreatment: A secondary analysis of the National Incidence Surveys. *Child Abuse and Neglect, 17*, 337–344.

Arias, I. (1999). Women's responses to physical and psychological abuse. In X. B. Arriaga & S. Oskamp (Eds.), *Violence in intimate relationships* (pp. 139–162). Thousand Oaks, CA: Sage.

Arroyo, J. A., Simpson, T. L., & Aragon, A. S. (1997). Childhood sexual abuse among Hispanic and non-Hispanic White college women. *Hispanic Journal of Behavioral Sciences, 19*, 57–68.

Asbury, J. E. (1999). What do we know *now* about spouse abuse and child sexual abuse in families of color in the United States? In R. L. Hampton (Ed.), *Family violence: Prevention and treatment* (pp. 148–167). Thousand Oaks, CA: Sage.

Ashton, V. (2001). The relationship between attitudes toward corporal punishment and the perception and reporting of child maltreatment. *Child Abuse and Neglect, 25*, 389–399.

Astin, M. C., Ogland-Hand, S. M., Coleman, E. M., & Foy, D. W. (1995). Posttraumatic stress disorder and childhood abuse in battered women: Comparison with mentally distressed women. *Journal of Consulting and Clinical Psychology, 63*, 308–312.

Austin, J., & Dankwort, J. (1998). *A review of standards for batterer intervention programs.* Retrieved January 30, 2003, from http://www.vaw.umn.edu/finaldocuments/vawnet/standard.htm

Axelrod, J., Myers, H. V., Durvasula, R. S., Wyatt, G. W., & Cheng, M. (1999). The impact of relationship violence, HIV, and ethnicity on adjustment in women. *Cultural Diversity and Ethnic Minority Psychology, 5*, 263–275.

Ayoub, C., Willett, J. B., & Robinson, D. S. (1992). Families at risk of child maltreatment: Entry-level characteristics and growth in family functioning during treatment. *Child Abuse and Neglect, 16*, 495–511.

Bachman, R. (1992). *Death and violence on the reservation.* New York: Auburn House.

Bachman, R., & Coker, A. L. (1995). Police involvement in domestic violence: The interactive effects of victim injury, offender's history of violence, and race. *Violence and Victims, 10*, 91–106.

Bailey, J. E., Kellerman, A. L., Somes, G. W., Banton, J. G., Rivara, F. P., & Rushforth, N. P. (1997). Risk factors for violent death of women in the home. *Archives of Internal Medicine, 157*, 777–782.

Baird, C., Ereth, J., & Wagner, D. (1999). *Research-based risk assessment: Adding equity to CPS decision making. The National Incidence Studies.* Madison, WI: Children's Research Center.

Baker, C. D. (1978). Preying on playgrounds: The sexploitation of children in pornography and prostitution. *Pepperdine Law Review, 5*, 816.

Barling, J., O'Leary, K. D., Jouriles, E. N., Vivian, D., & MacEwen, K. E. (1987). Factor similarity of the Conflict Tactics Scales across samples, spouses, and sites: Issues and implications. *Journal of Family Violence, 2*, 37–54.

Barlow, A., & Walkup, J. T. (1998). Developing mental health services for Native American children. *Child and Adolescent Psychiatry Clinic of North America, 7*, 555–577.

Baron, L., & Straus, M. A. (1984). Sexual stratification, pornography, and rape in the United States. In N. M. Malamuth & E. Donnerstein (Eds.), *Pornography and sexual aggression* (pp. 186–210). New York: Academic Press.

Baron, S., & Welty, A. (1996). Elder abuse. *Journal of Gerontological Social Work, 25*, 33–57.

Barter, E. R., & Barter, J. T. (1974). Urban Indians and mental health problems. *Psychiatric Annals, 4*, 37–43.

Bartholet, E. (1999). *Nobody's children: Abuse and neglect, foster drift, and the adoption alternative.* Boston: Beacon.

Bass, E., & Davis, L. (1988). *The courage to heal: A guide for women survivors of child sexual abuse*. New York: Harper & Row.

Bauer, H. M., Rodriguez, M. A., & Perez-Stable, E. J. (2000). Prevalence and determinants of intimate partner abuse among public hospital primary care patients. *Journal of General Internal Medicine, 15*, 811–817.

Beadnell, B., Baker, S. A., Morrison, D. M., & Knox, K. (2000). HIV/STD risk factors for women with violent male partners. *Sex Roles, 42*, 661–689.

Beals, J., Piasecki, J., Nelson, S., Jones, M., Keane, E., Dauphinais, P., et al. (1997). Psychiatric disorder among American Indian adolescents: Prevalence in Northern Plains youth. *Journal of the American Academy of Child and Adolescent Psychiatry, 36*, 1252–1259.

Beauvais, F., Chavez, E. L., Oetting, E. R., Deffenbacher, J. L., & Cornell, G. R. (1996). Drug use, violence, and victimization among White American, Mexican American, and American Indian dropouts, students with academic problems, and students in good academic standing. *Journal of Counseling Psychology, 43*, 292–299.

Beiser, M. (1974). Editorial: A hazard to mental health. Indian boarding schools. *American Journal of Psychiatry, 131*, 305–306.

Beiser, M., & Attneave, C. L. (1982). Mental disorder among Native American children: Rates and risk periods for entering treatment. *American Journal of Psychiatry, 139*, 193–198.

Belle, D., & Doucet, J. (2003). Poverty, inequality, and discrimination as sources of depression among U.S. women. *Psychology of Women Quarterly, 27*, 101–113.

Belsky, J. (1993). Etiology of child maltreatment: A developmental-ecological approach. *Psychological Bulletin, 114*, 413–434.

Benedict, M. I., Zuravin, S., Brandt, D., & Abbey, H. (1994). Types and frequency of child maltreatment by family foster care providers in an urban population. *Child Abuse and Neglect, 18*, 577–585.

Benedict, M. I., Zuravin, S., & Stallings, R. Y. (1996). Adult functioning of children who lived in kin versus nonrelative family foster homes. *Child Welfare, 75*, 529–549.

Benokraitis, N. V. (1996). *Marriages and families: Changes, choices, and constraints*. Upper Saddle River, NJ: Prentice-Hall.

Benton, D. (1998). Risk factors for elder mistreatment among African Americans. In Archstone Foundation (Ed.), *Understanding and combating elder abuse in minority communities: An exploration of the growing epidemic of elder abuse* (pp. 178-181). Long Beach, CA: Archstone Foundation.

Benton, D. (1999). African Americans and elder mistreatment: Targeting information for a high-risk population. In T. Tatara (Ed.), *Understanding elder abuse in minority populations* (pp. 49–64). Philadelphia: Brunner/Mazel.

Bergen, R. K. (1996). *Wife rape: Understanding the response of survivors and service providers*. Thousand Oaks, CA: Sage.

Berk, R. A., Newton, P. J., & Berk, S. F. (1986). What a difference a day makes: An empirical study of the impact of shelters for battered women. *Journal of Marriage and the Family, 48*, 481–490.

Berkowitz, L. (1983). The goals of aggression. In D. Finkelhor, R. J. Gelles, G. T. Hotaling, & M. A. Straus (Eds.), *The dark side of families: Current family violence research* (pp. 166–181). Beverly Hills, CA: Sage.

Berliner, L., & Elliott, D. M. (2002). Sexual abuse of children. In J. E. Myers, L. Berliner, J. Briere, C. T. Hendrix, C. Jenny, & T. A. Reid (Eds.), *The APSAC handbook on child maltreatment* (2nd ed., pp. 55–78). Thousand Oaks, CA: Sage.

Berrick, J. D., & Gilbert, N. (1991). *With the best of intentions: The child sexual abuse prevention movement*. New York: Guilford.

Besharov, D. J. (1993). Overreporting and underreporting are twin problems. In R. J. Gelles & D. R. Loseke (Eds.), *Current controversies on family violence* (pp. 257–272). Newbury Park, CA: Sage.

BigFoot, D. S. (2000). *History of victimization in Native communities*. Norman: University of Oklahoma Health Sciences Center, Native American Topic-Specific Monograph Series.

Binggeli, N. J., Hart, S. N., & Brassard, M. R. (2001). *Psychological maltreatment of children*. Thousand Oaks, CA: Sage.

Bluestone, C., & Tamis-LeMonde, C. S. (1999). Correlates of parenting styles in predominantly working- and middle-class African American mothers. *Journal of Marriage and the Family*, *61*, 881–893.

Boehnlein, J. K., Leung, P. K., & Kinzie, J. D. (1997). Cambodian American families. In E. Lee (Ed.), *Working with Asian Americans* (pp. 37–45). New York: Guilford.

Bograd, M. (1984). Family systems approaches to wife battering. *American Journal of Orthopsychiatry*, *54*, 558–568.

Bohn, D. K. (1993). Nursing care of Native American battered women. *AWHONN's Clinical Issues in Perinatal and Women's Health Nursing*, *4*, 424–436.

Bohn, D. K. (1998). Clinical interventions with Native American battered women. In J. C. Campbell (Ed.), *Empowering survivors of abuse: Health care for battered women and their children* (pp. 241–258). Thousand Oaks, CA: Sage.

Bohn, D. K. (2002). Lifetime and current abuse, pregnancy risks, and outcomes among Native American women. *Journal of Health Care for the Poor and Underserved*, *13*, 184–198.

Bonner, B. L., Crow, S. M., & Logue, M. B. (1999). Fatal child neglect. In H. Dubowitz (Ed.), *Neglected children: Research, practice, and policy* (pp. 156–173). Thousand Oaks, CA: Sage.

Bottoms, B. L., Shaver, P. R., Goodman, G. S., & Qin, J. (1995). In the name of God: A profile of religion-related child abuse. *Journal of Social Issues*, *51*, 85–111.

Boyatzis, C. J., Matillo, G. M., & Nesbitt, K. M. (1995). Effects of the "Mighty Morphin Power Rangers" on children's aggression with peers. *Child Study Journal*, *25*, 45–55.

Braveheart-Jordan, M., & DeBruyn, L. (1995). So she may walk in balance: Integrating the impact of historical trauma in the treatment of Native American women. In J. Adleman & G. M. Enuidanos (Eds.), *Racism in the lives of women: Testimony, theory, and guides to antiracist practice* (pp. 345–368). New York: Harrington Park.

Brenes Jette, C., & Remien, R. (1988). Hispanic geriatric residents in a long-term care setting. *The Journal of Applied Gerontology*, *7*, 350–366.

Brenner, S. L., Fischer, H., & Mann-Gray, S. (1987). Race and the shaken baby syndrome: Experience at one hospital. *Journal of the National Medical Association*, *81*, 183–184.

Brice-Baker, J. R. (1994). Domestic violence in African-American and African-Caribbean families. *Journal of Social Distress and the Homeless*, *3*, 23–38.

Brisson, N. J. (1981). Battering husbands: A survey of abusive men. *Victimology*, *6*, 338–344.

Bronfenbrenner, U. (1979). *The ecology of human development: Experiments by nature and design*. Cambridge, MA: Harvard University Press.

Brown, A. S. (1989). A survey on elder abuse at one Native American tribe. *Journal of Elder Abuse and Neglect*, *1*, 17–37.

Brown, A. S. (1998). *Perceptions and attitudes toward mistreatment and reporting: A multicultural study (an analysis of the Native American data)*. A report submitted to the National Indian Council on Aging and the National Center on Elder Abuse.

Brown, A. S. (1999). Patterns of abuse among Native American elderly. In T. Tatara (Ed.), *Understanding elder abuse in minority populations* (pp. 143–159). Philadelphia: Brunner/Mazel.

Brown, A. S., Fernandez, R., & Griffith, T. M. (1990). *Service provider perceptions of elder abuse among the Navajo* (Research Report RR-90-3). Flagstaff, AZ: Northern Arizona University, Social Research Laboratory.

Brown, D. R., & Gary, L. E. (1987). Stressful life events, social support networks, and physical and mental health of urban Black adults. *Journal of Human Stress*, *13*, 165–174.

Brown, E. A. (2001). *Elder mistreatment in the African American community*. Retrieved February 17, 2003, from http://www.rcgd.isr.umich.edu/prba/perspectives/springsummer2000/ebrown.pdf

Brown, E. R., Ojeda, V. D., Wyn, R., & Levan, R. (2000). *Racial and ethnic disparities in access to health insurance and health care*. Los Angeles: UCLA Center for Health Policy Research and the Henry J. Kaiser Family Foundation.

Brown, J., Cohen, P., Johnson, J. G., & Salzinger, S. (1998). A longitudinal analysis of risk factors for child maltreatment: Findings of a 17-year prospective study of officially recorded and self-reported child abuse and neglect. *Child Abuse and Neglect*, *22*, 1065–1078.

Brown, R. M. (2002). The development of family violence as a field of study and contributions to family and community violence among low-income fathers. *Aggression and Violent Behavior*, *7*, 499–511.

Browne, A. A., Miller, B., & Maguin, E. (1999). Prevalence and severity of lifetime physical and sexual victimization among incarcerated women. *Journal of Law and Psychiatry*, *22*, 301–322.

Browne, K., & Herbert, M. (1997). *Preventing family violence*. New York: John Wiley & Sons.

Buffalohead, P. (1985). Farmers, warriors, traders: A fresh look at Ojibway women. *Minnesota History*, *21*, 236–244.

Bui, H. N., & Morash, M. (1999). Domestic violence in the Vietnamese immigrant community: An exploratory study. *Violence Against Women*, *5*, 769–795.

Burgess, B. J. (1980). Parenting in the Native American community. In M. D. Fantini & R. Cardinas (Eds.), *Parenting in a multicultural society* (pp. 63–73). New York: Longman Press.

Buriel, R., Loya, P., Gonda, T., & Klessen, K. (1979). Child abuse and neglect referral patterns of Anglo and Mexican Americans. *Hispanic Journal of Behavioral Sciences*, *1*, 215–227.

Buzawa, E. S., & Buzawa, C. G. (1996). *Domestic violence: The criminal justice response* (2nd ed.). Thousand Oaks, CA: Sage.

Caetano, R., Cunradi, C. B., Clark, C. L., & Schafer, J. (2000). Intimate partner violence and drinking patterns among White, Black, and Hispanic couples in the U.S. *Journal of Substance Abuse*, *11*, 123–138.

Caetano, R., Schafer, J., Clark, C. L., Cunradi, C. B., & Raspberry, K. (2000). Intimate partner violence, acculturation, and alcohol consumption among Hispanic couples in the United States. *Journal of Interpersonal Violence*, *15*, 30–45.

Caetano, R., Schafer, J., & Cunradi, C. B. (2001). *Alcohol-related intimate partner violence among White, Black, and Hispanic couples in the United States*. Retrieved December 3, 2002, from http://www.niaaa.nih.gov/publications/arh25-1/58-65.htm

Caldwell, C. H., & Koski, L. R. (1997). Child rearing, social support, and perceptions of parental competence among African American mothers. In R. J. Taylor, J. S. Jackson, & L. M. Chatters (Eds.), *Family life in Black America* (pp. 185–200). Thousand Oaks, CA: Sage.

California Children's Services Archive (2002, July). *Child abuse referral highlights from CWS/CMS*. Retrieved February 17, 2003, from http://cssr.berkeley.edu/CSWMSreports/Highlights/data/referrals_Q2_02_v6_text.pdf

Campbell, D. W., Campbell, J., King, C., Parker, B., & Ryan, J. (2001). The reliability and factor structure of the Index of Spouse Abuse with African American women. In K. D. O'Leary & R. D. Maiuro (Eds.), *Psychological abuse in violent domestic relationships* (pp. 101–118). New York: Springer.

Campbell, D. W., & Gary, F. A. (1998). Providing effective interventions for African American battered women. In J. C. Campbell (Ed.), *Empowering survivors of abuse: Healthcare for battered women and their children* (pp. 229–240). Thousand Oaks, CA: Sage.

Campbell, D. W., Masaki, B., & Torres, S. (1997). Changing domestic violence perceptions in the African American, Asian American, and Latino communities. In E. Klein, J. Campbell, E. Soler, & M. Ghez (Eds), *Ending domestic violence: Changing public perceptions/halting the epidemic* (pp. 64–87). Thousand Oaks, CA: Sage.

Campbell, J. C., & Alford, P. (1989). The dark consequences of marital rape. *American Journal of Nursing*, *89*, 946–949.

Campbell, J. C., Rose, L., Kub, J., & Nedd, D. (1998). Voices of strength and resistance: A contextual and longitudinal analysis of women's responses to battering. *Journal of Interpersonal Violence*, *13*, 743–762.

Campbell, J. C., & Soeken, K. L. (1999). Women's responses to battering over time: An analysis of change. *Journal of Interpersonal Violence*, *14*, 21–40.

Campbell, J. C., Soeken, K. L., McFarlane, J., & Parker, B. (1998). Risk factors for femicide among pregnant and nonpregnant battered women. In J. C. Campbell (Ed.), *Empowering survivors of abuse: Health care for battered women and their children* (pp. 90–97). Thousand Oaks, CA: Sage.

Campbell Reay, A. M., & Browne, K. D. (2002). The effectiveness of psychological interventions with individuals who physically abuse or neglect their elderly dependents. *Journal of Interpersonal Violence, 17,* 416–431.

Camras, L. A., & Rappaport, S. (1993). Conflict behaviors of maltreated and nonmaltreated children. *Child Abuse and Neglect, 17,* 453–464.

Cano, A., & Vivian, D. (2001). Life stressors and husband-to-wife violence. *Aggression and Violent Behavior, 6,* 459–480.

Cappell, C., & Heiner, R. B. (1990). The intergenerational transmission of family aggression. *Journal of Family Violence, 5,* 135–152.

Cappelleri, J. C., Eckenrode, J., & Powers, J. L. (1993). The epidemiology of child abuse: Findings from the Second National Incidence and Prevalence Study of Child Abuse and Neglect. *American Journal of Public Health, 83,* 1622–1624.

Carillo, R., & Goubaud-Reyna, R. (1998). Clinical treatment of Latino domestic violence offenders. In R. Carrillo & J. Tello (Eds.), *Family violence and men of color* (pp. 53–73). New York: Springer.

Carson, D. K. (1995). American Indian elder abuse: Risk and protective factors among the oldest Americans. *Journal of Elder Abuse and Neglect, 7,* 17–39.

Carson, D. K., & Hand, C. (1999). Dilemmas surrounding elder abuse and neglect in Native American communities. In T. Tatara (Ed.), *Understanding elder abuse in minority populations* (pp. 161–184). Philadelphia: Brunner/Mazel.

Cate, R. M., Henton, J. M., Koval, J., Christopher, F. S., & Lloyd, S. (1982). Premarital abuse: A social psychological perspective. *Journal of Family Issues, 3,* 79–90.

Cazenave, N. A., & Straus, M. A. (1979). Race, class, network embeddedness and family violence: A search for potent support systems. *Comparative Family Studies, 10,* 282–300.

Cazenave, N. A., & Straus, M. A. (1990). Race, class, network embeddedness, and family violence: A search for potent support systems. In M. A. Straus & R. J. Gelles (Eds.), *Physical violence in American families: Risk factors and adaptations to violence in 8,145 families* (pp. 321–339). New Brunswick, NJ: Transaction Books.

Cecil, H., & Matson, S. C. (2001). Psychological functioning and family discord among African-American adolescent families with and without a history of childhood sexual abuse. *Child Abuse and Neglect, 25,* 973–988.

Centers for Disease Control. (2001). *American Indian/Alaska Natives and intimate partner violence.* Retrieved September 1, 2001, from http://www.cdc.gov/ncipc/factsheets/natamer.htm

Centers for Disease Control and Prevention. (1998). Self-reported frequent mental distress among adults—United States, 1993–1996. *Morbidity and Mortality Weekly Report, 47,* 326–331.

Chaffin, M., Kelleher, K., & Hollenberg, J. (1996). Onset of physical abuse and neglect: Psychiatric substance abuse and social risk factors from prospective community data. *Child Abuse and Neglect, 29,* 194–203.

Chaiken, J. M. (1998). *Violence by inmates: Analysis of data on crimes by current or former spouses, boyfriends, and girlfriends* (NCJ No.167237). Washington, DC: U.S. Department of Justice, Bureau of Justice Statistics.

Chanda, M. (1995, June). Two recent Native American women's health education resource center projects address domestic violence in the Yankton Sioux community. *South Dakota Nurse,* 15.

Chang, J., & Moon, A. (1997). Korean American elderly's knowledge and perception of elder abuse: A qualitative analysis of cultural factors. *Journal of Multicultural Social Work, 6,* 139–154.

Chapa, J. (1988). The question of Mexican American assimilation: Socioeconomic parity or underclass formation? *Public Affairs Comment, 35,* 1–14.

Chavez, G. F., Cordero, J. F., & Becerra, J. E. (1988). Leading major congenital malformations among minority groups in the United States, 1981–1986. *Morbidity and Mortality Weekly, 37,* 17–24.

Chester, B., Mahalish, P., & Davis, J. (1999). Mental health needs assessment of off-reservation American Indian people in Northern Arizona. *American Indian and Alaskan Native Mental Health Research, 8,* 25–40.

Chester, B., Robin, R. W., Koss, M. P., Lopez, J., & Goldman, D. (1994). Grandmother dishonored: Violence against women by male partners in American Indian communities. *Violence and Victims, 9*, 249–258.

Child Abuse Prevention and Treatment Act, 42 U.S.C. § 5101 *et seq.*; 42 U.S.C. § 5116 *et seq.* Retrieved August 8, 2002, from http://www.acf.dhhs.gov/programs/cb/laws/capta

Child Welfare League of America. (2002). *Promoting safe and stable families program.* Retrieved February 4, 2003, from http://www.cwla.org/advocacy/pssfsummary.htm

Chin, K. L. (1994). Out-of-town brides: International marriage and wife abuse among Chinese immigrants. *Journal of Comparative Family Studies, 25*, 53–70.

Clifton, J. (Ed.). (1989). *Being and becoming Indian: Biographical studies of North American frontiers.* Chicago, IL: Dorsey.

Coalition for Immigrant and Refugee Rights and Service. (1990). *A needs assessment of undocumented women.* San Francisco: Author.

Cohen, M., Deamant, C., Barkan, S., Richardson, J., Young, M., Holman, S., et al. (2000). The domestic violence and childhood sexual abuse in HIV-infected women and women at risk for HIV. *American Journal of Public Health, 90*, 560–565.

Cohn, A. H., & Daro, D. (1987). Is treatment too late? What ten years of evaluative research tells us. *Child Abuse and Neglect, 11*, 433–442.

Coker, A. L., Davis, K. E., Arias, I., Desai, S., Sanderson, M., Brandt, H. M., et al. (2002). Physical and mental health effects of intimate violence for men and women. *American Journal of Preventive Medicine, 223*, 260–268.

Coker, A. L., Derrick, C., Lumpkin, J. L., Aldrich, T. E., & Oldendick, R. (2000). Help-seeking for intimate partner violence and forced sex in South Carolina. *American Journal of Preventive Medicine, 19*, 316–320.

Coker, A. L., Smith, A. L., McKeown, R. E., & King, M. J. (2000). Frequency and correlates of intimate partner violence by type: Physical, sexual, and psychological battering. *American Journal of Public Health, 90*, 553–559.

Columbus, I., Day-Garcia, B., Wallace, B., & Walt, M. A. (1980). *Battering and the Indian woman.* Unpublished manuscript.

Comas-Diaz, L. (1995). Puerto Ricans and sexual child abuse. In L. A. Fontes (Ed.), *Sexual abuse in nine North American cultures: Treatment and prevention* (pp. 31–66). Thousand Oaks, CA: Sage.

Connelly, C. D., & Straus, M. A. (1992). Mother's age and risk for child abuse. *Child Abuse and Neglect, 16,* 709–718.

Coohey, C. (2000). The role of friends, in-laws, and other kin in father-perpetrated child abuse. *Child Welfare, 79*, 373–402.

Coohey, C., & Braun, N. (1997). Toward an integrated framework for understanding child physical abuse. *Child Abuse and Neglect, 21*, 1081–1094.

Cook, P. W. (1997). *Abused men: The hidden side of domestic violence.* Westport, CT: Praeger.

Corvo, K., & Carpenter, E. (2000). Effects of parental substance abuse on current levels of domestic violence: A possible elaboration of intergenerational transmission processes. *Journal of Family Violence, 15*, 123–137.

Costanzo, M. (1997). *Just revenge: Costs and consequences of the death penalty.* New York: St. Martin's.

Costello, E. J., Farmer, E. M., Angold, A., Burns, B. J., & Erkanli, A. (1997). Psychiatric disorders among American Indian and White youth in Appalachia: The Great Smoky Mountains Study. *American Journal of Public Health, 87*, 827–832.

Council of Economic Advisors. (1998, September). *Changing America: Indicators of social and economic well-being by race and Hispanic origin.* Retrieved January 2003 from http://w3.access.gpo.gov/eop/ca/index.html

Council on Domestic Violence and Sexual Assault. (1997). *Alaska's status report.* Juneau: Alaska Department of Public Safety.

Crenshaw, K. W. (1994). Mapping the margins: Intersectionality, identity politics, and violence against women of color. In M. A. Fineman & R. R. Mykitiuk (Eds.), *The public nature of private violence* (pp. 93–119). New York: Routledge.

Crenshaw, W. B., Crenshaw, L. M., & Lichtenberg, J. W. (1995). When educators confront child abuse: An analysis of the decision to report. *Child Abuse and Neglect, 19*, 1095–1113.

Crites, L. (1991). Cross-cultural counseling in wife beating cases. *Response to the Victimization of Women and Children, 13*, 8–12.

Cross, T. (1986). Drawing on cultural traditions in Indian child welfare practice. *Social Casework, 67*, 283–289.

Cross, T., Earle, K. A., & Simmons, D. (2000). Child abuse and neglect in Indian country: Policy issues. *Families in Society: The Journal of Contemporary Human Services, 81*, 49–58.

Cross, W. E. (1998). Black psychological functioning and the legacy of slavery: Myths and realities. In Y. Danieli (Ed.), *International handbook of multigenerational legacies of trauma* (pp. 387–400). New York: Plenum.

Crouch, J. L., & Behl, L. E. (2001). Relationships among parental beliefs in corporal punishment, reported stress, and physical child abuse potential. *Child Abuse and Neglect, 25*, 413–419.

Culp, R. E., Little, V., Letts, D., & Lawrence, H. (1991). Maltreated children's self-concept: Effects of a comprehensive treatment program. *American Journal of Orthopsychiatry, 61*, 114–121.

Cunradi, C. B., Caetano, R., Clark, C., & Schafer, J. (2000). Neighborhood poverty as a predictor of intimate partner violence among White, Black, and Hispanic couples in the United States: A multilevel analysis. *Annals of Epidemiology, 10*, 297–308.

Curley, L. (1987). Native American aged. In G. L. Maddox (Ed.), *The encyclopedia of aging* (pp. 469–470). New York: Springer.

Dabinoo'Igan: A place of new beginnings. (1999, July 4). *Duluth Budgeteer News.* Retrieved September 17, 2001, from http://www.duluth.com/placed/story/07-04-1999dabinoo.html

Daniel, J., Hampton, R., & Newberger, E. H. (1983). Child abuse and accidents in Black families: A controlled comparative study. *American Journal of Orthopsychiatry, 53*, 645–653.

Daro, D. (1988). *Confronting child abuse.* New York: Free Press.

Daro, D. (1991). Prevention programs. In C. Hollin & K. Howells (Eds.), *Clinical approaches to sex offenders and their victims* (pp. 285–306). New York: John Wiley.

Daro, D., & Cohn, A. (1988). Child maltreatment evaluation efforts? What have we learned? In G. Hotaling, D. Finkelhor, J. Kirkpatrick, & M. A. Straus (Eds.), *Coping with family violence: Research and policy perspectives* (pp. 275–287). Newbury Park, CA: Sage.

Daro, D., & Connelly, A. C. (2002). Child abuse prevention: Accomplishments and challenges. In J.E.B. Myers, L. Berliner, J. Briere, C. T. Hendrix, C. Jenny, & T. A. Reid (Eds.), *The APSAC handbook on child maltreatment* (2nd ed., pp. 431–448). Thousand Oaks, CA: Sage.

Daro, D., & Gelles, R. J. (1992). Public attitudes and behaviors in respect to child abuse prevention. *Journal of Interpersonal Violence, 7*, 517–531.

Dasgupta, S. D. (1998). Women's realities: Defining violence against women by immigration, race, and class. In R. K. Bergen (Ed.), *Issues in intimate violence* (pp. 209–219). Thousand Oaks, CA: Sage.

Dasgupta, S. D., & Warrier, S. (1996). In the footsteps of "Arundhati": Asian Indian women's experience of domestic violence in the United States. *Violence Against Women, 2*, 238–259.

Davidson, H. (1988). Failure to report child abuse: Legal penalties and emerging issues. In A. Maney & S. Wells (Eds.), *Professional responsibility in protecting children* (pp. 93–103). New York: Praeger.

Davidson, H. (1997). The legal aspects of corporal punishment in the home: When does physical discipline cross the line to become child abuse? *Children's Legal Rights Journal, 17*, 18–29.

Davis, R. E. (2000). Cultural health care of child abuse? The Southeast Asian practice of *cao gio*. *Journal of the American Academy of Nurse Practitioners, 12*, 89–95.

Dawson, S. E. (1994). Fieldwork among the Navajo: Implications for social work research and practice. *Journal of Multicultural Social Work, 3*, 101–111.

DeBaryshe, B. D., Yuen, S., & Stern, I. R. (2001). Psychosocial adjustment in Asian American/Pacific Islander youth: The role of coping strategies, parenting practices, and community social support. *Adolescent and Family Health, 2*, 63–71.

DeBruyn, L. M., Chino, M., Serna, P., & Fullerton-Gleason, L. (2001). Child maltreatment in American Indian and Alaska Native communities: Integrating culture, history, and public health for intervention and prevention. *Child Maltreatment, 6*, 89–102.

DeBruyn, L. M., Lujan, C. C., & May, P. A. (1992). A comparative study of abused and neglected American Indian children in the southwest. *Social Science and Medicine, 35,* 305–315.

DeBruyn, L. M., Wikens, B. J., & Artichoker, K. (1990, November). *"It's not cultural": Violence against Native American women.* Paper presented at the 89th American Anthropological Association Meeting, New Orleans, LA.

DeJong, A. R., Hervada, A. R., & Emmett, G. A. (1983). Epidemiologic variations in childhood sexual abuse. *Child Abuse and Neglect, 7,* 155–162.

DeLillo, D., Giuffre, D., Tremblay, G. C., & Peterson, L. (2001). A closer look at the nature of intimate partner violence reported by women with a history of child sexual abuse. *Journal of Interpersonal Violence, 16,* 116–132.

Dietz, T. L. (2000). Disciplining children: Characteristics associated with the use of corporal punishment. *Child Abuse and Neglect, 24,* 1529–1542.

Dimah, K. P. (2001). Patterns of elder abuse and neglect in an Illinois elder abuse and neglect provider agency: A comparative analysis. *Journal of Elder Abuse and Neglect, 13,* 27–43.

Dixon, P. (1998). Employment factors in conflict in African American heterosexual relationships: Some perceptions of women. *Journal of Black Studies, 28,* 491–505.

Dole, A. A. (1995). Why not drop race as a term? *American Psychologist, 50,* 40.

Doll, L. S., Joy, D., Bartholow, B. N., Harrison, J. S., Bolan, G., Douglas, J. M., et al. (1992). Self-reported childhood and adolescent sexual abuse among adult homosexual and bisexual men. *Child Abuse and Neglect, 16,* 855–864.

Donato, K. M., & Bowker, L. H. (1984). Understanding the help-seeking behavior of battered women: A comparison of traditional service agencies and women's groups. *International Journal of Women's Studies, 7,* 99–109.

Douglas, H. (1991). Assessing violent couples. *Families in Society, 72,* 525–535.

Douglas, K. S., & Dutton, D. G. (2001). Assessing the link between stalking and domestic violence. *Aggression and Violent Behavior, 6,* 519–546.

Dressler, W. W. (1985). Extended family relationships, social support, and mental health in a Southern Black community. *Journal of Health and Social Behavior, 26,* 39–48.

Dubanoski, R. A. (1982). Child maltreatment in European- and Hawaiian-Americans. *Child Abuse and Neglect, 5,* 457–465.

Dubanoski, R. A., & Snyder, K. (1980). Patterns of child abuse and neglect in Japanese and Samoan Americans. *Child Abuse and Neglect, 4,* 217–225.

Dubowitz, H., Black, M. M., Kerr, M. A., Starr, R. H., & Harrington, D. (2000). Fathers and child neglect. *Archives of Pediatrics & Adolescent Medicine, 154,* 135–141.

Dubowitz, H., Papas, M. A., Black, M. M., & Starr, R. H. (2002). Poverty and child neglect: Outcomes in high-risk urban preschoolers. *Pediatrics, 109,* 573–580.

Dukepoo, F. (1980). *The elder American Indian.* San Diego, CA: Campanile.

Duran, E., & Duran, B. (1995). *Native American postcolonial psychology.* Albany: State University of New York Press.

Duran, E., Duran, B., Braveheart, M.Y.H., & Yellow Horse-Davis, S. (1998). Healing the American Indian soul wound. In Y. Danieli (Ed.), *International handbook of multigenerational legacies of trauma* (pp. 341–354). New York: Plenum.

Duran, E., Duran, B., Woodis, W., & Woodis, P. (1998). A postcolonial perspective on domestic violence in Indian country. In R. Carillo & J. Tello (Eds.), *Family violence and men of color: Healing the wounded male spirit* (pp. 95–113). New York: Springer.

Durodoye, B. A. (1997). Factors of marital satisfaction among African American couples and Nigerian male/African American female couples. *Journal of Cross-Cultural Psychology, 28,* 71–80.

Durst, D. (1991). Conjugal violence: Changing attitudes in two northern Native communities. *Community Mental Health Journal, 27,* 359–373.

Dutton, D. G. (1995). Male abusiveness in intimate relationships. *Clinical Psychology Review, 15,* 567–581.

Dutton, D. G. (2002). The neurobiology of abandonment homicide. *Aggression and Violent Behavior, 7,* 407–421.

Dutton, D. G., & Kerry, G. (1999). Modus operandi and personality disorder in incarcerated spousal killers. *International Journal of Law and Psychiatry, 22*, 287–299.

Dutton, M. A., Goodman, L. A., & Bennett, L. (2001). Court-involved battered women's responses to violence: The role of psychological, physical, and sexual abuse. In K. D. O'Leary & R. D. Maiuro (Eds.), *Psychological abuse in violent domestic relationships* (pp. 177–195). New York: Springer.

Eamon, M. K. (2001). Antecedents and socioemotional consequences of physical abuse on children in two-parent families. *Child Abuse and Neglect, 25*, 787–802.

Earle, K. A. (2000). *Child abuse and neglect: An examination of American Indian data.* Retrieved December 15, 2001, from http://www.nicwa.org

Edwards, E. D. (1983). Native American elders: Current issues and social policy implications. In R. L. McNeely & J. L. Colen (Eds.), *Aging in minority groups* (pp. 74–82). Beverly Hills, CA: Sage.

Elliott, D. M., & Briere, J. (1994). Forensic sexual abuse evaluations of older children: Disclosures and symptomatology. *Behavioral Sciences and the Law, 12*, 261–277.

Elliot, N. L., Quinless, F. W., & Parietti, E. S. (2000). Assessment of a Newark neighborhood: Process and outcomes. *Journal of Community Health Nursing, 17*, 211–224.

Ellison, C. G., & Sherkat, D. E. (1993). Conservative Protestantism and support for corporal punishment. *American Sociological Review, 58*, 131–144.

Emery, R. E., & Laumann-Billings, L. (1998). An overview of the nature, causes, and consequences of abusive family relationships. *American Psychologist, 53*, 121–135.

Endabuse. (2002). *Programs for battered immigrant women.* Retrieved February 25, 2002, from http://endabuse.org/programs/immigrant

Erickson, M. F., & Egeland, B. (2002). Child neglect. In J. E. Myers, L. Berliner, J. Briere, C. T. Hendrix, C. Jenny, & T. A. Reid (Eds.), *The APSAC handbook on child maltreatment* (2nd ed., pp. 3–20). Thousand Oaks, CA: Sage.

Ernst, A. V., Nick, T. G., Weiss, S. J., Houry, D., & Mills, T. (1997). Domestic violence in an inner-city ED. *Annals of Emergency Medicine, 30*, 190–197.

Eron, L. D. (1987). The development of aggressive behavior from the perspective of a developing behaviorism. *American Psychologist, 42*, 425–442.

Eron, L. D., & Huesmann, L. R. (1980). Adolescent aggression and television. *Annals of the New York Academy of Sciences, 347*, 319–331.

Eron, L. D., & Huesmann, L. R. (1985). The role of television in the development of prosocial and antisocial behavior. In D. Olweus, M. Radke-Yarrow, & J. Block (Eds.), *Development of antisocial and prosocial behavior.* Orlando, FL: Academic Press.

Espino, D. V., Neufeld, R. R., Mulvihill, M., & Libow, L. S. (1988). Hispanic and non-Hispanic elderly on admission to the nursing home: A pilot study. *The Gerontologist, 28*, 821–824.

European Network of Ombudsmen for Children. (2002). *The European Network of Ombudsmen for Children (ENOC) seeks an end to all corporal punishment of children in Europe.* Retrieved August 17, 2002, from http://www.ombudsnet.org/ENOCStandards.htm#corp

Everett, J. E., Chipungu, S. S., & Leashore, B. R. (1991). *Child welfare: An Afrocentric perspective.* New Brunswick, NJ: Rutgers University Press.

Fagan, J. A., Stewart, D. K., & Hansen, K. V. (1983). Violent men or violent husbands? Background factors and situational correlates. In D. Finkelhor, R. J. Gelles, G. T. Hotaling, & M. A. Straus (Eds.), *The dark side of families* (pp. 49–67). Beverly Hills, CA: Sage.

Fairchild, D. G., Fairchild, M. W., & Stoner, S. (1998). Prevalence of adult domestic violence among women seeking routine care in a Native American health care facility. *American Journal of Public Health, 88*, 1515–1517.

Falchikov, N. (1996). Adolescent attitudes to abuse of women: Are wives and nonmarital partners viewed differently? *Journal of Interpersonal Violence, 11*, 391–409.

Falicov, C. J. (1998). *Latino families in therapy: A guide to multicultural practice.* New York: Guilford Press.

Family Violence Prevention Fund. (1993). *Men beating women: Ending domestic violence— A qualitative and quantitative study of public attitudes on violence against women.* San Francisco: Author.

Fang, L. (1998). Elder abuse in the Chinese community. In Archstone Foundation (Ed.), *Understanding and combating elder abuse in minority communities: An exploration of the growing epidemic of elder abuse* (pp. 178–181). Long Beach, CA: Archstone Foundation.

Feiring, C., Coates, D. L., & Taska, L. S. (2001). Ethnic status, stigmatization, support, and systems development following sexual abuse. *Journal of Interpersonal Violence, 16*, 1307–1329.

Feminist Daily News Wire. (2002, October 25). Sniper held on violation of federal domestic violence law. Retrieved Oct 26, 2002, from www.feminist.org/lnew/newsbyte/printnews.asp?id=7219

Finkelhor, D. (1979). *Sexually victimized children*. New York: Free Press.

Finkelhor, D. (1993). The main problem is still underreporting, not overreporting. In R. J. Gelles & D. R. Loseke (Eds.), *Current controversies on family violence* (pp. 273–287). Newbury Park, CA: Sage.

Finkelhor, D. (1994). Current information on the scope and nature of child sexual abuse. *Future of Children, 4*, 31–53.

Finkelhor, D., & Dziuba-Leatherman, J. (1994). Victimization of children. *American Psychologist, 49*, 173–183.

Finkelhor, D., Hotaling, G. T., Lewis, I. A., & Smith, C. (1990). Sexual abuse in a national survey of adult men and women: Prevalence, characteristics, and risk factors. *Child Abuse and Neglect, 14*, 19–28.

Finkelhor, D., & Korbin, J. (1988). Child abuse as an international issue. *Child Abuse and Neglect, 12*, 3–23.

Finkelhor, D., & Strapko, N. (1992). Sexual abuse prevention education: A review of evaluation studies. In D. J. Willis, E. Holden, & M. Rosenberg (Eds.), *Prevention of child maltreatment: Developmental and ecological perspectives* (pp. 150–167). New York: John Wiley.

Finkelhor, D., & Yllo, K. (1983). Rape in marriage: A sociological view. In D. Finkelhor, R. J. Gelles, G. T. Hotaling, & M. A. Straus (Eds.), *The dark side of families* (pp. 119–130). Beverly Hills, CA: Sage.

Finkelhor, D., & Yllo, K. (1985). *License to rape: Sexual abuse of wives*. New York: Holt, Rinehart, & Winston.

Finn, J. (1986). The relationship between sex role attitudes and attitudes supporting marital violence. *Sex Roles, 14*, 235–244.

Fischler, R. S. (1985). Child abuse and neglect in American Indian communities. *Child Abuse and Neglect, 9*, 95–106.

Flanzer, J. P. (1993). Alcohol and other drugs are key causal agents of violence. In R. J. Gelles & D. R. Loseke (Eds.), *Current controversies on family violence* (pp. 171–181). Newbury Park, CA: Sage.

Fluke, J. D., Yuan, Y. Y., & Edwards, M. (1999). Recurrence of maltreatment: An application of the National Child Abuse and Neglect Data System (NCANDS). *Child Abuse and Neglect, 23*, 633–650.

Fogelman, E. (1988). Therapeutic alternatives of survivors. In R. L. Braham (Ed.), *The psychological perspectives of the Holocaust and of its aftermath* (pp. 79–108). New York: Columbia University Press.

Fogelman, E. (1991). Mourning without graves. In A. Medvene (Ed.), *Storms and rainbows: The many faces of death* (pp. 25–43). Washington, DC: Lewis Press.

Follingstad, D. R., Rutledge, L. L., Berg, B. J., Hause, E. S., & Polek, D. S. (1990). The role of emotional abuse in physically abusive relationships. *Journal of Family Violence, 5*, 107–120.

Follingstad, D. R., Wright, S., Lloyd, S., & Sebastian, J. A. (1991). Sex differences in motivations and effects in dating violence. *Family Relations, 40*, 51–57.

Fontes, L. A. (1993). Disclosures of sexual abuse by Puerto Rican children: Oppression and cultural barriers. *Journal of Child Sexual Abuse, 2*, 21–35.

Fontes, L. A. (1997). Evaluating the cultural sensitivity of child abuse research: Sampling issues. *The APSAC Advisor, 10*, 8–10.

Fontes, L. A. (2002). Child discipline and physical abuse in immigrant Latino families: Reducing violence and misunderstandings. *Journal of Counseling and Development, 80*, 31–40.

Fontes, L. A., Cruz, M., & Tabachnick, J. (2001). Views of child sexual abuse in two cultural communities: An exploratory study among African Americans and Latinos. *Child Maltreatment, 6*, 103–117.

Foo, L. (2002). *Asian American women: Issues, concerns, and responsive human and civil rights advocacy.* New York: Ford Foundation.

Foo, L., & Margolin, G. (1995). A multivariate investigation of dating aggression. *Journal of Family Violence, 10*, 351–375.

Forjuoh, S. N. (2000). Child maltreatment related injuries: Incidence, hospital charges, and correlates of hospitalization. *Child Abuse and Neglect, 8*, 1019–1025.

Foster, H. J. (1983). African patterns in the Afro-American family. *Journal of Black Studies, 14*, 201–232.

Fowler, L. (1990). Colonial context and age group relations among Plains Indians. *Journal of Cross-Cultural Gerontology, 5*, 149–168.

Franklin, A. J., Boyd-Franklin, N., & Draper, C. V. (2002). A psychological and educational perspective on Black parenting. In H. P. McAdoo (Ed.), *Black children: Social, educational, and parental environments* (2nd ed., pp. 119–140). Thousand Oaks, CA: Sage.

Fraser, B. (1986). A glance at the past, a gaze at the present, a glimpse at the future: A critical analysis of the development of child abuse reporting statutes. *Journal of Juvenile Law, 10*, 641–686.

Gabler, M., Stern, S., & Miserandino, M. (1998). Latin American, Asian, and American cultural differences in perception of spousal abuse. *Psychological Reports, 83*, 587–592.

Gaines, R., Sandgrund, A., Green, A. H., & Power, E. (1978). Etiological factors in child maltreatment: A multivariate study of abusing, neglecting, and normal mothers. *Journal of Abnormal Psychology, 87*, 532–540.

Gambrill, E. (1983). Behavioral interventions with child abuse and neglect. *Progress in Behavior Modification, 15*, 1–56.

Garbarino, J. (1977). The human ecology of child maltreatment. *Journal of Marriage and the Family, 39*, 721–736.

Garbarino, J. (1987). The consequences of child maltreatment: Biosocial and ecological issues. In R. J. Gelles & J. Lancaster (Eds.), *Child abuse and neglect* (pp. 200–325). Hawthorne, NY: Aldine de Gruyter.

Garbarino, J., & Collins, C. C. (1999). Child neglect: The family with a hole in the middle. In H. Dubowitz (Ed.), *Neglected children: Research, practice, and policy* (pp. 1–23). Thousand Oaks, CA: Sage.

Garbarino, J., Guttman, E., & Seeley, J. (1986). *The psychologically battered child: Strategies for identification, assessment, and intervention.* San Francisco: Jossey-Bass.

Garbarino, J., & Kostelny, K. (1992). Child maltreatment as a community problem. *Child Abuse and Neglect, 16*, 455–464.

Garbarino, J., & Sherman, D. (1980). High-risk neighborhoods and high-risk families: The human ecology of child maltreatment. *Child Development, 51*, 188–198.

Garcia, J. G., & Marotta, S. (1997). Characterization of the Latino population. In J. G. Garcia and M. C. Zea (Eds.), *Psychological interventions and research with Latino populations* (pp. 1–14). Needham Heights, MA: Allyn & Bacon.

Geiger, B., & Fischer, M. (1999). Poor, abused, and neglected children's prospects in a fair society. *Aggression and Violent Behavior, 4*, 249–258.

Gelles, R. J. (1974). *The violent home: A study of physical aggression between husbands and wives.* Beverly Hills, CA: Sage.

Gelles, R. J. (1983). An exchange/social control theory. In D. Finkelhor, R. J. Gelles, G. T. Hotaling, & M. A. Straus (Eds.), *The dark side of families: Current family violence research* (pp. 151–165). Beverly Hills, CA: Sage.

Gelles, R. J. (1987). The family and its role in the abuse of children. *Psychiatric Annals, 17*, 229–232.

Gelles, R. J. (1993). Alcohol and other drugs are associated with violence—they are not its cause. In R. J. Gelles & D. R. Loseke (Eds.), *Current controversies on family violence* (pp. 182–196). Newbury Park, CA: Sage.

George, L. J. (1997). Why the need for the Indian Child Welfare Act? *Journal of Multicultural Social Work, 5,* 165–175.

Gershoff, E. T. (2002). Corporal punishment by parents and associated child behaviors and experiences: A meta-analytic and theoretical review. *Psychological Bulletin, 128,* 539–579.

Gershoff, E. T., Miller, P. C., & Holden, G. W. (1999). Parenting influences from the pulpit: Religious affiliation as a determinant of parental corporal punishment. *Journal of Family Psychology, 13,* 307–320.

Gil, D. G. (1979). Unraveling child abuse. In R. Bourne & E. H. Newberger, *Critical perspectives on child abuse* (pp. 69–79). Lexington, MA: Lexington Books.

Gil, V. E. (1988). In thy father's house: Self-report findings of sexually abused daughters from conservative Christian homes. *Journal of Psychology and Theology, 16,* 144–152.

Gilbert, L., El-Bassel, N., Schilling, R. F., & Friedman, E. (1997). Childhood abuse as a risk for partner abuse among women in methadone maintenance. *American Journal of Drug and Alcohol Abuse, 23,* 581–595.

Giles-Sims, J., Straus, M. A., & Sugarman, D. B. (1995). Child, maternal, and family characteristics associated with spanking. *Family Relations, 44,* 170–176.

Gillum, T. L. (2002). Exploring the link between stereotypic images and intimate partner violence in the African American community. *Violence Against Women, 8,* 64–86.

Ginorio, A. B., Gutierrez, A. M., & Acosta, M. (1995). Psychological issues for Latinas. In H. Landrine (Ed.), *Bringing cultural diversity to feminist psychology: Theory, research, and practice* (pp. 241–263). Washington, DC: American Psychological Association.

Giovannoni, J. (1989). Definitional issues in child maltreatment. In D. Cicchetti & V. Carlson (Eds.), *Child maltreatment* (pp. 3–37). Cambridge, MA: Cambridge University Press.

Giovannoni, J., & Becerra, R. M. (1979). *Defining child abuse.* New York: Free Press.

Giovannoni, J., & Billingsley, A. (1970). Child neglect among the poor: A study of parental adequacy in families of three ethnic groups. *Child Welfare, 49,* 196–204.

Glascock, A. P. (1990). In any other name, it is still killing: A comparison of the treatment of the elderly in America and other societies. In J. Sokolvsky (Ed.), *The cultural context of aging: Worldwide perspectives* (pp. 43–56). New York: Bergin & Garvey.

Goddard, I. (1996). *Handbook of North American Indians: Vol. 17. Languages.* Washington, DC: Smithsonian Institution.

Goebert, D., Nahulu, L., Hishinuma, E., Bell, C., Yuen, N., Carlton, B., et al. (2000). Cumulative effect of family environment on psychiatric symptomatology among multiethnic adolescents. *Journal of Adolescent Health, 27,* 34–42.

Goetting, A. (1988). When parents kill their young children: 1982–1986. *Journal of Family Violence, 3,* 339–346.

Goldsen, R. (1978). Letter to the editors of *Human Behavior. Human Behavior, 7,* 7–8.

Gomby, D., Culross, P., & Behrman, R. (1999). Home visiting: Recent program evaluations: Analysis and recommendations. *Future of Children, 9,* 4–26.

Gondolf, E. W. (1988). The effect of batterer counseling on shelter outcome. *Journal of Interpersonal Violence, 3,* 275–289.

Gondolf, E. W. (1990). An exploratory survey of court-mandated batterer programs. *Response to the Victimization of Women and Children, 13,* 7–11.

Gondolf, E. W. (1995). *Discharge criteria for batterer programs.* Retrieved January 30, 2003, from http://www.mincava.umn.edu/papers/gondolf/discharg.htm

Gondolf, E. W. (1999). Characteristics of court-mandated batterers in four cities. *Violence Against Women, 5,* 1277–1293.

Gondolf, E. W., & Fisher, E. (1988). *Battered women as survivors: An alternative to treating learned helplessness.* Lexington, MA: Lexington Books.

Gondolf, E. W., Fisher, E., & McFerron, J. R. (1988). Racial differences among shelter residents: A comparison of Anglo, Black, and Hispanic battered women. *Journal of Family Violence, 3,* 39–51.

Gondolf, E. W., & Foster, R. A. (1991). Preprogram attrition in batterer programs. *Journal of Family Violence, 6,* 337–349.

Gonzalez, G. (2002). *Barriers and consequences for battered immigrant Latinas*. Retrieved February 24, 2002, from http://www.aad.berkeley.edu/96journal/gloriagonzalez.html

Goode, W. J. (1971). Force and violence in the family. *Journal of Marriage and the Family, 33*, 624–636.

Gottlich, V. (1994). Beyond granny bashing: Elder abuse in the 1990s. *Clearinghouse Review, 28*, 371–381.

Graburn, N. (1987). Severe child abuse among the Canadian Inuit. In N. Scheper-Hughes (Ed.), *Child survival: Anthropological perspectives on the treatment and maltreatment of children* (pp. 211–225). Norwell, MA: Kluwer Academic Press.

Gray, E., & Cosgrove, J. (1985). Ethnocentric perception of childrearing practices in protective services. *Child Abuse and Neglect, 9*, 389–396.

Gray, S. S., & Nybell, L. M. (1990). Issues in African-American family preservation. *Child Welfare, 59*, 513–523.

Greenberg, J. R., McKibben, M., & Raymond, J. A. (1990). Dependent adult children and elder abuse. *Journal of Elder Abuse and Neglect, 2*, 73–86.

Greenfeld, L. A., & Smith, S. K. (1999). *American Indians and crime* (U.S. Department of Justice, Office of Justice Programs, NCJ 173386). Retrieved January 27, 2003, from http://www.ojp.usdoj.gov/bjs/abstract/aic.htm

Gridley, M. (1974). *American Indian women*. New York: Hawthorn Books.

Griffin, L. W. (1999a). Elder mistreatment in the African American community: You just don't hit your mama!!! In T. Tatara (Ed.), *Understanding elder abuse in minority communities* (pp. 13–26). Philadelphia: Brunner/Mazel.

Griffin, L. W. (1999b). Understanding elder abuse. In R. L. Hampton (Ed.), *Family violence: Prevention and treatment* (pp. 260–287). Thousand Oaks, CA: Sage.

Griffin, L. W., & Williams, O. J. (1992). Abuse among African American elderly. *Journal of Family Violence, 7*, 19–35.

Griffin, L. W., Williams, O. J., & Reed, J. G. (1998). Abuse of African American elders. In R. K. Bergen (Ed.), *Issues of Intimate Violence* (pp. 267–284). Thousand Oaks, CA: Sage.

Grisso, J. A., Schwartz, D. F., Hirschinger, N., Samuel, M., Bensinger, C., Santanna, J., et al. (1999). Violent injuries among women in an urban area. *The New England Journal of Medicine, 541*, 1899–1906.

Gross, A. B., & Keller, H. R. (1992). Long-term consequences of childhood physical and psychological maltreatment. *Aggressive Behavior, 18*, 171–185.

Guemple, L. (1995). Gender in Inuit society. In L. Klein & L. Ackerman (Eds.), *Women and power in Native North America* (pp. 17–27). Norman: University of Oklahoma Press.

Gyimah-Brempong, K. (2001, July). Alcohol availability and crime: Evidence from census tract data. *Southern Economic Journal, 68*, 2–21.

Hall, J. M. (1999). Abuse of Black elders in Rhode Island. In T. Tatara (Ed.), *Understanding elder abuse in minority populations* (pp. 13–26). Philadelphia: Brunner/Mazel.

Hall, P. A. (1987). Minority elder maltreatment: Ethnicity, gender, age, and poverty. *Ethnicity and Gerontological Social Work, 9*, 81–93.

Hamby, S. L. (1998). Partner violence: Prevention and intervention. In J. L. Jasinski & L. M. Williams, *Partner violence: A comprehensive review of 20 years of research* (pp. 210–258). Thousand Oaks, CA: Sage.

Hamby, S. L. (2000). The importance of community in a feminist analysis of domestic violence among American Indians. *American Journal of Community Psychology, 28*, 649–669.

Hamby, S. L., & Skupien, M. B. (1998). Domestic violence on the San Carlos Apache reservation: Rates, associated psychological symptoms, and current beliefs. *The IHS Provider, 23*, 103–106.

Hampton, R. L. (1987). Race, class, and child maltreatment. *Journal of Comparative Family Studies, 18*, 113–126.

Hampton, R. L., & Gelles, R. J. (1994). Violence toward Black women in a nationally representative sample of Black families. *Journal of Comparative Family Studies, 25*, 105–119.

Hampton, R. L., & Newberger, E. H. (1985). Child abuse incidence and reporting by hospitals: Significance of severity, class, and race. *American Journal of Public Health, 75*, 56–60.

Haney, C., & Logan, D. D. (1994). Broken promise: The Supreme Court's response to social science research on capital punishment. *Journal of Social Issues, 50,* 75–101.

Hansen, K. K. (1997). Folk remedies and child abuse: A review with emphasis on *caida de mollera* and its relationship to shaken baby syndrome. *Child Abuse and Neglect, 22,* 117–127.

Harrell, A. (1991). *Evaluation of court-ordered treatment for domestic violence offenders.* Raleigh: North Carolina Supreme Court Library.

Harrington, D., & Dubowitz, H. (1999). Preventing child maltreatment. In R. L. Hampton (Ed.), *Family violence: Prevention and treatment* (2nd ed., pp. 122–147). Thousand Oaks, CA: Sage.

Harrykissoon, S. D., Rickert, V. I., & Wiemann, C. M. (2002). Prevalence and patterns of intimate partner violence among adolescent mothers during the postpartum period. *Archives of Pediatrics & Adolescent Medicine, 156,* 325–330.

Hartz, D. T. (1995). Comparative conflict resolution patterns among parent-teen dyads of four ethnic groups in Hawaii. *Child Abuse and Neglect, 19,* 681–689.

Hass, G. A., Dutton, M. A., & Orloff, L. E. (2000). Lifetime prevalence of violence against Latina immigrants: Legal and policy implications. *Domestic Violence: Global Responses, 7,* 93–113.

Hauswald, E. (1987). External pressure/internal change: Child neglect on the Navajo reservation. In N. Schepter-Hughes (Ed.), *Child survival* (pp. 145–164). Boston: Reidel.

Hawkins, D. F. (1987). Devalued lives and racial stereotypes: Ideological barriers to the prevention of family violence among Black populations. In R. L. Hampton (Ed.), *Violence in the Black family: Correlates and consequences* (pp. 189–205). Lexington, MA: Lexington Books.

Health Resources and Services Administration. (2002). *Healing shattered lives: Assessment of selected domestic violence programs in primary health care settings. A publication of the BPHC Office of Minority and Women's Health.* Retrieved February 12, 2003, from http://www.bphc.hrsa.gov:80/OMWH/domesticviolence.htm

Heffer, R. W., & Kelly, M. L. (1987). Mothers' acceptance of behavioral interventions for children: The influence of parental race and income. *Behavior Therapy, 2,* 153–163.

Heinrich, R. K., Corbine, J. L., & Thomas, K. R. (1990). Counseling Native Americans. *Journal of Counseling and Development, 69,* 128–133.

Heise, L. L. (1998). Violence against women: An integrated, ecological framework. *Violence Against Women, 4,* 262–290.

Helms, J. E., & Talleyrand, R. M. (1997). Race is not ethnicity. *American Psychologist, 52,* 1246–1247.

Henson, C. L. (2002). *From war to self-determination: A history of the Bureau of Indian Affairs.* Retrieved December 2, 2002, from http://www.americansc.org.uk/indians.htm

Henton, J., Cate, R., Koval, J., Lloyd, S., & Christopher, S. (1983). Romance and violence in dating relationships. *Journal of Family Issues, 4,* 467–482.

Herman-Giddens, M. E., Kotch, J. B., Browne, D. C., Ruina, E., Winsor, J. R., Jung, J. W., et al. (1998). Childbearing patterns in a cohort of women sexually abused as children. *Journal of Interpersonal Violence, 13,* 504–513.

Hernandez, J. T., Lodico, M., & DeClemente, R. J. (1993). The effects of child abuse and race on risk-taking in male adolescents. *Journal of the National Medical Association, 85,* 593–597.

Herrerias, C. (1988). Prevention of child abuse and neglect in the Hispanic community: The MADRE parent education program. *Journal of Primary Prevention, 9,* 104–119.

Hien, D., & Bukszpan, C. (1999). Interpersonal violence in a "normal" low-income control group. *Women & Health, 29,* 1–15.

Hill, R. (1972). *The strengths of Black families.* New York: Emerson Hall.

Hines, D. A., & Malley-Morrison, K. (2001). Psychological effects of partner abuse against men: A neglected research area. *Psychology of Men & Masculinity, 2,* 75–85.

Hines, D. A., & Saudino, K. J. (2002). Intergenerational transmission of intimate partner violence: A behavioral genetic perspective *Trauma, Violence, & Abuse, 3,* 210–225.

Hines, D. A., & Saudino, K. J. (2003). Gender differences in psychological, physical, and sexual aggression among college students using the Revised Conflict Tactics Scales. *Violence and Victims, 18*, 197–218.

Ho, C. K. (1990). An analysis of domestic violence in Asian American communities: A multicultural approach to counseling. *Women & Therapy, 9*, 129–150.

Ho, M. K. (1992). *Minority children and adolescents in therapy*. Newbury Park, CA: Sage.

Hobfoll, S. E., Bansal, A., Schurg, R., Young, S., Pierce, C. A., Hobfoll, I., et al. (2002). The impact of perceived child physical and sexual abuse history on Native American women's psychological well-being and AIDS risk. *Journal of Consulting and Clinical Psychology, 70*, 252–257.

Holtzworth-Munroe, A., Markman, H., O'Leary, K. D., Neidig, P., Leber, D., Heyman, R. E., et al. (1995). The need for marital violence prevention efforts: A behavioral-cognitive secondary prevention program for engaged and newly married couples. *Applied and Preventive Psychology: Current Scientific Perspectives, 4*, 77–88.

Homma-True, R. (1997). Japanese American families. In E. Lee (Ed.), *Working with Asian Americans* (pp.114–124). New York: Guilford Press.

Hong, G. K., & Hong, L. K. (1991). Comparative perspectives in child abuse and neglect: Chinese versus Hispanics and Whites. *Child Welfare, 70*, 463–475.

Horejsi, C., Craig, B. H., & Pablo, J. (1992). Reactions by Native American parents to child protection agencies: Cultural and community factors. *Child Welfare, 71*, 329–342.

Hotaling, G. T., & Sugarman, D. B. (1986). An analysis of risk markers in husband to wife violence: The current state of knowledge. *Violence and Victims, 1*, 101–124.

Huang, C. J., & Gunn, T. (2001). An examination of domestic violence in an African American community in North Carolina: Causes and consequences. *Journal of Black Studies, 31*, 790–811.

Hudson, M. F., Armachain, W. D., Beasley, C. M., & Carlson, J. R. (1998). Elder abuse: Two Native American views. *The Gerontologist, 38*, 538–548.

Hudson, M. F., & Carlson, J. R. (1999). Elder abuse: Its meaning to Caucasians, African Americans, and Native Americans. In T. Tatara (Ed.), *Understanding elder abuse in minority populations* (pp. 187–204). Philadelphia: Brunner/Mazel.

Huisman, K. A. (1996). Wife battering in Asian American communities. *Violence Against Women, 2*, 260–283.

Hutchison, I. A. (1999). Alcohol, fear, and woman abuse. *Sex Roles, 40*, 893–921.

Ima, K., & Hohm, C. F. (1991). Child maltreatment among Asian and Pacific Islander refugees and immigrants: The San Diego case. *Journal of Interpersonal Violence, 6*, 267–275.

Indian Health Service. (1997). *1997 trends in Indian health*. Rockville, MD: Author.

Ingraham v. Wright, 430 U.S. 651 (1977).

Ingram, K., Corning, A., & Schmidt, L. (1996). The relationship of victimization experiences to psychological well-being among homeless women and low-income housed women. *Journal of Counseling Psychology, 43*, 218–227.

Ishisaka, H. (1978). American Indians and foster care: Cultural factors in separation. *Child Welfare, 57*, 299–308.

Jackson, S., Thompson, R. A., Christiansen, E. H., Colman, R. A., Wyatt, J., Buckendahl, C. W., et al. (1999). Predicting abuse-prone parental attitudes and discipline practices in a nationally representative sample. *Child Abuse and Neglect, 23*, 15–29.

Jantzen, K., Ball, S. A., Leventhal, J. M., & Schottenfeld, R. S. (1998). Types of abuse and cocaine use in pregnant women. *Journal of Substance Abuse Treatment, 15*, 319–323.

Jasinski, J. L. (1996). *Structural inequalities, family and cultural factors, and spousal violence among Anglo and Hispanic Americans*. Unpublished doctoral dissertation. University of New Hampshire, Durham.

Jasinski, J. L. (2001). Physical violence among Anglo, African American, and Hispanic couples: Ethnic differences in persistence and cessation. *Violence and Victims, 16*, 479–490.

Jasinski, J. L., Asdigian, N. L., & Kaufman Kantor, G. (1997). Ethnic adaptations to occupational strain: Work-related stress, drinking, and wife assault among Anglo and Hispanic husbands. *Journal of Interpersonal Violence, 12*, 814–831.

Jasinski, J. L., & Kaufman Kantor, G. (2001). Pregnancy, stress, and wife assault: Ethnic differences in prevalence, severity, and onset in a national sample. *Violence and Victims, 16,* 219–232.

Jasinski, J. L., Williams, L. M., & Siegel, J. (2000). Childhood physical and sexual abuse as risk factors for heavy drinking among African-American women: A prospective study. *Child Abuse and Neglect, 24,* 1061–1071.

Jayakody, R., & Chatters, L. M. (1997). Differences among African American single mothers: Marital status, living arrangements, and social support. In R. J. Taylor, J. S. Jackson, & L. M. Chatters (Eds.), *Family life in Black America* (pp. 167–184). Thousand Oaks, CA: Sage.

Jenkins, E. J., Bell, C. C., Taylor, J., & Walker, L. (1989). Circumstances of sexual and physical victimization of Black psychiatric outpatients. *Journal of the National Medical Association, 81,* 246–252.

John, R. (1988). The Native American family. In C. H. Mindel, R. W. Habenstein, & R. Wright Jr. (Eds.), *Ethnic families in America: Patterns and variations* (3rd ed., pp. 325–363). New York: Elsevier Science.

Johnson, H. R., Gibson, R. C., & Luckey, I. (1990). Health and social characteristics: Implications for services. In Z. Harel, E. A. McKinney, & M. Williams (Eds.), *Black aged: Understanding diversity and service needs* (pp. 69–81). Newbury Park, CA: Sage.

Johnson, I. M., & Sigler, R. T. (2000). Public perceptions: The stability of the public's endorsements of the definition and criminalization of the abuse of women. *Journal of Criminal Justice, 28,* 165–179.

Johnson, M. P. (1995). Patriarchal terrorism and common couple violence: Two forms of violence against women. *Journal of Marriage and the Family, 57,* 283–294.

Jones, J. S. (1994). Elder abuse and neglect: Responding to a national problem. *Annals of Emergency Medicine, 23,* 845–848.

Jonson-Reid, M., & Barth, R. P. (2000). From maltreatment report to juvenile incarceration: The role of child welfare services. *Child Abuse and Neglect, 24,* 505–520.

Joseph, J. (1997). Woman battering: A comparative analysis of Black and White women. In G. Kaufman Kantor & J. L. Jasinski (Eds.), *Out of the darkness: Contemporary perspectives on family violence* (pp. 161–169). Thousand Oaks, CA: Sage.

Jurich, A. P. (1990). Families who physically abuse adolescents. In S. M. Stith & M. B. Williams (Eds.), *Violence hits home: Comprehensive treatment approaches to domestic violence. Springer series on social work* (Vol. 19, pp. 126–150). New York: Springer.

Kahn, M. W. (1982). Cultural clash and psychopathology in three aboriginal cultures. *Academic Psychology Bulletin, 4,* 553–561.

Kalichman, S. C., Craig, M. E., & Follingstad, D. R. (1989). Factors influencing the reporting of father-child sexual abuse: Study of licensed practicing psychologists. *Professional Psychology: Research and Practice, 20,* 84-89.

Kalmuss, D. (1984). The intergenerational transmission of marital aggression. *Journal of Marriage and the Family, 46,* 11–19.

Kang, S.-Y., Magura, S., Laudet, A., & Whitney, S. (1999). Adverse effects of child abuse victimization among substance-using women in treatment. *Journal of Interpersonal Violence, 14,* 657–670.

Kanuha, V. (1994). Women of color in battering relationships. In L. Comas-Diaz & B. Greene (Eds.), *Women of color: Integrating ethnic and gender identities in psychotherapy* (pp. 428–454). New York: Guilford Press.

Kapitanoff, S. H., Lutzker, J. R., & Bigelow, K. M. (2000). Cultural issues in the relation between child disabilities and child abuse. *Aggression and Violent Behavior, 5,* 227–244.

Kaplan, S. J., Pelcovitz, D., & Lubruna, V. (1999). Child and adolescent abuse and neglect research: A review of the past 10 years: Part I. Physical and emotional abuse and neglect. *Journal of the American Academy of Child and Adolescent Psychiatry, 8,* 1214–1222.

Kashani, J. H., & Allan, W. D. (1998). *The impact of family violence on children and adolescents.* Thousand Oaks, CA: Sage.

Kaslow, N. J., Thompson, M. P., Okun, A., Price, A., Young, S., Bender, M., et al. (2002). Risk and protective factors for suicidal behavior in abused African American women. *Journal of Consulting and Clinical Psychology, 70,* 311–319.

Katz, R., & Rolde, E. (1981). Community alternatives to psychotherapy. *Psychotherapy: Theory, Research and Practice, 18*, 365–374.

Kaufman, J., & Zigler, E. (1987). Do abused children become abusive parents? *American Journal of Orthopsychiatry, 57*, 186–192.

Kaufman Kantor, G., Jasinski, J. L., & Aldarondo, E. (1994). Sociocultural status and incidence of marital violence in Hispanic families. *Violence and Victims, 9*, 207–222.

Keefe, S. E. (1984). Real and ideal extended familism among Mexican Americans and Anglo Americans: On the meaning of "close" family ties. *Human Organization, 43*, 65–70.

Keefe, S. E., & Padilla, A. M. (1987). *Chicano ethnicity*. Albuquerque: University of New Mexico Press.

Kehoe, A. B. (1989). *The Ghost Dance: Ethnohistory and revitalization*. Fort Worth, TX: Holt, Rinehart & Winston.

Keller, T. E., Wetherbee, K., Le Prohn, N. S., Payne, V., Sim, K., & Lamont, E. R. (2001). Problem behaviors of children in family foster care: Variations by kinship placement status and race. *Children and Youth Services Review, 23*, 915–940.

Kelley, M. L., Power, T. G., & Wimbush, D. D. (1992). Determinants of disciplinary practices in low-income Black mothers. *Child Development, 63*, 573–582.

Kelley, S. J., Whitley, D., Sipe, T. A., & Yorker, B. C. (2000). Psychological distress in grandmother kinship care providers: The role of resources, social support, and physical health. *Child Abuse and Neglect, 24*, 311-321.

Kenny, M. C., & MacEachern, A. G. (2000). Racial, ethnic, and cultural factors of childhood sexual abuse: A selected review of the literature. *Clinical Psychology Review, 20*, 905–922.

Kercher, G., & McShane, M. (1984). The prevalence of child sexual abuse victimization in an adult sample of Texas residents. *Child Abuse and Neglect, 8*, 495–501.

Kessler, R. C., Molnar, B. E., Feurer, I. D., & Appelbaum, M. (2001). Patterns and mental health predictors of domestic violence in the United States: Results from the National Comorbidity Survey. *International Journal of Law and Psychiatry, 24*, 487–508.

Kestenberg, J. S. (1990). A metapsychological assessment based on an analysis of a survivor's child. In M. S. Bergmann & M. E. Jucovy (Eds.), *Generations of the Holocaust* (pp. 137–158). New York: Columbia University Press.

Kilpatrick, D. G., Acierno, R., Saunders, B., Resnick, H. S., Best, C. L., & Schnurr, P. P. (2000). Risk factors for adolescent substance abuse and dependence: Data from a national sample. *Journal of Consulting and Clinical Psychology, 68*, 19–30.

Kim, D. S. (1986). How physicians respond to child maltreatment cases. *Health and Social Work, 11*, 95–106.

Kim, J. Y., & Sung, K. T. (2000). Conjugal violence in Korean American families: A residue of the cultural tradition. *Journal of Family Violence, 15*, 331–345.

Kim, S. C. (1997). Korean American families. In E. Lee (Ed.), *Working with Asian Americans* (pp. 125–135). New York: Guilford Press.

Kolko, D. J. (1996). Clinical monitoring of treatment course in child physical abuse: Psychometric characteristics and treatment comparisons. *Child Abuse and Neglect, 20*, 23–43.

Kolko, D. J. (2002). Child physical abuse. In J.E.B. Myers, L. Berliner, J. Briere, C. T. Hendrix, C. Jenny, & T. A. Reid (Eds.), *The APSAC handbook on child maltreatment* (2nd ed., pp. 21–54). Thousand Oaks, CA: Sage.

Kolko, D. J., Seleyo, J., & Brown, E. J. (1999). The treatment histories and service involvement of physically and sexually abusive families: Description, correspondence, and clinical correlates. *Child Abuse and Neglect, 23*, 459–476.

Korbin, J. E., Anetzberger, G. J., Thomasson, R., & Austin, C. (1991). Abused elders who seek legal recourse against their adult offspring: Findings from an exploratory study. *Journal of Elder Abuse and Neglect, 3*, 1–16.

Korbin, J. E., Coulton, C. J., Lindstrom-Ufuti, H., & Spilsbury, J. (2000). Neighborhood views on the definition and etiology of child maltreatment. *Child Abuse and Neglect, 24*, 1509–1527.

Kowal, L. W., Kottmeier, C. P., Ayoub, C. C., Komives, J. A., Robinson, D. S., & Allen, J. P. (1989). Characteristics of families at risk of problems in parenting: Findings from a home-based secondary prevention program. *Child Welfare, 68*, 529–538.

Koyano, W. (1989). Japanese attitudes toward the elderly: A review of research findings. *Journal of Cross Cultural Psychology*, *4*, 335–345.

Kozu, J. (1999). Domestic violence in Japan. *American Psychologist*, *54*, 50–54.

Krieger, N., Rowley, D. L., Herman, A. A., Avery, B., & Phillips, M. T. (1993). Racism, sexism, and social class: Implications for studies of health, disease, and well-being. *American Journal of Preventative Medicine*, *9*, 82–122.

Krishnan, S. P., Hilbert, J. C., & VanLeeuwen, D. (2001). Domestic violence and help-seeking behaviors among rural women: Results from a shelter-based study. *Family and Community Health*, *24*, 28–38.

Krishnan, S. P., Hilbert, J. C., VanLeeuwen, D., & Kolia, R. (1997). Documenting domestic violence among ethnically diverse populations: Results from a preliminary study. *Family and Community Health*, *20*, 32–48.

Kucklinski, D. M., & Buchanan, C. B. (1997). Assault injuries on the Hualapai Indian reservation: A descriptive study. *The IHS Provider*, *22*, 60–64.

Kuhl, A. (1982). Community responses to battered women. *Victimology*, *7*, 49–59.

Kunitz, S. J., Levy, J. E., McCloskey, J., & Gabriel, K. R. (1998). Alcohol dependence and domestic violence as sequelae of abuse and conduct disorder in childhood. *Child Abuse and Neglect*, *22*, 1079–1091.

Kyriacou, D. N., McCabe, F., Anglin, D., Lapesarde, K., & Winer, M. R. (1998). Emergency department-based study of risk factors for acute injury from domestic violence against women. *Annals of Emergency Medicine*, *31*, 502–506.

Lachs, M. S., Berkman, L., Fulmer, T., & Horwitz, R. I. (1994). Prospective community-based pilot-study of risk factors for the investigation of elder mistreatment. *Journal of the American Geriatrics Society*, *42*, 169–173.

Lachs, M. S., Williams, C., O'Brien, S., Hurst, L., & Horwitz, R. (1997). Risk factors for reported elder abuse and neglect: A nine-year observational cohort study. *The Gerontologist*, *17*, 469–474.

LaFromboise, T. (1988). American Indian mental health policy. *American Psychologist*, *43*, 388–397.

LaFromboise, T., & Dixon, D. (1981). American Indian perceptions of trustworthiness in a counseling interview. *Journal of Counseling Psychology*, *28*, 135–139.

Lai, T. A. (1986). Asian women: Resisting the violence. In M. C. Burns (Ed.), *The speaking profits us: Violence in the lives of women of color* (pp. 8–11). Seattle, WA: Center for the Prevention of Sexual and Domestic Violence.

Lassiter, R. F. (1987). Child rearing in Black families: Child-abusing discipline? In R. L. Hampton (Ed.), *Violence in the Black family: Correlates and consequences* (pp. 39–53). Lexington, MA: Lexington Books.

Lauderdale, M. A., Valiunas, A., & Anderson, M. (1980). Race, ethnicity, and child maltreatment: An empirical analysis. *Child Abuse and Neglect*, *4*, 163–169.

Le, Q. K. (1997). Mistreatment of Vietnamese elderly by their families in the United States. *Journal of Elder Abuse and Neglect*, *9*, 51–62.

Lebert, N., & Lebert, S. (2000). *My father's keeper: Children of Nazi leaders: An intimate history of damage and denial*. New York: Back Bay.

Lee, E. (1997). Chinese American families. In E. Lee (Ed.), *Working with Asian Americans* (pp. 46–78). New York: Guilford Press.

Lee, L. C. (1998). An overview. In L. C. Lee & N.W.S. Zane (Eds.), *Handbook of Asian American Psychology* (pp. 1–19). Thousand Oaks, CA: Sage.

Lee, M. Y. (2000). Understanding Chinese battered women in North America: A review of the literature and practice implications. *Journal of Multicultural Social Work*, *8*, 215–241.

Lee, R. K., Thompson, V. L., & Mechanic, M. B. (2002). Intimate partner violence and women of color: A call for innovations. *American Journal of Public Health*, *92*, 530–534.

Lemberg, J. (2002, July 21). Spouse abuse in South Asian marriages may be high. *Women's E News*. Retrieved December, 2002, from http://www.womensenews.org/article.cfm/dyn/aid/979/context/archive

Leventhal, J. M., Horwitz, S. M., Rude, C., & Stier, D. M. (1993). Maltreatment of children born to teenage mothers: A comparison between the 1960s and 1980s. *The Journal of Pediatrics*, *122*, 314–319.

Levesque, R. J. R. (2001). *Culture and family violence: Fostering change through human rights law*. Washington, DC: American Psychological Association.

Levine, M., Doucek, H. J., Freeman, J. B., & Compaan, C. (1996). African American families and child protection. *Children and Youth Services Review*, *18*, 693–711.

Levinson, D. (1989). *Family violence in a cross-cultural perspective*. Newbury Park, CA: Sage.

Lindholm, K. J., & Willey, R. (1986). Ethnic differences in child abuse and sexual abuse. *Hispanic Journal of Behavioral Sciences*, *8*, 111–125.

Littlejohn-Blake, S. M., & Darling, C. A. (1993). Understanding the strengths of African American families. *Journal of Black Studies*, *23*, 460–471.

Lockhart, L. L. (1985). Methodological issues in comparative racial analyses: The case of wife abuse. *Social Work Research and Abstracts*, *21*(2), 35–41.

Lockhart, L. L. (1991). Spousal violence: A cross-racial perspective. In R. L. Hampton (Ed.), *Black family violence: Current research and theory* (pp. 85–101). Lexington, MA: Lexington Books.

Lodico, M. A., Gruber, E., & DiClemente, R. J. (1996). Childhood sexual abuse and coercive sex among school-based adolescents in a midwestern state. *Journal of Adolescent Health*, *18*, 211–217.

Logan, T. K., Walker, R., Staton, M., & Luekefeld, C. (2001). Substance use and intimate violence among incarcerated males. *Journal of Family Violence*, *16*, 93–114.

Lohrmann-O'Rourke, S., & Zirkel, P. A. (1998). The case law on aversive interventions for students with disabilities. *Exceptional Children*, *65*, 101–123.

Lown, E. A., & Vega, W. A. (2001). Intimate partner violence and health: Self-assessed health, chronic health, and somatic symptoms among Mexican American women. *Psychosomatic Medicine*, *63*, 352–360.

Lujan, C., DeBruyn, L. M., May, P. A., & Bird, M. E. (1989). Profile of abused and neglected American Indian children in the southwest. *Child Abuse and Neglect*, *13*, 449–461.

Lum, J. L. (1998). Family violence. In L. C. Lee & N.W.S. Zane (Eds.), *Handbook of Asian psychology* (pp. 505–525). Thousand Oaks, CA: Sage.

Lund, L. E. (2002). Incidence of non-fatal intimate partner violence against women in California, 1998–1999. *Epicgram*, *4*, 1–4.

Lung, C. T., & Daro, D. (1996). *Current trends in child abuse reporting and fatalities: The results of the 1995 annual 50-state survey*. Chicago: National Committee to Prevent Child Abuse.

Lutzker, J. R., Bigelow, K. M., Doctor, R. M., Gershater, R. M., & Greene, B. F. (1998). An ecobe-havioral model for the prevention and treatment of child abuse and neglect. In J. R. Lutzker (Ed.), *Handbook on child abuse research and treatment* (pp. 239–266). New York: Plenum.

MacEachron, A. E., Gustavsson, N. S., Cross, S., & Lewis, A. (1996). The effectiveness of the Indian Child Welfare Act of 1978. *Social Service Review*, *70*, 451–463.

MacEwen, K. E. (1994). Refining the intergenerational transmission hypothesis. *Journal of Interpersonal Violence*, *9*, 350–365.

Macfie, J., Cicchetti, D., & Toth, S. L. (2001). Dissociation in maltreated versus nonmaltreated preschool-aged children. *Child Abuse and Neglect*, *25*, 1253–1267.

Maciak, B. J., Guzman, R., Santiago, A., Villalobos, G., & Israel, B. A. (1999). Establishing LA VIDA: A community-based partnership to prevent intimate violence against Latina women. *Health Education and Behavior*, *26*, 821–840.

Mackner, L. M., Starr, R. H., & Black, M. M. (1997). The cumulative effect of neglect and failure to thrive on cognitive functioning. *Child Abuse and Neglect*, *21*, 691–700.

Macolini, R. M. (1995). Elder abuse policy: Consideration in research and legislation. *Behavioral Sciences and the Law*, *13*, 349–363.

Makepeace, J. M. (1981). Courtship violence among college students. *Family Relations*, *30*, 97–100.

Malley-Morrison, K., You, H. S., & Mills, R. B. (2000). Young adult attachment styles and perceptions of elder abuse: A cross-cultural study. *Journal of Cross-Cultural Gerontology*, *15*, 163–184.

Mandel, D. R., Lehman, D. R., & Yuille, J. C. (1994). Should the child be removed from home? Hypothesis generation and information seeking as predictors of case decisions. *Child Abuse and Neglect*, *18*, 1051–1062.

Mandel, D. R., Lehman, D. R., & Yuille, J. C. (1995). Reasoning about the removal of a child from home: A comparison of police officers and social workers. *Journal of Applied Social Psychology*, *10*, 906–921.

Mann, C. R. (1991). Black women who kill their loved ones. In R. L. Hampton (Ed.), *Black family violence: Current research and theory* (pp. 129–146). Lexington, MA: Lexington Books.

Mannes, M. (1993). Seeking the balance between child protection and family preservation in Indian child welfare. *Child Welfare*, *72*, 141–152.

Manson, S. M., Shore, J. H., Bloom, J. D., Keepers, G., & Neligh, G. (1989). Alcohol abuse and major affective disorders: Advances in epidemiological research among American Indians. In D. L. Spiegler, D. Tate, S. Aiken, & C. Christian (Eds.), *Alcohol use among U.S. ethnic minorities* (pp. 291–300). Rockville, MD: NIAAA Research, Department of Health and Human Services.

Marshall, L. L., & Rose, P. (1990). Premarital violence: The impact of family of origin on violence, stress, and reciprocity. *Violence & Victims*, *5*, 51–64.

Martin, M. (1981). Native American medicine, thoughts for posttraditional healers. *The Journal of the American Medical Association*, *245*, 141–143.

Martinez, R., & Wetli, C. (1982). Santeria: A magico-religious system of Afro-Cuban origin. *Journal of Social Psychiatry*, *2*, 32–39.

Masaki, B., & Wong, L. (1997). Domestic violence in the Asian community. In E. Lee (Ed.), *Working with Asian Americans* (pp. 37–45). New York: Guilford Press.

Maxwell, E. K., & Maxwell, R. J. (1992). Insults to the body civil: Mistreatment of elderly in two Plains Indian tribes. *Journal of Cross-Cultural Gerontology*, *7,* 3–23.

Mayhall, M. P. (2001). *Kiowa Indians*. Retrieved October 7, 2001, from http://www.tsha.utexas.edu/handbook/online/articles/view/KK/bmk10.html

Mayo, Y. (1997). Machismo, fatherhood, and the Latino family: Understanding the concept. *Journal of Multicultural Social Work*, *5*, 49–61.

Mayo, Y., & Resnick, R. P. (1996). The impact of machismo on Hispanic women. *Affilia*, *11*, 257–277.

McAdoo, H. P. (Ed.). (2002). *Black children: Social, educational, and parental environments* (2nd ed.). Thousand Oaks, CA: Sage.

McCarroll, J. E., Newby, J. H., Thayer, L. E., Norwood, A. E., Fullerton, C. S., & Ursano, R. J. (1999). Reports of spouse abuse in the U.S. Army Central Registry. *Military Medicine*, *164*, 77–84.

McClain, P. D. (1982). Black females and lethal violence: Has time changed the circumstances under which they kill? *Omega*, *13*, 13–25.

McClain, P. W., Sacks, J. J., Froehlke, R. G., & Ewigman, B. G. (1993). Estimates of fatal child abuse and neglect, United States, 1979 through 1988. *Pediatrics*, *91*, 338–343.

McFarlane, J., Campbell, J. C., Sharps, P., & Watson, K. (2002). Abuse during pregnancy and femicide: Urgent implications for women's health. *Obstetrics & Gynecology*, *100*, 27–36.

McFarlane, J., Parker, B., & Soeken, K. (1995). Abuse during pregnancy: Frequency, severity, perpetrator and risk factors of homicide. *Public Health Nursing*, *12*, 284–289.

McFarlane, J., Soeken, K., Campbell, J., Parker, B., Reel, S., & Silva, C. (1998). Severity of abuse to pregnant women and associated gun access of the perpetrator. *Public Health Nursing*, *15*, 201–206.

McFarlane, J., Wiist, W., & Watson, M. (1998). Characteristics of sexual abuse against pregnant Hispanic women by their male intimates. *Journal of Women's Health*, *7*, 739–745.

McIntire, M. (1988, Summer). Societal barriers faced by American Indian battered women. *Women of Nations Newsletter*.

McKelvey, R. S., & Webb, J. A. (1995). A pilot study of abuse among Vietnamese Amerasians. *Child Abuse and Neglect*, *19*, 545–553.

McKinnon, J. (2001, August). The Black population: 2000. U.S. Bureau of the Census. Retrieved May 9, 2003, from http://www.census.gov/population/www/cen2000/briefs.html

McKinnon, J. (2003, April). The Black population in the United States: March 2002. U.S. Census Bureau of Current Population Reports. Retrieved June 30, 2003, from http://www.census. gov/prod/2003pubs/p20–541.pdf

McLeod, J. D., Kruttschitt, C., & Dornfield, M. (1994). Does parenting explain the effects of structural conditions on children's antisocial behavior? A comparison of Blacks and Whites. *Social Forces, 73*, 575–604.

McNutt, L. M., Carlson, B. E., Rose, I., & Robinson, D. A. (2002). Partner violence intervention in the busy primary care environment. *American Journal of Preventative Medicine, 22*, 84–91.

Mederos, F. (1999). Batterer intervention programs: The past and future prospects. In M. F. Shepard & E. L. Pence (Eds.), *Coordinating community responses to domestic violence: Lessons from Duluth and beyond* (pp. 127–150). Thousand Oaks, CA: Sage.

Mehrotra, M. (1999). The social construction of wife abuse: Experiences of Asian Indian women in the United States. *Violence Against Women, 5*, 619–640.

Melton, G. B. (2002). Chronic neglect of family violence: More than a decade of reports to guide U.S. policy. *Child Abuse and Neglect, 26*, 569–586.

Melton, G. B., & Limber, S. (1989). Psychologists' involvement in cases of child maltreatment: Limits of role and expertise. *American Psychologist, 44*, 1225–1233.

Mending the Sacred Hoop. (2001). *Program overview.* Retrieved September 1, 2001, from http://www.msh-ta.org/overview.htm

Mennen, F. E. (1994). Sexual abuse in Latina girls: Their functioning and a comparison with White and African American girls. *Hispanic Journal of Behavioral Sciences, 16*, 475–486.

Mennen, F. E. (1995). The relationship of race/ethnicity to symptoms in childhood sexual abuse. *Child Abuse and Neglect, 19*, 115–124.

Mennen, F. E. (2000). Psychological symptoms in a sample of Latino abused children. *Journal of Multicultural Social Work, 8*, 193–213.

Mercy, J. A., & Saltzman, L. E. (1989). Fatal violence among spouses in the United States, 1976-1985. *American Journal of Public Health, 79*, 595–599.

Meyerson, L. A., Long, P. J., Miranda, R., & Marx, B. P. (2002). The influence of childhood sexual abuse, physical abuse, family environment, and gender on the psychological adjustment of adolescents. *Child Abuse and Neglect, 26*, 387–405.

Mignon, S. I. (1998). Husband battering: A review of the debate over a controversial social phenomenon. In N. A. Jackson & G. C. Oates (Eds.), *Violence in intimate relationships: Examining sociological and psychological issues* (pp. 137–160). Boston: Butterworth-Heinemann.

Milburn, M. A., & Conrad, S. D. (1996). *The politics of denial.* Cambridge, MA: MIT Press.

Millan, F., & Rabiner, S. S. (1992). Toward a culturally sensitive child sexual abuse prevention program for Latinos. *Journal of Social Distress and the Homeless, 1,* 311–320.

Miller, J., & Bukva, K. (2001). Intimate violence perceptions: Young adults' judgments of abuse escalating from verbal arguments. *Journal of Interpersonal Violence, 16*, 133–150.

Mills, R. B., & Malley-Morrison, K. (1998). Emotional commitment, normative acceptability, and attributions for abusive partner behaviors. *Journal of Interpersonal Violence, 13*, 682–699.

Mills, R. B., Vermette, V., & Malley-Morrison, K. (1998). Judgments about elder abuse and college students' relationship with grandparents. *Gerontology and Geriatrics Education, 19*, 17–30.

Milner, J. S. (1994). Assessing physical child abuse risk: The Child Abuse Potential Inventory. *Clinical Psychology Review, 14*, 547–583.

Milner, J. S., Gold, R. G., Ayoub, C., & Jacewitz, M. M. (1984). Predictive validity of the Child Abuse Potential Inventory. *Journal of Consulting and Clinical Psychology, 52*, 879–884.

Mitchell, B. M., Festa, N. A., Franco, A. C., Juarez, D., & Lamb, L. L. (1999). Issues in the provision of adult-protective services to Mexican American elders in Texas. In T. Tatara (Ed.), *Understanding elder abuse in minority populations* (pp. 79–92). Philadelphia: Brunner/Mazel.

Mitchell, C. M., O'Nell, T. D., Beals, J., Dick, R., Keane, E., & Manson, S. M. (1995). Dimensionality of alcohol use among American Indian adolescents: Latent structure, construct validity, and implications for development research. *Journal of Research on Adolescence, 6*, 151–180.

Mitchell, M. C. (1990). Attachment antecedents and socio-cultural factors in Hispanic mothers' physical abuse of their children. In K. Pottharst (Ed.), *Research explorations in adult attachment* (pp. 129–198). New York: Peter Lang.

Moeller, T. P., Bachman, G. A., & Moeller, J. R. (1993). The combined effects of physical, sexual, and emotional abuse during childhood: Long-term health consequences for women. *Child Abuse and Neglect, 17,* 623–640.

Moisan, P. A., Sanders-Phillips, K., & Moisan, P. M. (1997). Ethnic differences in circumstances of abuse and symptoms of depression and anger among sexually abused Black and Latino boys. *Child Abuse and Neglect, 21,* 473–488.

Moody, L. E., Voss, A., & Lengacher, C. A. (2000). Assessing abuse among the elderly living in public housing. *Journal of Nursing Measurement, 8,* 61–70.

Moon, A. (1999). Elder abuse and neglect among the Korean elderly in the United States. In T. Tatara (Ed.), *Understanding elder abuse in minority populations* (pp. 109–118). Philadelphia: Brunner/Mazel.

Moon, A., & Benton, D. (2000). Tolerance of elder abuse and attitudes toward third-party intervention among African American, Korean American, and White elderly. *Journal of Multicultural Social Work, 6,* 283–303.

Moon, A., Tomita, S. K., & Jung-Kamei, S. (2001). Elder mistreatment among four Asian American groups: An exploratory study on tolerance, victim blaming and attitudes toward third-party intervention. *Journal of Gerontological Social Work, 36,* 153–169.

Moon, A., & Williams, O. (1993). Perceptions of elder abuse and help-seeking patterns among African American, Caucasian American, and Korean American elderly women. *The Gerontologist, 33,* 386–395.

Morse, B. J. (1995). Beyond the Conflict Tactics Scale: Assessing gender differences in partner violence. *Violence and Victims, 10,* 251–272.

Morton, T. D. (1999). The increasing colorization of America's child welfare system. *Policy and Practice of Public Human Services, 57,* 23–26.

Mosby, L., Rawls, A. W., Meehan, A. J., Mays, E., & Pettinari, C. J. (1999). Troubles in interracial talk about discipline: An examination of African American child rearing narratives. *Journal of Comparative Family Studies, 30,* 489–521.

Murphy, C. M., & Cascardi, M. (1999). Psychological abuse in marriage and dating relationships. In R. L. Hampton (Ed.), *Family violence prevention and treatment* (2nd ed., pp. 198–226). Thousand Oaks, CA: Sage.

Murphy, C. M., & Hoover, S. A. (2001). Measuring emotional abuse in dating relationships as a multifactorial construct. In K. D. O'Leary & R. D. Maiuro (Eds.), *Psychological abuse in violent domestic relations* (pp. 29–46). New York: Springer.

Murphy, C. M., & O'Leary, K. D. (1989). Psychological aggression predicts physical aggression in early marriage. *Journal of Consulting and Clinical Psychology, 57,* 579–582.

Myers, J. E. B. (1998). *Legal issues in child abuse and neglect practice* (2nd ed.). Thousand Oaks, CA: Sage.

Myers, J. E. B. (2002). The legal system and child protection. In J. E. B. Myers, L. Berliner, J. Briere, C. T. Hendrix, C. Jenny, & T. A. Reid (Eds.), *The APSAC handbook on child maltreatment* (2nd ed., pp. 305–328). Thousand Oaks, CA: Sage.

Nahmiash, D., & Reis, M. (2000). Most successful intervention strategies for abused older adults. *Journal of Elder Abuse and Neglect, 12,* 53–70.

Nalepka, C., O'Toole, R., & Turbett, J. P. (1981). Nurses' and physicians' recognition and reporting of child abuse. *Issues in Comprehensive Pediatric Nursing, 5,* 33–44.

Nam, Y., & Tolman, R. (2002). Partner abuse and welfare receipt among African American and Latino women living in a low-income neighborhood. *Social Work Research, 26,* 241–252.

National American Indian Court Judges Association. (2001). *Violence against Indian women tribal code project.* Retrieved September 16, 2001, from http://www.naicja.org/vawa/htm

National Center for Health Statistics. (2000). *Live births, infant deaths, and infant mortality rates by plurality, birthweight, race of mother, and gestational age: United States, 2000 period data.* Retrieved January 28, 2003, from http://www.cdc.gov/nchs/data/dvs/LINK00.WK46.pdf

National Center on Elder Abuse. (1998). *The National Elder Abuse Incidence Study.* Retrieved October 1, 2002, from http://www.aoa.dhhs.gov/abuse/report/cexecsum.htm

National Clearinghouse on Family Violence. (1996). *Family violence in Aboriginal communities: An Aboriginal perspective.* Retrieved April 11, 2002, from http://www.hc-sc.gc.ca/hppb/familyviolence/html/labor.htm

National Coalition Against Domestic Violence. (2002). *Summary of organization's history.* Retrieved March 15, 2002, from http://www.ncadv.org/about.htm

National Coalition of Hispanic Health and Human Services Organization. (n.d.). *What is COSSMHO?* Retrieved February 4, 2003, from http://clnet.ucr.edu/community/ cossmho. html

National Coalition to Abolish Corporal Punishment in the Schools. (2001). *Facts about corporal punishment.* Retrieved February 4, 2003, from http://www.stophitting.com/disatschool/facts.php

National Institute of Justice. (2002). *Elder justice: Medical forensic issues concerning abuse and neglect (draft report): Medical forensic roundtable discussion.* Retrieved March 15, 2002, from http://www.ojp.usdoj.gov/nij/elderjust/elder_05.html

Navajo Nation. (1988). *Navajo Nation FAX 88: A statistical abstract.* Window Rock, AZ: Navajo Nation.

Navarro, J., & Miranda, M. R. (1985). Stress and child abuse in the Hispanic community: A clinical profile. In W. A. Vega & M. R. Miranda (Eds.), *Stress and Hispanic mental health: Relating research to service delivery* (pp. 239–260). Rockville, MD: National Institute of Mental Health.

Needel, B., & Barth, R. P. (1998). Infants entering foster care compared to other infants using birth status indicators. *Child Abuse and Neglect, 22*, 1179–1187.

Neff, A. J., Holamon, B., & Schluter, T. D. (1995). Spousal violence among Anglos, Blacks, and Mexican Americans: The role of demographic variables, psychosocial predictors, and alcohol consumption. *Journal of Family Violence, 10*, 1–21.

Nelson, B. (1984). *Making an issue of child abuse.* Chicago: University of Chicago Press.

Nelson, K., Cross, T., Landsman, M. J., & Tyler, M. (1996). Native American families and child neglect. *Children and Youth Services Review, 18*, 505–521.

Nelson, S. H., McCoy, G. F., Stetter, M., & Vanderwagen, W. C. (1992). An overview of mental health services for American Indians and Alaska Natives in the 1990s. *Hospital and Community Psychiatry, 43*, 257–261.

Nerenberg, L. (1999). Culturally specific outreach in elder abuse. In T. Tatara (Ed.), *Understanding elder abuse in minority populations* (pp. 205–220). Philadelphia: Brunner/Mazel.

Newberger, C. M., & Newberger, E. H. (1981). The etiology of child abuse. In N. S. Ellerstein (Ed.), *Child abuse and neglect* (pp. 11–20). New York: John Wiley & Sons.

Newberger, E. H., & Bourne, R. (1978). The medicalization and legalization of child abuse. *American Journal of Orthopsychiatry, 48*, 593–607.

Newberger, E. H., Reed, R., Daniel, J., Hyde, J., & Kotelchuck, M. (1977). Pediatric social illness: Toward an etiologic classification. *Pediatrics, 60*, 178–185.

Newby, J. H., McCarroll, J. E., Thayer, L. E., Norwood, A. E., Fullerton, C. S., & Ursano, R. J. (2000). Spouse abuse by Black and White offenders in the U.S. Army. *Journal of Family Violence, 15*, 199–208.

Northern Navajo Medical Center. (1996). *The Navajo health status report.* Shiprock, NM: U.S. Indian Health Service.

Northwest Tribal Court Judges Association. (1999). *Tribal court bench book for domestic violence cases.* Washington, DC: The Violence Against Women Grants Office.

Norton, I. M., & Manson, S. M. (1995). A silent minority: Battered American Indian women. *Journal of Family Violence, 10*, 307–318.

Norton, I. M., & Manson, S. M. (1996). Research in American Indian and Alaska Native communities: Navigating the cultural universe of values and process. *Journal of Consulting and Clinical Psychology, 64*, 856–860.

Norton, I. M., & Manson, S. M. (1997). Domestic violence intervention in an urban Indian health center. *Community Mental Health Journal, 33*, 331–337.

Nunez, R. (2001). Family homelessness in New York City: A case study. *Political Science Quarterly, 116*, 367–379.

Oates, R. K., & Bross, D. C. (1995). What have we learned about treating child physical abuse? A literature review of the last decade. *Child Abuse and Neglect, 19*, 463–473.

O'Brien, S. (1989). *American Indian tribal governments.* Norman: University of Oklahoma Press.

O'Campo, P., Gielen, A. C., Faden, R. R., Xue, X., Kass, N., & Wang, M. C. (1995). Violence by male partners against women during the childbearing years: A contextual analysis. *American Journal of Public Health, 85*, 1092–1097.

O'Campo, P., McDonnell, K., Gielen, A., Burke, J., & Chen, Y-h. (2002). Surviving physical and sexual abuse: What helps low-income women? *Patient Education and Counseling, 46*, 205–212.

Oetting, E. R., Swaim, R. C., Edwards, W. R., & Beauvais, F. (1989). Indian and Anglo adolescent alcohol use and emotional distress: Path models. *American Journal of Drug and Alcohol Abuse, 15*, 153–172.

Office of Juvenile Justice. (2000). *Children as victims* (1999 National Report Series, Juvenile Justice Bulletin). Retrieved March 16, 2002, from http://www.ncjrs.org/html/ojjdp/2000_5_2/child_09.html

Office on Violence Against Women. (2000). *Violence Against Women Act of 2000.* Retrieved March 25, 2002, from http://www.ojp.usdoj.gov/vawo/laws/vawo2000/stitle_b.htm

Oglala Sioux Tribe Social Services. (1999). *Cangleska domestic violence program.* Retrieved September 17, 2001, from http://www.innovations.harvard.edu/winners/1999/cangleska99.htm

Okamura, A., Heras, P., & Wong-Kerberg, L. (1995). Asian, Pacific Island, and Filipino Americans and sexual child abuse. In L. A. Fontes (Ed.), *Sexual abuse in nine North American cultures: Treatment and prevention* (pp. 67–96). Thousand Oaks, CA: Sage.

O'Keefe, M. (1994). Racial/ethnic differences among battered women and their children. *Journal of Child and Family Studies, 3*, 283–305.

Olds, D. L., Eckenrode, J., Henderson, C. R., Kitzman, H., Powers, J., Cole, R., et al. (1997). Long-term effects of home visitation on maternal life course and child abuse and neglect. *Journal of the American Medical Association, 278*, 637–642.

O'Leary, K. D., Barling, J., Arias, I., Rosenbaum, A., Malone, J., & Tyree, A. (1989). Prevalence and stability of physical aggression. *Journal of Consulting and Clinical Psychology, 57*, 263–268.

Opler, M. E. (1996). *An Apache life-way: The economic, social, and religious institutions of the Chiricahua Indians.* Lincoln: University of Nebraska Press.

O'Sullivan, M. J., & Lasso, B. (1992). Community mental health services for Hispanics: A test of the culture compatibility hypothesis. *Hispanic Journal of the Behavioral Sciences, 14*, 455–468.

Pablo, S. (1998). Perceptions of elder abuse and neglect and help-seeking patterns among Filipino and Korean elderly women in Honolulu. In Archstone Foundation (Ed.), *Understanding and combating elder abuse in minority communities: An exploration of the growing epidemic of elder abuse* (pp. 183–188). Long Beach, CA: Archstone Foundation.

Padgett, D. K., Patrick, C., Burns, B. J., & Schlesinger, H. J. (1994). Ethnicity and the use of outpatient mental health services in a national insured population. *American Journal of Public Health, 84*, 222–226.

Padilla, A. M., Ruiz, R. A., & Alvarez, R. (1989). Community mental health services for the Spanish-speaking/surnamed population. In M. R. Miranda (Ed.), *Psychotherapy with the Spanish-speaking: Issues in research and service delivery* (pp. 9–19). Los Angeles: Spanish Speaking Mental Health Research Center.

Padilla, Y. C. (1996). Incorporating social science concepts in the analysis of ethnic issues in social work: The case of Latinos. *Journal of Multicultural Social Work, 4*, 1–12.

Panitz, D. R., McConchie, R. D., Sauber, S. R., & Fonseca, J. A. (1983). The role of machismo and the Hispanic family in the etiology and treatment of alcoholism in Hispanic American males. *American Journal of Family Therapy, 11*, 31–44.

Park, M. S. (2001). The factors of child physical abuse in Korean immigrant families. *Child Abuse and Neglect, 25*, 945–958.

Paulsen, M., Parker, G., & Adelman, L. (1966). Child abuse reporting laws: Some legislative history. *George Washington Law Review, 34*, 482–506.

Peacock, P. L. (1995). Marital rape. In V. R. Wiehe & A. L. Richards (Eds.), *Intimate betrayal: Understanding and responding to the trauma of acquaintance rape*. Thousand Oaks, CA: Sage.

Pennsylvania v. Ritchie, 480 U.S. 39 (1987).

Perez, D. M. (2001). Ethnic differences in property, violent, and sex offending for abused and nonabused adolescents. *Journal of Criminal Justice, 29*, 407–417.

Perilla, J. L. (1999). Domestic violence as a human rights issue: The case of immigrant Latinos. *Hispanic Journal of Behavioral Sciences, 21*, 107–133.

Perilla, J. L. (2000). Cultural specificity in domestic violence interventions: A Latino model. *The Family Psychologist, 16*, 6–7.

Perilla, J. L., Bakeman, R., & Norris, F. H. (1994). Culture and domestic violence: The ecology of abused Latinas. *Violence and Victims, 9*, 325–339.

Pharris, M. D., Resnick, M. D., & Blum, R. W. (1997). Protecting against hopelessness and suicidality in sexually abused American Indian adolescents. *Journal of Adolescent Health, 21*, 400–406.

Phinney, J. S. (1996). When we talk about American ethnic groups, what do we mean? *American Psychologist, 51*, 918–927.

Piasecki, J. M., Manson, S. M., Biernoff, M. P., Hiat, A. B., Taylor, S. S., & Bechtold, D. W. (1989). Abuse and neglect of American Indian children: Findings from a survey of federal providers. *American Indian and Alaska Native Mental Health Research, 3*, 43–62.

Pillemer, K. (1986). Risk factors in elder abuse: Results from a case-control study. In K. Pillemer & R. S. Wolf (Eds.), *Elder abuse: Conflict in the family* (pp. 236–263). Dover, MA: Auburn House.

Pillemer, K. (1993). Abuse is caused by the deviance and dependence of abusive caregivers. In R. J. Gelles & D. R. Loseke (Eds.), *Current controversies on family violence* (pp. 237–250). Newbury Park, CA: Sage.

Pillemer, K., & Finkelhor, D. (1988). The prevalence of elder abuse: A random sample survey. *Gerontologist, 28*, 51–57.

Pillemer, K., & Finkelhor, D. (1989). Causes of elder abuse: Caregiver stress versus problem relatives. *American Journal of Orthopsychiatry, 59*, 179–187.

Pillemer, K., & Wolf, R. (Eds.). (1986). *Elder abuse: Conflict in the family*. Dover: Auburn House.

Pinderhughes, E. E., Dodge, K. A., Bates, J. E., Peettit, G. S., & Zelli, A. (2000). Discipline responses: Influences of parents' socioeconomic status, ethnicity, beliefs about parenting, stress, and cognitive-emotional processes. *Journal of Family Psychology, 14*, 380–400.

Plantz, M. C., Hubbell, R., Barrett, B. J., & Dobrec, A. (1988). *Indian child welfare: A status report—Final report on the Survey of Indian Child Welfare and Implementation of the Indian Child Welfare Act and Section 428 of the Adoption Assistance and Child Welfare Act of 1980* (CSR Incorporated and Three Feathers Associates, 105-82-1602). Washington, DC: U.S. Department of Health and Human Services, Administration for Children, Youth, and Families; U.S. Department of the Interior, Bureau of Indian Affairs.

Pleck, E. (1987). *Domestic tyranny: The making of social policy against family violence from colonial times to the present*. New York: Oxford University Press.

Pleck, E., Pleck, J. H., Grossman, M., & Bart, P. B. (1977-1978). The battered data syndrome: A comment on Steinmetz's article. *Victimology: An International Journal, 2*, 680–683.

Plummer, C. A. (1993). Prevention is appropriate, prevention is successful. In R. J. Gelles & D. R. Loseke (Eds.), *Current controversies on family violence* (pp. 288–305). Newbury Park, CA: Sage.

Plunkett, M., & Mitchell, C. M. (2000). Substance use among American Indian adolescents: Regional comparisons with Monitoring the Future high school seniors. *Journal of Drug Issues, 30*, 575–591.

Population Reference Bureau. (2000). *2000 United States population data sheet*. Washington, DC: Author.

Portwood, S. G. (1998). The impact of individuals' characteristics and experiences on their definitions of child maltreatment. *Child Abuse and Neglect, 22*, 437–452.

Powers, J. L., & Eckenrode, J. (1988). The maltreatment of adolescents. *Child Abuse and Neglect, 12*, 189–199.

Powers, M. N. (1986). *Oglala women*. Chicago: University of Chicago Press.

Prathikanti, S. (1997). East Indian American families. In E. Lee (Ed.), *Working with Asian Americans* (pp. 79–100). New York: Guilford Press.

Price, B. K., & McNeill, B. W. (1992). Cultural commitment and attitudes toward seeking counseling services in American Indian college students. *Professional Psychology: Research and Practice, 23*, 376–381.

Raj, A., & Silverman, J. G. (2002). Violence against immigrant women: The roles of culture, context, and legal immigrant status on intimate partner violence. *Violence Against Women, 8*, 367–398.

Ramos Lira, L., Koss, M. P., & Russo, N. F. (1999). Mexican American women's definitions of rape and sexual assault. *Hispanic Journal of Behavioral Sciences, 21*, 236–265.

Rao, K., DiClemente, R. J., & Ponton, L. E. (1992). Child sexual abuse of Asians compared with other populations. *Journal of the American Academy of Child and Adolescent Psychiatry, 31*, 880–886.

Rasche, C. E. (1988). Minority women and domestic violence: The unique dilemma of battered women of color. *Journal of Contemporary Criminal Justice, 4*, 150–171.

Ray, M. C., & Smith, E. (1991). Black women and homicide: An analysis of the subculture of violence thesis. *The Western Journal of Black Studies, 15*, 144–158.

Raymond, J. (2002). Building a statewide network of services for older abused women. *Nexus, 8*, 10–11.

Rennison, C. M. (2001a). *Intimate partner violence and age of victim, 1993–1999*. Retrieved February 3, 2003, from http://www.ojp.usdoj.gov/bjs/abstract/ipva99.htm

Rennison, C. M. (2001b). *Violence victimization and race, 1993–98*. Retrieved February 4, 2003, from http://www.ojp.usdoj.gov/bjs/abstract/vvr98.htm

Rennison, C. M. (2002). *Rape and sexual assault: Reporting to police and medical attention, 1992–2000*. Retrieved February 12, 2003, from http://www.ojp.usdoj.gov/bjs/abstract/rsarp00.htm

Rennison, C. M., & Welchans, S. (2000). *Intimate partner violence*. Retrieved February 12, 2003, from http://www.ojp.usdoj.gov/bjs/abstract/ipv.htm

Reppucci, N. D., & Haugaard, J. J. (1993). Problems with child sexual abuse prevention programs. In R. J. Gelles & D. R. Loseke (Eds.), *Current controversies on family violence* (pp. 306–322). Newbury Park, CA: Sage.

Richie, B. (1985). Battered Black women: A challenge for the Black community. *Black Scholar, 16*, 40–44.

Richie, B., & Kanuha, V. (1993). Battered women of color in public health care systems: Racism, sexism, and violence. In B. Blair & S. E. Cayleff (Eds.), *Wings of gauze: Women of color and the experience of health and illness* (pp. 288–299). Detroit, MI: Wayne State University Press.

Riger, S., Raja, S., & Camacho, J. (2002). The radiating impact of intimate partner violence. *Journal of Interpersonal Violence, 17*, 184–205.

Rimonte, N. (1989). Domestic violence among Pacific Asians. In Asian Women United of California (Ed.), *Making waves: An anthology of writings by and about Asian American women* (pp. 327–337). Boston: Beacon Press.

Rittman, M., Kuzmeskus, L. B., & Flum, M. A. (1999). A synthesis of current knowledge on minority elder abuse. In T. Tatara (Ed.), *Understanding elder abuse in minority populations* (pp. 221–238). Philadelphia: Brunner/Mazel.

Roberts, A. R. (1987). Psychosocial characteristics of batterers: A study of 234 men charged with domestic violence offenses. *Journal of Family Violence, 2*, 81–93.

Roberts, D. (2001). *Shattered bonds: The color of child welfare*. New York: Basic Books.

Robin, R. W., Chester, B., & Goldman, D. (1996). Cumulative trauma and PTSD in American Indian communities. In A. J. Marsella, M. J. Friedman, E. T. Gerrity, & R. M. Scurfield (Eds.), *Ethnocultural aspects of Posttraumatic Stress Disorder: Issues, research, and clinical applications* (pp. 239–253). Washington, DC: American Psychological Association.

Robin, R. W., Chester, B., & Rasmussen, J. K. (1998). Intimate violence in a southwestern American Indian tribal community. *Cultural Diversity and Mental Health, 4*, 335–344.

Robin, R. W., Chester, B., Rasmussen, J. K., Jaranson, J. M., & Goldman, D. (1997). Prevalence, characteristics, and impact of childhood sexual abuse in a southwestern American Indian tribe. *Child Abuse and Neglect, 21,* 769–787.

Robison, D. I., Bubb, J. L., Jr., Beach, G., Brown, D., & Sutton, C. (1998). Elder abuse prevention campaigns for special audiences: African American, Hispanic, and rural elderly. In Archstone Foundation (Ed.), *Understanding and combating elder abuse in minority communities: An exploration of the growing epidemic of elder abuse* (pp. 73-86). Long Beach, CA: Archstone Foundation.

Rodriguez, C. M., & Green, A. J. (1997). Parenting stress and anger expression as predictors of child abuse potential. *Child Abuse and Neglect, 21,* 367–377.

Rodriguez, M. A., Bauer, H. M., Flores-Ortiz, Y., & Szkupinski-Quiroga, S. (1998). Factors affecting patient-physician communication for abused Latina and Asian immigrant women. *The Journal of Family Practice, 47,* 309–311.

Rodriguez, M. A., McLoughlin, E., Nah, G., & Campbell, J. C. (2001). Mandatory reporting of domestic violence injuries to the police: What do emergency department patients think? *Journal of the American Medical Association, 286,* 580–583.

Romero, G. J., Wyatt, G. E., Loeb, T. B., Carmona, J. V., & Solis, B. M. (1999). The prevalence and circumstances of child sexual abuse among Latina women. *Hispanic Journal of Behavioral Sciences, 21,* 351–365.

Rooney, J., & Hanson, R. K. (2001). Predicting attrition from treatment programs for abusive men. *Journal of Family Violence, 16,* 131–149.

Roosa, M. W., Reinholtz, C., & Angelini, P. J. (1999). The relations of child sexual abuse and depression in young women: Comparisons across four ethnic groups. *Journal of Abnormal Child Psychology, 27,* 65–76.

Root, M. P. P. (1996). The psychology of Asian American women. In H. Landrine (Ed.), *Bringing cultural diversity to feminist psychology: Theory, research, and practice* (pp. 265-301). Washington, DC: American Psychological Association.

Rose, S. (1999). Reaching consensus on child neglect: African American mothers and child welfare workers. *Children and Youth Services Review, 21,* 463–479.

Rose, S., & Meezan, W. (1995). Child neglect: A study of the perceptions of mother and child welfare workers. *Children and Youth Services Review, 17,* 471–486.

Rosenthal, C. (2000). Latino practice outcome research: A review of the literature. *Smith College Studies in Social Work, 70,* 217–238.

Rosner, D., & Markowitz, G. (1997). Race, foster care, and the politics of abandonment in New York City. *American Journal of Public Health, 87,* 1844–1849.

Rouse, L. P. (1988). Abuse in dating relationships: A comparison of Blacks, Whites, and Hispanics. *Journal of College Student Development, 29,* 312–319.

Rueda, R., & Martinez, I. (1992). Fiesta Educativa: One community's approach to parent training in developmental disabilities. *Journal of Severe Handicaps, 17,* 95–103.

Ruggiero, K. J., McLeer, S. V., & Dixon, J. F. (2000). Sexual abuse characteristics associated with survivor psychopathology. *Child Abuse and Neglect, 24,* 951–964.

Runyan, D. K., & Gould, C. L. (1985). Foster care for child maltreatment: Impact on delinquent behavior. *Pediatrics, 75,* 562-568.

Runyan, D. K., Gould, C. L., Trost, D. C., & Loda, F. A. (1981). Determinants of foster care placement for the maltreated child. *American Journal of Public Health, 71,* 706–710.

Rural Policy Research Institute. (1999). *Rural by the numbers: Information about rural America. Demographics.* Retrieved December 15, 2001, from http://www.rupri.org/policyrcs/rnumbers/demopop/demo.html

Russell, D. E. (1986). *The secret trauma: Incest in the lives of girls and women.* New York: Basic Books.

Russell, D. E. (1990). *Rape in marriage.* Indianapolis: Indiana University Press.

Sabogal, F., Marin, B., & Otero-Sabogal, R. (1987). Hispanic familism and acculturation: What changes and what doesn't. *Hispanic Journal of Behavioral Sciences, 9,* 397–412.

Sacred Shawl Women's Society. (2002). *A sharing: Traditional Lakota thought and philosophy regarding domestic violence.* Pine Ridge, SD: Author.

Sales, P., & Murphy, S. (2000). Surviving violence: Pregnancy and drug use. *Journal of Drug Issues, 30*, 695–723.

Sanchez, C. D. (1992). Mental health issues: The elderly Hispanic. *Journal of Geriatric Psychiatry, 25*, 69–84.

Sanchez, Y. M. (1999). Elder mistreatment in Mexican American communities: The Nevada and Michigan experiences. In T. Tatara (Ed.), *Understanding elder abuse in minority populations* (pp. 67–77). Ann Arbor, MI: Taylor & Francis.

Sanders-Phillips, K. (1994). Correlates of healthy eating habits in low-income Black women and Latinas. *Preventive Medicine, 23*, 781–787.

Sanders-Phillips, K., Moisan, P., Wadlington, S., Morgan, S., & English, K. (1995). Ethnic differences in psychological functioning among Black and Latino sexually abused girls. *Child Abuse and Neglect, 19*, 691–706.

Saunders, B. E., Kilpatrick, D. G., Hanson, R. F., Resnick, H. S., & Walker, M. E. (1999). Prevalence, case characteristics, and long-term psychological correlates of child rape among women: A national survey. *Child Maltreatment, 4*, 187–200.

Saunders, D. G. (1986). When battered women use violence: Husband-abuse or self-defense? *Victims and Violence, 1*, 47–60.

Saunders, E. J., Nelson, K., & Landsman, M. J. (1993). Racial inequality and child neglect: Findings in a metropolitan area. *Child Welfare, 72*, 341–354.

Scannapieco, M. (1999). Kinship care in the public child welfare system: A systematic review of the research. In R. L. Hegar & M. Scannapieco (Eds), *Kinship foster care: Policy, practice, and research* (pp. 141–154). New York: Oxford University Press.

Schafer, J. R., & McIllwaine, B. D. (1992). Investigating child abuse in the American Indian community. *American Indian Quarterly, 16*, 157–167.

Scheper-Hughes, N. (1987). Introduction: The cultural politics of child survival. In N. Scheper-Hughes (Ed.), *Child survival* (pp. 1–32). Norwell, MA: Kluwer Academic.

Schiamberg, L. B., & Gans, D. (2000). Elder abuse by adult children: An applied ecological framework for understanding contextual risk factors and the intergenerational character of quality of life. *International Journal of Aging & Human Development, 50*, 329–335.

Schuck, A. M., & Widom, C. S. (2001). Childhood victimization and alcohol symptoms in females: Causal inferences and hypothesized mediators. *Child Abuse and Neglect, 25*, 1069–1092.

Schweitzer, M. M. (1983). The elders: Cultural dimensions of aging in two American Indian communities. In J. Sokolovsky (Ed.), *Growing old in different societies: Cross-cultural perspectives* (pp. 168–178). Belmont, CA: Wadsworth.

Scully, M., Kuoch, T., & Miller, R. A. (1995). Cambodians and sexual child abuse. In L. A. Fontes (Ed.), *Sexual abuse in nine North American cultures: Treatment and prevention* (pp. 97–127). Thousand Oaks, CA: Sage.

Sedlak, A. J., & Broadhurst, D. D. (1996). *Executive summary of the Third National Incidence Study of child abuse and neglect.* Retrieved January 14, 2003, from http://www.calib.com/ nccanch/pubs/statinfo/nis3.cfm#national

Segal, U. A. (2000). A pilot exploration of family violence among nonclinical Vietnamese. *Journal of Interpersonal Violence, 15*, 523–533.

Shaw, J. A., Lewis, J. E., Loeb, A., Rosado, J., & Rodriguez, R. A. (2001). A comparison of Hispanic and African-American sexually abused girls and their families. *Child Abuse and Neglect, 25*, 1363–1379.

Shepherd, J. (2001). Where do you go when it's 40 below? Domestic violence among rural Alaska Native women. *Affilia, 16*, 488–510.

Shinkwin, A. (1983). *Homes in disruption: Spouse abuse in Yupik Eskimo society.* Fairbanks: University of Alaska Press.

Shinn, M., Weltzman, B. C., Stojanovic, D., Knickman, J. R., Jimenez, L., Duchon, L., et al. (1998). Predictors of homelessness among families in New York City: From shelter request to housing stability. *American Journal of Public Health, 88*, 1651–1657.

Shomaker, D. (1990). Health care, cultural expectations, and frail elderly Navajo grandmothers. *Journal of Cross-Cultural Gerontology, 5*, 21–34.

Shore, N., Sim, K. E., Le Prohn, N. S., & Keller, T. E. (2002). Foster parent and teacher assessments of youth in kinship and non-kinship foster care placements: Are behaviors perceived differently across settings? *Children and Youth Services Review, 24,* 109–134.

Shorris, E. (1992). *Latinos: A biography of the people.* New York: Norton.

Siegel, J. M., Sorenson, S. B., Golding, J. M., Burnam, M. A., & Stein, J. A. (1987). The prevalence of childhood sexual assault: The Los Angeles epidemiologic catchment area project. *American Journal of Epidemiology, 126,* 1141–1153.

Simonelli, C. J., & Ingram, K. M. (1998). Psychological distress among men experiencing physical and emotional abuse in heterosexual dating relationships. *Journal of Interpersonal Violence, 13,* 667–681.

Simoneti, S., Scott, E. C., & Murphy, C. M. (2000). Dissociative experiences in partner-assaultive men. *Journal of Interpersonal Violence, 15,* 1262–1283.

Singelis, T. M., Triandis, H. C., Bhawuk, D. P. S., & Gelfand, M. J. (1995). Horizontal and vertical dimensions of individualism and collectivism: A theoretical and measurement refinement. *Cross-Cultural Research, 29,* 240–275.

Smith, J. C., Rudolph, C., & Swords, P. (2002). Kinship care: Issues in permanency planning. *Children and Youth Services Review, 24,* 175–188.

Smith, P. B., & Bond, M. H. (1994). *Social psychology across cultures: Analysis and perspectives.* Boston: Allyn & Bacon.

Song, Y. I. (1996). *Battered women in Korean immigrant families: The silent scream.* New York: Garland.

Song-Kim, Y. I. (1992). Battered Korean women in the United States. In S. M. Furuto, R. Biswas, D. K. Chung, K. Murase, & R. Ross-Sheriff (Eds.), *Social work practice with Asian Americans* (pp. 202–212). Newbury Park, CA: Sage.

Sorenson, S. B. (1996). Violence against women: Examining ethnic differences and commonalities. *Evaluation Review, 20,* 123–145.

Sorenson, S. B., & Golding, J. M. (1988). Suicide attempts in Mexican Americans: Prevention implications of immigration and cultural issues. *Suicide and Life Threatening Behavior, 18,* 322–333.

Sorenson, S. B., & Peterson, J. G. (1994). Traumatic child death and documented maltreatment history, Los Angeles. *American Journal of Public Health, 84,* 623–627.

Sorenson, S. B., & Telles, C. A. (1991). Self-reports of spousal violence in a Mexican-American and Non-Hispanic White population. *Violence and Victims, 6,* 3–15.

Spearly, J. L., & Lauderdale, M. (1983). Community characteristics and ethnicity in the prediction of child maltreatment rates. *Child Abuse and Neglect, 7,* 91–105.

Stacey, W. A., Hazlewood, L. R., & Shupe, A. (1994). *The violent couple.* Westport, CT: Praeger.

Staples, R., & Mirande, A. (1980). Racial and cultural variations among American families: A decennial review of the literature on minority families. *Journal of Marriage and the Family, 42,* 887–903.

Stapp, J., Tucker, A. M., & VandenBos, G. R. (1985). Census of psychological personnel: 1983. *American Psychologist, 40,* 1317–1351.

Stein, J. A., Golding, J. M., Siegel, J. M., Burnam, M. A., & Sorenson, S. B. (1988). Long-term psychological sequelae of child sexual abuse: The Los Angeles epidemiologic catchment area study. In G. E. Wyatt & G. J. Powell (Eds.), *Lasting effects of child sexual abuse* (pp. 135–154). Newbury Park, CA: Sage.

Stein, J. A., Leslie, M. B., & Nyamathi, A. (2002). Relative contributions of parent substance use and childhood maltreatment to chronic homelessness, depression, and substance abuse problems among homeless women: Mediating roles of self-esteem and abuse in adulthood. *Child Abuse and Neglect, 26,* 1011–1027.

Steinmetz, S. K. (1977). Wifebeating, husbandbeating—A comparison of the use of physical violence between spouses to resolve marital fights. In M. Roy (Ed.), *Battered women: A psychosociological study of domestic violence* (pp. 63–72). New York: Van Nostrand Reinhold.

Steinmetz, S. K. (1978). Battered parents. *Society, 15,* 54–55.

Steinmetz, S. K. (1988). *Duty bound: Elder abuse and family care.* Newbury Park, CA: Sage.

Steinmetz, S. K. (1993). The abused elderly are dependent: Abuse is caused by the perception of stress associated with providing care. In R. J. Gelles & D. R. Loseke (Eds.), *Current controversies on family violence* (pp. 222–236). Newbury Park, CA: Sage.

Sternberg, R. J. (1985). Implicit theories of intelligence, creativity, and wisdom. *Journal of Personality and Social Psychology, 49,* 607–627.

Sternberg, R. J. (1998). A balance theory of wisdom. *Review of General Psychology, 2,* 347–365.

Stets, J. E. (1990). Verbal and physical aggression in marriage. *Journal of Marriage and the Family, 52,* 501–514.

Stevens, E. (1973). Machismo and marianismo. *Transaction-Society, 10,* 57–63.

Stevenson, H. C., & Renard, G. (1993). Trusting ole' wise owls: Therapeutic use of cultural strengths in African-American families. *Professional Psychology: Research and Practice, 24,* 433–442.

Stevenson, T., & Love, C. (1999). *Herstory of domestic violence: A timeline of the battered women's movement.* Sacramento, CA: SafeNETWORK.

Stith, S. M., Rosen, K. H., & McCollum, E. E. (2002). Developing a manualized couples treatment for domestic violence: Overcoming challenges. *Journal of Marital and Family Therapy, 28,* 21–25.

Stolley, K. S., & Szinovacz, M. (1997). Caregiving responsibilities and child spanking. *Journal of Family Violence, 12,* 99–112.

Straus, M. A. (1979). Measuring intrafamily conflict and violence: The Conflict Tactics (CT) Scales. *Journal of Marriage and the Family, 41,* 465–499.

Straus, M. A. (1980a). Stress and physical child abuse. *Child Abuse and Neglect, 4,* 75–88.

Straus, M. A. (1980b). Wife-beating: How common and why? In M. A. Straus & G. T. Hotaling (Eds.), *The social causes of husband-wife violence.* Minneapolis: University of Minnesota Press.

Straus, M. A. (1990). The Conflict Tactic Scales and its critics: An evaluation and new data on validity and reliability. In M. A. Straus & R. J. Gelles (Eds.), *Physical violence in American families: Risk factors and adaptations to violence in 8,145 families* (pp. 49–73). New Brunswick, NJ: Transaction Books.

Straus, M. A. (1994). *Corporal punishment of children and crime in ethnic group context.* Retrieved February 13, 2003, from http://pubpages.unh.edu/~mas2/CP10.pdf

Straus, M. A. (1996). Spanking and the making of a violent society. *Pediatrics, 98,* 837–842.

Straus, M. A. (2000). Corporal punishment by parents: The cradle of violence in the family and society. *The Virginia Journal of Social Policy and the Law, 8,* 7–60.

Straus, M. A., & Donnelly, D. (2001). *Beating the devil out of them: Corporal punishment and its effects on children.* Boston: Lexington Books.

Straus, M. A., & Gelles, R. J. (1986). Societal change and change in family violence from 1975 to 1985 as revealed by two national surveys. *Journal of Marriage and the Family, 48,* 465–479.

Straus, M. A., & Gelles, R. J. (1988). How violent are American families? Estimates from the national family violence resurvey and other studies. In G. T. Hotaling, D. Finkelhor, J. T. Kirkpatrick, & M. A. Straus (Eds.), *Family abuse and its consequences: New directions in research* (pp. 14–36). Beverly Hills, CA: Sage.

Straus, M. A., & Gelles, R. J. (1990). How violent are American families? Estimates from the National Family Violence Resurvey and other studies. In M. A. Straus & R. J. Gelles (Eds.), *Physical violence in American families: Risk factors and adaptations to violence in 8,145 families* (pp. 95–112). New Brunswick, NJ: Transaction Books.

Straus, M. A., Gelles, R. J., & Steinmetz, S. (1980). *Behind closed doors: Violence in the American family.* Garden City, NY: Anchor.

Straus, M. A., Hamby, S. L., Boney-McCoy, S., & Sugarman, D. B. (1996). The revised Conflict Tactics Scales (CTS2): Development and preliminary psychometric data. *Journal of Family Issues, 17,* 283–316.

Straus, M. A., Hamby, S. L., Finkelhor, D., Moore, D. W., & Runyan, D. (1998). Identification of child maltreatment with the Parent-Child Conflict Tactics Scales: Development and psychometric data for a national sample of American parents. *Child Abuse and Neglect, 22,* 249–270.

Straus, M. A., Kaufman Kantor, G., & Moore, D. W. (1997). Change in cultural norms approving marital violence from 1968 to 1994. In G. Kaufman Kantor & J. L. Jasinski (Eds.), *Out of darkness: Contemporary perspectives on family violence* (pp. 3–16). Thousand Oaks, CA: Sage.

Straus, M. A., & Smith, C. (1990a). Family patterns and child abuse. In M. A. Straus & R. J. Gelles (Eds.), *Physical violence in American families: Risk factors and adaptations to violence in 8,145 families* (pp. 245–262). New Brunswick, NJ: Transaction Books.

Straus, M. A., & Smith, C. (1990b). Violence in Hispanic families in the United States: Incidence rates and structural interpretations. In M. A. Straus & R. J. Gelles (Eds.), *Physical violence in American families: Risk factors and adaptations to violence in 8,145 families* (pp. 305–313). New Brunswick, NJ: Transaction Books.

Straus, M. A., & Stewart, J. H. (1999). Corporal punishment by American parents: National data on prevalence, chronicity, severity, and duration, in relation to child and family characteristics. *Clinical Child and Family Psychology Review, 2,* 55–70

Straus, M. A., & Sweet, S. (1992). Verbal symbolic aggression in couples: Incidence rates and relationships to personal characteristics. *Journal of Marriage and the Family, 54,* 346–367.

Strube, M. J. (1988). The decision to leave an abusive relationship: Empirical evidence and theoretical issues. *Psychological Bulletin, 104,* 236–250.

Strube, M. J., & Barbour, L. S. (1984). Factors related to the decision to leave an abusive relationship. *Journal of Marriage and the Family, 46,* 837–844.

Suarez-Al-Adam, M., Raffaelli, M., & O'Leary, A. (2000). Influence of abuse and partner hypermasculinity on the sexual behavior of Latinas. *AIDS Education and Prevention, 12,* 263–274.

Suarez-Orozco, C., & Suarez-Orozco, M. M. (1995). *Transformations: Immigration, family life, and achievement motivation among Latino adolescents.* Stanford, CA: Stanford University Press.

Sudarkasa, N. (1993). Female-headed African American households: Some neglected dimensions. In H. P. McAdoo (Ed.), *Family ethnicity: Strength in diversity.* Newbury Park, CA: Sage.

Sue, S., Fujino, D. C., Hu, L. T., Takeuchi, D. T., & Zane, N. W. (1991). Community mental health services for ethnic minority groups: A test of the cultural responsiveness hypothesis. *Journal of Consulting and Clinical Psychology, 59,* 533–540.

Sugarman, D. B., & Frankel, S. L. (1996). Patriarchal ideology and wife-assault: A meta-analytic review. *Journal of Family Violence, 1,* 13–35.

Sugarman, D. B., & Hotaling, G. T. (1989). Dating violence: Prevalence, context and risk markers. In M. A. Pirog-Good & J. E. Stets (Eds.), *Violence in dating relationships: Emerging social issues* (pp. 3–32). New York: Praeger.

Sullivan, C. M., Parisian, J. A., & Davidson, W. S. (1991). *Index of Psychological Abuse: Development of a measure.* Presented at the 99th annual convention of the American Psychological Association, San Francisco.

Sullivan, C. M., & Rumptz, M. H. (1994). Adjustment and needs of African-American women who utilized a domestic violence shelter. *Violence and Victims, 9,* 275–286.

Sullivan, C. M., Tan, C., Basta, J., Rumptz, M., & Davidson, W. S. (1992). An advocacy intervention program for women with abusive partners: Initial evaluation. *American Journal of Community Psychology, 20,* 309–332.

Sustento-Sereniches, J. (1997). Filipino American families. In E. Lee (Ed.), *Working with Asian Americans* (pp. 101–113). New York: Guilford.

Takeuchi, D. T., Sue, S., & Yeh, M. (1995). Return rates and outcomes from ethnicity-specific mental health programs in Los Angeles. *American Journal of Public Health, 85,* 638–643.

Tang, C. S. (1997). Psychological impact of wife abuse: Experiences of Chinese women and their children. *Journal of Interpersonal Violence, 12,* 466–478.

Taussig, H. N., & Talmi, A. (2001). Ethnic differences in risk behaviors and related psychosocial variables among a cohort of maltreated adolescents in foster care. *Child Maltreatment, 6,* 180–192.

Taylor, J. Y. (2000). Sisters of the yam: African American women's healing and self-recovery from intimate male partner violence. *Issues in Mental Health Nursing, 21,* 515–531.

Taylor, M. C., & Hammond, P. V. (1987). See how they run: Women in a domestic violence center in the Old Dominion. In R. L. Hampton (Ed.), *Violence in the Black family: Correlates and consequences* (pp. 107–119). Lexington, MA: Lexington Books.

Telles, C., Karno, M., Mintz, J., Paz, G., Arias, M., Tucker, D., et al. (1995). Immigrant families coping with schizophrenia: Behavioural Family Intervention versus case management with a low-income Spanish-speaking population. *British Journal of Psychiatry, 167,* 473–479.

Thomas, E. K. (2000). Domestic violence in the African-American and Asian-American communities: A comparative analysis of two racial minority cultures and implications for mental health service provision for women of color. *Psychology: A Journal of Human Behavior, 37,* 32–43.

Tjaden, P., & Thoennes, N. (2000). *Extent, nature, and consequences of intimate partner violence: Findings from the National Violence Against Women Survey.* Retrieved January 10, 2003, from http://www.ojp.usdoj.gov/nij/victdoc.htm#2000

Tolman, R. M. (1989). The development of a measure of psychological maltreatment of women by their male partners. *Violence and Victims, 4,* 159–178.

Tomita, S. K. (1994). The consideration of cultural factors in the research on elder mistreatment with an in-depth look at the Japanese. *Journal of Cross-Cultural Gerontology, 9,* 39–52.

Tomita, S. K. (2000). Elder mistreatment: Practice modifications to accommodate cultural differences. *Journal of Multicultural Social Work, 8,* 305–326.

Tong, B. R. (1998). Asian-American domestic violence: A critical psychohistorical perspective. In R. Carillo & J. Tello (Eds.), *Family violence and men of color.* New York: Springer.

Torres, S. (1986). *A comparative analysis of wife abuse among Anglo-American and Mexican-American battered women: Attitudes, nature, severity, frequency, and response to the abuse.* Unpublished doctoral dissertation, University of Texas, Austin.

Torres, S. (1987). Hispanic-American battered women: Why consider cultural differences? *Response to the Victimization of Women and Children, 10,* 20–21.

Torres, S. (1991). A comparison of wife abuse between two cultures: Perceptions, attitudes, nature, and extent. *Issues in Mental Health Nursing, 12,* 113–131.

Torres, S., Campbell, J., Campbell, D. W., Ryan, J., King, C., Price, P., et al. (2000). Abuse during and before pregnancy: Prevalence and cultural correlates. *Violence and Victims, 15,* 303–321.

Tran, C. G. (1997). *A cultural analysis and model for understanding domestic violence among Vietnamese women.* Unpublished doctoral dissertation, Boston University.

Tran, C. G., & Des Jardins, K. (2000). Domestic violence in Vietnamese refugee and Korean immigrant communities. In J. L. Chin (Ed.), *Relationship among Asian American women: Psychology of women* (pp. 71–96). Washington, DC: American Psychological Association.

Tribal Court Clearinghouse. (2001). *Domestic violence.* Retrieved September 16, 2001, from http://www.tribal-institute.org/lists/domestic.htm

Trimble, J. E., & Hayes, S. (1984). Mental health interventions in the psychosocial contexts of American Indian communities. In W. O'Connor & B. Lubin (Eds.), *Ecological models: Ecological approaches to clinical and community mental health* (pp. 293–321). New York: Wiley.

Trimble, J. E., & Thurman, P. J. (2002). Ethnocultural considerations and strategies for providing counseling services to Native American Indians. In P. B. Pedersen, J. G. Draguns, W. J. Lonner, & J. E. Trimble (Eds.), *Counseling across cultures* (5th ed., pp. 53–91). Thousand Oaks, CA: Sage.

Tzeng, O., & Schwarzin, H. (1990). Gender and race differences in child sexual abuse correlates. *International Journal of Intercultural Relations, 14,* 35–161.

Ucko, L. G. (1994). Culture and violence: The interaction of Africa and America. *Sex Roles, 31,* 185–204.

Ullman, S. E., & Siegel, J. M. (1993). Victim-offender relationship and sexual assault. *Violence and Victims, 8,* 121–134.

United Nations. (1990). *United Nations Convention on the Rights of the Child.* Retrieved August 28, 2002, from http://www.unhchr.ch/html/menu3/b/k2crc.htm

Urquiza, A. J., & Goodlin-Jones, B. L. (1994). Child sexual abuse and adult revictimization with women of color. *Violence and Victims, 9,* 223–232.

U.S. Bureau of the Census. (1993). *We, the first Americans.* Retrieved December 15, 2001, from http://minneapolisfed.org/pubs/cd/98-sum/WeFirst.html

U.S. Bureau of the Census. (1999). *Statistical abstract of the United States: The national data book.* Washington, DC: Author.

U.S. Bureau of the Census. (2001a). *The American Indian and Alaska Native population: 2000*. Retrieved January 27, 2003, from http://www.census.gov/population/www/cen2000/briefs.html

U.S. Bureau of the Census. (2001b). *The Hispanic population, Census 2000 brief*. Retrieved January 31, 2003, from http://www.census.gov/population/www/cen2000/briefs.html

U.S. Bureau of the Census. (2002). *The Asian population: 2000*. Retrieved January 2003 from http://www.census.gov/population/www/cen2000/briefs.html

U.S. Department of Education. (1982). *A study of alternative definitions and measures relating to eligibility and service under Part A of the Indian Education Act*. Unpublished report.

U.S. Department of Health and Human Services. (1999). *10 years of reporting child maltreament*. Washington, DC: Administration for Children and Families, Administration on Children, Youth, and Families Children's Bureau.

U.S. Department of Health and Human Services. (2000). *Summary of key findings from calendar year 2000*. Retrieved July 9, 2002, from http://www.calib.com/nccanch/prevmnth/scope/ncands.cfm

U.S. Department of Health and Human Services. (2001). *Mental health: Culture, race, and ethnicity—A supplement to mental health: A report to the surgeon general*. Retrieved January 28, 2003, from http://www.mentalhealth.org/cre/toc.asp

U.S. Department of Health and Human Services, Administration on Children, Youth, and Families. (1999). *Child maltreatment 1999*. Retrieved January 14, 2003, from http://www.acf.dhhs.gov/programs/cb/publications/cm99/index.htm

U.S. Department of Health and Human Services, Administration on Children, Youth, and Families. (2002). *Child maltreatment 2000*. Retrieved November 20, 2002, from http://www.acf.dhhs.gov/programs/cb/publications/cm00/index.htm

U.S. Office of Technology Assessment. (1986). *Indian health care* (Tech. Rep. OTA-H-290). Washington, DC: Government Printing Office.

U.S. Senate Hearing 100-981. (1988). *The American Indian elderly: The forgotten population*. Hearing before the Special Committee on Aging, United States Senate, 100-98, Pine Ridge, South Dakota, July 21, Serial No. 100-25.

Utsey, S. O., Bolden, M. A., & Brown, A. L. (2001). Visions of revolution from the spirit of Frantz Fanon: A psychology of liberation for counseling African Americans confronting societal racism and oppression. In J. B. Ponterotto, J. M. Casas, L. A. Suzuki, & C. M. Alexander (Eds.), *Handbook of multicultural counseling* (2nd ed., pp. 311–336). Thousand Oaks, CA: Sage.

Van Hightower, N. R., & Gorton, J. (1998). Domestic violence among patients at two rural health care clinics: Prevalence and social correlates. *Public Health Nursing, 15*, 355–362.

Van Hightower, N. R., Gorton, J., & DeMoss, C. L. (2000). Predictive models of domestic violence and fear of intimate partners among migrant and seasonal farm worker women. *Journal of Family Violence, 15*, 137–154.

Vasquez, M. J. (1998). Latinos and violence: Mental health implications and strategies for clinicians. *Cultural Diversity and Mental Health, 4*, 319–334.

Vazquez, C. I., & Rosa, D. (1999). An understanding of abuse in the Hispanic older person: Assessment, treatment, and prevention. *Journal of Social Distress and the Homeless, 8*, 193–206.

Verlarde-Castillo, A. R. (1992). *Spouse abuse among Hopi women*. Unpublished manuscript.

Verlinden, S., Hersen, M., & Thomas, J. (2000). Risk factors in school shootings. *Clinical Psychology Review, 20*, 3–56.

Vernon, I. S., & Bubar, R. (2001, Spring). Child sexual abuse and HIV/AIDS in Indian country. *Wicazo SA Review, 14*, 47–63.

Violence Policy Center. (2001). *When men murder women: An analysis of 1999 homicide data*. Retrieved September 29, 2002, from http://www.vpc.org/studies/dv4three.htm

Vissing, Y. M., Straus, M. A., Gelles, R. J., & Harrop, J. W. (1991). Verbal aggression by parents and psychosocial problems of children. *Child Abuse and Neglect, 15*, 223–238.

Wah, L. M. (1998). Asian men and violence. In R. Carillo & J. Tello (Eds.), *Family violence and men of color: Healing the wounded male spirit* (pp. 128–146). New York: Springer.

Walker, L. E. A. (1979). *The battered woman*. New York: Harper & Row.

Walker, L. E. A. (1983). Victimology and the psychological perspectives of battered women. *Victimology, 8*, 82–104.

Walker, L. E. A. (1995). Racism and violence against women. In J. Adelman & G. Enguidanos (Eds.), *Racism in the lives of women: Testimony, theory, and guides to antiracist practice* (pp. 239-250). Binghamton, NY: Haworth Press.

Walker, L. E. A. (1999). Psychology and domestic violence around the world. *American Psychologist, 54*, 21–29.

Walker, L. E. A. (2000). *The battered woman syndrome* (2nd ed.). New York: Springer.

Wallace, H. (2002). *Family violence: Legal, medical, and social perspectives* (3rd ed.). Boston: Allyn & Bacon.

Wallach, V. A., & Lister, L. (1995). Stages in the delivery of home-based services to parents at risk of child abuse: A Healthy Start experience. *Scholarly Inquiry for Nursing Practice: An International Journal, 9*, 159–173.

Wares, D. M., Wedel, K. R., Rosenthal, J. A., & Dobrec, A. (1994). Indian child welfare: A multicultural challenge. *Journal of Multicultural Social Work, 3*, 1–15.

Warrier, S. (2000). *(Un)heard voices: Domestic violence in the Asian American community*. San Francisco: Family Violence Prevention Fund.

Warters, B. (1989, Winter). Native American men and domestic violence. *Ending Men's Violence Newsletter*. Retrieved on September 17, 2001, from http://www.mincava.umn.edu/ documents/warters/wartersi.shtml

Waters, J., Robert, A. R., & Morgen, K. (1997). High risk pregnancies: Teenagers, poverty, and drug abuse. *Journal of Drug Issues, 27*, 541–562.

Watkins, B., & Bentovim, A. (1992). The sexual abuse of male children and adolescents: A review of the current research. *Journal of Child Psychology & Psychiatry, 33*, 197–248.

Wauchope, B. A., & Straus, M. A. (1990). Physical punishment and physical abuse of American children: Incidence rates by age, gender, and occupational class. In M. A. Straus & R. J. Gelles (Eds.), *Physical violence in American families: Risk factors and adaptations to violence in 8,145 families* (pp. 133–150). New Brunswick, NJ: Transaction Books.

Weibel-Orlando, J. (1990). Grandparenting styles: Native American perspectives. In J. Sokolovsky (Ed.), *The cultural context of aging: Worldwide perspectives* (pp. 109–125). New York: Bergin & Garvey.

Weinbaum, Z., Stratton, T. L., Chavez, G., Motylewski-Link, C., Barrera, N., & Courtney, J. G. (2001). Female victims of intimate partner physical domestic violence (IPP-DV), California 1998. *American Journal of Preventive Medicine, 21*, 313–319.

Weis, L., Centrie, C., Valentin-Juarbe, J., & Fine, M. (2002). Puerto Rican men and the struggle for place in the United States: An exploration of cultural citizenship, gender, and violence. *Men and Masculinities, 4*, 286–302.

Weiss, R. P. (2001). Charitable choice as neoliberal social welfare strategy. *Social Justice, 28*, 1–21.

West, C. M. (2003). *Violence in the lives of Black women: Battered, black, and blue*. Binghamton, NY: Haworth Press.

West, C. M., Kaufman Kantor, G., & Jasinski, J. L. (1998). Sociodemographic predictors and cultural barriers to help-seeking behavior by Latina and Anglo American battered women. *Violence and Victims, 13*, 361–375.

White, E. C. (1986). Life is a song worth singing: Ending violence in the Black family. In M. C. Burns (Ed.), *The speaking profits us: Violence in the lives of women of color*. Seattle, WA: Center for the Prevention of Sexual and Domestic Violence.

White, E. C. (1995). *Chain, chain, change: For Black women in abusive relationships*. Seattle, WA: Seal Press.

White, R. (1977). *Navajo child abuse and neglect study*. Baltimore: Johns Hopkins University, Department of Maternal and Child Health.

White, R., & Cornely, D. (1981). Navajo child abuse and neglect study. *Child Abuse and Neglect, 2*, 9–17.

Whiteman, M., Fanshel, D., & Grundy, J. F. (1987). Cognitive-behavioral interventions aimed at anger of parents at risk of child abuse. *Social Work, 32*, 469–474.

Whittaker, J., Kinney, J., Tracy, E. M., & Booth, C. (1990). *Reaching high-risk families: Intensive family preservation in human services*. New York: Aldine.

Wichlacz, C., Lane, J., & Kempe, C. (1978). Indian child welfare: A community team approach to protective services. *Child Abuse and Neglect, 2*, 29–35.

Wichlacz, C., & Wechsler, J. G. (1983). American Indian law on child abuse and neglect. *Child Abuse and Neglect, 7*, 347–350.

Widom, C. S. (1989). The cycle of violence. *Science, 244*, 160–166.

Wiist, W. H., & McFarlane, J. (1998). Severity of spousal and intimate partner abuse to pregnant Hispanic women. *Journal of Health Care for the Poor and Underserved, 9*, 248–261.

Willett, J. B., Ayoub, C. C., & Robinson, D. (1991). Using growth modeling to examine systematic differences in growth: An example of change in the functioning of families at risk of maladaptive parenting, child abuse, or neglect. *Journal of Consulting and Clinical Psychology, 59*, 38–47.

Williams, O. J. (1992). Ethnically sensitive practice to enhance treatment participation of African American men who batter. *Families in Society, 73*, 588–595.

Williams, O. J., & Becker, R. L. (1994). Domestic partner abuse treatment programs and cultural competence: The results of a national survey. *Violence and Victims, 9*, 287–296.

Williams, O. J., & Griffin, L. W. (1996). Elderly maltreatment and cultural diversity: When laws are not enough. *Journal of Multicultural Social Work, 4*, 1–13.

Willson, P., McFarlane, J., Malecha, A., Watson, K., Lemmey, D., Schultz, P., et al. (2000). Severity of violence against women by intimate partners and associated use of alcohol and/or illicit drugs by the perpetrator. *Journal of Interpersonal Violence, 15*, 996–1008.

Wohl, J. (1989). Integration of cultural awareness into psychotherapy. *American Journal of Psychotherapy, 43*, 343–355.

Wolf, R. S., Strugnell, C. P., & Godkin, M. A. (1982). *Preliminary findings from three model projects on elder abuse*. Worcester: University of Massachusetts Medical Center, University Center on Aging.

Wolfner, G. D., & Gelles, R. J. (1993). A profile of violence toward children: A national study. *Child Abuse and Neglect, 17*, 197–212.

Wolk, L. E. (1982). *Minnesota's American Indian battered women: The cycle of oppression; a cultural awareness training manual for non-Indian professionals*. St. Paul, MN: St. Paul Indian Center.

W.O.M.A.N. Inc. (2002). *Latina and bicultural services*. Retrieved February 24, 2002, from http://dvp.best.vwh.net/womaninc/latina.html

Wood, J. M. (1997). Risk predictors for re-abuse or re-neglect in a predominantly Hispanic population. *Child Abuse and Neglect, 21*, 379–389.

Wood, W., Wong, F. Y., & Chachere, J. G. (1991). Effects of media violence on viewers' aggression in unconstrained social interaction. *Psychological Bulletin, 109*, 371–383.

Wyatt, G. E. (1985). The sexual abuse of Afro-American and White-American women in childhood. *Child Abuse and Neglect, 9*, 507–519.

Wyatt, G. E., Axelrod, J., Chin, D., Carmona, T. B., & Loeb, G. E. (2000). Examining patterns of vulnerability to domestic violence among African American women. *Violence Against Women, 6*, 495–514.

Wyatt, G. E., Loeb, T. B., Solis, B., & Carmona, J. B. (1999). The prevalence and circumstances of child sexual abuse: Changes across a decade. *Child Abuse and Neglect, 23*, 45–60.

Wyatt, G. E., & Riederle, M. (1994). Sexual harassment and prior sexual trauma among African-American and White American women. *Violence and Victims, 9*, 233–247.

Wyatt, G. E., Strayer, R., & Lobitz, W. C. (1976). Issues in treatment of sexually dysfunctioning couples of Afro-American descent. *Psychotherapy, Theory, Research and Practice, 13*, 44–50.

Yates, A. (1987). Current status and future directions of research on the American Indian child. *American Journal of Psychiatry, 144*, 1135–1142.

Yax, L. K. (2000). *Racial and ethnic classifications used in Census 2000 and beyond* (U.S. Census Bureau). Retrieved May 30, 2002, from http://www.census.gov/population/www/socdemo/race/racefactcb.html

Yick, A. (2000). Domestic violence beliefs and attitudes in the Chinese American community. *Journal of Social Service Research, 27*, 29–47.

Yick, A., & Agbayani-Siewert, P. (1997). Perceptions of domestic violence in a Chinese-American community. *Journal of Interpersonal Violence, 12*, 832–846.

Yllo, K. A., & Straus, M. A. (1990). Patriarchy and violence against wives: The impact of structural and normative factors. In M. A. Straus & R. J. Gelles (Eds.), *Physical violence in American families* (pp. 383–399). New Brunswick, NJ: Transaction Books.

Yololink. (2002). *Wallace and Vannucci Shelter: Sexual assault and domestic violence center.* Retrieved February 22, 2002, from http://www.dcn.davis.ca.us/yololink/programs/pWallacVannucShelte-7288.html

Yoshihama, M. (1999). Domestic violence against women of Japanese descent in Los Angeles: Two methods of estimating prevalence. *Violence Against Women, 5*, 869–897.

Yoshihama, M. (2000). Reinterpreting strength and safety in socio-cultural context: Dynamics of domestic violence and experiences of women of Japanese descent. *Journal of Human Behavior in the Social Environment, 3*, 201–224.

Yoshihama, M., & Horrocks, J. (2002). Posttraumatic stress symptoms and victimization among Japanese American women. *Journal of Consulting and Clinical Psychology, 70*, 205–215.

Yoshioka, M. R., Dang, Q., Shewmangal, N., Chan, C., & Tan, C. I. (2000). *Asian family violence report.* Prepared for the Asian Task Force Against Domestic Violence, Inc. Retrieved December 15, 2002, from http://www.atask.org

Yoshioka, M. R., DiNoia, J., & Ullah, K. (2001). Attitudes toward marital violence: An examination of four Asian communities. *Violence Against Women, 7*, 900–926.

Zambrano, M. M. (1985). *Mejor sola que mal acompanada: For the Latina in an abusive relationship.* Seattle, WA: Seal Press.

Zayas, L. H., & Palleja, J. (1988). Puerto Rican familism: Implications for family therapy. *Family Relations, 37*, 260–264.

Zea, M. C., Diehl, V. A., & Porterfield, K. S. (1997). Central American youth exposed to war violence. In J. G. Garcia & M. C. Zea (Eds.), *Psychological interventions and research with Latino populations* (pp. 39–55). Boston: Allyn & Bacon.

Zellman, G. L. (1992). The impact of case characteristics on child abuse reporting decisions. *Child Abuse and Neglect, 16*, 57–74.

Zellman, G. L., & Fair, C. C. (2002). Preventing and reporting abuse. In J.E.B. Myers, L. Berliner, J. Briere, C. T. Hendrix, C. Jenny, & T. A. Reid (Eds.), *The APSAC handbook on child maltreatment* (2nd ed., pp. 449–478). Thousand Oaks, CA: Sage.

Zlotnick, C., Kohn, R., Peterson, J., & Pearlstein, T. (1998). Partner physical violence in a national sample of American families: Relationship to psychological functioning, psychosocial factors, and gender. *Journal of Interpersonal Violence, 13*, 156–166.

Zuniga, M. E. (1992). Families with Latino roots. In E. Lynch & M. Hanson (Eds.), *Developing cross cultural competence.* Baltimore: Paul H. Brookes.

Zuravin, S. J., & Starr, R. H., Jr. (1991). Psychosocial characteristics of mothers of physically abused and neglected children: Do they differ by ethnicity? In R. Hampton (Ed.), *Black family violence: Current research and theory* (pp. 35–71). Lexington, MA: Lexington Books.

AUTHOR INDEX

SUBJECT INDEX

Abuse, 4-5
  criteria, 6
  implicit theories of, 8-11
  multicultural society and, 12-13
  perpetrator dependency and, 20
  reporting laws, 9-10
  socioeconomic status and, 12
  terroristic abuse, 48
  See also Maltreatment; Research approaches;
    Theoretical framework
Acculturation, 159-161, 166-167
Adoption Assistance and Child Welfare Act
  of 1980, 222
Adoption and Safe Families Act, 222
Adult maltreatment:
  adult dependent children, elder
    maltreatment by, 55
  caregiving relatives, elder maltreatment by, 55
  elder maltreatment, 53-55, 89-90
  husband abuse, 51-53, 52 (box), 88-89
  Native American experience, 60-61, 64, 66,
    67, 84-90
  spousal elder maltreatment, 54-55
  spousal maltreatment, 40, 48-53, 84, 87-89
  United States, incidence studies, 40-55,
    41-47 (table)
  wife emotional abuse, 48-49
  wife physical abuse, 40, 48, 84, 87-88
  wife sexual abuse, 49-51, 50 (box), 88
Adult maltreatment prevention/intervention, 236
  African Americans and, 240, 242, 246, 248-249
  Asian Americans and, 241-242, 246, 249-250
  battered women's shelters, 238-239, 243
  church organizations and, 250
  couples therapy, 243-244
  elder maltreatment, 247-251
  exosystem efforts, 238-243, 248-250
  feminist philosophy and, 241-242
  Hispanics/Latinos and, 240, 243, 246, 249
  immigrant issues, 238

  individual-level efforts, 244-247, 250-251
  macrosystem efforts, 236-238, 247-248
  male batterers, programs for, 244-246
  male victims of abuse, 247
  microsystem efforts, 243-244
  minority communities, prevention program
    specificity, 239-240, 242-243
  Native Americans and, 237, 242, 246
  outreach efforts, 248-250
  problems with, 237, 238, 240-243
  racism, service delivery and, 240
  services, utilization barriers, 237-238, 249-250
  spouse maltreatment, 236-247
Adult protective services (APS), 11, 28, 53, 54,
  141, 154, 189
African American child maltreatment, 109,
  111-117 (table)
  community services, 230-231
  consequences of, 124-125
  exosystem factors in, 122-123
  individual characteristics and, 123-124
  macrosystem factors in, 121-122
  microsystem factors in, 123
  neglect, 119, 123, 124-125, 126 (box)
  physical maltreatment/corporal punishment,
    110, 118-119
  predictors/correlates of, 121-124
  reporting issues in, 109-110, 118-121
  sexual abuse, 119-120, 121 (box), 123, 125
African American cultural contexts, 97-98
  child maltreatment, 98-100, 99 (box)
  child neglect, 101
  child-rearing, elder role in, 105
  child sexual abuse, 101
  cultural value systems, 104-106
  elder maltreatment, 102
  family/kinship systems, 104-105
  immigration histories, 103
  oppression/racism and, 106-107
  population characteristics, 102-104

ABOUT THE AUTHORS

Kathleen Malley-Morrison, Ed.D., is a Professor of Psychology at Boston University. She has completed considerable research on family violence since 1980 when she was a postdoctoral fellow on the family violence team at Children's Hospital in Boston. She also regularly teaches undergraduate and graduate courses focusing on family violence. She is first author of several books, including *Treating Child Abuse and Family Violence in Hospitals* with Eli Newberger, Richard Bourne, and Jane Snyder, as well as second author, with Anne Copeland, of the Sage book *Studying Families*. Her current focus is primarily on cross-cultural and international perspectives on family violence and abuse.

Denise A. Hines, Ph.D., completed her doctoral degree in the Human Development program in the Psychology Department at Boston University. Her dissertation, a behavioral genetic study of violence in intimate relationships, was supported by a National Research Service Award from the National Institute of Mental Health. Her primary research interests include genetic influences on aggressive behaviors in family relationships, female-perpetrated intimate violence, and cultural issues in family violence. She has published several articles on these topics and has made numerous conference presentations relating to issues in family violence. She is currently a postdoctoral fellow with Murray Straus at the University of New Hampshire.